THE CAMBRIDGE COMPANION TO
GERMAN ROMANTICISM

The late eighteenth and early nineteenth centuries saw an extraordinary flowering of arts and culture in Germany which produced many of the world's finest writers, artists, philosophers and composers. This volume offers students and specialists an authoritative introduction to that dazzling cultural phenomenon, now known collectively as German Romanticism. Individual chapters not only introduce the reader to writers such as Friedrich Schlegel, Novalis, Eichendorff, Heine, Hoffmann, Kleist, Schiller and Tieck, but also treat key concepts of Romantic music, painting, philosophy, gender and cultural anthropology, science and criticism in concise and lucid language. All German quotations are translated to make this volume fully accessible to a wide audience interested in how Romanticism evolved across Europe. Brief biographies and bibliographies are supplemented by a list of primary and secondary further reading in both English and German.

A complete list of books in the series is at the back of this book

T0364216

THE CAMBRIDGE
COMPANION TO
GERMAN ROMANTICISM

EDITED BY
NICHOLAS SAUL

CAMBRIDGE
UNIVERSITY PRESS

CAMBRIDGE UNIVERSITY PRESS
Cambridge, New York, Melbourne, Madrid, Cape Town,
Singapore, São Paulo, Delhi, Mexico City

Cambridge University Press
The Edinburgh Building, Cambridge CB2 8RU, UK

Published in the United States of America by Cambridge University Press, New York

www.cambridge.org
Information on this title: www.cambridge.org/9780521613262

© Cambridge University Press 2009

This publication is in copyright. Subject to statutory exception
and to the provisions of relevant collective licensing agreements,
no reproduction of any part may take place without the written
permission of Cambridge University Press.

First published 2009

A catalogue record for this publication is available from the British Library

Library of Congress Cataloguing in Publication data
Saul, Nicholas.
The Cambridge companion to German romanticism / Nicholas Saul.
p.   cm.
ISBN 978-0-521-84891-6 (hardback)
1. Arts, German–19th century.   2. Romanticism–Germany.   I. Title.
II. Title: Cambridge companion to German romanticism.
NX 550. A 1 S 278 2009
830.9′145–dc22
2009016995

ISBN 978-0-521-61326-2 Hardback
ISBN 978-0-521-84891-6 Paperback

Cambridge University Press has no responsibility for the persistence or
accuracy of URLs for external or third-party internet websites referred to in
this publication, and does not guarantee that any content on such websites is,
or will remain, accurate or appropriate. Information regarding prices, travel
timetables, and other factual information given in this work is correct at
the time of first printing but Cambridge University Press does not guarantee
the accuracy of such information thereafter.

CONTENTS

LIST OF ILLUSTRATIONS

NOTES ON CONTRIBUTORS

JÜRGEN BARKHOFF is Associate Professor of German at Trinity College Dublin. He has published widely on the interface of literature with anthropology, medicine and psychology, on eco-literature and contemporary Swiss literature. His publications include *Magnetische Fiktionen: Literarisierung des Mesmerismus in der Romantik* (1995).

ANDREW BOWIE is Professor of Philosophy and German at Royal Holloway, University of London. His books include *Aesthetics and Subjectivity: From Kant to Nietzsche* (1990; 2nd edn 2003); *Schelling and Modern European Philosophy* (1993); *From Romanticism to Critical Theory* (1997); *Introduction to Modern German Philosophy from Kant to Nietzsche* (2003); and *Music, Philosophy, and Modernity* (2007).

JANE K. BROWN, Professor of Germanics and Comparative Literature at the University of Washington, is best known for her work on Faust and on European literature and music from the seventeenth to the nineteenth centuries. Her most recent book is *The Persistence of Allegory: Drama and Neoclassicism from Shakespeare to Wagner* (2007).

GESA DANE teaches at Göttingen University and currently holds a Guest Professorship at the University of Vienna. She has published on German Literature from the seventeenth to the twentieth centuries. Her most recent monograph, on the issue of rape in German literature and law, is '*Zeter und mordio*': *Vergewaltigung zwischen Literatur und Recht* (2005).

MARGARETE KOHLENBACH is Reader in German and Comparative Literature at the University of Sussex. She works on literature, culture and critical theory from the eighteenth century to the present. Her books include *Das Ende der Vollkommenheit: Zum Verständnis von Thomas Bernhards*

'*Korrektur*' (1986) and *Walter Benjamin: Self-Reference and Religiosity* (2002).

RICHARD LITTLEJOHNS is Emeritus Professor of Modern Languages at the University of Leicester. He has published extensively on literature and the visual arts in German Classicism and Romanticism, and on theoretical aspects of life-writing and literary history. In 2007, with Sara Soncini, he co-edited *Myths of Europe*, to which he also contributed an essay.

CHARLIE LOUTH is Lecturer in German at Oxford University and a Fellow of the Queen's College. He has published *Hölderlin and the Dynamics of Translation* (1998).

JOHN A. MCCARTHY directs the Max Kade Center for European and German Studies at Vanderbilt University. Widely published on literature and philosophy, literature and science, and modes of writing and reading, his most recent book is *Remapping Reality: On Creativity in Science and Literature (Goethe–Nietzsche–Grass)* (2006).

ETHEL MATALA DE MAZZA is Professor of Cultural Theory at the University of Konstanz. Her research focuses on the history of the political imaginary, on interrelations between law and literature, and on cultural analysis in general. Her latest, co-edited book is *Der fiktive Staat: Konstruktionen des politischen Körpers in der Geschichte Europas* (2007).

CARL NIEKERK is Associate Professor of German, Comparative and World Literature at the University of Illinois (Urbana-Champaign). In 2005 he published *Zwischen Naturgeschichte und Anthropologie: Lichtenberg im Kontext der Spätaufklärung*. He is currently working on the intersections of literature and music in Vienna around 1900.

ROGER PAULIN is Emeritus Schröder Professor of German in the University of Cambridge and a Fellow of Trinity College. He has published extensively on the *Goethezeit*, Romanticism and the nineteenth century. His latest book is the edited volume *Shakespeare im 18. Jahrhundert* (2007).

ANTHONY PHELAN is Professor of German Romantic Literature at Oxford and a Fellow of Keble College. He has written widely on German literature and thought, from Wieland and Goethe to Benjamin and Brecht. His latest book is *Reading Heinrich Heine* (2007).

NICHOLAS SAUL is Professor of German at the University of Durham. He has published widely on literature and philosophy, literature and science, literature and homiletics. His latest book is *Gypsies and Orientalism in German Literature and Anthropology of the Long Nineteenth Century* (2007).

RICARDA SCHMIDT is Professor of German at the University of Exeter. She has published on twentieth-century women writers from East and West Germany and Austria, on E. T. A. Hoffmann and questions of periodization, and on Kleist. Her latest book is *Wenn mehrere Künste im Spiel sind: Intermedialität bei E. T. A. Hoffmann* (2006).

AZADE SEYHAN is the Fairbank Professor in the Humanities at Bryn Mawr College. She has lectured and published extensively on German Romanticism, Heinrich Heine, Walter Benjamin, cultural diversity in modern German society and literature and exile in the United States and Europe. She is the author of *Representation and Its Discontents: The Critical Legacy of German Romanticism* (1992), *Writing Outside the Nation* (2001) and the forthcoming *Tales of Crossed Destinies* (2008).

PREFACE

In a way it is odd that German Romantics should feature as the collective subject of a *Cambridge Companion*. This series contains volumes devoted to writers such as Thomas Mann, Goethe and Kafka. But there is no *Companion* to Friedrich von Hardenberg (Novalis), Friedrich Schlegel, Ludwig Tieck, Clemens Brentano or Ernst Theodor Amadeus Hoffmann. Traditionally scholarship has treated the German Romantics as a collective, so that we implicitly value Hardenberg, Schlegel and the rest less as autonomous creative individuals than as a composite entity greater than the sum of its parts, a cultural and social grouping which is at its most effective and significant when united. And indeed, whilst no one would argue that these gifted individuals do not each merit a volume of their own, it must be conceded that the collective approach both reflects the German Romantics' self-understanding and offers an apt category to capture their achievement – especially for a volume designed to introduce. The Romantics were a heterogeneous collection of individuals, men and women, hailing from metropolitan Berlin (or Vienna or Paris), but also from pious Barby, dull Hanover, remote Eutin, Catholic Cologne, strict Stuttgart and sleepy Bayreuth, from the military or administrative lower aristocracy, from patrician *bürgerlich* and impoverished preaching, teaching or artisan families (if not from the peasantry). They all believed in individual genius. But they also all believed that genius was even more creative when fused 'sympoetically' with another's. Hardenberg had no reservations about asking Schlegel collaboratively to edit his *Fragment* collections or songs, so that scholars today are still uncertain where Schlegel's contribution begins and ends. Clemens Brentano published Sophie Mereau's work under his name, and his under hers. One Romantic novel has four authors, and most present themselves in any case as unauthorized, collaborative continuations of the much-admired and – criticized – *Wilhelm Meister*, Goethe's *Bildungsroman*. Hardenberg, Schlegel and Schleiermacher even held the Bible to be cooperative work in progress down the centuries and seriously considered adding another New

Testament (or thought they had done so). And the Romantics did tend to collect and collaborate in spontaneously self-constituting bohemian artist colonies, in Jena, Berlin, Heidelberg, Coppet, Munich and Vienna. If they did not quite invent it, they nonetheless institutionalized the received notion of marriage as androgynous dissolution of discrete personal identity in gender exchange. They both elevated reciprocal sociability into a foundational principle and lived it. Above all they propagated collective change: restoral of the overarching totality of the organism and the *Volk*.

So ambitious and ambiguous a project, and one conducted in such a style, was from the start open to misprision and manipulation. Schlegel, conscious of genuine affinities between the Classical duo and the Romantics, had included 'classicity' as a gesture to Goethe and Schiller in his most important definition of the Romantic. But that did not prevent Romanticism becoming for Goethe a slogan of artificial ideological division. Nor did the collectivist practice of the Romantics prevent unwitting self-misrepresentation. Hardenberg's fragmentary writings were subjected posthumously to 'sympoetic' editorship by Schlegel and Tieck, with the consequence that – uncontested – a mystical, escapist and politically reactionary light was cast on them for generations. Thus Hardenberg, and with him Romanticism, was cast as the opponent of the French Revolution and legitimist restorer of monarchy, as the apostle of primal Germanness in a threateningly cosmopolitan age, as the enemy of emancipatory Enlightenment and life, and preacher of beautiful morbidity. Before the First World War it took brave scholars – Walter Benjamin and Thomas Mann among them – to dispute these labellings. Against this background, the Romantic writings of Hardenberg and Kleist, Müller and Körner offered easy pickings for nationalist, and finally National Socialist, readings designed to invent a self-serving tradition. Worse, these readings were paradoxically taken over at face value by scholars intending to make a fresh start after the Second World War.

That view of the collective Romantic project has now, thankfully, changed. Post-war editions of all the major German Romantics have surprised us with wholly unfamiliar texts, radically changed the face of once-familiar ones, or reintroduced forgotten central actors (usually women). As a result, in the 1970s, an 'other', radical and anti-establishment Romanticism emerged. Hardenberg's blue flower, once smeared with brown, was said to have been red all along. Far from opposing the Enlightenment, energies prefiguring the political and aesthetic ideas of the alternative thinkers of the left – Adorno, Habermas and the deconstructivists – were discerned. Affinities have been recognized in the Romantics' critical understanding of nation and culture with today's post-colonial theories. In a still later phase, the pendulum has swung back, and a fundamental polyvalence has been detected. Perhaps equally important, these newly recognized epistemological dynamics have exposed pioneering, thoroughly modern critiques of established science.

Romanticism, then, has after all come to be recognized as a kind of classic, with something important to say to each generation, and like any classic demands and repays new readings. Our volume seeks, in the briefest of compasses so refreshingly demanded by the *Companion* format, to do justice to the complex phenomenon of this movement in literature, thought, music and art both to introduce new readers to Romantic work, to familiarize them with the movement's chequered history and to sensitize them to today's appreciation of its true richness. The essays which follow focus initially on the origin, nature and progress of the movement. An entire section is devoted to exposition and interpretation of Romantic achievements in the diverse genres of literary writing, including criticism and journalism, writing by women and the troubled relation with Schiller and Goethe. All the contributors have an eye on the European dimension of Romanticism, but a further section focuses on characteristic issues put by our contemporary understanding of the movement, in its relation to cultural alterity and the different otherness of death. Finally, the volume includes essays which recognize the contribution of Romanticism not merely to literature, but also to other spheres of human thought and experience, philosophy and religion, politics and society, science and psychology, fine art and music. An analysis of Romanticism's changing image down the successive generations concludes the volume. Each chapter contains a list of further reading, and the volume also offers a general bibliography.

My thanks go to all the contributors for their energy and perspicuity, and especially to Linda Bree for sound advice and criticism; also to the faculty of Arts and Humanities at the University of Durham for financial support, and to Janet Starkey for her fine work on the index.

Nicholas Saul

ABBREVIATIONS

The following standard abbreviations are used throughout the book:

KFSA   Friedrich Schlegel, *Kritische Friedrich-Schlegel-Ausgabe*, eds. Ernst Behler, Hans Eichner and Jean-Jaques Anstett, 35 vols. (Munich, Paderborn, Vienna: Schöningh, 1958–)

NS   *Novalis: Schriften*, eds. Paul Kluckhohn, Richard Samuel, Hans-Joachim Mähl, Gerhard Schulz, 7 vols. (Stuttgart, Berlin, Cologne, Mainz: Kohlhammer, 1960–)

CHRONOLOGY

1749   28 August: birth of Johann Wolfgang Goethe, Frankfurt am Main

1759   10 November: birth of Friedrich Schiller, Marbach am Neckar

1762   19 May: birth of Johann Gottlieb Fichte, Bischofswerda

1765   21 March: birth of Jean Paul, Wunsiedel

1767   8 September: birth of August Wilhelm Schlegel

1768   21 November: birth of Friedrich Schleiermacher, Breslau
      (Wroclaw)

1770   20 March: birth of Friedrich Hölderlin, Lauff am Neckar
      27 August: birth of Friedrich Hegel, Stuttgart
      16 December: birth of Ludwig van Beethoven, Bonn

1772   10 March: birth of Friedrich Schlegel, Hanover
      2 May: birth of Friedrich von Hardenberg (Novalis),
      Oberwiederstedt

1773   2 May: birth of Henrik Steffens, Stavanger
      31 May: birth of Ludwig Tieck, Berlin
      13 July: birth of Wilhelm Wackenroder, Berlin

1774   5 September 1774: birth of Caspar David Friedrich, Greifswald

1775   27 January: birth of Friedrich Schelling, Leonberg/Württemberg
      4 April: birth of Bettine Brentano, Frankfurt am Main
      Goethe, *Die Leiden des jungen Werthers*

1776   Adam Smith, *Wealth of Nations*

1777   23 July: birth of Philipp Otto Runge, Wolgast/Sweden
      10 October: birth of Heinrich von Kleist, Frankfurt an der Oder

1778   9 September: birth of Clemens Brentano, Ehrenbreitstein/Coblenz

1780   11 February: birth of Karoline von Günderrode, Karlsruhe
      20 November: death of Holy Roman Empress Maria Theresia;
      succeeded by co-regent Joseph II
      Frederick II, *De la littérature allemande*

1781   Kant, *Kritik der reinen Vernunft*

1786   17 August: death of Frederick II (the Great) of Prussia, succeeded
       by Frederick William II
       18 November: birth of Carl Maria von Weber, Eutin
1787   Kant, *Kritik der praktischen Vernunft*
1788   First steam engine in operation in Germany (Friedrich-Grube,
       Silesia)
       10 March: birth of Joseph von Eichendorff, Ratibor
1789   Outbreak of the French Revolution, Paris
1790   20 February: death of Joseph II, Holy Roman Emperor, succeeded
       by Leopold II
       Edmund Burke, *Reflections on the Revolution in France*
1791   5 December: Wolfgang Amadeus Mozart dies in Vienna
       Kant: *Kritik der Urteilskraft*
1792   1 March: death of Leopold II, Holy Roman Emperor, succeeded by
       Franz II
       Georg Forster joins the Jacobin Club in Mainz
       First War of Coalition, Austria and Prussia, later Russia and Great
       Britain against Revolutionary France (–1797)
1793   Outbreak of the Terror in Paris under Robespierre
1794   Fichte, *Grundlage der gesammten Wissenschaftslehre*
       Fichte takes Chair of Philosophy at Jena University, as does
       Schelling
1795   Goethe, *Wilhelm Meisters Lehrjahre* (–1796)
       Schiller, *Ästhetische Briefe*
       Kant, *Zum ewigen Frieden*
1796   Schiller, *Über naive und sentimentalische Dichtung*
       F. Schlegel, *Versuch über den Republikanismus*
1797   31 January: birth of Franz Schubert, Vienna
       16 November: death of Frederick William II of Prussia, succeeded
       by Frederick William III
       Tieck/Wackenroder, *Herzensergießungen*
       Tieck, *Der gestiefelte Kater, Shakespeares Behandlung des
       Wunderbaren*
       F. Schlegel, Georg Forster, *Über das Studium der griechischen
       Poesie, Fragmente*
       Canonical Shakespeare translation by A. W. Schlegel and Tieck
       begins
1798   13 February: death of Wackenroder, Berlin
       August: Hardenberg, Schelling, Schlegels in Dresden at the
       Gemäldegalerie
       Schlegel brothers, *Athenæum* (–1800)

Hardenberg, *Glauben und Liebe, oder der König und die Königin*

Tieck, *Franz Sternbalds Wanderungen*

Kant, *Die Religion innerhalb der Grenzen der reinen Vernunft*

C. D. Friedrich, *Wrack im Eismeer*

1799   Second War of Coalition (–1802)

Peace of Lunéville: de facto dissolution of Holy Roman Empire; Germany loses left bank of Rhine (occupied since 1794) to France

First steam engine in Berlin

11–14 November: first 'summit' meeting of Early Romantics (Hardenberg, Ritter, Schelling, Schlegels, Tieck), Jena

Atheismusstreit; Fichte loses Chair of Philosophy at Jena

Schleiermacher, *Über die Religion; Versuch einer Theorie des geselligen Betragens*

Hardenberg, *Die Christenheit oder Europa* (unpublished)

F. Schlegel, *Lucinde*

Tieck/Wackenroder, *Phantasien über die Kunst*

Schiller, *Wallenstein* (–1800)

1800   Hardenberg, *Hymnen an die Nacht, Heinrich von Ofterdingen*

C. Brentano, *Godwi*

1801   25 March: death of Friedrich von Hardenberg, Weißenfels

1803   *Reichsdeputationshauptschluß*: German ecclesiastical states and property secularized

Schelling moves to Chair of Philosophy at Würzburg

Runge, *Die Zeiten* (drawings)

Werner, *Die Söhne des Thals* (–1804)

Jean Paul, *Titan*

F. Schlegel, *Europa*

1804   Napoleon Buonaparte crowned as Emperor of France

Heidelberger Romantik, centred on Arnim, Brentano, Creuzer, Görres

Günderrode ('Tian'), *Gedichte und Phantasien*

1805   Third War of Coalition

Battle of Trafalgar and Continental Blockade

9 May: death of Friedrich Schiller, Weimar

11 September: Hölderlin admitted to psychiatric clinic, Tübingen

Klingemann, *Nachtwachen von Bonaventura*

Arnim, *Zeitung für Einsiedler*

1806   Fourth War of Coalition (–1807) ends in catastrophic defeat of Prussia at Jena-Auerstädt and French occupation

Fichte, *Reden an die deutsche Nation*

Arnim/Brentano, *Des Knaben Wunderhorn*
Juridical abolition of Holy Roman Empire; Federation of the Rhine constituted
26 July 1806: death of Günderrode, Winkel am Rhein

1807 Edict on Emancipation of the Peasants
Hegel, *Phänomenologie des Geistes*
Kleist/Müller, *Phöbus*

1808 Hoffmann *Kapellmeister* in Bamberg
Kleist, *Die Hermannsschlacht*
G. H. Schubert, *Ansichten von der Nachtseite der Naturwissenschaft*
F. Schlegel, *Über die Sprache und Weisheit der Indier*

1809 Fifth War of Coalition
Failed insurrection in Austria (Andreas Hofer)
Goethe, *Die Wahlverwandtschaften* (-1810)
Adam Müller, *Elemente der Staatskunst*
A. W. Schlegel, *Vorlesungen über dramatische Kunst und Literatur*

1810 Karl August von Hardenberg becomes Prussian Chancellor, introduces radical reforms
Foundation of Berlin University (today: Humboldt University); W. von Humboldt, Fichte, Savigny, Schleiermacher join
Kleist, *Das Erdbeben in Chili, Berliner Abendblätter*
Arnim, *Gräfin Dolores*
2 December: death of Runge, Hamburg
C. D. Friedrich, *Der Mönch am Meer*

1811 Edict on Freedom of Trade; Edict on Landowners' and Peasants' Relations (abolition of feudalism)
Kleist, *Prinz Friedrich von Homburg*
21 November: death of Kleist, Wannsee/Berlin

1812 Edict on the Civil Relations of the Jews (emancipation of the Jews)
Christlich-teutsche Tischgesellschaft, Berlin

1813 Frederick William III institutes the Iron Cross
Prussia declares war on France
Wars of Liberation (–1815)
16–18 October, Leipzig, Battle of the Nations; collapse of Napoleonic system
Theodor Körner, *Leyer und Schwert*

1814 29 January 1814: death of Fichte, Berlin
Hoffmann resumes legal career in Berlin
Beethoven, *Fidelio*
Hoffmann, *Undine* (opera after Fouqué)

Schubert, *Gretchen am Spinnrade, Erlkönig*

G. H. Schubert, *Symbolik des Traumes*

1815   18 June: Battle of Waterloo

Congress of Vienna brings restoration, legitimism, balance of power, Holy Alliance

German Federation (–1866) Creates thirty-nine states, Frankfurt Parliament

Clemens Prince Metternich becames Austrian Chancellor

Hegel elected to Chair of Philosophy at Berlin

Neo-Pietist *Erweckungsbewegung* arrives in North Germany

First German *Burschenschaften* (student clubs)

Brentano, *Die Schachtel mit der Friedenspuppe, Die Gründung Prags*

Hoffmann, *Die Elixiere des Teufels*

Eichendorff, *Ahnung und Gegenwart*

1816   *Berliner Romantik* centres on the *salon* of Rahel Levin-Varnhagen (Brentano, Fouqué, Hoffmann)

1817   18 October: Wartburg Festival, student clubs against Metternich's repressive system

Brentano, *Die mehreren Wehmüller und ungarischen Nationalgesichter*

Arnim, *Die Kronenwächter*

Karl Ludwig von Haller, *Restauration der Staatswissenschaft* (–1825); book burned at Wartburgfest

Union of Protestant Churches in Prussia to form Evangelical Church

1819   Murder of August von Kotzebue, popular writer and diplomat, prompts Carlsbad Decrees, intensifying censorship and ban on student clubs

Görres: *Teutschland und die Revolution*

Brentano retires to obscurity in Westphalia, tending visionary nun Anna Katharina Emmerick (–1825)

1820   Schelling takes Chair of Philosophy at Erlangen

Hoffmann, *Lebens-Ansichten des Katers Murr* (–1822)

1821   Weber, *Der Freischütz*

1822   Hoffmann embroiled in legal difficulty and controversy when he defends civil rights against repression

22 June: death of Hoffmann

1823   Beethoven, 9th Symphony

1825   14 November: death of Jean Paul, Bayreuth

Tieck Dramaturge of Court Theatre, Dresden

1826   5 June: death of Weber, London
Görres to Chair at Munich University

1827   Schelling moves to Chair of Philosophy at Munich
26 March: death of Beethoven, Vienna
Heine, *Buch der Lieder*

1828   19 November: death of Schubert, Vienna

1829   12 January: death of Friedrich Schlegel, Dresden

1830   July Revolution in Paris
Stockton to Darlington railway

1831   14 November: death of Hegel, Berlin
Bettine Brentano, *Goethe's Briefwechsel mit einem Kinde*

1832   22 March: death of Goethe, Weimar
Goethe, *Faust: Zweiter Teil*

1833   Heine, *Die romantische Schule*

1834   North German Customs Union
12 February: death of Schleiermacher, Berlin
Eichendorff, *Dichter und ihre Gesellen*

1835   First German railway Nuremberg–Fürth

1837   Protest of the 'Göttingen Seven'

1840   7 June: death of Frederick William III of Prussia; successor
Frederick William IV
608 steam engines now operating in Germany
7 May 1840: death of C. D. Friedrich

1841   Schelling called to Chair of Philosophy at Berlin

1842   28 July: death of Clemens Brentano, Aschaffenburg
Tieck as Dramaturge in Berlin

1843   7 June: death of Hölderlin, Tübingen

1844   Heine, *Die Weber, Deutschland: Ein Wintermärchen*

1845   13 February: death of Henrik Steffens, Berlin
12 May: death of August Wilhelm Schlegel, Bonn

1848   March: Protest and Revolution in Mannheim, Frankfurt am Main,
Munich and finally across all Germany and Austria

1853   28 April: death of Tieck, Berlin

1854   20 August: death of Schelling, Bad Ragaz

1857   26 November: death of Eichendorff, Neisse

1859   20 January: death of Bettine Brentano, Berlin

I

AZADE SEYHAN

What is Romanticism, and where did it come from?

Since the significance and history of German Romanticism is embedded in an exceptionally complex configuration of sociopolitical, religious and aesthetic phenomena, this chapter comprises three sections. The first focuses on the larger historical and political context of the Romantic movement in Germany, the second on the philosophical, cultural and aesthetic coordinates of German Romanticism, and the final section investigates the critical aesthetics of the Jena or early German Romantics, as articulated in the fragments and aphorisms of the journals *Lyceum der schönen Künste* (1797) and *Athenaeum* (1798–1800). The term 'Romanticism', as defined in this chapter, refers predominantly to the eighteenth- and nineteenth-century concept of an era informed by the profound experience of momentous political, social and intellectual revolutions. The term also has its own history, which calls for a short introduction.

The etymology of the word 'Romantic' can be traced to the old French *romanz,* which referred to the vernacular 'romance' languages, Italian, French, Spanish, Catalan, Portuguese and Provençal, which were developed from Latin. Subsequently, tales of chivalry, written in one of these romance languages, came to be known as medieval *romance* or *romaunt.* These were often composed in verse and narrated a quest. Later, the authors of the Middle Ages and the Renaissance, such as Dante, Ariosto, Torquato Tasso, Cervantes and Shakespeare, who abandoned classical forms, were seen as inventors of a romantic, fantastical style. In the eighteenth century, the semantic field of the word 'romantic' in common English usage had expanded to include the picturesque, the fanciful and the fantastic with not altogether positive connotations. Romantic imagination was seen as impeding the purity of the art form and pushing it beyond the limits of proper subject matter. At the end of the eighteenth century, the concept of the 'romantic' came to inhabit permanently the vocabularies of European languages and referred simultaneously and variously to landscape, feeling (predominantly love), or eccentric character. It was in the work of the late eighteenth-century German literary and cultural critics that 'romantische

Poesie' (Romantic poesy) was transformed into a critical mode of thought and came to be seen as a contemporary and autonomous literary tradition. In 1798, Friedrich Schlegel (1772–1829), the leading critic of the early German Romantic movement, defined *romantische Poesie* as 'a progressive universal poesy'. This kind of poesy both emphasised its links to classical and medieval literatures and its future-orientated mission and focused on foregrounding its critical capabilities, which had been disregarded or missed by traditional literary criticism. How was it that in less than half a century, the negative connotations of the concept 'romantic' were transformed into notions that denoted revolutionary, innovative, modern, critical and universal? The trajectory of the term needs to be understood in the context of several revolutions – the American, the French, the industrial revolution and Immanuel Kant's 'Copernican Revolution' – that inaugurated the Age of Enlightenment in Europe. This seismic transformation of European culture required new modes of understanding the world, and Romanticism came to symbolise the consciousness of the new age.

Although a tremendous amount of scholarship on the critical legacy of early German Romanticism (*Frühromantik*) has emerged in the last decades, many works on the subject are dedicated to specific or specialised topics. A more differentiated view of the emergence of Romanticism in Germany calls for a broader historico-philosophical approach. As Friedrich Schlegel had famously remarked, the French Revolution, Fichte's *Wissenschaftslehre* (1794; *Theory of Knowledge*) and Goethe's *Wilhelm Meisters Lehrjahre* (1795–6; *Wilhelm Meister's Apprenticeship*) constituted the three major culture-changing trends at the close of the eighteenth century. In Schlegel's view, whoever rejected the logic of this juxtaposition or the idea of a revolution that was not loud and physical had failed to achieve a broad perspective on the history of humanity. In the final analysis, political and philosophical revolution and literary innovation participated equally in the genesis of Romanticism. The coincidence of the rise of Romanticism with the rapid expansion of the European reading public, the efflorescence of German culture at the close of the eighteenth century and the French occupation of all of Germany west of the Rhine by 1794 calls for a multiple-field approach to a critical understanding of the Romantic movement. In this spirit, the present chapter provides a condensed reading map of the complex historical and critical directions that led to the *Frühromantik* and beyond.

Historical and political background

At the onset of the German Romantic movement, the political map of Germany represented an unusual configuration of multiple federations under the nominal suzerainty of the Holy Roman Empire. German territories constituted a diverse assemblage of states with different political and cultural institutions and practices, economies and religious professions. Writing in *Zur Geschichte der Religion und Philosophie in Deutschland* (*On the History of Religion and Philosophy in Germany*) as late as 1835, Heinrich Heine (1797–1856) remarks that the only unity a politically and religiously fragmented Germany possesses consists in its literary language, as created in Martin Luther's masterly Bible translation. The titular political protection and the juridical framework of the Empire made it possible for a diverse group of principalities to coexist without being taken over by more powerful neighbouring or rival states. This pattern of territorial power and the decentralisation of political rule encouraged a practice of absolutist rule by individual princes who were not accountable to a parliament or an estate. The political landscape was a mosaic of medieval remnants reminiscent of feudal administrative machinery. Seen in the historical continuum, the ascendancy of territorial power was set in motion by the cumulative socioeconomic consequences of the Thirty Years War (1618–48) and the succession wars that followed it. The way that led to the Thirty Years War was, in turn, paved by the political destabilisation that accompanied the Protestant revolution. The Catholic emperor was unable to stop the conversion of many powerful princes to Protestantism. Furthermore, Luther's revolutionary zeal not only broke the undisputed power of the Catholic Church but also heralded the possibility of a critical sensibility that questioned any form of absolutist rule. The Peace of Westphalia that had marked the end of the Thirty Years War in 1648 was followed by a multitude of wars that were increasingly disengaged from the Empire, as individual principalities engaged in conflicts or otherwise signed treaties with states outside the Empire.

The German states after 1648 varied greatly in size and constitution. Habsburg Austria with its court in Vienna included a sizeable number of non-German dynasties along with its territories within the Empire. Other major courts were Protestant Saxony, with its magnificent capital city of Dresden, and Catholic Bavaria, with its capital Munich. Important ecclesiastical territories included the prince bishoprics of Mainz and Würzburg. Toward the end of the seventeenth century, as the centres of European trade moved westwards to the Atlantic seaboard, urban life began to decline. This recession enabled rulers to curtail the autonomy of German towns. The downtrend of burgher life and the increasing dependence of the aristocracy, already impoverished by successive wars, on the patronage of rulers, advanced the realisation of the absolutist state in the form of Brandenburg-Prussia. The Hohenzollerns of Brandenburg, who were given the title of 'Elector' of the Holy Roman Empire, ruled over an amalgamated state with culturally and socio-economically diverse territories. Eighteenth-century German states, courts and rulers featured a great diversity of sociopolitical and cultural practices, ways of post-war economic rehabilitation and inter-state relations. In some areas agricultural production could not sustain peasants, whereas in others farms prospered. Aristocracy ranged from powerful nobles to impoverished knights. The League of Princes formed by Frederick II in 1780 included the Archbishop of Mainz, the Elector of Saxony and Britain's George III in the latter's capacity as Elector of Hanover. *Hansestadt* Hamburg (a member of the Hanseatic League) represented an oligarchic tradition of urban government, and, in one exceptional case, in the Duchy of Württemberg, a parliamentary form of government representing rural, urban and church interests endured until the rise of the modern German nation state in the nineteenth century. From this disunity of state and territory, Austria and Prussia emerged as the two competing powers of the German political landscape toward the end of the eighteenth century. When the French Revolution broke out, Germany was a very long way from being a unified nation state. Among German intellectuals, the ideal of a unified Germany amounted to a revolutionary vision. Although Brandenburg-Prussia rose to great power from the fragmented ground of German territories and undertook ambitious administrative, economic and military reforms, it was the French Revolution and the Napoleonic wars that spelled the end of the Holy Roman Empire, buried the last remnants of feudal social practices and forced an overhaul of administrative, judicial, economic and military systems.

If the legacy of a revolution were to be measured by the seismic upheavals it triggers, then the French Revolution, as a major quake that sent tremors through the European terrain, could be seen as an agent of momentous political, economic and social reconfigurations that took place within and beyond the borders of France. Although there had been signs of political discontent among German intellectuals at the onset of the French Revolution, most Germans seemed happy to observe the developments in France with a sense of curiosity, sometimes coupled with a sigh of relief that Germany had been able to ward off a revolution by measured reforms. All but the most conservative thinkers saw the French Revolution in a positive light and were happy that the French were finally setting their house in order. The German aristocracy and intelligentsia had long regarded France as the epitome of civilisation, and German thinkers lauded the achievements of the French Enlightenment. Nevertheless, they also realised that the French state apparatus and society were in dire need of reform. However, even those Germans most sympathetic to the French cause were in no way inclined to import the Revolution to Germany. Many German writers saw the French Revolution as a great and inspiring world drama performed on the stage of history, but they were not enthusiastic about joining it. Writer and critic Christoph Martin Wieland (1733–1813) regarded his generation as fortunate to have witnessed so momentous an event as a bystander. Johann Gottfried Herder (1744–1803), one of the leading language historians of German pre-Romanticism, maintained that Germans would not expose themselves to such clear and imminent danger but rather watch the 'shipwreck' on the open sea from a safe haven. Other writers, such as the revolutionary-minded popular essayist Georg Forster (1754–94), opposed the spread of revolution to Germany for fear that the people were not enlightened enough to prevent its disastrous consequences.[1] Thus, if there was any lesson to be learned from the French Revolution, it had to be reflected on and theorised, but not put into practice.

The French Revolution itself was in no small way indebted to the legacy of the American Revolution in theory and practice. Humanistic secular ideals had informed the moral and intellectual character of both the American and French Revolutions. The American Revolution represented the most concrete expression of emancipation and subject sovereignty for a Europe suffering in the oppressive climate of absolutist regimes. Rulers and those who occupied the highest levels of society who should have provided moral leadership for their nations were hopelessly corrupt and resistant to reform. The founding fathers of the American rebellion were bourgeois or patrician dissidents who sought parity with their British peers. Like the French Revolution, the American one had embraced the secular humanistic ideals of the Enlightenment. The Declaration of Independence signed by the founding fathers in 1776 further incorporated the empirical signature of Francis Bacon (1561–1626) and David Hume's (1711–76) reception of Enlightenment ideas. On the eve of the French Revolution, one of the major sources of public discontent in France was the disastrous state of government finances, since the French, as allies of the uprising American colonies, borrowed heavily to support the American revolutionaries against Great Britain. Since Germany was not a unified state at this time, its financial backing of the American Revolution could not be a sustained effort. An exception was the Hessian mercenary state, which provided the revolutionaries with paid soldiers. Although the intellectual and moral spirit of the American Revolution generated a strong spark in the German Romantic movement, its political implications for Germany were more indirect or perhaps less immediate, as they first travelled through the momentous upheavals in France on their way to Germany.

The intellectuals of the French Enlightenment were aware that, in contrast to America's situation, the poor and disaffected masses in France could be a potentially destructive force in any radical political transformation. Their insight proved true, when in the second phase of the French Revolution in 1792–3, the Jacobins, a democratic republican group affiliated with the revolutionary leader Maximilien Robespierre (1758–94), had to give in to the demands of hardline *sans culottes*. 1793–4 ushered in the reign of Terror, when mass executions, including that of King Louis XVI, turned the promise of liberty into a bloodbath. When the Revolution changed from a declaration of freedom and equality to bloodshed and anarchy, it became increasingly difficult for German intellectuals to remain sympathetic observers. With the subsequent invasion and exploitation of German territories by the French revolutionary army and the occupation of all of Germany west of Rhine by 1794, any remaining sympathy for the Gallic spirit turned into fear and hate. Friedrich Schlegel saw the French Revolution as both an 'outstanding allegory of the system of transcendental idealism'[2] and 'the most frightful grotesque of the age where the most deep-seated prejudices and their most brutal punishments are joined in a gruesome chaos' (*KFSA* II, p. 248, No. 424). The various indigenous sociopolitical developments in Germany from the end of the Thirty Years War and the Peace of Westphalia to the Congress of Vienna (1814–15) were deflected by the French Revolution and the subsequent French invasion. This sea change resulted in major cultural and administrative transformations in the German territories.

Although the French Revolution, which Friedrich Schlegel regarded 'an almost universal earthquake' in the political order, was initially met with enthusiasm by German thinkers who yearned for a consolidation of Germany's discontinuous and fragmented political landscape, by 1794 it had come to represent the loss of a once whole world. German Romanticism's real and symbolic links to the French Revolution inhere both in the passion generated by ideals of equality, fraternity and freedom that resounded beyond French borders in 1789 and in mourning an irretrievably lost world of unity and harmony. Thus, the French Revolution also came to represent a shift in the understanding of movement in history. The Judaeo-Christian tradition had represented time as the agent of sacred history, whereas the Revolution became in the Romantic mind an allegory of disruption in time, the eclipse of teleology and the rise of chaos. Neither the Enlightenment ideal of progress nor a millennarian belief could make sense of the explosive and destructive course of history. Romanticism can thus be seen as originating in our human anxiety about the interlinked crises of the political turmoil that engulfed Europe and the limits of understanding introduced by Immanuel Kant's critiques. Thus, Romanticism came to view expressive freedom in life, writing and art as an end toward which humanity had to strive in order to rise above mere physical and natural existence.

Philosophical and cultural context

Considered by many intellectual historians to be a major turning point in the history of political and critical thought, Romanticism emerged at the end of the eighteenth century in Europe, principally in Germany (but also in Britain and France), as simultaneously a cultural, political and socio-economic movement of revolutionary vision and ambition. Various cultural discourses, both complementary and oppositional, including Pietism, the Enlightenment, Weimar Classicism and *Sturm und Drang* (Storm and Stress), converged in early German Romanticism. Pietism, one of the several sociocultural threads that made up the complicated web of German Romanticism's larger historical context, was an earlier and relatively less-known influence on the genesis of Romantic thought. In the late seventeenth century, Pietism rose up against Lutheran orthodoxy and played an important role in the development of Enlightenment's world view. Founded by Philipp Jakob Spener (1635–1705), whose *Pia desideria* (1675; *Pious Longings*) endeavoured to free the Church from the weight of dogma, Pietism emphasised Bible study and spiritual experience. Its regard for Christian fellowship and community dictated that laity should share in the spiritual government of the Church. One of the six reform proposals of *Pia desideria* called for tolerance toward non-believers and their kindly treatment. Another pleaded for a new form of preaching that supplanted lofty rhetoric with the desire to instil Christianity in the inner person. The influence of Pietism lasted from the end of the seventeenth to the middle of the eighteenth century and was felt most strongly in northern and central Germany. As Pietism placed the spirit of Christian life above the letter of doctrine and stressed the role of individual will in spiritual life, its more liberal concepts endured in European intellectual history through its influence on Immanuel Kant (1724–1804), Friedrich Schleiermacher (1768–1834) and Søren Kierkegaard (1813–55).

An important influence on the early German Romantic critics' views on language and literary genealogies were the language theoreticians and philologists Johann Gottfried Herder and Jacob (1785–1863) and Wilhelm Grimm (1786–1859). However, unlike Herder and the Grimm brothers, the early Romantics were not interested in mining language for the riches of a specifically Germanic culture. Whereas in Herder and the Grimms the Romantic sensibility took a turn toward cultural origins or the *Volk*, for the Schlegel brothers Friedrich and August Wilhelm (1767–1845) and their circle the 'Romantic' ethos resided in a universal and unifying discourse. Herder, a student of Kant's, challenged the universalist orientation of his teacher's philosophy. Like Johann Georg Hamann (1730–88) before him, Herder felt that the fundamental cognitive and communicative function of language had been underrated by Kant and other Enlightenment philosophers. He endeavoured to show that language was inseparable from thought, and that each language constituted the unique expression of a particular culture. This linguistic turn in the study of culture advanced the study of philology, a field the Grimm brothers cultivated extensively. Both the Grimms and Herder collected folk tales (*Volksmärchen*) and folk songs (*Volkslieder*) as material evidence of indigenous culture. Herder traced the influence of 'folk' traditions in Shakespeare, Ossian, the fictitious Gaelic bard (James Macpherson), and the Bible. He maintained that Shakespeare's tragedies presented an organic, unifying vision of a world buffeted by the storm of history.

In the tumultuous 1770s, this storm was to become the dominant symbol of the Storm and Stress movement that took its name from a play, *Wirrwarr, oder Sturm und Drang* (1776; *Confusion or Storm and Stress*) by Friedrich Klinger (1752–1831). The Storm and Stress, characterised by stirrings of idealism, nationalism, faith in nature and scorn for artistic convention, had its heyday long before the French Revolution. Nevertheless, it was a full dress rehearsal for the coming German Romanticism. Romanticism has often been viewed as a critique of Enlightenment modernity and a paradigm shift that problematised the entire conceptual framework of the age. However, in the German context, Romanticism cannot be seen as a movement that reacted to and replaced the German Enlightenment. Rather, the intellectual thrust of the Romantic movement in Germany arose from the critical practice instituted by the Enlightenment itself. The relationship of Weimar Classicism, as exemplified in the work of Johann Wolfgang von Goethe (1749–1832) and Friedrich Schiller (1759–1805), to early German Romanticism has been variously interpreted in literary history as one of continuity, antagonism or reconciliation. More recent critical views agree that the last decade of the eighteenth century represented an enriching juxtaposition of Classical and Romantic views. It is important to remember that the authors of early German Romanticism did not refer to themselves as 'Romantics', but rather as members of a 'new school'. Likewise, Goethe and Schiller did not consider themselves 'Classicists'. They did, however, aspire to develop a dynamic concept of Classicism that did not exclude the idea of infinite perfectibility.[3] Friedrich Schlegel, for his part, understood the truly Classical text to be one with infinite possibilities for interpretation, just as he considered the inexhaustibility of interpretation Romantic poesy's most distinguishing feature. Recent German scholarship sees the last five years of the eighteenth century as a dynamic cultural encounter of the Classical and the Romantic. Textual historical evidence supports this view as reflecting the spirit of that period most accurately. Even Goethe viewed the last decade of the eighteenth century as an unusually fruitful age of German intellectual and cultural history, and considered the Romantics an integral part of that history.

The various echoes of these political and cultural movements crystallised in the project of early German Romanticism, which responded to an intellectual and moral crisis that marked the end of the rationalist and Classical world view. Romanticism's critical anxiety was prompted by the radical eruptions in the historical and intellectual landscape of the age. The social and political upheaval set off by the 'earthquake' and the aftershocks of the French Revolution ran parallel to a crisis of understanding the conditions and limits of human reason. The chaos that threatened to erase the pillars of reason necessitated new paradigms of understanding and counter-order. The uneasy confrontation with an uncertain future and the impossibility of accessing a truth hidden in the noumenal world, an occult code or a forgotten past characterised the many crises of an age that seemed to have lost its place in the order of history. Kant's institution of critical philosophy represented in his own words 'a Copernican Revolution', by placing the human mind, in an analogy to the place of the sun in the solar system, at the centre of all operations of knowledge. However, the cognitive powers of the mind famously cannot for Kant ascertain the reality of things in themselves. The 'Ding an sich' ('thing in itself') is not accessible by the faculties and so presents a limit to human understanding. Although Kant's transcendental idealism was both daunting and liberating, it offered no possibility for reflective praxis. It was, in the first instance, purely epistemological and could not transcend the historical reality of political and moral deliquescence. Also known as formal or critical idealism, this position maintains that all theoretical knowledge is restricted to the world of experience via appearances and refutes claims to knowledge of anything beyond this realm. At the same time, although the form of experience is subjective, it corresponds to a reality independent of this form. Therefore, the laws of nature are universally applicable, as they are located in the subject. The moral law is also a priori given to the subject and legislated by the faculty of reason.

While Kant rescued science from epistemological scepticism and secured the status of idealism, he did not account for an understanding of the 'real' world, of an independent and totally unknowable thing-in-itself, and thus thwarted the natural desire for a unity of knowledge. Johann Gottlieb Fichte (1762–1814) set out to overcome the duality of Kantian philosophy by positing an absolute consciousness that would guarantee a systematic unity of conception from which a multiplicity of experience could be deduced. For Fichte, the major weakness of Kantian philosophy lay in its lack of self-representation. In other words, it failed to posit an absolute first principle from which self-consciousness could be deduced. This first principle in Fichte's transcendental system is the absolute *Ich* (I/self) that posits itself as an object of cognition. This act of positing is not directed at any object, as Fichte claims, but represents the self to itself by limiting the infinity of the self. Thus, reflection, which is a mode of cognition in Fichte, is rendered possible in the condition of a self-limiting self. This absolute *Ich* bridges the duality of theoretical and practical reason and becomes the ground where the subject is only one manifestation of the Absolute whose history subsumed all modes of human cognitive and moral activity. Because of the inherent self-representation (and thus self-critique) of the *Ich*, forms of cognition and moral consciousness are informed by an infinite progression. Picking up the thread of Kantian-Fichtean idealisms, Friedrich Wilhelm Joseph Schelling (1775–1854) seeks further to erase all forms of discontinuity between the conscious mind and objective nature by setting up a dialectic wherein nature becomes the objectified self and the self the reflected nature. His *Identitätsphilosophie* (philosophy of identity) renders subject and object identical in the Absolute. As this Absolute manifests itself in human consciousness, the harmony of mind and nature gives rise to aesthetic contemplation. For Schelling the path of absolute idealism ultimately leads to art, where human consciousness finds expression in sensuous form.

One of the earliest sceptical responses to the possibility of a first or overarching principle of philosophy (even if this were to be understood as an all-encompassing experience of aesthetics à la Schelling) came from the Jena Romantics. The most uncompromising form of subjective idealism, as represented in the Fichtean model, does not admit of an independently postulated 'real' world. In Fichte, the reflecting self converts the 'pure form' (*reine Form*) of all objectifications of perception into the content of a new form, that of 'knowledge' (*Wissen*) or consciousness (*Bewußtsein*). In the Romantics' interpretation of Fichte's self-reflexive activity, the world emerges as a realm of infinite representations captured in form. By emphasising Idealist philosophy's inability to grasp the absolute securely within a method, the early Romantics credit art with the power of representing the unrepresentable, in other words, to intimate the absolute that eluded all reason. As Friedrich Schlegel famously remarked, 'Das Höchste kann man, eben weil es unaussprechlich ist, nur allegorisch sagen' ('the absolute, because it is inexpressible, can only be expressed allegorically'; *KFSA* II, p. 324). Nevertheless, the source of the early German Romantic inspiration for raising the cognitive and expressive potency of poetry to ever-higher levels was transcendental idealism. Friedrich Schlegel saw 'higher poetry' (*höhere Poesie*) as yet another expression of the same transcendental understanding of the world.

In a similar vein, a short and fragmentary text, *Das älteste Systemprogramm des deutschen Idealismus* (1795; *The Earliest System Programme of German Idealism*), variously attributed to Friedrich Hölderlin (1776–1843), Schelling and Georg Wilhelm Friedrich Hegel (1770–1831), contends that philosophy realises itself only when it represents itself in art. The highest act of reason that embraces all ideas is an aesthetic act that takes transcendental philosophy beyond the 'monotheism' of reason. The decisive insight of the fragment that the philosophy of the spirit reveals itself as an aesthetic philosophy legitimises the idea of beauty as the mediator between consciousness, knowledge and ethics. Beauty, as the ideal idea, resolves the opposition between system and freedom. Qualitative *Romantisieren* (Romanticising), a notion of Friedrich Schlegel's close collaborator and friend Friedrich von Hardenberg (Novalis; 1772–1801), implies that knowledge cannot be limited to the pure forms of perception and verifiable experience. Poetic imagination calls upon images, dreams and memory to endlessly expand the human capacity for understanding. In Hardenberg's well-known novel fragment *Heinrich von Ofterdingen*, for example, *Romantisieren* enables the representation of time and place both in the real world of experience and beyond the world of representable reality by seeing them in a continuum of dream, memory and anticipation.

For the early German Romantics, the monumental political and cultural events at the turn of the century called for a 'new mythology'. This new mythology was conceived not as an archaic but rather as a restorative principle of modern life, fragmented by opposing intellectual and cultural drives, as illustrated in Friedrich Schiller's famous essay on the aesthetic education of humanity. *Über die ästhetische Erziehung des Menschen* (1795–6; *On the Aesthetic Education of Humanity*) validates *avant la lettre* early German Romantics' appointment of aesthetics to the highest court of understanding. Schiller sees the modern age as riven by the conflicting impulses of reason and sensibility. Philosophy may have identified this malaise of the modern age – fragmentation – but it cannot heal it. Schiller sees the role of aesthetic education as reconciling opposed states ('entgegengesetzte Zustände') of matter and form, passivity and activity, and feeling and thought. Like Kant, Schiller tries to reconcile sensibility with reason in the realm of the aesthetic. Unlike Kant, however, he is interested in the far-reaching social consequences of such reconciliation. Humanity was once in a state of harmony with nature. The advent of civilisation disrupted this accord, and human beings became trapped between the competing forces of reason and nature and self and state. Schiller's remedy rests on the concept of the play impulse that arbitrates between that of form (reason) and that of matter (sensibility). Schiller associates the play impulse with art, which combines the fullness of material existence with the highest intellectual autonomy. The experience of the beautiful is necessary, as it can overcome the historically overdetermined claims of rationality and sensuousness and secure the well-being of humanity in freedom. Art in the form of free play redefines the Kantian notion of aesthetic autonomy and creates a disposition toward moral goodness.

Friedrich Schlegel's early essay *Über das Studium der griechischen Poesie* (*On the Study of Greek Poetry*), written in 1795 and published in 1797, proposes an aesthetic revolution that would set the highest goals for an art which, in turn, would reconcile the conflicting demands of ancient and modern aesthetic *Bildung* (education). In a way, this essay represents a response to a debate on aesthetic culture, known as the *Querelle des anciens et des modernes* (*Quarrel of the ancients and the moderns*) that began in the late seventeenth and the early eighteenth centuries in France. This literary and artistic quarrel that heated up in the early 1690s and made its way to England and Germany opposed the merits of the ancient writers to modern scholarship. Critics such as Charles Perrault (1628–1703) and Bernhard le Bouvier de Fontenelle (1657–1757) in France and David Hume and John Dryden (1631–1700) in England attempted to free modern letters from the yoke of classical antiquity and recognise its originality and self-assurance.

The quarrel of the ancients and moderns was a disguise for a profound opposition of the ideas of progress and innovation on the one hand and tradition and authority on the other. The attack on authority in literary criticism had analogues in the rise of scientific inquiry. The moderns strove to demonstrate that the spirit of progress that marked the modern age had not only gone beyond Aristotle's *Physics* but also beyond his *Poetics*. They believed that the ideas of progress and perfectibility upheld by modern philosophy and natural science had to be translated into poetic terms. However, the moderns' endeavour to infuse the arts with a strong consciousness of modernity did not come to fruition until the end of the eighteenth century. Even then, the proponents of the modern in France and England did not see themselves as the true heirs of the moderns, such as Shakespeare and the literary giants of the age of Louis XIV, Corneille and Racine. The quarrel of the ancients and the moderns was belatedly imported to Germany by Herder, who in his essay 'Shakespeare' (1772) advanced the thesis that, in the larger framework of historical progress and transformation, Shakespeare's drama can be seen as having achieved its own undeniably unique status against that of Sophocles. Herder stated that he saw himself closer to Shakespeare than to the Greeks.

The early writings of the Jena Romantics resounded with praise of the ancients because of the historical breadth of their critical vision that took into its purview world literature from its earliest emergent forms through the Middle Ages to their day. Although *Über das Studium der griechischen Poesie* appears to confirm Schiller's notion of Schlegel's 'Grecomania', this early essay, which considered Greek poetry as 'the highest peak of free beauty', also concluded that art was 'infinitely perfectible', thus paving the way to the idea of endlessly progressive Romantic poesy. The completion of the study of Greek poesy marks Schlegel's abandonment of classical antiquity in favour of advancing the Romantic discourse of humanism that endeavoured to transcend multiple forms of division – ancient and modern, philosophy and poetry, subject and object – in order to secure expressive freedom. The whole of the Schlegel brothers' oeuvre is informed by a profound historical and comparative understanding of literature and an astounding perspicacity of aesthetic appreciation. This literary-historical acumen was an important factor in the early Romantics' revaluation and restoration of underestimated or forgotten literary traditions that did not necessarily conform to cherished classical standards. The recovery of fairy tales, troubadour songs, literature of the European Middle Ages and of ancient India and the enthusiastic reception of Dante, Boccaccio, Cervantes, Calderón and Shakespeare marked a new appreciation of the diversity of literary forms, histories and mythologies. The early Romantics' notion of a 'new mythology' rested on a vision that strove to synthesise diverse literary traditions to create the most artistic form of all arts, art to the highest power.[4]

Aesthetic criticism in early German Jena Romanticism

Athenaeum, a journal of cultural and literary criticism, published by the brothers August Wilhelm and Friedrich Schlegel in Jena, witnessed the birth of German Romanticism from the spirit of a universal aesthetics. During its brief yet revolutionary life span, *Athenaeum* laid the critical foundations of literary study. Influenced by the work of their literary forebears, Gotthold Ephraim Lessing (1729–81) and Herder, and drawing on the intellectual fruits of philosophical idealism, the Schlegels and the *Athenaeum* contributors relieved modern poesy of its burden of adherence to classical models and recognised it as the decisive aesthetic expression of modern consciousness. Besides the Schlegel brothers, the journal's contributors included Hardenberg, Caroline Schlegel (1763–1809), August Schlegel's wife at the time, Friedrich's wife Dorothea Schlegel (1764–1839), theologian-philosopher Friedrich

Schleiermacher, writer Ludwig Tieck (1773–1853) and philosopher Friedrich Wilhelm Joseph Schelling. The contributions to this lively forum not only addressed an extraordinary range of historico-political, philosophical, and aesthetic questions but also reflected the critical anxiety of an age poised at the threshold of major epochal changes.

While Friedrich Schlegel and Hardenberg were the leading philosophical and poetic visionaries of Jena Romanticism, August Wilhelm Schlegel was arguably the most learned member of the group. A prodigious man of letters, linguist, classicist and Orientalist, he was also one of the most prolific and accomplished translators of his time. In A.W. Schlegel's university lectures at Berlin and Vienna (1801–8), the critical labour of early German Romanticism finds its most comprehensive expression. Schlegel reads the role of the history of art as a record of what transpired in that history and the role of theory as a demonstration of what art should accomplish. Without an intermediate term between art history and theory, however, art history and theory alone cannot explain their respective functions and remain inadequate forms of inquiry. Thus, criticism enters the picture as the mediating third party that provides the cognitive link between history and conceptual framework. Like Romantic poetry, Romantic criticism is a generative force and does not operate as a closed system. Schlegel maintains that nations and individuals who are fettered by educational dictates, entrenched habits of mind and strict conventions of taste lack the capacity for genuine criticism. He concludes that no person can be a true critic without an understanding of other times, places and systems of thought. Based on the elaborate historical and critical ground of his literary studies, Schlegel observes that the reverent reception of the art of antiquity is seriously misguided and poses a challenge to a genuine appreciation of modern art by judging it only in terms of its imitation of classical models.

A. W. Schlegel's lectures, which followed the age of *Athenaeum*, articulated the difference between classical antiquity and Romantic modernity in terms of stasis and movement. Classical art represents a finished product. Romantic art, on the other hand, is informed by a sense of becoming that implies infinite perfectibility. The Grecian ideal of human nature sees an accord between faculties, where no gap separates fantasy and understanding, and the world appears as a coherent myth. But the modern age is marked by a deep anxiety arising from the separation of impression and reflection. Therefore, the poetry of the new age needs to heal the breach in modern consciousness by recreating the consolation of the mythical. Although in recent scholarship the theoretical acumen of Friedrich Schlegel's work has eclipsed his brother's more historicising style, A. W. Schlegel's lectures reflect the critical breadth of early German Romantics' imagination.

Poesy, A. W. Schlegel maintains, is a self-creation, an aesthetic invention that transforms everything it touches. Ultimately, all poetry is undeniably poetry raised to a higher power, poetry of poetry (*Poesie der Poesie*). For Friedrich Schlegel, this felicitous phrase refers to the notion that poetry is at bottom also always a reflection on poetry, an aesthetic form of reflexive thought. Borrowing Kant's philosophical idiom, Friedrich Schlegel also named this reflecting activity of modern poetry *Transzendentalpoesie* (transcendental poesy). Indeed, as the aesthetic analogue of transcendental philosophy, this poetry represents the representer along with the represented and is both poetry and poetry of poetry.

It is important to remember that, although the critical project of early German Romanticism rested on an abiding interest in idealistic philosophy, it also challenged the latter's rejection of metaphorical accounts of experience. Hardenberg's *Fichte-Studien* (1795–6; *Fichte Studies*) were by no means a tribute to Fichtean idealism but a further departure from the idea of some absolute principle that is epistemically an end in itself. For Hardenberg, Fichte's unquestioned representation of the world as a reflexive activity of the self remains a purely theoretical premise, totally lacking in poetic sense. Hardenberg's theoretical imagination reveals the idea of an absolute foundation as an invention. Both Hardenberg and Schlegel see allegory as a metaphorical intimation of the real. In Hardenberg's view, 'real' poetry can at best have an allegorical meaning. For Schlegel, allegory forms the philosophical ground of all poetry. The dichotomy of identity and difference as a formal construct of philosophy fails to capture the diversity of human experience that is manifested in the signs and symbols of language and art. The Romantics turn the tables on philosophy's reliance on analytic rigour and its resistance to figural language by showing that it consistently relies on analogies, heuristic fictions and rhetorical ploys in its quest for truth and certainty.

Recent scholarship on early German Romanticism, particularly the work of Walter Benjamin, Ernst Behler, Manfred Frank, Jochen Hörisch, Philipp Lacoue-Labarthe and Jean-Luc Nancy, has shown how all articulations of Romantic idealism are registered at the level of form – Romantic irony, allegory, *Witz*, fragment – which, in turn, reflect at the level of ideas.[5] In his Jena lectures on transcendental philosophy, Friedrich Schlegel maintains that the infinite field of perception is brought to the level of understanding in representational forms, specifically in 'allegory', which itself points to the infinity of form. The form commands an endless field of transfigurations. The value of aesthetic form lies in its generative energies that transform both the subject and the world. Thus, it is within the boundaries of the figural that human understanding moves from the field of amorphous data to that of specific representations. Its proper locus is not the cognition of primal grounds of being but the multiplicity of particular forms. These forms, particularly as they were developed and theorised by Schlegel, presented a persuasive answer to the dilemma of the subject sceptical of philosophical faith in ultimate principles, while adhering to the belief in the power of expressive articulation.

Most recent studies on the critical legacy of early German Romanticism portray the *Frühromantiker* as creative thinkers who not only introduced models that could be adopted by those after them but also created a space for the introduction of differences with respect to their writings, concepts and hypotheses. Hardenberg and Friedrich Schlegel translated Kantian notions of critique and the autonomous work of art and Fichte's philosophy of reflection into usable terms of literary and aesthetic criticism. Although the Romantics embraced Kant's principle of the autonomy and self-referentiality of the work of art, they disagreed with the subordinate status he assigned to imagination with respect to reason and understanding. In Kant, the judgement of beauty is not related to the cognition of the object, but through imagination the subject experiences pleasure (or pain in the case of negative judgement). Thus, judgement is not concerned with the knowledge of an object but with a subjective experience. Here judgement is 'disinterested', as the free condition of aesthetic pleasure is without utilitarian purpose and cannot be represented either as self-assured truth or as a moral postulate. The possibility of a judgement of beauty arises from a 'free play' of faculties that are common to all subjects and thus make intersubjectively valid judgements possible. Although imagination does not relate to a determinate concept of understanding, it synthesises 'the manifold of intuition' and understanding to provide a unity of concepts that connects representations to render judgement universally communicable. Ultimately, Kant does not grant imagination either a cognitive or a legislative function, as he does with understanding and reason. Schlegel reverses Kant's judgement by claiming that all human beings are endowed with the same faculty of reason, but imagination and inner poetry are unique to each individual. For the Romantics, the cognitive power of imagination in its freedom transcended that of reason, bound as reason was by transcendental concepts and laws.

The Romantics' meditation on Fichte's work took a much more extended and intensive form than their critique of Kant. Whereas absolute idealism à la Fichte posits self-consciousness as the grounding principle of philosophy, the early Romantics establish the primacy of Being over self-consciousness or reflection. The transcendence of Being urges philosophy to take the path of infinite progression, and the search for the Unknowable unfolds in aesthetic experience. With the establishment of the concept of foundations as a fiction, art is given the mandate to represent the absolute allegorically. Friedrich Schlegel's voluminous oeuvre, comprising critical essays, fragments, lectures, letters and fiction, chronicles the genesis of the early Romantic theory of art and the development of the idea of form. The importance of the concept of form in early German Romanticism had been extensively and eloquently analysed by Walter Benjamin (1892–1940) in his doctoral dissertation, *Der Begriff der Kunstkritik in der deutschen Romantik* (1920; *The Concept of Art Criticism in German Romanticism*). The main argument of Benjamin's thesis is that in early German Romanticism the idea of form replaces the idea of the absolute. The Romantic theory of art is the theory of its forms in a continuum of transformations. 'The representational form' (*Darstellungsform*) functions as the medium of reflection and reveals itself in criticism. For Friedrich Schlegel and Hardenberg, figural form as sign, symbol, allegory, fragment and irony mediates between the infinity of being and the sensible finitude of art. 'Every allegory means God,' writes Schlegel, and 'one cannot speak of God, save allegorically.' Thus, allegory or allegorical imagination represents the very impossibility of reflective thought to understand the absolute or highest truth. Like allegory, irony points to the failure of philosophy to represent the infinite adequately. Since for Schlegel philosophy does not have its own form and language in a real sense, irony becomes 'the duty of all philosophy that is yet neither history nor system' (*KFSA* XVIII, p. 86, No. 678). Schlegel sees irony as a play between the finite and the infinite and destruction and creation, where one thing cleaves to its opposite. Like life itself, irony is dialectical and represents the authentic contradiction of our selves, thereby revealing the 'innermost mystery of critical philosophy' (p. 285, No. 1067). Ultimately, irony and allegory represent a creative liberation from the prison of the merely phenomenal world and the representational limitations of philosophical language.

Friedrich Schlegel's and Hardenberg's reflections on Romantic poesy and art share a number of characteristics that came to define early Romanticism's critical legacy. Disillusioned by the political turmoil and what they saw as the crass materialism of the age, both writers revive various forms and images of the exotic as alternatives to Western culture. They reimagine ancient Indian religions and medieval Christianity as cultures that once endowed societies with meaning and integrity. They appreciate liminal and incomplete forms, tropes and histories as opposed to figures of arrest and closure and resist classical ideals of completion. In their elliptical and fragmentary texts, including their *Athenaeum* fragments, Friedrich Schlegel's novel *Lucinde* (1799) and *Kritische Fragmente* (*Critical Fragments*), Hardenberg's *Heinrich von Ofterdingen* (1800–2) and

Blüthenstaub (1798; *Pollen*), they point to possibilities of self-revision and the generative power of poetic consciousness that transcends the structural and thematic limits of any given work of art. The early Romantics valued alliances of misalliances. Hardenberg contended that genuine philosophical thought called for the introduction of systemlessness (*Systemlosigkeit*) into a system. Only such an interruption could address the flaws of the system while avoiding the anarchy of systemlessness. The form that best captured a systemless system would be the Fragment, a form complete in itself but connected to the larger world like a microcosm. Fragment also became the form of choice for Hardenberg's encyclopedia project, *Das allgemeine Brouillon* (1798–9; *The General Notebook*). When, in 1797, Hardenberg envisioned an integration and reconciliation of all the sciences and arts within the covers of a universal encyclopedia, he consulted Schlegel about the form such a major undertaking would be cast in. Hardenberg's list of possible genres included a collection of Fragments, a story, a speech, a monologue, a review, a treatise, or fragments of a dialogue. Clearly, a coherent and closed system would have functioned against the spirit of Romantic poesy with its penchant for universal and transformative movement. Schlegel's preference was for fragments of a dialogue, as the only viable design for synthesising disparate ideas and modes of knowledge. If the encyclopedia were to be composed as parts of a dialogue, the multiplicity of knowledge could be represented in the form of conversation that would progress in a temporal continuum and be disseminated across time and space by participants in the discussion. Such a progressive conversation would prevent the stagnation of ideas and ensure that knowledge is not determined for all time, as if it were an invariable given. In a conversation without final statements, philosophy emerges as 'Symphilosophie' or 'Sympoesie', a symphonic sounding of ideas in an ongoing collaboration in the pursuit of knowing and understanding. Like other favourite tropes and figures of Romantic aesthetics, the fragment is a form of ironic inquiry about the reliability of truth constructs and thus a mode of critical self-reflection. The novel, as early Romantics' idea of a genre of genres, a *Mischgedicht* ('mixed poem'), also assumed the form of a Fragment, albeit a large one. It was a hybrid form that incorporated a mixture of genres, dialogue, philosophical musing, letters, song, poem and novella. The novel was both an art form and a forum for critical reflection. For Schlegel's famous formulation, the theory of the novel had to be a novel itself. Its hermeneutic encounter with other works of art lent it its inherently intertextual and generative character. Ultimately, Romanticism's critical openness and self-correcting disposition comes to inhabit the form of the Fragment, which momentarily captures a transcendental insight yet ensures its incompleteness in the generativity of its articulation. In the final analysis, for Schlegel the symbolic import of poetry, where the ideas and forms of Romantic imagination converge, speaks where philosophy falls silent.

The extent of the influence of Romanticism's critical cultural legacy, its transfigurations and continuities in modernism and postmodernism, in post-structuralist theories remains an area of disputed claims.[6] Yet, the trials of our modernity still carry the not so distant echoes of German Romanticism's anxiety of a world in which individuals, communities and nations struggle for freedom and agency, as they face the seemingly insurmountable challenges of consumerism, intolerance, lack of ethical vision, religious fanaticism and the twilight of creative reason and empowering art.

NOTES

1. For the summary of the views of German intellectuals on the French Revolution, I have drawn on Thomas P. Saine's excellent study, *Black Bread-White Bread: German Intellectuals and the French Revolution* (Columbia, S.C.: Camden House, 1988).
2. Friedrich Schlegel, *KFSA* II, p. 366. All translations are my own.
3. This view is held by Ernst Behler, *Frühromantik* (Berlin and New York: Walter de Gruyter, 1992), p. 5.
4. In addition to Ernst Behler's voluminous work on German Romanticism, Hans Eichner's edited volume, *Romantic and Its Cognates: The European History of a Word* (Toronto: University of Toronto Press, 1972) and his *Friedrich Schlegel* (New York: Twayne, 1970), Rudolf Haym's *Die romantische Schule: Ein Beitrag zur Geschichte des deutschen Geistes* (Berlin: Weidemann, 1906), Ricarda Huch's *Die Romantik* (Leipzig: H. Hassel, 1924), Raymond Immerwahr's *Romantisch: Genese und Tradition einer Denkform* (Frankfurt am Main: Athenäum, 1972), and Lothar Pikulik's *Romantik als Ungenügen an der Normalität* (Frankfurt am Main: Suhrkamp, 1979) have contributed to a critically more nuanced understanding of German Romanticism.
5. See Walter Benjamin, *Der Begriff der Kunstkritik in der deutschen Romantik*, ed. Hermann Schweppenhäuser (Frankfurt am Main: Suhrkamp, 1973), Behler, *Frühromantik*, Manfred Frank, *Unendliche Annäherung* (Franfurt am Main: Suhrkamp, 1997), Jochen Hörisch, *Die fröhliche Wissenschaft der Poesie* (Frankfurt am Main: Suhrkamp, 1976), Philipp Lacoue-Labarthe and Jean-Luc Nancy, *The Literary Absolute: The Theory of Literature in German Romanticism*, trans. Philip Barnard and Cheryl Lester (Albany: State University of New York Press, 1988).
6. See the chapter by Margarete Kohlenbach in this volume.

FURTHER READING

Behler, Ernst, *German Romantic Literary Theory* (Cambridge: Cambridge University Press, 1993)
Beiser, Frederick C., *The Romantic Imperative: The Concept of Early German Romanticism* (Cambridge, Mass.: Harvard University Press, 2003)

Berman, Antoine, *The Experience of the Foreign: Culture and Translation in Romantic Germany*, trans. S. Heyvaert (Albany: State University of New York Press, 1992)

Brown, Marshall, *The Shape of German Romanticism* (Ithaca, N.Y.: Cornell University Press, 1979)

Calhoon, Kenneth S., *Fatherland: Novalis, Freud, and the Discipline of Romance* (Detroit, Mich.: Wayne State University Press, 1992)

Frank, Manfred, *Einführung in die frühromantische Ästhetik* (Frankfurt am Main: Suhrkamp, 1989)

Kluckhohn, Paul, *Das Ideengut der deutschen Romantik* (Tübingen: Niemeyer, 1961)

Kuzniar, Alice A., *Delayed Endings: Nonclosure in Novalis and Hölderlin* (Athens: University of Georgia Press, 1987)

Molnár, Geza von, *Romantic Vision, Ethical Context: Novalis and Artistic Autonomy* (Minneapolis: University of Minnesota Press, 1987)

O'Brien, William Arctander, *Novalis: Signs of Revolution* (Durham, N.C., and London: Duke University Press, 1995)

Pfefferkorn, Kristin, *Novalis: A Romantic's Theory of Language and Poetry* (New Haven, Conn.: Yale University Press, 1988)

Seyhan, Azade, *Representation and Its Discontents: The Critical Legacy of German Romanticism* (Berkeley, Los Angeles and Oxford: University of California Press, 1992)

Ziolkowski, Theodore, *German Romanticism and Its Institutions* (Princeton, N.J.: Princeton University Press, 1992)

2

RICARDA SCHMIDT

From early to late Romanticism

The Romantic epoch has, as is well known, been associated with diametrically opposed evaluations, with Romanticism being regarded as escapist or realist, reactionary or progressive in many variations. In addition to that, however, there are still unresolved debates as to whether Romanticism is an epochal movement with a single, clearly identifiable character, or falls into different phases which are more different from each other than from other literary movements.

The conceptualisation of a clear split between early and late Romanticism was advanced most notably by Ricarda Huch, employing a botanical model, the organic sequence of blossoming and decay. Huch examines August Wilhelm and Friedrich Schlegel, Friedrich von Hardenberg (Novalis), Wilhelm Heinrich Wackenroder and Ludwig Tieck as exponents of early Romanticism. Its 'blossoming' consists, for Huch, in utopian thinking, namely the striving to balance reason and fantasy, mind and body, and developing the idea of human perfectibility, within an all-pervasive religious framework, as a task for everybody. Huch evaluates the early Romantics' interest in illness merely as a symptom of a necessary and transitory stage of development in their pursuit of unity and wholeness. However this model works more on a social and metaphoric than on a biological level. For while Friedrich Schlegel and, to a lesser extent, Ludwig Tieck could possibly be said to follow a route from blossoming to decay in their works, many of the late Romantic writers only began writing after the most prominent early Romantics (Wackenroder and Hardenberg) had died. Thus the 'decay' Huch laments in late Romanticism – renouncing the balance between mind and nature, giving up the spiritual side in favour of indulging in natural drives, leaning towards simplistic folklore and myth, demonstrating lack of receptivity and self-destructive tendencies – is the culturally mediated difference in approach of a new generation of writers. Huch counts the dramatist Zacharias Werner, the lyric poet and novelist Clemens Brentano, the dramatist and novelist Achim von Arnim, the latter's wife (and Clemens's sister) the novelist Bettine von Arnim, the poet and medical writer Justinus Kerner, the historical novelist Friedrich de la Motte-Fouqué and the novelist Count Loeben among the most (in this sense) decadent late Romantics, while attributing at least some merit to E. T. A. Hoffmann,[1] Eduard Mörike and Joseph von Eichendorff.

The opposing strategy of outlining different stages in Romanticism, but emphasising their overarching unity, is embodied in Paul Kluckhohn's 1941 classic *Das Ideengut der deutschen Romantik* (*The Ideas of German Romanticism*). Kluckhohn distinguishes three phases on geographical and thematic grounds.[2] First, the philosophically minded *Frühromantik* (early Romanticism) is centred on Berlin. Beginning with Wackenroder's *Herzensergießungen eines kunstliebenden Klosterbruders* (1796, *Heartfelt Outpourings of an Art-Loving Friar*) and extending to A. W. Schlegel's Berlin lectures in 1802–4, it encompasses the writers Wackenroder, Tieck, Hardenberg, the Schlegel brothers and the philosopher Friedrich Schleiermacher. The second phase, *Jüngere Romantik, Mittlere Romantik, Hochromantik* or *Heidelberger Romantik* (younger Romanticism, middle Romanticism, high Romanticism or Heidelberg Romanticism), extends from 1804 to 1815 and centres on Heidelberg, Dresden and Berlin. It encompasses the writers Achim von Arnim, Clemens Brentano, Zacharias Werner, the journalist Joseph Görres, the popular philosopher Gotthilf Heinrich Schubert, the literary critic Adam Müller and the painters Philipp Otto Runge and Caspar David Friedrich. Heinrich von Kleist was associated in his last years. This phase is regarded as less philosophical than early Romanticism and more orientated towards German history and culture, theories of German nationhood and the formation of the state. Painting comes to the fore. The third phase is geographically and conceptually still more diverse. It extends to the 1830s and beyond. It is associated with the older Friedrich Schlegel in Vienna, the poet Eichendorff in Silesia, Justinus Kerner and the poet Ludwig Uhland in Swabia; finally the writers E. T. A. Hoffmann, Fouqué, Bettine von Arnim, as well as the Grimms (collectors of fairy tales and philological scholars) and the law professor Friedrich von Savigny in Berlin. It manifests itself in the form of natural philosophy, natural sciences, medicine, poetry, painting and music, and adopts a distinctly pious (Catholic and Protestant) tenor.

Nevertheless, Kluckhohn emphasises the common features of these different Romantics which distinguish Romanticism from other literary movements. He sees shared philosophical assumptions: dialectical and cyclical rather than linear thinking; ideas of infinite unity and infinite multiplicity, of the sublime and yearning for the infinite, of hovering above unresolved contradictions, and enthusiasm.[3] A merging of the sacred and the profane, of the sublime and trivial, characterizes Romantic yearning. But this is often expressed in irony, the awareness of the contrast between ideal and reality, which emerges through self-reflection and seeks distance from the self (Romantic irony). At times this leads to the conscious destruction of aesthetic illusions, escape from an identity which is little more than role-play.

Finally, Kluckhohn identifies at the core of Romanticism an empathetic understanding of nature (as opposed to dissecting nature), a participation in its creativity, an emphasis on the unity of body, soul and spirit, an interest in the unconscious forces of the soul, in the so-called 'vegetative' life of the psyche in which dream has a prophetic function and provides a connection to the transcendental or divine. Fantasy and emotion play the central role in forming Romantic individuality.[4]

By contrast to the understanding of Romanticism as a distinct movement, there is the tendency to link Romanticism with other literary movements of the age and emphasise what they have in common. This sometimes overlaps with a differentiation between early and late Romanticism. Such a careful balancing of similarities and differences between Romanticism and other literary movements on the one hand, and between early and late Romanticism on the other hand, is a position with a long history, going back to H. A. Korff's *Geist der Goethezeit* (1923–58; *The Spirit of the Age of Goethe*). In it Korff argues that there was a single spirit which evolved from Storm and Stress to Classicism and Romanticism, and that Storm and Stress, Classicism and Romanticism are merely phases of an overarching organic overall process. The Romantic generation, he argues, is divided into two generational groups, as early and high Romanticism. Korff sees early Romanticism as characterised by hyperidealism and the interest in metaphysics, the marvellous, Christianity and the Middle Ages and the form of the fairy tale, whereas high Romanticism is primarily a return to realism and nationalist-historical tendencies of patriotic Germanness in fantastic historical novels.[5]

While these characterisations largely fit Hardenberg as paradigmatic early Romantic, and to some extent Arnim as equivalent late Romantic, many other writers seem to fall outside these categories: Hölderlin, Friedrich Schlegel, Karoline von Günderrode and Jean Paul do not situate their fictional work in the Middle Ages, but in the present. The anonymously published *Nachtwachen* (1804, *Nightwatches*) are more nihilistic than idealistic. Hölderlin lacks the supernatural dimensions, and Hoffmann the German patriotism and the religious commitment, whereas Jean Paul already has realist tendencies. Hölderlin's *Hyperion, oder der Eremit in Griechenland* (1797–9; *Hyperion, or the Hermit in Greece*) is set in Greece around 1770 and naturally extends its imaginative reach to classical antiquity. As well as depicting the yearning for ideal friendship, love and society, it deals with depression, the loss of hope and purpose, the disappointment of revolutionary ardour, personal loss. Arnim is critical of both the present and the Middle Ages, and by no means realistic in style. Brentano is too interested in the quaint, comic and symbolic aspects of life to employ a realistic style.

Korff's generational division is further complicated by the fact that both Kleist and Hoffmann, whom Korff regards as the most talented writers, are also most distant from the spiritual centre of high Romanticism,[6] and that Tieck's writing spans over half a century. Tieck's early novel *William Lovell* (1796) would have to be discounted from early Romanticism, either because of its lack of a utopian trajectory (for it portrays instead a subjectivity in crisis which rejects any religious ties and ends fatally) or because it unmasks the belief in the marvellous, promoted by Wackenroder and Hardenberg, as false. While a narrow thematic definition of early Romanticism tends to fit some writers well,[7] it excludes certain others altogether or at least some of their work.

More recently, Korff's nuanced insights have been radicalised and applied to literary movements which Korff sees as entirely separate, such as the Enlightenment. While until the 1970s Romanticism used to be seen as a reaction against Enlightenment and classed as irrational by self-styled progressive critics, it has become accepted opinion in the last few decades to view Romanticism as a turn merely against the reductive, mechanistic tendencies of the Enlightenment, not as a rejection of Enlightenment altogether.[8]

A dialectical approach to early Romanticism, as developed by Silvio Vietta, goes some way to help explain the fact that the literary exploration of a philosophical problem or cultural conflicts can manifest itself in diverse ways. Vietta argues that early Romanticism portrays a contradiction in the very philosophical premises of the European Enlightenment, between Enlightenment's attempt to make rational concepts prescriptive and the attempt to restrict the validity of absolute reason with reference to emotion, the finality of the subject and its contingency with nature.[9] The Romantic response to Enlightenment can thus lead either to the attempt to compensate for the lack of meaning with a new mytho-poetic teleology, expressed in utopian or religious fiction (Wackenroder and Hardenberg), or critically to explore failed subjectivity (Tieck's *William Lovell*).

Building on Vietta's dialectical concept of Romanticism's relation with Enlightenment as well as on Korff's insights into the shared spirit of Classicism and Romanticism, but suspending his generational model of the differences within that period and replacing it with a model of differences in political and cultural experiences, Nicholas Saul suggests a unified approach to what Korff's title had made into a household name as *Goethezeit* (*Age of Goethe*). Looking at the literature of 1790–1830 as a creative response to the crisis provoked by the political problems of the age (revolution, collapse of the Holy Roman Empire, war of German liberation, Restoration, *Vormärz*) and to the decline and fall of traditional religion, Nicholas Saul identifies as the underlying consensus

> a new, anthropologically orientated vision of human fulfilment, which continues the Enlightenment project, yet differs clearly from it, and is not without its own contradiction. Human fulfilment, in the wake of the Revolution and secularisation, was to be realized through *aesthetic* means.[10]

Radicalising this approach, Richard Littlejohns proposes a 'new literary historical periodisation'[11] in which he emphasises the shared features of early Romanticism with Enlightenment, *Empfindsamkeit* (sensibility), and German Classicism, and of late Romanticism with *Biedermeier* (Restoration) and realism. He proposes a division of the epoch on the basis of either an optimistic or a pessimistic stance towards the course of history expressed in the literature in question, with the watershed lying around 1806, i.e. the historical demise of the Holy Roman Empire, splitting Romanticism in half. This neat pinpointing of change by collapsing a historical with a literary epoch, however, is then retracted when the breakdown of literary optimism is spun out into 'a succession of setbacks from the mid-1790s through to the final petrification of the Restoration anti-climax in the Karlsbad Decrees',[12] that is, extending from early to late Romanticism, and so spanning the very period it was said to divide.

The impasses created by this attempt at outlining stark divisions inside a literary movement suggest a more gradualist approach to literary history. Taking as my starting point Saul's position on the characteristics of the period, i.e. the idea that political crises and the experience of secularisation had prompted writers to look for human fulfilment via aesthetic means, I would like to add one more characteristic which writers of that period shared, and then examine the diversity within it. What writers also widely shared, I believe, is a triadic concept of historical development, a deep yearning to overcome the disharmony and disintegration experienced in the present, and to remake wholeness and unity. Claus Sommerhage called the Romantic experience of disharmony a 'potenzierte Weltungenügsamkeit' ('amplified dissatisfaction with the world'), by which he means less a generalised frustration than the conviction of the inadequacy of the world as such, the destruction of which thus appears both unavoidable and desirable.[13] This in fact amounts to little more than a modern version of Goethe's equation of Romanticism with sickness – a questionable, because totalising and essentialising view of Romanticism. There are in truth individual and historic differences with regard to the ideal of wholeness against which

Romantic writers judge the world: the personal or political, the spiritual or the sensual, the metaphysical or the patriotic, the aesthetic or religious dimensions of human life. Furthermore, there are differences in how the aesthetic is conceptualised as supporting the process of achieving the ideal of wholeness. Therefore, instead of establishing a one-dimensional binary model, I aim to account both for synchronic diversity and diachronic changes within Romanticism. I will do so by tracing the synchronic spectrum and the diachronic shifts in the deployment of one central motif in Romantic writing: the depiction of the love of the artist for a muse. Although historic changes can be observed, this is a motif which is not developed following a universal linear pattern, or a pattern of radical ruptures. Rather, it serves to demonstrate the historic simultaneity of different artistic practices and concepts, and it allows me to focus on gradual shifts in emphasis of the concept of love.

What, then, is Romantic love? In what is probably the oldest standard work on the topic, Paul Kluckhohn's *Die Auffassung der Liebe in der Literatur des 18. Jahrhunderts und in der deutschen Romantik* (1922; *The Conception of Love in the Literature of the Eighteenth Century and German Romanticism*) argues that Romantic love is the conviction of the unity of physical and spiritual love.[14] Kluckhohn derives this concept primarily from his analysis of Hardenberg and Friedrich Schlegel. While accentuating the more religious-transcendental emphasis in Hardenberg's *Heinrich von Ofterdingen* (1800) by contrast with the synthesis of sensuality and spirituality in Friedrich Schlegel's *Lucinde* (1799), Kluckhohn views the Romantic concept of love as the means of achieving an all-embracing harmony. Love for the beloved and love for the universe become one, leading towards harmony with nature and the whole universe. Love becomes the decisive formative factor in the Romantic human being. It is directed at the centre of the personality and capable of making it visible or letting it shine and thus of making the beloved person conscious of themselves.[15] The beloved in some of early Romantic fiction does indeed become an intermediary to God and infinity, a priestess, a Madonna whose death no longer constitutes a barrier to the feelings of love for her and unity with her which the man experiences. From Kluckhohn's proclamation of Friedrich Schlegel's and Hardenberg's concept of love as the essence of Romanticism follows his rejection of other Romantic writers' concept of love as 'not Romantic'. Thus hedonistic sexual encounters in Tieck's *Franz Sternbalds Wanderungen* (1798; *The Wanderings of Franz Sternbald*) are dismissed as not yet Romantic, but emerging rather from Wilhelm Heinse's hedonistic strand of Enlightenment.[16] Given Kluckhohn's view that the synthesis between sensual and spiritual love is renounced as an aim by Clemens Brentano and Zacharias Werner after a vain struggle, and that Tieck and Hoffmann aimed at it only half-heartedly or not at all, they too fail the Romanticism test.[17] This means that, contrary to Kluckhohn's later more inclusive approach to Romanticism in *Das Ideengut der deutschen Romantik*, only Hardenberg, Friedrich Schlegel and Hölderlin fulfil his criteria in *Die Auffassung der Liebe*. And indeed, it is their concept of love which to this day is mostly conceived of as *the* Romantic notion of love.

In order to avoid definitions of Romanticism or early Romanticism which exclude large sections of works whose authors are commonly regarded as Romantic, I would argue we need to widen the parameters and allow for differences, even within the subsection of early Romanticism, and so suggest the following extended hypothesis.

Most early Romantic protagonists are young men who seek their (artistic) destiny in travelling the world and whose relationship with the world is symbolized in their relationship to a female muse. This preponderance of male heroes even extends to the work of female writers, as in Dorothea Schlegel's novel *Florentin* (1801), or Karoline von Günderrode's poems 'Don Juan' and 'Wandel und Treue' ('Change and Fealty'). Inspiration through love is a key factor in Romantic protagonists' development to maturity. But the nature of this love and its literary presentation vary greatly. There is, in Wackenroder's short stories, dreams and allegedly historical accounts, the fervent exploration of art as sacred in both production and reception. Thus the asexual worshipping of the Divine in the form of the Madonna inspires the completion of a work of art in Wackenroder's fiction. By contrast, in Tieck's *Sternbald* and Hardenberg's *Ofterdingen*, both of which remained fragments, love for the elusive, absent, but human, woman has a vital function in making the protagonists realise their artistic potential – without tying them down in domesticity. For, as Hans-Joachim Mähl pointed out, the aim of history, utopia, lies beyond the process in which it is realized, and the novels can depict only the process.[18] In the tightly constructed *Ofterdingen*, each incident on the medieval poet's journey to Augsburg and each genre convention in the multi-faceted narrative has symbolic meaning, and Ofterdingen's love for Mathilde is exclusive. By contrast, *Sternbald*, with its vague imaginary landscapes and looser mixture of genres (including many letters), invites more emotional identification with the protagonist, who fairly effortlessly combines, in his search for artistic mastery on his journey from Dürer's Nuremberg to Italy, a number of sexual experiences with his love for Marie, the elusive idealised woman. In *Hyperion*, an epistolary novel narrated in a fervent and elevated tone, but set in the context of modern Greece's fight for liberty, love for a beautiful woman inspires a feeling of unity with nature as well as patriotism in the elegiac hero: Diotima asks Hyperion not to close himself off in the heaven of his love, but to become 'Erzieher unsers Volks' ('educator of our people').[19] *Hyperion*'s ideals of friendship and love, where art and religion, poetry and philosophy are seen as one, functioning as the crowning glory of a state which would be 'ein dürr Gerippe ohne Leben und Geist' ('dry bones without life and spirit')[20] if the love of beauty has not attained the status of a religion, are, however, counteracted by references to gender norms which, from a twenty-first-century perspective, threaten to turn pathos into bathos. When Diotima expresses a desire to join Hyperion in the revolutionary activities she had originally advised against, he requests her to stay at home and quietly to guard the sacred flame and beauty for his regeneration on his return.[21] This Schillerian role division between the female sphere of the pure and beautiful home and the male sphere of the hostile world, reinforced by the equation of a girl's cooking with nature's provision for mankind,[22] or with 'ein heilig priesterlich Geschäft' ('a holy priestly business'),[23] cause one to feel uneasy about ideals of the state, art, religion, love and friendship which are built on such essentialised gender segregation. Yet, despite lofty idealism being rooted in conventional gender norms of the time, *Hyperion*, in its epistolary form, is on the other hand wide enough to give a voice to Diotima, even though it is only in the form of a swan song – letters she writes to Hyperion before her death give evidence of the reflective depth a female protagonist is endowed with.

While all these different forms of love are associated with successful artistic inspiration and longing, none is consummated in the texts. Thus Friedrich Schlegel's *Lucinde*, with its celebration of sexual love as an explicit part of male–female relationships, and even gender-swapping in love-making, was scandalously different from Hardenberg's, Tieck's and Hölderlin's representations of love as ever-unfulfilled longing which drives the male protagonist's development forward, or Wackenroder's mystically religious love of art.

Although there are a number of well-known women associated with the Romantic movement, in most Romantic texts the beloved is female, and the artist desiring her is male. This reflects the fact that, in spite of some remarkable changes to gender roles practised in Romantic circles, many patriarchal structures nevertheless prevailed on a psychological and social level. Even women in the Romantic circle rebelling against the restrictions of patriarchal society had either internalised the assumption that the human condition was generically embodied in the male (thus creating male protagonists) or were finding the social hurdles to become a creative artist as a woman hard to overcome. Many of the famous Romantic women did not create fiction. They were primarily known for their personalities, lifestyle, *salons* and influence on the men around them, rather than for their own writing. Some of them published little or nothing under their own name:

Caroline Schlegel is known to have contributed to the 'Gemäldegespräche' in the journal *Athenaeum*, published under the name of her husband, August Wilhelm Schlegel. Most of them did not engage much with recognised literary genres in the public sphere, but were active primarily in secondary kinds of writing like translation and reviews, or private writing, like letters or diaries (as opposed to epistolary fiction as practised widely by eighteenth-century male novelists): Dorothea Schlegel translated extensively, but only published one (unfinished) novel, *Florentin* (1801), and in it depicts a male protagonist. Rahel von Varnhagen became famous for her posthumously published letters, but never wrote fiction. Bettine von Arnim only started publishing in 1834, after her husband's death, and when Romanticism as a movement on any definition was virtually over. Although her edited and revised collections of authentic correspondences were highly successful at the time – and her writing was revived again, together with that of Karoline von Günderrode, by Christa Wolf and feminist researchers in the late twentieth century – she has remained better known for her quirky personality than for her writing. Very few women worked in recognised, 'serious' literary genres (poetry, drama, novella); of these, Sophie Mereau and Karoline von Günderrode, who published under the gender-neutral pseudonym Tian, produced a very slender body of work and died young. Caroline de la Motte-Fouqué, on the other hand, the most prolific and commercially successful female writer of fiction in the Romantic circle (and towards the end of her life a better-known author than her husband Friedrich), has been forgotten. While feminist scholarship has tried to reclaim the writing of Romantic women (above all their letter writing) as part of the canon, they have neither had a lasting influence on the style of other writers in the course of literary history, nor has their writing gained popular acclaim among a contemporary readership.

The fact that the notion of love depicted within early Romantic writing is much wider than is often assumed in critical writing is confirmed by Jean Paul's *Siebenkäs*, first published in 1796–7, and republished after extensive revisions in 1818. The comedy of provincial life in *Siebenkäs* stands in sharp contrast to the seriousness in most other early Romantic writing, in particular to *Hyperion*'s high elegiac tone. Rather than focusing on the longing for an elusive beloved who functions as muse because of her elusiveness (a longing which is maintained because of the fragmentary form of *Sternbald* and *Ofterdingen*), or even through her death (*Hyperion* and *Lucinde*), *Siebenkäs* explores the frustrations of wedded bliss which threaten to destroy the artistic endeavours of the eponymous hero. *Siebenkäs* focuses mainly on the trials and tribulations of the mundane in married life: hearing, and, worse, in the absence of any noise waiting to hear, his young wife do the housework destroys the old man's power to concentrate on his masterpiece – a work conceived to alleviate the couple's financial problems. This is a marriage made not in heaven, but in the German provinces, here the humorously named 'Kuhschnappel' (roughly: 'cow snap'), and ends in separation thanks to the fake death of the husband and his 'widow's' innocently bigamous remarriage. Her death in childbirth finally leaves him free to marry a more congenial lover, thus demonstrating that irony does not necessarily imply a rejection of faith in utopia. In the depiction of incompatibility in marriage, there is a noteworthy discrepancy in the causes suggested for this. On the one hand, the narrator humorously describes the alienation between Siebenkäs and his wife Lenette as caused by both his neurotic behaviour and her clinging to the material tokens of bourgeois rank. On the other hand, there is the narrator's explicit judgement that the marriage fails because of Lenette's lack of idealism and preference for petty bourgeois values. The ironic stance towards the protagonist, who is nevertheless presented affectionately, is something which unites the early Romantic Jean Paul with the late Romantic E. T. A. Hoffmann, despite many differences in their concepts of love and art.

There are other exceptions to the notion that early Romantic writing depicts love for a woman as overcoming the split between body and soul, sensuality and reason, temporality and eternity, as an ideal which is instrumentalised for the self-realisation and artistic perfection of the male lover and the evocation of harmony on a social scale. In Tieck's *William Lovell*, William is unmasked as incapable of love, and such a pessimistic trajectory would fit better with many critics' definition of the characteristics of late Romanticism. In the *Nachtwachen*, the nightwatchman Kreuzgang rhapsodically and mockingly comments on his experiences in a world which lacks meaning. Social cruelty towards lovers is satirically exposed, but the utopian concept of love and the poet dreaming it are ridiculed just as much by the emphasis on the gulf between ideal and real. Kreuzgang claims: 'Die Liebe ist nicht schön – es ist nur der Traum der Liebe, der entzückt' ('Love is not beautiful – it is only the dream of love which delights').[24] The narrator recognises that the ideal of eternal love demands the death of the beloved, as 'Nur die Lebende stirbt, die Todte bleibt bei mir, und ewig ist unsere Liebe und unsere Umarmung!' ('Only the living woman dies, the dead one remains with me, and our love and embrace last for eternity!').[25] The concept of the visionary power of the poet, and the notion of the poet as social educator, on the other hand, is debunked as an aggrandising illusion, when a weak and self-centred poet commits suicide on having his manuscript rejected, using the very string with which the publisher had tied the returned manuscript to hang himself.

In Schlegel's *Florentin*, the male protagonist's longing for an ideal love grows out of a troubled past (as it does in Dorothea Schlegel's husband's structurally much more arabesque novel *Lucinde*). But in *Florentin* this longing is not even temporarily fulfilled. In addition, *Florentin* explores the complicated – and often less than exalted – feelings in a triangular relationship in the novel's present. Combining adventure with the theme of the artist, the discussion of social reform with a search for the secrets of the protagonists' past, the novel hints at many different kinds of experiencing and expressing love, beyond the love between artist and muse, thus opening up the path to a more realistic than idealistic depiction of love.

Diametrically opposed concepts of love can even be found in the work of one and the same writer. Thus Günderrode, in 'Wandel und Treue', on the one hand redefines the notion of faithful love as a 'faithful' giving in to the innate fluctuation of feelings, rather than as faithfulness to one person. On the other hand, in Günderrode's poem 'Don Juan', the archetype of the male wandering lover eventually focuses all his desire on one woman and dies for love of her. This depiction of Don Juan as having engaged in philandering because he had not yet found his one true love anticipates Hoffmann's Romantic rendering of the myth in his fictional interpretation of Mozart's opera in 'Don Juan'.

Thus not all early Romantic texts promote the idealisation of love, and those that do demonstrate a range of diverse notions of love. Similarly, late Romantic texts do not entirely renounce the idealisation of love. In some late Romanticism (Eichendorff's *Marmorbild* [1818; *Marble Statue*], Arnim's *Raphael und seine Nachbarinnen* [1824; *Raphael and the Women Next Door*]) there is a tendency to split the feminine into the Venus and the Madonna type and put the male to the test of making the 'right' choice. The wrong choice (or loving the right woman in the wrong way) can lead to the early death of the male protagonist (Arnim's *Raphael*, Hoffmann's *Die Elixiere des Teufels* [1815–16; *The Devil's Elixirs*]).

On the other hand, many later Romantic texts portray the artist's love for the muse less as a way of achieving artistic inspiration and greatness (as was the case with Wackenroder, Tieck, Hölderlin and Hardenberg), and more like Jean Paul, in order to explore the gap between expectation and outcome. The refusal to merge the ideal and the real has perhaps contributed to the view that late Romanticism is pessimistic and gave up idealism. However, just as Siebenkäs does not end in despair, but finds a new love, late Romanticism still retains a serious concept of love and the ideal of art as a secularised religion, with the artist's task being to impart a vision of the ideal and transcendental. The difference is, that in late Romanticism there is a more pronounced interest in exploring what can go wrong in the course of an individual's artistic development. And it is again love that symbolises what can go wrong. Rather than evoking ideals directly, much of later Romantic art depicts ideals of love, art and of the artist indirectly, by focusing in the first instance on psychological problems in achieving creativity and love, or on the effect of social decline on the artist, or on satirical portraits of failed artists wrongly held in high esteem by society. Love is portrayed more as a task which requires self-discipline than as a utopian state of being which symbolises ecstatic fulfilment. Moreover, it is a task at which the protagonist can fail (for example in Hoffmann's *Der Sandmann* [1814; *The Sandman*] and *Die Jesuiterkirche in G.* [1817; *The Jesuit Church in G.*]) and which can even lead to murder (Tieck's *Tannhäuser*). But that does not imply that the ideal itself is rejected.

In *Armut, Reichtum, Schuld und Buße der Gräfin Dolores* (1810, *Poverty, Wealth, Guilt and Penance of Countess Dolores*) Achim von Arnim argues against the concept of free love and for the sanctity of and responsibility in marriage. As a human being, the muse proves hollow and does not fulfil the expectations her lover had of her. But after confronting his wife's unfaithfulness the Count steadfastly performs the work of educating her to be the ideal he had first dreamed of when he met her. Rather than being lifted to a higher plane through the rapturous union with his beloved (as in *Lucinde*, and suggested in *Franz Sternbald* and *Heinrich von Ofterdingen*), the Count aspires to, and achieves, a higher level through moral effort and steadfastness in the face of disillusionment. Yet, despite Arnim's overt commitment to the sacredness of marriage, it is remarkable how often he depicts triangular relationships in his fiction. Time and again, the reality of temptation, conflicting desires and human weakness is juxtaposed in Arnim's work with the ideal of moral behaviour – an ideal which Arnim with his art is trying to help achieve. In his *Kronenwächter* (1817, *Guardians of the Crown*), he critically portrays an obsession with reviving the historical German past as doomed: the secretly surviving heir to the Hohenstaufen throne is brought up by poor foster parents (a triangular set!) and rises in bourgeois society. Yet he only survives a serious illness by a kind of Faustian pact – in his case a blood transfusion. His magic revival results in the transference of his love for his childhood beloved to her daughter whom he marries. A love triangle ensues in which his young wife feels she takes second place in her husband's affections to her mother and, in turn, is attracted to a young artist, of whom her husband then becomes jealous. The protagonist's orientation towards the past in both social and personal terms makes him fail to deal adequately with the bourgeois present, leading to the fall of the man who tried to unite the ideals of the bourgeoisie, in his rise through work and merit, with the elitist ideals of aristocracy. Thus failure in love and social vision, instead of the prospect of success, is thematised in Arnim's novel, encouraging a critical rather than an identificatory view of the importance of the Middle Ages for a revival of society, and suggesting a concept of love which stresses the reality of renunciation and loss. However, the fact that this novel remained unfinished, with a second part, still unfinished, only published posthumously, means that the positive ideal of love presented or implied in Arnim's other work is less evident here.

In his later story *Raphael und seine Nachbarinnen*, Arnim explores one of the conundrums in the reception of art in Romanticism. Raphael was seen by the Romantics mainly as the artist of the divine and transcendental. This view obscures part of his oeuvre and what art historians knew about his promiscuous lifestyle (mainly from Vasari's biographical account as the source). Via a narrator who poses as Raphael's close friend and collaborator, Arnim's story tries to give a psychological explanation for the historical Raphael's promiscuity, to account for some of Raphael's less 'divine' works as being wrongly attributed to him, as well as to indicate the regret and loss the artist suffers as a consequence of this lifestyle. In an echo of the choice the protagonist in Eichendorff's *Marmorbild* has to make between a virginal woman and a femme fatale, with the telling names Bianca and Venus, Raphael is portrayed as a man between two women: the ethereal potter and fellow artist Benedetta, who is spiritually pure and impeccably chaste, and plump Ghita, bakerwoman and embodiment of base physical needs. Losing Benedetta, Raphael also loses sight of the spiritual aspect of love and becomes dependent for artistic creation on the sensual satisfaction Ghita provides. Yet this sensuality is deplored as something paltry and sinful, made even more despicable by Ghita's repeated unfaithfulness to Raphael and her secret marriage to an ape-like man, who however paints in Raphael's style and sells his work as Raphael's. Thus a fictional 'excuse' is provided to attribute some of the historical Raphael's more sensual paintings to this base alter ego. Although the narrator emphasises that Raphael needed physical fulfilment to be creative (thus leaving a sting in the contrast between Raphael's sensuality in life and his divine art), it is made clear in a play of words evoking the ordinary and the Biblical connotations of bread that, having got used to Ghita's earthly bread, he lost the divine bread of life. Having chosen the 'bread of destruction' over the 'bread of grace', he contracts a fatal illness on rediscovering Benedetta and learning that, Madonna-like, she has cared for the two children which Ghita has secretly borne him. His early death is thus presented as the result of his recognition that he chose the wrong muse. However, the fact that the historical Raphael produced great art in spite of having chosen the wrong muse, or even that low sensual experience was the foundation of transcendent art, points to the impossibility of making idealism merge with historical reality.

Arnim's contemporary success in conveying a notion of ideal moral behaviour in love (rather than portraying the expectation of an imminent synthesis between the individual, his beloved, and the world) is demonstrated by Eichendorff attributing a fundamental change of heart to a character in his *Ahnung und Gegenwart* (1815; *Presentiment and Presence*) due to her reading Arnim's *Gräfin Dolores*. In *Ahnung und Gegenwart*, Countess Romana is negatively portrayed as a power-hungry, amoral libertine, and most relationships of the fictional characters end in despair, with the protagonist Friedrich choosing renunciation in a hermit-like existence on top of a mountain. In Eichendorff's *Das Marmorbild*, the dangerous enticement of the senses is represented by the heathen statue of Venus, and the ethical alternative, sacred Christian love in marriage, by the tellingly named Bianca. The didacticism of the choice presented here is to reinforce the reader's morality and preference for the ideal over seduction. Nonetheless, seduction remains the more alluring alternative, and the protagonist's ethical choice in *Das Marmorbild* does not convey the glowing intensity of feeling which Hardenberg portrays in Heinrich's all-encompassing love for Mathilde.

Some writers from the period of late Romanticism, it is true, choose to focus less on the love of the artist, but create protagonists with a different spectrum of experiences. In Adelbert von Chamisso's *Peter Schlemihl* (1814), the protagonist's disappointment in love triggers his replacement of love by the adventures of scientific exploration of the world. Heinrich von Kleist explores the extremes characters display in the context of war, revolution, or excessive demands by the state on the individual: the possibility of the coexistence, in a noble character, of love and rape in war in his *Marquise von O...*; of love and murder in the context of the danger and dissimulation brought about by violent revolution in *Die Verlobung in St Domingo*; of love and cannibalistic destruction in *Penthesilea*. Yet even Kleist, so famous for the violent actions of his characters, and for exploring extreme and contradictory states of feeling, holds on to an idea of love. In *Das Käthchen von Heilbronn*, set in fairy-tale-like Middle Ages, he envisages the unconditional love of a woman successfully overcoming all obstacles, including the rejection by a lover with a sadistic streak.

By contrast to the explorations of the difficulties of love which most of her male contemporaries engage in, Bettine von Arnim in *Goethe's Briefwechsel mit einem Kinde* (1834; *Goethe's Correspondence with a Girl*) evokes, under the guise of a naive and 'natural' child (a 'Feldblume' or wild flower),[26] an eroticised love for an idealised, even deified, writer. While the idealisation of the beloved recalls the artist-muse constellations in some of early Romantic literature, there are decisive differences. Above all, the muse is male and an established writer, whose kindness to her is to elevate the female correspondent-editor from insignificance because of his acknowledged greatness. The female would-be artist in this epistolary fiction thus partly feeds on reflected glory (made more effective as she styles herself as much younger and more naive than the author was at the time), and partly presents herself as a precocious genius. Since this fictionalised epistolary text is based on real letters, exchanged between historical persons about whom we know extra-literary historical facts, the process of idealisation is, I would suggest, from a twenty-first-century perspective, less convincing than pure fictional idealisation.

While Bettine von Arnim had a great influence on the liberal student movement of her day, women writers do not necessarily adopt a progressive position socially or aesthetically in their writing. Paradoxically, the most commercially successful of them often owe their success to the conservative (thus non-threatening) social message and the epigonal (thus familiar) aesthetic structures they employ. This is the case in Caroline von Motte-Fouqué's best-known story, *Der Delphin* (1817; *The Dolphin*). A male first-person narrator, Guilio Franchino, spends an eerie night in a castle-like inn: the portraits in his room frighten him, as they seem to come not only alive, but to resemble him, thus hinting at the Romantic motif of making discoveries about his ancestors. Adopting motifs from Hoffmann's *Elixiere*, *Die Abenteuer der Sylvester-Nacht* (1815; *The Adventures of New Year's Eve*) and *Don Juan* (even giving a cameo to Hoffmann as Gottmund, the slight, agile, expressive musician who drinks hard and caricatures everyone), Fouqué evokes an atmosphere of the uncanny, but without giving insights into the workings of the unconscious, as Hoffmann did, or questioning the relationship between love and art. This story, like many of hers, uses the supernatural conservatively to promote the sanctity of marriage. The superiority of the aristocracy is emphasised, in the story's closing sentence, through the destruction of the signs of the castle's bourgeois instrumentalisation as an inn, and through the castle's emblematic position towering over the neighbouring houses.

E. T. A. Hoffmann appears to be diametrically opposed to key tenets of early Romanticism when, in his early work, he depicts the necessity for the artist to renounce the possession of the beloved woman in order to pursue his ideals in art, i.e. instead of a synthesis between love and art he appears to promote division. Yet, despite the overt Gothic tendencies of his *Die Elixiere des Teufels*, the novel has also many links to Hardenberg's sublime notion of transcendental love, with the love of the dead woman being an uplifting presence for the surviving Medardus, and the lovers achieving ultimate union only in death. But religious vocabulary is for Hoffmann only a metaphor for a philosophical problem and for the high esteem in which he holds art. Thus

Hoffmann consciously draws on and subconsciously transforms Hardenberg's and Tieck's tenets on love and art. In his later writing, Hoffmann depicts an internalisation of what to him is a necessary separation between the love for an idealised woman and a real woman. Whereas Anselmus in *Der goldene Topf* (1814; *The Golden Pot*) has to choose between the real girl, Veronika, and the symbolic representation of art, the green snake Serpentina, Giglio Fava in *Prinzessin Brambilla* (1821; *Princess Brambilla*) has to recognise the coexistence of the real and the ideal, both in himself and in his beloved. Only this act of reflection, symbolised by the mirror images of a pair of lovers reflected in the lake of Urdar, can liberate them, enable them to produce good art and let them enter into a fulfilled, loving relationship. The clarity of the psychological insight, the positive belief in art's contribution towards achieving transcendence, as well as the humorous, self-reflective and complex form make *Prinzessin Brambilla* one of the most important works of German Romanticism.[27]

Hoffmann's 'Serapiontic principle' argues that imagination and enthusiasm, whilst vital to human fulfilment, must be balanced by 'Besonnenheit' (reason). This insight into the ambiguity of the artistic process and of life, while deriving from Hardenberg's insistence that the artist must remain detached and rational, nevertheless leads to a highly ironic form of writing which has often, wrongly, been thought to refute everything Hardenberg stood for. But Hoffmann, as so many other late Romantics, does cling to aesthetic humanism. However, he explores primarily the difficulties, dangers and failures an artist may encounter in love for his muse and putting a notion of the utopian function of art into practice. Instead of evoking an ideal directly, Hoffmann often enables his readers to deduce it from the structurally complex suggestion of the mistakes his fictional protagonists are making.

Tieck's *Vittoria Accorombona* (1840) reaches perhaps beyond Romanticism. Set in Renaissance Italy, for the first time in German Romanticism a woman writer is portrayed positively, by a man, as an original, independent, gifted, spirited and strong artist, one who moreover has a fulfilling sexual relationship with the man of her dreams. But as an artist, she has no conflict. Her exceptional talent is never questioned either by her or the people around her. The conflict in her life merely arises from the contrast between her purity and superiority of mind and her decadent environment. In this struggle she bows to necessity, is physically crushed, but her spirit soars. Her cause is finally avenged by society on those who murdered her, and thus she achieves social recognition in death.

Yet her purity and her lack of internal conflict or development on the one hand point to her function as a symbol of beauty to others, rather than embodying the growing and struggling of a creative artist. Furthermore, the alleged purity of her mind stands in contradiction to the fact that she loves a man who she knows has murdered his wife and her husband. Tieck's creation seems finally not to face up to the irreconcilability between the generally high moral standards attributed to her and the fact that she loves a man who murdered two people in order to be close to her.

Martin Neuhold argues that early Romanticism portrays the unrepresentable by hinting at its absence through poetological means: use of the Fragment, the motif of yearning, of sentimental material and irony.[28] While much (but by no means all) of early Romanticism uses religious or mystical metaphors to depict the task of art, late Romanticism deploys philosophical terminology of the absolute and tries to portray a realistic presence. A possibility, hinted at, can loom larger than a reality. Implicitly or explicitly, late Romanticism develops an ideal of love which has its base less in emotional symbiosis and ecstatic sensuality than in reflection and responsibility, although the attraction of Dionysian sensuality continues to be thematised. Where, as in Tieck's *Vittoria Accorombona*, the ideal of emotional symbiosis and ecstatic sensuality in love is depicted, it remains restricted to the personal realm and contrasts with the alienation between the loving couple and society, rather than envisaging social harmony via personal love.

This chapter has explored a range of different concepts of Romantic human fulfilment in love and of aesthetic means to achieve it. Rather than mapping literary development on a model of sudden ruptures and as direct reflections of historical experiences, I suggest that cultural and political experiences, literary examples and above all the dynamics of relating creatively to earlier forms of writing (even if they are much admired) all contribute to producing different answers and aesthetic forms. Any would-be rigorous definition of a movement may paradoxically exclude texts from the historical corpus whence the definition was derived. By nature, any literary grouping is always in flux, and the setting of boundaries has to bear in mind the simultaneity of continuity and change. What I think all the Romantic writers share is the belief in the imaginative possibilities of the human mind, the exploration of experiences beyond narrow concepts of enlightened reason, and the notion that art should strive for an ideal and thus contribute towards human perfectibility. The belief in the possibility of a triadic concept of historical development, to which their work is to contribute, separates Romantic artists from those in modernism and postmodernism. The positive evocation of a utopian trajectory on a symbolic level distinguishes many (but not all) early Romantic texts from later Romantics' tendency to explore, often humorously, the obstacles in reaching, in real life, a utopian ideal of love and art, which they nevertheless still share and sometimes still have their protagonists reach.

NOTES

 1. R. Huch, *Die Romantik*, 2 vols. (Leipzig: Haessel, 1931), vol. II, pp. 194–215.
 2. P. Kluckhohn, *Das Ideengut der deutschen Romantik*, 3rd edn (Tübingen: Niemeyer, 1953; 1st edn 1941), pp. 8–9.
 3. Ibid., pp. 11–17.
 4. Ibid., pp. 28–38.
 5. See H. A. Korff, *Geist der Goethezeit: Versuch einer ideellen Entwicklung der klassisch-romantischen Literaturgeschichte* (Leipzig: Koehler & Amelung, 1964; 1st edn 1923–58), vol. III, pp. 1, 13; vol. IV, pp. 20, 132.
 6. Ibid., vol. IV, p. 20.
 7. For example, Mähl's five forms of utopian writing describe Hardenberg's writing well. See H.-J. Mähl, 'Philosophischer Chiliasmus: Zur Utopiereflexion bei den Frühromantikern', in *Die literarische Frühromantik*, ed. S. Vietta (Göttingen: Vandenhoeck & Ruprecht, 1983), pp. 149–79.
 8. S. Vietta, 'Frühromantik und Aufklärung', in Vietta (ed.), *Die literarische Frühromantik*, pp. 7–84.
 9. Ibid., p. 48.
 10. N. Saul, 'Aesthetic Humanism (1790–1830)', in *The Cambridge History of German Literature*, ed. H. Watanabe-O'Kelly (Cambridge: Cambridge University Press, 1997), pp. 202–71, at p. 205.
 11. R. Littlejohns, 'Crossing a Threshold: The Example of German Romanticism', in *Schwellen. Germanistische Erkundungen einer Metapher*, eds. N. Saul, D. Steuer, F. Möbus (Würzburg: Königshausen & Neumann, 1999), pp. 152–63, at p. 157.
 12. Ibid., p. 159.
 13. C. Sommerhage, *Romantische Aporien: Zur Kontinuität des Romantischen bei Novalis, Eichendorff, Hofmannsthal und Handke* (Paderborn, Munich, Vienna, Zurich: Schöningh, 1993), p. 156.
 14. P. Kluckhohn, *Die Auffassung der Liebe in der Literatur des 18. Jahrhunderts und in der deutschen Romantik* (Tübingen: Niemeyer, 1966; first edn 1922), p. 571.
 15. Ibid. p. 381. See also pp. 386–90 and 503.
 16. Ibid., pp. 558–60.
 17. Ibid., p. 605, note 5.
 18. Mähl, 'Philosophischer Chiliasmus', p. 167.
 19. Friedrich Hölderlin, *Hyperion oder Der Eremit in Griechenland*, in *Hölderlin: Sämtliche Werke*, III, ed. Friedrich Beissner (Stuttgart: Kohlhammer, 1957), p. 89.
 20. Ibid., p. 80.
 21. Ibid., p. 100.
 22. Ibid., pp. 56–7.
 23. Ibid., p. 99.
 24. A. Klingemann, *Nachtwachen von Bonaventura*, ed. and with an afterword by Jost Schillemeit (Frankfurt am Main: Insel, 1974), p. 123.
 25. Ibid.

38

26. B. von Arnim, *Goethe's Briefwechsel mit einem Kinde*, in *Bettine von Arnim: Werke und Briefe in vier Bänden*, II, ed. Walter Schmitz and Sibylle von Steinsdorff (Frankfurt am Main: Deutscher Klassiker Verlag, 1992), p. 97.
27. Compare R. Schmidt, 'Male Foibles, Female Critique and Narrative Capriciousness: On the Function of Gender in Conceptions of Art and Subjectivity in E. T. A. Hoffmann', in *From Goethe to Gide: Feminism, Aesthetics and the French and German Literary Canon 1770–1936*, ed. Mary Orr and Lesley Sharpe (Exeter: University of Exeter Press, 2005), pp. 49–64; and *Wenn mehrere Künste im Spiel sind: Intermedialität bei E. T. A. Hoffmann* (Göttingen: Vandenhoeck & Ruprecht, 2006), pp. 141–92.
28. See M. Neuhold, *Achim von Arnims Kunsttheorie und sein Roman 'Die Kronenwächter' im Kontext ihrer Epoche* (Tübingen: Niemeyer, 1994), p. 102.

FURTHER READING

Brecht, C., *Die gefährliche Rede: Sprachreflexion und Erzählstruktur in der Prosa Ludwig Tiecks* (Tübingen: Niemeyer, 1993)

Brinkmann, R. (ed.), *Romantik in Deutschland: Ein interdisziplinäres Symposion* (Stuttgart: Metzler, 1978)

Brown, H. M., *E. T. A. Hoffmann and the Serapiontic Principle: Critique and Creativity* (Rochester, N.Y.: Camden House, 2006)

Dürbeck, Gabriele, '"Sibylle", "Pythia" oder "Dame Lucifer": Zur Idealisierung und Marginalisierung von Autorinnen der Romantik in der Literaturgeschichtsschreibung des 19. Jahrhunderts', *Zeitschrift für Germanistik*, 2 (2000), pp. 258–80

Feldges, B. and Stadler, U., *E. T. A. Hoffmann: Epoche – Werk – Wirkung* (Munich: Beck, 1986)

Kastinger-Riley, H. M., *Clemens Brentano* (Stuttgart: Metzler, 1985)

Paulin, R., *Ludwig Tieck: A Literary Biography* (Oxford: Oxford University Press, 1985)

Reuchlein, G., *Bürgerliche Gesellschaft, Psychiatrie und Literatur: Zur Entwicklung der Wahnsinnsthematik in der deutschen Literatur des späten 18. und frühen 19. Jahrhunderts* (Munich: Fink, 1986)

Ries, F. X., *Zeitkritik bei Joseph von Eichendorff*, ed. Bernd Engler, Volker Kapp, Helmuth Kiesel and Günter Niggl (Berlin: Duncker & Humblot, 1997)

Saul, N., *'Prediger aus der neuen romantischen Clique': Zur Interaktion von Romantik und Homiletik um 1800* (Würzburg: Königshausen & Neumann, 1999)

Stopp, E. C., *German Romantics in Context. Selected Essays 1971–86*, collected by P. Hutchinson, R. Paulin and J. Purver (London: Bristol Classical Texts, 1992)

Strohschneider-Kohrs, I., *Die romantische Ironie in Theorie und Gestaltung* (Tübingen: Niemeyer, 1977; (1st edn 1960)

Vietta, S., 'Frühromantik und Aufklärung', in *Die literarische Frühromantik* (Göttingen: Vandenhoeck & Ruprecht, 1983), pp. 7–84.

3

ANTHONY PHELAN

Prose fiction of the German Romantics

Goethe

Goethe's novel *Wilhelm Meisters Lehrjahre* (1795–6, *Wilhelm Meister's Apprenticeship*) was decisively important for the development of prose fiction among the Romantic authors who (to a greater or lesser degree) admired it. There is more than one reason for its powerful impact on Friedrich Schlegel and Friedrich von Hardenberg (Novalis) and their contemporaries. In the words of Nicholas Saul, 'with his *Bildungsroman* [Goethe] adapted the market's major genre to the common cause of aesthetic education. It was to establish the epoch's dominant novel-paradigm.'[1]

Goethe's hero journeys through various romantic attachments, but also through a practical and aesthetic education in the theatre, towards the recognition of personal responsibility and social integration, not least towards marriage. Among the early Romantic authors Goethe's novel provoked a differentiated reflection on the purposes that the novel as a genre might be supposed to serve. Three authors made decisive contributions: Friedrich Schlegel, Hardenberg-Novalis and Ludwig Tieck. In his 'Brief über den Roman' (1800; 'Letter on the Novel'), Schlegel high-handedly dismisses the kind of popular novel distributed by the circulating libraries when he writes: 'Mit Erstaunen und mit innerm Grimm habe ich oft den Diener die Haufen zu Ihnen hereintragen sehn. Wie mögen Sie nur mit Ihren Händen die schmutzigen Bände berühren?' ('I have often watched your servant carrying the heaps of books in to you, with astonishment and inner fury. How can you even touch the filthy volumes?').[2] For Schlegel, Goethe's model provides above all a more urgently *modern* alternative.

Schlegel claimed that an adequate critical account of Goethe's achievement would be tantamount to a definition of the current task of literature (*Kritische Fragmente*, No. 120; *KFSA* I/2, p. 162). His own conviction that the novel had set a canonical standard for contemporary literature was echoed a year later in the *Athenaeumsfragmente*, No. 216: alongside the

French Revolution and Fichte's *Wissenschaftslehre* (theory of knowledge), it stood as one of the three greatest tendencies of the age. Finally, Schlegel responded to *Wilhelm Meister* in a review, 'Über Goethes *Meister*' (1797, 'On Goethe's *Meister*'). This points to certain formal characteristics of the work which gave it its unusual authority. Stressing mode of presentation in the book, Schlegel models the form of *Wilhelm Meister* as a set of metamorphoses. His review identifies this kind of narrative organisation with an understanding of the text as a network of seemingly independent but interrelated elements: 'so wird jeder notwendige Teil des einen und unteilbaren Romans ein System für sich' ('thus each necessary part of the unified and indivisible novel becomes a system in itself', *KFSA* I/2, p. 135). This systematic integration of any particular episode or element within the work as a totality offers an unmistakeable structural analogy to the ostensible narrative theme of Goethe's story, in which the individual is integrated in a greater social whole. But Schlegel also sees parallels to his own burgeoning understanding of the *Fragment* as a ground-breaking aesthetic form.

Early Romantics

Wilhelm Meister bequeathed to its Romantic successors a conception of the novel that required full autonomy in each of its parts to be integrated with the absolute canonical authority of the whole. However, what is still a conformity of narrative substance with textual structure in Goethe is reformulated by Schlegel as an avant-garde emphasis on form. Both Friedrich and his wife Dorothea Schlegel engage formally, thematically and critically with Goethe's text in their own novels of identity and development. In *Lucinde* (1799) Friedrich Schlegel makes his debt to Goethe clear in the central section. 'Lehrjahre der Männlichkeit' ('apprenticeship of masculinity') establishes a direct relation to *Wilhelm Meisters Lehrjahre*, but also inflects development towards social and cultural wholeness by insisting on gender, and the sexual component in the emergence of a complete humanity. (Hints of a sentimental education in Goethe's novel remain less than central.) Seduction and libertinage lead the young Julius to melancholy and cynicism. An encounter with a prostitute, Lisette, ends in her suicide. Recognising the tragic consequences of sensuality, Julius plunges into male bonding, driven by aesthetic enterprises which are close to the real concerns of the Jena circle. Yet this homosociality, however noble its ideals, does not bring any of his many projects to fruition. After further false starts he encounters Lucinde, who perfectly matches him. This new relationship gives him a meaningful view of his own life as a coherent narrative: 'Auch er erinnerte sich an die Vergangenheit und sein Leben ward ihm, indem er es ihr erzählte, zum erstenmal zu einer gebildeten Geschichte.' ('He too remembered the past, and, as he recounted his life to her, for the first time it took on for him the form of a shaped history'; *KFSA* I/5, p. 53.) What had seemed dissipated and fragmented is now drawn into a higher unity, as Julius and Lucinde are fully united in their sexual difference.

With adequate elaboration this central narrative sketch could make a novel in its own right. Instead it provides the nucleus for a different kind of work, *Lucinde* itself. After a prologue, Schlegel's novel consist of a series of heterogeneous texts arranged symmetrically around the 'Lehrjahre der Männlichkeit'. Some relate to the central characters, others are cast as fantasies, allegories, idylls and dreams; after the 'Lehrjahre', letters, meditations and dialogues reflect on the ethics of marriage, friendship and family life. None of this amounts to a continuous prose narrative. Instead the framing texts and the variety of genres they set in play offer a model of the unity-in-diversity that emerges through Julius's love for Lucinde. Or so, at least, Schlegel seems to have intended. At the same time, through their sheer variety the component texts challenge the very basis of the novel genre as a sequential narrative. For Schlegel a dispersed unity in the differences and variety of the parts is everywhere present but never uniquely apparent. It was exactly the kind of coherence he had claimed to find in *Wilhelm Meister*, as part of its 'mode of presentation'. For subsequent exponents of the novel, this question of textual and narrative coherence returns.

As a result of her affair with Schlegel, Brendel Veit (daughter of the Jewish Enlightenment philosopher Moses Mendelssohn) was rabbinically divorced in 1799, the year *Lucinde* appeared, and under her new Christian name, Dorothea, married Friedrich in 1804. His novel, with its allusions to their affair, was widely felt to be scandalous and even pornographic. Dorothea's book has been understood as a response to Friedrich's. The symmetries are plain: Friedrich, the male author, publishes a text with a woman's name as its one-word title; Dorothea replies with a text written by a woman, but bearing the name of its central male protagonist: *Florentin* (1801). Thematically, Dorothea's novel challenges the male assumptions of *Lucinde*, and their oppression of women. Fatherhood, the metaphor of male creativity in Friedrich's novel, is confronted by the suicide of Florentin's lover at the very point where she finds herself pregnant. The emergent self-discovery of Julius after his sequence of amorous adventures is trumped by a 'hero', in Florentin, who knows neither his parentage nor his true identity. Thus Friedrich's novel is systematically dismantled.[3]

Alongside its particular challenges to Friedrich, *Florentin* continues the critical dialogue with Goethe. Dorothea too places the narrative of the hero's life at the centre. Florentin is attracted to Juliane, daughter of an aristocratic house and already engaged to Eduard. A pastoral excursion and a convenient storm provide the occasion for Florentin's account of his childhood and experience abroad. On the day of the wedding, Florentin heads for the nearby town where Juliane's aunt, the mysterious Clementine lives. When he finally encounters her, she faints away.

What drives this narrative is the enigma of Florentin's origins. It remains unresolved when the reader reaches the last line of this unfinished work: 'Florentin war nirgends zu finden' ('Florentin was nowhere to be found').[4] What Goethe reveals as the hidden hand of a secret society, shaping his hero's experience to give the contours of a meaningful life, is reduced by Dorothea Schlegel to the enigmatic itself. Clementine's fainting fit and even their names point towards undiscovered kinship. Beyond all Florentin's amorous adventures or the derring-do that might take him to the American War of Independence, it is the unresolved potential of his unknown identity that dominates.

If *Lucinde* remakes the novel through its form and symmetries, *Florentin* seeks a possible coherence through half-remembered details and half-recognised figures from the past. The same mystery presents itself to the hero of Ludwig Tieck's *Franz Sternbalds Wanderungen* (1798; *Franz Sternbald's Wanderings*): the young painter is told by his father, 'Du bist mein Sohn nicht, liebes Kind' (p. 49: 'You are not my son, dear child').[5] A promise of further enlightenment 'tomorrow' is frustrated by the sudden death of this adoptive parent. From his mother Franz learns that she was his ersatz father's second wife, and therefore not his birth mother either. The mystery of origins is complete.

The plot of *Franz Sternbald* is highly attenuated. The journeyman painter's conversations with Lucas van Leyden and Dürer, and Sternbald's intention to study Raphael and Michelangelo in Italy, raise questions about the relationship between Northern art and its Italian contemporaries – issues first raised in Wackenroder's *Herzensergießungen eines kunstliebenden Klosterbruders* (1795–7; *Heartfelt Outpourings of an Art-Loving Friar*), to which Tieck had contributed several chapters. Yet Sternbald is easily distracted, and none of the questions that look as though they will motivate the action carry it beyond fits and starts.

The mystery of Sternbald's parentage is never resolved; this novel too is incomplete. Repeated interruptions to the ostensible narrative enigma are matched by the intermittent storyline that deals with the girl Sternbald falls in love with. In playing up but frustrating any impulse to resolve the plot, Tieck makes room for an itinerant narrative that can accommodate extensive reflections on the nature of art and the painter's calling. Like Goethe, he contrasts the artist with the more conventional vocations of trade; but Sternbald's defence of art as a vehicle of mystical cognition can subsequently include landscape painting as a subject independent of any religious or historical theme. Such freer approaches open up in *Franz Sternbald* the whole question of abstraction, meaning and 'content'. Like many Romantic fictions, *Sternbald* is punctuated by lyrical texts. So questions of genre are raised by the juxtaposition of poetry and prose in a novel about painting. By canvassing the limitations of occasional poetry – drinking songs – in a contest of poets, the novel allows Florestan to argue for a higher poetry as a kind of free play that avoids closure, only to cap his own argument with a lyric demonstration of exactly such closure. In its turn, Florestan's case for a freer treatment of poetic composition in the spirit of Romantic improvisation is caught out by the even freer spirit of Ludoviko. Florestan requests a theme for a song he is about to improvise, and is asked in return: 'warum soll eben Inhalt den Inhalt eines Gedichts ausmachen?' (p. 316: 'why should content determine the content of a poem?'). In an ironic double-take, this again gives primacy to form. Tieck is more explicit than Schlegel in drawing a parallel between the discovery of identity and the integration of experience into the realm of the aesthetic. Sternbald stands for the artist in general, including the poet or writer; as for them, experience and imagination can only achieve their full meaning in some future moment of integration. That understanding of temporality in relation to an essentially hermeneutic life-project makes Tieck's novel an important text in the development of Romantic fiction: 'So ist die Seele des Künstlers oft von wunderlichen Träumereien befangen, denn jeder Gegenstand der Natur, jede bewegte Blume, jede ziehende Wolke ist ihm eine Erinnerung, oder ein Wink in die Zukunft' (p. 70: 'The soul of the artist is often caught up in mysterious dreams, for every object of nature, every moving flower, every passing cloud is a memory or a hint of the future').

Friedrich von Hardenberg's first experiment in narrative, *Die Lehrlinge zu Sais* (1797–1800; *The Apprentices at Sais*),[6] announces its relation to Goethe's novel by its very title. If Goethe told of an apprenticeship, Hardenberg has a tale of apprentices. This work too challenges the very idea of linear narrative and the expectations of story-telling. Instead of unfolding a continuous action, the text moves between scientific or linguistic speculation and philosophical dialogue in an almost essayistic style that can nevertheless include fragmentary stories and a fairy tale. The apprentices are initiated into the taxonomy of a mystical geology. When one of the students returns with a seemingly insignificant pebble, his trophy reveals the underlying pattern that reflects the organising principle – and therefore the meaning – of Nature itself.

This discovery offers a model for the second part. Hardenberg's experiment with narrative was long thought to be a chaotic fragment, but it has become clear that the second part, 'Nature', with its different voices and perspectives, is carefully arranged. The novel's opening sentences proclaim that within the manifold of nature the attentive observer will detect mysterious patterns ('Figuren'), part of that great cipher read 'überall, auf Flügeln, Eierschalen, in Wolken, im Schnee, in Krystallen und in Steinbildungen, auf gefrierenden Wassern, im Innern und Äußern der Gebirge, der Pflanzen, der Thiere, …' (p. 199: 'everywhere, on wings, egg-shells, in clouds, snow, crystals and rock-formations, in freezing waters, the interior and exterior of mountains, of plants, of animals …'). Tieck's Sternbald had borne witness to the same intuition that nature and the unfolding of a human life can be read for their 'wunderbare Bedeutsamkeit und rätselhafte Winke' (*Sternbald*, p. 264: 'mysterious significance and enigmatic clues'). The search for meaning is enacted as a pursuit of these signs, but self-knowledge within an understanding of Nature must be part of Nature's own harmonious being. Only secret correspondences between the natural realm and the human mind will be able to activate the living understanding that Hardenberg promotes.

In the second part, the exploration is conducted through the interplay of a series of 'voices', responding to and outdoing one another in a kind of fugue. The Apprentice at the centre of the narrative 'hört mit Bangigkeit die sich kreuzenden Stimmen' (*Lehrlinge*, p. 213: 'listens apprehensively to the conflicting voices'). As he grows calmer, another form of understanding is made available: a universal 'mood' ('Stimmung'), attained through the experience of love. Mood and love invoke a further genre: the fairy tale. The Apprentice's companion expounds the role of love through a 'Märchen' (fairy tale) of Hyacinth and Rosenblüthchen (Roseblossom). The articulate world surrounding him – as so often in Hardenberg, animals, plants, and even stones are involved in a continuous dialogue – reveals that Hyacinth's melancholia is the symptom of his love for Rosenblüthchen. No sooner is this quietly recognised than the young man is drawn away by his intellectual curiosity. Hyacinth leaves home to pursue a higher knowledge in a pilgrimage-cum-quest to the 'Mutter der Dinge … die verschleyerte Jungfrau' (p. 216: 'the mother of things, the veiled virgin'), identified as Isis. When he finally reaches his goal, he lifts the veil in a dream and encounters none other than Rosenblüthchen – a *different* virgin, who falls into his arms.

This moment returns the questing hero to where he began, but raises that origin to a higher power. Love, an understanding of nature, and self-knowledge are indistinguishably identical in the *Märchen* of Hyacinth and Rosenblüthchen, but the tale reveals that Hyacinth's longing for a different knowledge requires interpretation, like the great cipher of nature itself. In his next novel project Hardenberg retains the idea of a significant organising principle and the use of fairy tale as a positive utopia of transcendent meaning, identified in his attempts to interpret Goethe's 'Märchen' in 1798. *Heinrich von Ofterdingen* was substantially written in the following year. The first part, 'Die Erwartung' ('Expectation'; *NS* I, 181–315), is complete. The second, 'Die Erfüllung' ('Fulfilment'), never progressed beyond tantalising sketches (*NS* I, pp. 317–69). The hero is a legendary poet of the Middle Ages, yet *Ofterdingen* is not a historical novel. Hardenberg's major impulse in writing was provided, once again, by *Wilhelm Meister*. His reading of the novel was intensive and sustained, but his enthusiasm for Goethe's text, which he initially thought was the novel par excellence, soon gave way to sceptical comments: *Wilhelm Meister* was an ultimately prosaic 'Candide', attacking poesy as Voltaire's *Candide* had railed against lazy philosophical optimism; Wilhelm's career offered merely a 'pilgrimage' up the social scale (*NS* IV, p. 323; III, p. 646). Thus *Heinrich von Ofterdingen,* instead of following the life of a young man who must be disabused of his imagined vocation to the theatre, traces the process by which a born poet discovers his true calling. Whatever happens to him turns out to contribute to his artistic development.

In one sense the plot is very straightforward. Heinrich travels with his mother from his home in Thuringia to visit his maternal grandfather in Augsburg. The journey is punctuated by a series of significant encounters: with merchants; with Crusaders long since returned from the Holy Land and a captive Saracen girl, Zulima; with a miner; and, in the descent into exhausted mine-workings, with Count Friedrich von Hohenzollern, a Romantic hermit like those to be found in many subsequent narratives of Arnim, Brentano, Eichendorff or Hoffmann. The merchants entertain the travellers with tales of poets in two interpolated *Märchen* – of Arion, and of the union of poetry and monarchy in an Atlantis of the imagination. The Crusader knights recall the Holy Sepulchre and encourage Heinrich to join in the next crusade himself; Zulima tells him he reminds her of her brother, who went to be close to a famous poet in Persia. This unexpected resemblance in an oriental context may well derive from Lessing's drama *Nathan der Weise* (1780; *Nathan the Wise*), but the feeling of an almost conscious familiarity is clearly a version of the family resemblances encountered in *Florentin* and of the search for origins that intermittently motivates *Franz Sternbald*. Such spontaneous recognition is recurrent but most striking when Heinrich finds an old book in Hohenzollern's cave. Although it is written in a language he does not know, he finds in it pictures which he recognises as scenes from his own life. Ultimately all these moments are deciphered by the poet Klingsohr. '[D]er Geist der Dichtkunst,' he tells him, '[ist] euer freundlicher Begleiter' (p. 331: 'The spirit of poetry has been your friendly companion'): warfare was present thematically with the knights, the Orient in the captive Zulima, while the Bohemian miner initiated him into the realm of nature, where he also encounters history, the theme of Hohenzollern's discourse. Klingsohr as poet draws this out, and it will be his daughter Mathilde who adds love to the repertoire. Even a world beyond death itself (Heinrich foresees Mathilde's death in a dream) is apparently opened up in the second part, in which figures from the first are to be reincarnated yet encountered afresh. The novel breaks off a few pages into this second part.

Its interest lies not only in its ostensible themes and encyclopedic scope. Warfare, the Orient, nature and history, poetry, love and death are drawn together through the movement of poetic imagination and the interplay of reality, interpolated narratives and dreams. Yet, threading their way through all this variety, a network of correspondences holds the fabric of the writing together in ways that transcend the apparent linearity of the journey. In the subterranean world, Hohenzollern describes miners as inverted astrologers. Earth and sky, macrocosm and microcosm correspond, and any single point can give access to a whole system of analogies. This principle organises Hardenberg's novel, so that narrative and metaphor constantly fold back into one another. Hardenberg's 'Wenn nicht mehr Zahlen und Figuren' ('When numbers and figures no longer ...') summarises this radical understanding of meaning as relational. A transformation of world and experience will be accomplished 'Wenn sich die Welt in's freie Leben / Und in die Welt wird zurück begeben' ('When the world moves into free life / And then back into the world') – the world will move into a sphere of freedom (from the constraints of empirical measurement) but will also move back *into itself*. Heinrich's experiences cannot signify without reference to those of the others, whence they too return to the condition and place they had left behind.

Circularity is signalled early in the journey: Heinrich sets out 'mit der seltsamen Ahndung ... als werde er nach langen Wanderungen von der Weltgegend her, nach welcher sie jetzt reisten, in sein Vaterland zurückkommen, und als reise er daher diesem eigentlich zu' (p. 251: 'with the strange sense that after long wanderings he would return from the part of the world he was now travelling towards, to his homeland, and that he was therefore actually travelling towards it'). Hardenberg subtly reworks a moment when Goethe's disturbed hero senses the lost unity of his life: 'alles erinnerte ihn an alles; er übersah den ganzen Ring seines Lebens, nur lag er leider zerbrochen vor ihm und schien sich auf ewig nicht schließen zu wollen' (everything recalled everything else; he viewed the whole circle of his life – only now it lay shattered before him').[7] *Ofterdingen* becomes at last a dense network of reminiscences, drawing us into an active participation in the magic of the imagination. Thus Heinrich's visit to the mine evokes what Ziolkowski called one of German Romanticism's 'institutions', as an emblematic descent into nature where history too is fully encountered.[8] Heinrich's encounter with the book, unfinished and therefore provisional, takes back Wilhelm Meister's 'Lehrbrief' ('Diploma of Apprenticeship'); but the mine also points back to the subterranean concealment of the pregnant princess in the Atlantis-*Märchen*, and forward to the mysterious world below the surface of the river in Heinrich's dream of Mathilde's death by drowning. The reader too is always en route and always at the moment of a homecoming. As Mathilde says to Heinrich in his dream, we are always on our way home. Such an inter-communication of significance between all its moments means that *Ofterdingen* can dispense with Goethe's Masonic jiggery-pokery. This Romantic fiction retains its author's political radicalism; for dispensing also with Goethe's implied aristocratic recuperation of the bourgeois professions, in *Heinrich von Ofterdingen* the meaning and purpose of a life are accessible always and everywhere and to all.

Thus by opening the journey of self-discovery to a sense that identity is available only in a fragmented or fragmentary way (*Lucinde*) or is an unattainable male fantasy (*Florentin*); by showing that the pursuit of the origin – even of a secure parentage – is practically impossible, or at any rate constantly interrupted (*Sternbald*); finally, by folding the line of narrative into a virtuous circularity (*Heinrich von Ofterdingen*), these early fictions model new ways to engage with the meaning and purpose of a life. In their different ways, they anticipate Ralph Waldo Emerson's perplexity in his essay 'Experience': 'Where do we find ourselves? In a series of which we do not know the extremes, and believe that it has none.'[9]

Later Romantics

The second of the sonnets that preface *Heinrich von Ofterdingen* announces as its guiding trope the secret power of poesy that greets us in eternal metamorphoses. What cannot be immediately grasped is the hidden power of creativity itself. If the mastery of *Ofterdingen* lies in the understated way in which the question of narrative coherence is opened, Clemens Brentano, in his novel *Godwi, oder das steinerne Bild der Mutter* (1800–2; *Godwi, or the Stone Image of the Mother*),[10] drives the disruption of linear narrative to its next extreme. He himself gives his work the ominous subtitle *ein verwilderter Roman*, and this novel has indeed 'run wild'.

Eric Blackall defined *Godwi* as the Romantic novel par excellence: 'Its form is confessional with arabesques, theme and variations, using all genres, frequently self-reflexive.'[11] Brentano's disruptive text works on narrative form itself. Like *Lucinde* with its false starts (prologue, the title announcing confessions, Julius's introductory letter explaining his editorial process), *Godwi* has an explanatory dedication followed by a kind of dedicatory statement. This text is unsigned, but is followed by a preface over the name *Maria*. In its very inception the novel is hesitant and generically ambiguous – as ambiguous as the gender and identity of the signatory. Maria is Brentano's own second name: he seems to speak *in propria persona* about the origin of his text; and yet another Maria will subsequently emerge as a character within the fiction shaping and ordering its narrative, at least until in exhaustion he dies and Godwi takes over the tale himself.

The first part of *Godwi* is an epistolary novel. In the course of twenty-eight letters Karl Godwi and his friend Karl Römer describe their travels and amorous adventures; yet the text provides no tidy chronology. Godwi begins the first letter in the midst of a storm, and already 'beyond' the point at which his journey began – when he was enamoured of Molly, who, recognising the child of a former lover, sends him packing. The sense that some dark and tragic circumstance hangs over Godwi's childhood is underlined by enigmatic disclosures which cannot be fully resolved until much later. Like the stormy *medias in res* beginning of the first part, the novel is forever trying to catch up with itself: the enigmas of the past, of personal identity and origin, as well as love and desire, carry the characters along. Yet the texture of the novel 'run wild' seems bewildering – caught between Godwi's pursuit of immediate pleasures and Römer's insight that the present (or presence: 'Gegenwart') is unattainable: 'man sieht nicht, man sieht nur nach und entgegen' (p. 57: 'we cannot see – we can only look back or forwards'). In the company of the hermit Werdo's daughter Joduno, Godwi finally glimpses the still centre that holds all together: 'Denn nach dem einzigen Punkt, der in der Mitte der Welt liegt, kannst du die meisten Linien ziehen, und nur von ihm aus zu allem gelangen' (p. 131: 'For given the single point that lies at the centre of the world, you can draw the most lines, and only by starting with it attain to all others'). Such symmetry of meaning is familiar from the geological taxonomy of Hardenberg's *Lehrlinge*. Yet the second part of *Godwi* upsets as well as clarifies what hesitantly emerges in the first. Maria is revealed as an editor given the task of shaping the correspondence by Römer himself. Dissatisfied by the outcome, he withdraws the commission, and Maria sets off to find Godwi and complete the task with first-hand information. The result is a famous moment when the 'author' identifies himself as such to one of the characters of his own book.

Chapter 18 of the second part of *Godwi* provides a classic instance of Romantic irony, which, we recall, Friedrich Schlegel had defined as a fundamental requirement of any Romantic work of art. As Godwi the character discusses the first part of *Godwi* the novel with its editor and co-author, the conceit generates famously anti-illusionistic moments, such as '"Dies ist der Teich, in den ich Seite 146 im ersten Band falle"' (p. 307: 'This is the pond I fell into on p. 146 of the first volume') and an amusing discussion of alternative resolutions of the plot. However, the disruption of narrative by the very act of narration is not simply an effect: like the characters themselves, this strategy raises the question of genre by putting the business of narration formally back into the narrative. The text, it turns out, has been moving from the start towards its own origin in Godwi, in the disclosure of Maria's creative (and according to Godwi, distorting and hence enfictioning) editorship, and the compilation of a second volume as a documentary commentary on the first. Finally Godwi himself takes over the task from his exhausted redactor. Maria's death brings a fragmentary autobiographical conclusion, and the text concludes with a biographical note about the now deceased editor and finally co-author, before his demise, of the text we have just read.

However unlike *Lucinde*, the model for all this, *Godwi* does not conclude as affirmation. The second part, with its mirror relation to the first, is not only anti-illusionistic but actively disillusioning. Godwi's idyllic encounter with Otilie (as edited and reconstructed in various letters by Maria) in the first part is subjected to a critique that strips away its pathos. The failing health and ultimately the death of the original narrator indicates a *failure* of reflexivity. Like so many of its predecessors, Brentano's *Godwi* ends with a promise of intelligibility and completion: the tangle of relationships and blood-ties between the characters is clarified; old conflicts and past hurts are recognised – but the underlying tragedies (the suicide of Godwi's mother; the death of his great love Violette whom he abandoned) remain unresolved. The monument to Violette bears witness to a 'wound', which resonates with violent and erotic imagery. The wound is sexual and, it has been suggested, incestuous: deep within the entanglements of the back story lies the primal scene of seduction (by Godwi senior) of Molly and incestuous desire (on the part of Godwi junior) for Molly, his mother. While Schlegel too has characters, including initially Julius, his hero/author, who are damaged by sexuality, his novel settles stably enough in marriage and family. But Brentano's novel starts in the middle of a journey and ends (rather than concludes) with a promise of further proliferating narratives. And yet in another sense the extremes of its narrative series, to use Emerson's phrase again, are tragically clear: at the origin there is violence or exploitation in paternity, at their term, suicide.

Brentano's close friend Achim von Arnim turns explicitly to these moral question in his quite remarkable novel *Armut, Reichtum, Schuld und Buße der Gräfin Dolores* (1810; *Poverty, Wealth, Guilt and Penance of Countess Dolores*).[12] Its plot practically defies summary. Arnim too writes in response to Goethe – not only to *Wilhelm Meister* but more particularly to Goethe's next novel *Die Wahlverwandtschaften* (1809; *Elective Affinities*), which had offered a sardonic and, at times, bizarre account of adultery and marriage in the minor aristocracy of the early nineteenth century. Arnim is keen to restore Christian order to the perceived decadence of the nobility. Dolores's career is mapped out by the title. The abandoned daughter of a rakish aristocrat, she moves from poverty to wealth, to the guilt of seduction – by a man who turns out to be her brother-in-law – and finally to penitence. Even her name indicates that the path of Christian morality, order and fidelity will be one of dolours.

Within its theological framework, the novel proceeds via a series of parallel ethical and aesthetic narratives. A character called Mad Ilse, Dolores's maid, conceives a passion for Karl, Dolores' suitor and subsequently her husband. Later a local aristocratic lady will fall in love with him and seek any and every means to secure him for her pleasure –with fatal consequences for herself, her secretary, and Dolores. The implication is that this moral laxity is the consequence of idleness and the collapse of traditional mores.

Gräfin Dolores makes its critique of *Die Wahlverwandtschaften* apparent in several ways: the chemical model of Goethe's work is echoed when her seducer reads aloud Christian Rosenkreutz's *Chemische Hochzeit* (1616; *Chymical Wedding*), which seems to hypnotise Dolores. In a counter-parallel, the child of their union is the strange and saintly Johannes, rather than the monster of adulterous imagination born to Goethe's Countess. Yet the focus on the aristocracy in Arnim's text is symptomatic of another shared concern. If *Wilhelm Meister* had defined its hero's career in terms of an ascent to nobility, Arnim's text is troubled by, but not simply resistant to, bourgeois social aspirations and questions of aristocratic survival in an egalitarian age. Although it has been claimed that the aesthetic radicalism of Arnim's text is incongruent with its socially conservative tenor, there is ample evidence of Arnim's serious engagement with questions of class and status after the French Revolution. Count Karl is identified as a reforming estate proprietor. In this respect, he is in line with the rationalism of Goethe's idealised aristocrats in *Wilhelm Meister* and with the modernising trend that is represented on the estate visited by Florentin in Dorothea Schlegel's novel. Preacher Frank, who corresponds to Goethe's Mittler (the signally unsuccessful proponent of marital fidelity in *Die Wahlverwandtschaften*) finally goes off to revolutionary Paris in search of freedom, justice and truth.

Karl's preferences, meanwhile, are more orthodox. He recognises that the ability even to conceive a radically new world demands a degree of ruthlessness of which he is ultimately incapable. Once this is understood, Karl can take as his watchword a paraphrase of lines from Hölderlin's ode 'Patmos', cited from Arnim's own journal *Zeitung für Einsiedler* (*Tidings for Hermits*): 'das Bestehende soll gut gedeutet werden, sagt ein tiefer Denker, dem folgt Deutschland in seiner Entwickelung' (p. 167: 'what exists should be interpreted well, says a profound thinker, that is what Germany follows in its development'). It is a familiar German view: revolutionary intervention requires a rupture in historical development so radical as to be counterproductive, if not impossible. That hermeneutics can provide an alternative is a characteristically Romantic twist.

These political and social issues are not dismissed or marginalised in Arnim's novel. Karl returns to Germany to assist an aristocratic friend from his student days, who seeks advice and support on his own accession to power. This project for the political and moral renewal of the aristocracy is also apparent in the career of Dolores's father. When his dilapidated castle burns down, he is astonished to learn that the local population think of him as a ghost still haunting his former home. Arnim's point seems to be that the decadence of the old, unmodernised aristocracy still haunts contemporary society and the polity of the German-speaking lands. But it can be transformed. The old Count becomes an adviser and minister to the Prince who had been his sworn enemy. The meliorist principles implied by Arnim's positive models clearly indicate that improvement is possible. The return of the Prince heralds the cultural restoration of his *Residenzstadt* after the (Napoleonic) wars: economic prosperity goes hand in hand with revival in the arts to generate a new spirit of community.

In its structure and narrative methods, Arnim's novel continues the line of experimentation that is most signally apparent in the work of Friedrich Schlegel and Brentano. The unfolding story is constantly interrupted by interpolated texts and subordinate narratives that offer parallels to or reflections on the questions of marriage, love and order. The variety of texts and genres that Arnim intersperses through the novel include novellas, anecdotes, sermons, drama, a whole range of verse (some of which is intended to exemplify 'bad' art), and aphorisms. This chaotic texture refracts the central issues, and any of them might communicate 'the sense of our book', as the narrator says of one animal fable in particular. Like Tieck, Arnim boldly challenges readers' assumptions about the content of narrative: 'Was ist uns denn in einer Geschichte wichtig', the narrator asks, 'doch wohl nicht, wie sie auf einer wunderlichen Bahn Menschen aus der Wiege ins Grab zieht, nein die ewige Berührung in allem, wodurch jede Begebenheit zu unserer eigenen wird, in uns fortlebt, ein ewiges Zeugnis, daß alles Leben aus Einem stamme und zu Einem wiederkehre' (pp. 425–6: 'What is important in a story? Surely not the way in which it drags people along a mysterious path from cradle to grave – no, the eternal connection in all things, through which every event becomes our own, lives on in us, an eternal witness that all life stems from the One and returns to the One'). In Arnim's case, the One refracted through all forms and circumstances is a divine transcendence: what is most striking in *Gräfin Dolores* is that the tense realities of the secular world nevertheless make their inexorable demands, and Count Karl sets out to meet them in the real and historical German world as he returns, with his sons, to his homeland from the realms of romance and pastoral in Sicily. Dolores dies on the precise anniversary of her seduction – on 14 July, Bastille Day. The war after which the Prince returns to make Dolores's father his minister is (presumably) the Coalition War of 1806. Yet Arnim's attempt to relate his novel to its own times (towards which Karl rides in the closing lines) remains attenuated.

The title of its most immediate successor in the Romantic genealogy, Joseph von Eichendorff's *Ahnung und Gegenwart* (1815; *Presentiment and Presence*) gives very little away; yet its implied abstraction is a significant factor in its style and texture. As his friend Friedrich de la Motte Fouqué recognised, Eichendorff's text, written 1810–12, breathes the air of the period *before* the defeat of Napoleon, and its factual chronology can be reconstructed. The central character Count Friedrich completes his studies at the end of the summer semester of 1808, the year of the Congress of Erfurt. Friedrich's travels take him from the country to the *Residenz* in 1809 but, repelled by its decadence and superficiality, his patriotism drives him into the Wars of Liberation, where he is wounded, defeated and finally dispossessed. It was in 1809, after the Austrian victories at Aspern and Eßling, that Napoleon achieved his decisive victory at the Battle of Wagram.[13] *Ahnung und Gegenwart* ends in 1811, when Friedrich enters a monastery, his brother sets off for Egypt in search of higher wisdom, and his friend Leontin for America. This history of national defeat and collapse thus provides a context for the narrative, but its action has a different focus. Friedrich is befriended by Leontin, who remarks that life (in its relation to the poet) is 'wie ein unübersehbar weitläufiges Hyerogliphenbuch von einer unbekannten, lange untergegangenen Ursprache' (p. 81: 'like an immense and extensive book of hieroglyphs from an unknown, long lost primal language').[14] The young count is moved by these words, because he is seeking the meaning of his life (in the face of his by now familiar loss of parents and family). The image of unreadability is a measure of Eichendorff's debt to Hardenberg's *Lehrlinge*, as is Friedrich's sense subsequently of being 'wie in den Mittelpunkt alles Lebens versenkt, wo alle die Farbenstrahlen, gleich Radien, ausgehn und sich an der wechselnden

Oberfläche zu dem schmerzlich-schönen Spiele der Erscheinung gestalten' (p. 130: 'as if immersed in the central point of all life, where all the coloured rays, like radii, begin and take form on the changing surface as the painful yet beautiful play of appearance'). Beyond that, the novel signals its intertextual debts to most of the novels considered here, from Goethe, through Tieck and Brentano, to Arnim. The hero's sense of an enciphered life to be decoded, coupled with the intimation of a central focal position within a projected circumference, illustrates once more Emerson's perplexity, in the midst of a potentially infinite series.

The image of the surface, however, opens up Eichendorff's greatest imaginative achievement. His novel becomes the exploration of a fantasy landscape, of Germany and Austria, through which Friedrich and his companions travel, gathering the signs of memory and meaning that can constitute identity, both personal and, perhaps, national. At the conclusion, however, the circularities and recursions of narrative and memory yield only a need to withdraw – to religion, to a Faustian pursuit of higher knowledge, or to Leontin's project of his own new and unapproachable America. Each of these offers an alternative foundation for the chain of meaning that they have pursued *genetically* in the recovery and reconstitution of family ties, *semiotically* by reading the meanings of nature and geography and *historically* through the national war. None will suffice, and the chain of signification must be secured or reforged in another transcendence.

Such a pursuit of transcendence provides the essential structure of many of Hoffmann's works. Exploring the psychological effects of pitting a fully described real world against the fantastical and imaginative, Hoffmann's so-called 'Serapiontic' principle is expounded in his framed collection of stories, *Die Serapions-Brüder* (1820–2; *The Serapion Brotherhood*),[15] named after a hermit who was unable to distinguish between the real and the imaginary: the principle enjoins the kind of self-conscious interplay between a 'plastic', three-dimensional representation of the world and the inner vision of imagination. A sense of what Hoffmann calls the 'duplicity that determines all earthly life' renders again the self-transcending dynamic of irony.

Hoffmann's first novel, *Die Elixiere des Teufels* (1815–16; *The Devil's Elixirs*: *Sämtliche Werke* 2/2) pursues this structure with many of the mechanisms that characterised its predecessors. When Medardus, the central, demonically driven character, witnesses (or perhaps causes) another man to plunge into a ravine, he is effortlessly able to assume the other's identity. Coincidences, parallels and substitutions proliferate, culminating in the appearance of a *Doppelgänger*. *Die Elixiere* thus combine Romantic reflexivity (the framework of prefaces, letters and a confessional manuscript) with popular Gothic horror. The trail of enigmas is resolved in terms of family relationships – the genealogical 'code' that we have already observed as a motor of Romantic plots. Slippages and coincidences of identity take the central figure towards incest, the collapse of identity and madness because he is the heir to a family curse that haunts him in the half-remembered, half-recognised faces of companions and casual encounters.

The drift of the *Elixiere* towards insanity goes hand in hand with a satirical pull towards rational explanation. And yet a 'Leichtigkeit des innern Seins' ('lightness of inner being') attaining 'in heitrer Ironie auf den hohen Standpunkt' ('the higher perspective of blithe irony'; p. 232) can adequately recognise this Serapiontic incompatibility. Hoffmann's insight is formulated à propos of bourgeois scholars and artists who find themselves entertained and patronised in a princely court, and who can only survive in a context of aristocratic hauteur by achieving such interior distance. With the exception of the earliest novels we have considered, an aristocratic world – with occasional *échappées* into the pastoral and the urban – has held centre stage. However, Hoffmann's irony more characteristically turns to the tension between a life of bourgeois regularity and the imaginative freedoms of the artist. Hoffmann's perhaps most important, final and unfinished narrative, *Lebens-Ansichten des Katers Murr, nebst fragmentarischer Biographie des Kapellmeisters Johannes Kreisler, in zufälligen Makulatur-Blättern* (1822–3; *The Life and Opinions of Tomcat Murr, together with the Fragmentary Biography of Kapellmeister Johannes Kreisler, on Random Scrap Paper: Sämtliche Werke* 5), also sets the artist and musician among the aristocrats of a petty German principality and opposes all that to the bourgeois aspirations of Murr, a cat owned by the author of the biography, Kreisler's friend Meister Abraham. The structural conceit of the novel puts it firmly in the tradition of generic experimentation. Indeed, the 'fragmentary' nature of the interpolated life itself pays tribute to the continuing influence on aesthetic practice of Schlegel's experiments with fragmentary form. For interleaved with the otherwise continuous autobiography of the smugly self-educated Murr are episodes from an eccentric biography of Kreisler. Hoffmann, presenting himself as the editor of this mixed text, explains that Murr, whilst writing his life and opinions, tore up a printed book that belonged to his owner, and used its pages for writing and blotting paper. These pages have in error remained in the manuscript and been printed along with it. Thus in the spirit of Romantic irony, the book as artefact – product of writing, editing and printing – becomes itself the critical object of reflection, and linearity is doubly disrupted: first by the episodic sequence of the cat's narrative, and again by the achronological order in which Kreisler's life-story appears in the interstices. The effect is probably closest to *Godwi*, but much more entertaining.

Hoffmann's realist impulse takes a sharply satirical turn in *Kater Murr*. On the one hand, Kreisler undermines the empty formalities of the court. Meister Abraham recognises this when he denounces aristocratic society, which is irritated because it cannot reckon Kreisler as its equal: 'Er will die Ewigkeit der Verträge, die ihr über die Gestaltung des Lebens geschlossen, nicht anerkennen' (p. 499: 'he refuses to recognise the eternal nature of the contracts you have concluded about the way life is to be arranged'). On the other, Murr's autobiography explicitly parodies the idea of an individual's development in general and Goethe's *Bildungsroman* in particular. In the meantime, Kreisler's life can only be perceived in discontinuous form, in torn pages. Like his predecessors, Godwi, Julius, and even Wilhelm Meister, he experiences love for different women, but not as any progressive development or even decadence: drawn simultaneously to the musically gifted Julia and to the wild Princess Hedwig, his emotional life is torn in two. His career at court is the occasion of complex intrigue, and its climax is to be a double wedding, of Julia to Ignatius, idiotic son of the ruling prince, and of Princess Hedwig to Prince Hector. Kreisler is summoned by Meister Abraham, at the end of the second part of the novel, to the celebration of the name-day of the ruling prince's consort, which in turn coincides with Julia's name-day. The structural trick of the novel is to move in a circle, for Meister Abraham's spectacular entertainment for this court occasion is described in the first fragmentary pages from Meister Abraham's biography. And we know, therefore, that in spite of being summoned, Kreisler was absent. The novel circles back to Kreisler ('Kreis': circle) – but Kreisler is absent, a void. The fold of reflexivity that made the circularity of Hardenberg's *Heinrich von Ofterdingen* a path homewards now encloses emptiness.

Shorter forms: *Novelle, Erzählung, Märchen*

The framework of radical experimentation in these novels readily makes possible the integration of short narrative forms alongside the exploration of fragmentary texts and episodic plots. Among these forms the fairy tale has definitive status. In *Das allgemeine Brouillon* (his *General Notebook* for a projected Romantic encyclopedia) Hardenberg defines the fairy tale: 'Das Mährchen ist gleichsam der *Canon* der *Poësie* – alles poëtische muß mährchenhaft seyn. Der Dichter betet den Zufall an' ('The fairy tale is as it were the *canon* of *poesy* – everything poetic must be as in a fairy story. The poet worships chance', *Das allgemeine Brouillon* [940], NS III, p. 449). Chance, chaos, anarchy: in another fragment on Romantic *Märchen* these terms all mark 'der *Naturstand* der *Natur* – die Zeit vor der *Welt* (Staat)' ('the *natural condition* of nature – the time before the *world* (state)', [234], NS III, pp.

280–1): the *Märchen* realm is prior to any world, ordered as state or society, and so is able to reveal the possibility of a higher order – the very *possibility of meaning*. *Poësie*, of which the fairy tale is the regulative canon, names the forms in which such meaning can be disclosed. For Hardenberg the *Märchen* has much the same function as the notion of *irony* for Friedrich Schlegel: it is not simply a model for Romantic narratives but a regulative principle. Hardenberg's thinking was guided here by another text of Goethe. The *Unterhaltungen deutscher Ausgewanderten* (1794–5; *Conversations of German Refugees*) concludes with 'Das Märchen', a densely symbolic story that ends, after the fulfilment of various magical conditions, in a utopian restoration when dwellers on opposing sides of a river are finally united in fruitful commerce and mystical harmony. A poem from the drafts of *Ofterdingen* points towards just such a transcendence: a time 'Wenn nicht mehr Zahlen und Figuren / Sind Schlüssel aller Kreaturen' ('when numbers and figures are no longer / The key to all creatures'; *NS* I, p. 344) – when it will be possible to divine the meaning of the world.

At about the time Goethe wrote his own model 'Märchen', Tieck had also become interested in traditional fairy tales. His *Volksmährchen* (1797; *Popular Fairy Tales*), include an original tale with *Märchen*-like characteristics, but a tragic outcome. In *Der blonde Eckbert* ('Blond Eckbert'), much that is disturbingly unstable in Tieck's longer fiction is prefigured – indeed, *Sternbald* appeared only a year later. Eckbert lives in retirement with his wife Bertha until a new friend disturbs their calm. Bertha's life-story of escape from rural poverty takes her into a magical landscape of woodland solitude ('Waldeinsamkeit'). She discovers unimaginable wealth when she takes refuge with an old woman in the forest, but is unable to control her hunger for 'experience'. Killing the old woman's magical bird and stealing her enchanted jewels, Bertha 'escapes' again into her relationship with Eckbert. When the framing of her retrospective story-telling is breached by Eckbert's mysterious friend Philipp Walther, who supplies the forgotten name of the dog Bertha had known in her forest retreat, the idyll of her life with Eckbert begins to unravel. The undoing of her narrative reveals Bertha and Eckbert as incestuous brother and sister – and leads, in turn, to madness and death.

Romantic novels make widespread use of enigmas ('hieroglyphs', déjà vu, lost parentage) and invoke reading as the hermeneutic resolution of the enigmatic in higher meaning. At their most radical, the Romantic *Märchen*, and forms like it, insist on the intractability of life, as resistant to our will to interpret: the higher sense turns out to be at best mere coincidence, and at worst neurotic fantasy. Tieck's later tale *Der Runenberg* (1804; *Rune Mountain*) is evidently influenced by Hardenberg's professional interest in mining and geology. But for Tieck, the intuition of a crystalline, metallic truth of nature, far from revealing the origins of gold, social order, commerce and even language, as it does in *Ofterdingen* (*NS* I, pp. 239–50), tears the central character Christian away from life and his love of the organic world. His existence is a series of assumed identities. Abandoning the agricultural world to which his rural birth calls him, he becomes a huntsman. Tempted into the mountains, he glimpses the beautiful Lady of the Mountain and a golden tablet on which magical lore is inscribed. For a time the charm of the landscape and a deep nostalgia for the familiar enables him to settle, but by the end he has become literally unrecognisable as the man he once was. Thus *Der Runenberg* offers a succinct parody of the process of (in this case Romantic) *Bildung*. For Tieck's hero, the inexplicable impulse to leave home relocates him in an alternative identity, and is replaced for a moment by illusory married bliss, before his fugue state brings him finally to dissociation and the loss of identity.

For Tieck, Hardenberg's 'time before the *world* (state)' is a fearful inorganic and therefore inhuman realm. Though he is generally at odds with the transcendental aspirations of his Romantic contemporaries, Heinrich von Kleist nevertheless reviews the possibility of a world remade from its very foundations in a parallel way. In *Das Erdbeben in Chili* (1810; first version 1807, *The Earthquake in Chile*), the earthquake liberates two lovers just before their executions. Through their escape, providence (or mere chance) opens the prospect of a new and apparently Edenic world as night falls: 'so silberglänzend und still, wie nur ein Dichter davon träumen mag' ('as silvery, gleaming and quiet as any poet could ever dream of').[16] Recognisably an aesthetic construct, this natural idyll also alludes to the liberty, equality and human solidarity of the French Revolution, widely regarded as a political earthquake; but the final part of Kleist's story underlines his scepticism, when the murderous authority of church and state is again unleashed. Kleist's longest tale, *Michael Kohlhaas*, projects a similar fantasy of renewed and humane justice after a catastrophic failure of the principle of law. The horse dealer Kohlhaas overturns order and due process when he realises that they will not guarantee the return of his sequestered horses. Obsessed by this project, he leaves his original personality behind – and in his wake a trail of havoc. His earlier encounter with a mysterious Gypsy grants him, at his very execution, a measure of moral victory over the Elector of Saxony. As in Tieck's *Runenberg*, though reason and law can be restored, at the end an unaccountable order of the world supervenes.

In Tieck and, however vestigially, in Kleist, the *Märchen* world discloses the profound uncertainty of identity in an unstable world. On the face of it, in other writers, this canon of poesy seems more positive. Brentano was also an exponent of the *Märchen*. Yet for all their inventive playfulness, patterns of proliferation in his fairy-tale collections introduce a disturbing instability. The first of his *Rheinmärchen* (1811–12, published 1846; *Fairy Tales of the Rhine*), *Das Märchen von dem Rhein und dem Müller Radlauf* (*The Rhine and Wheelturn the Miller*), deploys legendary material (the Pied Piper, gluttonous Bishop Hatto of Mainz, the Bingen Mouse-Tower, the siren Loreley) and even elements drawn from Runge's tale 'Von dem Fischer un syner Fru' ('The Fisherman and His Wife'). From this traditional base Brentano unfolds a series of sub-narratives, each leading the plot into further complexities. Miller Wheelturn becomes King of Mainz and the children of the city, confined beneath the waters of the Rhine, can only be released if a fairy tale is told for each lost child. In a parody of national ambitions, this tumbling, interrupted narrative is echoed in the drummed commands that distract Prince Mousear's rag-tag army: a stork 'trommelte mit solcher Kraft *Parenthesis* und *Claudatur*, daß das Heer, wie in Klammern festgebannt, im Bache stehen blieb' (*Werke* 3: *Märchen*, p. 77: 'drummed *parenthesis* and *claudatur* with such force that the army, as if spellbound in brackets, came to a halt in the stream'). The earlier drum command '*et cetera*' gives the game away. There is no foreseeable end.

Although he made use of popular elements and even borrowed and read their core collection in 1810, the Grimm Brothers – authors of the paradigmatic *Kinder- und Hausmärchen* (1812–15; *Fairy Tales for Household and Nursery*) – were not convinced that Brentano's tales counted as *Märchen* at all. Their own *Märchen* rarely exceed a few pages and pursue very different literary ends. Fundamental patterns here range from firm moral categories, transgression of rules and the breaking of conditions to the imposition of taboos. But such structures are also reflected in literary *Märchen*. More importantly, many of the popular tales depend on the essentially literary device of evoking a world beyond, index of an alternative order which might make sense of reality. Finally, the Grimms coined a literary style for the miraculous. But they too took as a model Runge's Pomeranian *Märchen* 'Von dem Fischer un syner Fru' and 'Vom Machandelboom' ('The Juniper Tree'), with their dry and laconic directness, delight in repeated, architectonic forms, highly visual style and quiet humour.

Thus what eventually emerges as the characteristic style of the Grimms' allegedly popular and authentic tales is in fact the product of considerable literary effort. As Rölleke shows, even the characteristic fairy-tale opening 'Es war einmal' ('Once upon a time') in the very first *Märchen*, 'Der Froschkönig und der eiserne Heinrich' ('The Frog King and Iron Henry') is added between manuscript and first publication – and it is not until 1837 that the famous proverbial opening of the final version is established as 'In alten Zeiten, als das Wünschen noch geholfen hat' ('In olden times, when wishing still worked').[17] In this highly wrought simplicity, ethical and psychological structures, even within a realm of wonders, remain quite secure.

In Brentano's *Märchen*, on the other hand, the multiple voices of Hardenberg's *Lehrlinge* have become an avalanche of narratives. In his finest fairy tale, *Gockel, Hinkel und Gackeleia* (1838), the main story of the dynastic rooster Alektryo, whose crop preserves the Ring of Solomon (which is lost and recovered), proceeds via the usual conditions, exclusions (no cats in the castle, no dolls for the child) and ritual sequences. But Brentano's style is ever more exuberant, full of puns and word play. Its repetitions and acoustic effects are mesmerising, and even lists of flowers take on lyrical qualities. A dynastic marriage between Gackeleia and Prince Kronovus looks set to bring the story to a satisfactory conclusion, but here too the open-endedness of the structure is apparent when the *prima donna* of Gelnhausen announces her intention of marrying the court organist to put an end to their '*Fuga perpetua*, eine immerwährende Flucht' (*Werke* 3: *Märchen*, p. 794: 'an everlasting flight'). In the 'Tagebuch der Ahnfrau' ('Diary of the Ancestress'), Brentano's back story for his tale, the figure for this fugal non-self-coincidence is the Wandering Jew: 'ich darf nicht ruhen, bis ans Ende der Tage, und doch muß ich immer dahin streben, wo ich Ruhe finden könnte, und komme ich dem Orte nahe, so verdoppelt sich meine Flucht' (p. 892: 'I may not rest, until the end of days, and yet I must strive towards where I might find rest, and if I come close to that place, my flight is redoubled'). Only the Christian revelation of ultimate truth can arrest this fugue state (p. 893), the dissociation of identity and the flight of meaning.

By promoting their folk-tales the Grimms seek to secure identity within a national order. In 1805 Arnim's essay 'Von Volksliedern' ('On Folk-songs'), written for another folk anthology, *Des Knaben Wunderhorn* (*The Boy's Magic Horn*), declared that anyone who collected words and music from the many German-speaking lands 'sammelt sein zerstreutes Volk ... singend zu einer neuen Zeit unter seiner Fahne' ('he gathers his scattered people ... in song, for a new age under his banner').[18] The Grimms' collection echoes this ambition. They note that the social world of the *Märchen* is closely circumscribed: there are kings, faithful servants, honest craftsmen – but the emphasis lies on fishermen, millers, charcoal-burners and shepherds: social groups who are close to nature. The Preface makes their central ideological tenet explicit: 'Diese unschuldige Vertraulichkeit des größten und kleinsten hat eine unbeschreibliche Lieblichkeit in sich' ('This innocent familiarity between the greatest and the least evinces an indescribable sweetness').[19] In their testimony to the almost forgotten unity and authority of the *Volk* in the sense of 'nation', the Grimm Brothers are at pains to promote the ideological illusion of a 'pastoral' union between the greatest and the least. Authentic folk-tales, Jacob Grimm insisted, bear witness to a *national* act of self-creation.

That sense of a secure national identity is still a crucial element in Eichendorff's *Aus dem Leben eines Taugenichts* (1826; *From the Life of a Good-for-Nothing*). Like his novels, *Taugenichts* again explores the national and psychological space of German and Austrian landscapes, contrasted with Italy and the city of Rome, but also in a dialectical relationship with village life, gardens and castles. The hero's sense of distance and open spaces engenders contrasting emotions of terror and elation in his youthful search for a fuller life; this further dialectic is resolved both by his joyous return to 'unser kühlgrünes Deutschland' (*Werke* 2, p. 526: 'our cool, green Germany'). Here love for his supposed Countess can end in marriage when she turns out to be only the castle porter's niece. The resolution of a byzantine plot, within the stable order of Christian providence, achieves exactly the 'familiarity between the greatest and the least' espoused by the Grimms' preface. In *Die Bergwerke zu Falun* (1819; *The Mines at Falun*, published in *Die Serapions-Brüder*), on the other hand, E. T. A. Hoffmann satirises the pastoral innocence of the Grimms' *Volk* figures. When the young fisherman Elis Fröbom heeds his calling to the mines but falls prey to supernatural forces in the subterranean world, Hoffmann's tale repeats the pattern of Tieck's *Runenberg* in a parody of Hardenberg's romance of mining, complete with an old miner.

What the Grimms decried in Brentano's literary *Märchen* is the ironic, dangerously playful aspect of Romantic writing. Thus Romantic irony points in a different aesthetic direction. In Hoffmann's version the tension is between the present, settled social order (whether bourgeois and professional or manual) and some other dimension which will disturb it; and the same strain is felt in the artist between the real and the imaginative. By repeatedly foregrounding the creative process, irony raises questions about reality and, in recognising the productivity of (real) authorship, invites a fuller 'realism'. Hoffmann confronts these issues starkly in an early story, *Ritter Gluck* (1809; *Sir Gluck*), subsequently collected in his *Fantasiestücke* (1814–15; *Fantasias: Sämtliche Werke* II/1, p. 46). Hoffmann's text registers the detail of a late autumn day in Berlin with dry precision. His careful notation of the promenading crowds and the cafés where second-rate musicians play tunes from popular operetta, frames an impossible encounter when the narrator tells of his conversations with the long-dead composer Gluck. The same dialectic also drives *Der goldene Topf* (1815; *The Golden Pot*), which characteristically sets the magical career of Anselmus the student and his poetic destiny in the midst of everyday life in Dresden. As Hoffmann's sub-title says, it is a fairy tale of modern times.

The quizzical pull of rational scepticism never quite overcomes the insta-bilities of a supernatural, Gothic vision, however. The companion piece to *Der goldene Topf, Der Sandmann* (1816; *The Sandman*), which caught Freud's attention in his landmark essay on the Uncanny (1918), follows the narrative of Nathaniel's descent into obsession and madness. Ultimately the reader too must face the undecidable ambiguity of the tale as an account of madness or, as a professor of rhetoric in the story says, as 'eine Allegorie, eine fortgeführte Metapher' (*Sämtliche Werke* III, p. 46: 'an allegory, an extended metaphor').

One of the stories in *Die Serapions-Brüder* explicitly returns the Romantic pursuit of significance in a higher order of meaning to the realist side of Romantic irony. *Der Zusammenhang der Dinge* (1820; *The Coherence of Things*) in *Die Serapions-Brüder* has the usual framework narrative among the 'brethren', but includes the account of a striking episode from the Peninsular War. The heroism of a German patriot who fights with the Spanish guerillas against Napoleon's army is curiously mixed up with remi-niscences of Goethe's Mignon-figure from *Wilhelm Meister*. This realistic tale is told in the context of friendship between a quietly modest man Euchar (who turns out to be telling his own story from the Spanish resistance) and the utterly effete Ludwig, who notes that he shares his name with Tieck. It is Ludwig who believes in some predetermined cosmic order, 'the coherence of things', which excuses all his inadequacies. Hoffmann's conviction seems to be that moral decision and historical action point towards a different kind of narrative: when the Serapion brethren consider the tale they have been told, it is Sir Walter Scott who is invoked as an author with 'das Geschick, die Wirklichkeit, das geschichtlich Wahre aufzufassen' (*Sämtliche Werke* IV, p. 1114: 'the skill to grasp reality, the historically true'). In the late tale *Des Vetters Eckfenster* (1822, *My Cousin's Corner Window*) it will be the obser-vation of the crowded Gendarmemarkt in Berlin which, coupled with the power of the imagination, will yield 'ein treues Abbild des ewig wechselnden Lebens' (*Sämtliche Werke* VI, p. 497: 'a true picture of the constant changes of life'). Such realism ultimately dispenses with the pursuit of signs that is at the heart of Romantic narratives.

NOTES

1. Nicholas Saul, 'Aesthetic Humanism (1790–1830)', in *The Cambridge History of German Literature*, ed. Helen Watanabe O'Kelly (Cambridge: Cambridge University Press, 1997), p. 215.
2. See *KFSA* II, p. 330.

3. See Elena Pnevmonidou, 'Die Absage an das romantische Ich: Dorothea Schlegels *Florentin* als Umschrift von Friedrich Schlegels *Lucinde*', *German Life and Letters*, 58 (2005), pp. 271–92; on this 'démontage' of *Lucinde* pp. 280–1.

4. Dorothea Schlegel, *Florentin: Ein Roman herausgegeben von Friedrich Schlegel*, ed. Wolfgang Nehring (Stuttgart: Reclam, 1993).

5. Ludwig Tieck, *Franz Sternbalds Wanderungen*, ed. Alfred Anger (Stuttgart: Reclam, 1966).

6. *Die Lehrlinge zu Saïs*, in *NS* I, pp. 71–112.

7. Goethe, *Wilhelm Meisters Lehrjahre*, in Goethe, *Werke* (Hamburger Ausgabe), ed. Erich Trunz, 14 vols. (Munich: Beck, 1948–60), vol. VII, p. 570.

8. Theodor Ziolkowski, *German Romanticism and Its Institutions* (Princeton, N.J.: Princeton University Press, 1990), pp. 18–63, esp. pp. 33–7.

9. Ralph Waldo Emerson, *Selected Essays*, ed. Larzer Ziff (New York and London: Penguin, 1985), p. 285.

10. Clemens Brentano, *Godwi, oder das steinerne Bild der Mutter, ein verwilderter Roman*, in *Clemens Brentano: Werke*, ed. Friedhelm Kemp, 4 vols. (Munich: Hanser, 1963–8), vol. II.

11. Eric Blackall, *The Novels of the German Romantics* (Ithaca, N.Y., and London: Cornell University Press, 1983), p. 185.

12. Ludwig Achim von Arnim, *Armut, Reichtum, Schuld und Buße der Gräfin Dolores* in *Werke*, eds. Roswitha Burwick *et al.*, 6 vols. (Frankfurt am Main: Deutscher Klassiker Verlag, 1989–94), vol. I.

13. See Claus Sommerhage, *Romantische Aporien* (Paderborn and Munich: Schöningh, 1993), pp. 145–8.

14. Joseph von Eichendorff, *Ahnung und Gegenwart: Erzählungen* in *Werke*, eds. Wolfgang Frühwald, Brigitte Schillbach and Hartwig Schulz, 6 vols. (Frankfurt am Main: Deutscher Klassiker Verlag 1985–93), vol. II.

15. E. T. A. Hoffmann, *Die Serapions-Brüder*, in *Sämtliche Werke*, eds. Wulf Segebrecht *et al.*, 6 vols. (Frankfurt am Main: Deutscher Klassiker Verlag 1985–2004), vol. IV, eds. Wulf Segebrecht and Ursula Segebrecht, 2001. (Hereafter *Sämtliche Werke*.)

16. Heinrich von Kleist, *Sämtliche Erzählungen*, ed. Klaus Müller-Salget (Frankfurt am Main: Deutscher Klassiker Verlag, 1990), p. 201.

17. See Brüder Grimm, *Kinder- und Hausmärchen*, ed. Heinz Rölleke, 3 vols. (Stuttgart: Reclam, 1980), vol. III, p. 607.

18. Achim von Arnim and Clemens Brentano, *Des Knaben Wunderhorn: Alte deutsche Lieder*, ed. Heinz Rölleke, 9 vols. (Stuttgart, Berlin, Cologne, Mainz: Kohlhammer, 1979), vol. I, p. 441.

19. This is the text of the first edition, cited from Hans-Jürgen Schmitt's anthology, *Romantik*, 2 vols. (Stuttgart: Reclam, 1978), vol. I, pp. 138–9.

FURTHER READING

Blackall, Eric, *The Novels of the German Romantics* (Ithaca, N.Y., and London: Cornell University Press, 1983)

Engel, Manfred, *Roman der Goethezeit* (Stuttgart: Metzler, 1993)

Jacobs, Jürgen, *Wilhelm Meister und seine Brüder: Untersuchungen zum deutschen Bildungsroman* (Munich: Wilhelm Fink Verlag, 1978)

Kaminski, Nicola, *Kreuzgänge: Romanexperimente der deutschen Romantik* (Paderborn: Ferdinand Schöningh, 2001)

Kremer, Detlef, *Prosa der Romantik* (Stuttgart: Metzler, 1997)

Minden, Michael, *The German Bildungsroman: Incest and Inheritance* (Cambridge: Cambridge University Press, 1997)

O'Brien, William Arctander, *Novalis: Signs of Revolution* (Durham, N.C., and London: Duke University Press, 1995)

Sommerhage, Claus, *Romantische Aporien* (Paderborn and Munich: Ferdinand Schöningh, 1993)

Ziolkowski, Theodor, *German Romanticism and Its Institutions* (Princeton, N.J.: Princeton University Press, 1990)

4

CHARLIE LOUTH

The Romantic lyric

Most of the poetry written by the German Romantics is remote from what we tend nowadays to appreciate in a poem. It lacks the concreteness, the precision, the dense texture and above all the love of the particular that we have largely come to associate with the modern lyric, and beyond that, in its reliance on a limited stock of themes and motifs (nightingales, the heart, stars, moonlight, gardens, spring, childhood, the soul ...), it seems to stand for what much modern poetry has worked against. More so than in the writings of the English Romantics its world can seem to join up with our own experience and our articulation of it only by stark contrast. At the same time, thanks in part to Schubert, Schumann, Brahms and other composers of the *Lied*, if we are familiar with any German Romantic work it is likely to be a poem; and to some extent modern poetry still depends on an implicit knowledge of the once-dominant forms of the Romantic lyric to point and nuance its workings.

Who, though, wrote the Romantic lyric? Conventionally German literary history, because of the virtual simultaneity of Classicism and Romanticism in the German tradition, excludes several writers who from a European perspective are clearly Romantic poets, chief among them Goethe and Hölderlin. Romantic poetry in the narrow sense is as unthinkable without the example of Goethe's early poetry as is the Romantic novel without his *Wilhelm Meister*, though the debt was much less fully acknowledged at the time. And as well as anticipating, Goethe later absorbed many aspects of Romanticism and sometimes actually worked with Romantic writers, as when he wrote his sonnet cycle alongside Zacharias Werner in Jena in 1807–8 (when the sonnet was virtually a Romantic form). Still, there are good reasons for observing a distinction between Goethe and the younger poets who are more commonly thought of as Romantics. Though it is obviously a generalisation, it is quite a useful one, to say that Goethe's poems are mostly anchored to a specific occasion and give the impression of being so whereas poems by Tieck, Brentano, Eichendorff and Heine, to name some of the main practitioners, tend not to give that impression. But even if one wants to see Goethe as outside Romanticism proper he feeds into it as an important source of imagery and as a poetic figure in his own right. In about 1807 Eichendorff noted: 'Es gibt gewisse Worte, die plötzlich, wie ein Blitzstrahl, ein Blumenland in meinem Innersten auftun, gleich Erinnerungen alle Saiten der Seelen-Äolsharfe berühren, als: Sehnsucht, Frühling, Liebe, Heimat, Goethe' ('There are certain words that of a sudden, like a lightning-flash, open up a vista of flowers within me, brush all the strings of the soul's Aeolian harp like memories. Such are: longing, spring, love, homeland, Goethe'); and Novalis (Friedrich von Hardenberg) had already called Goethe 'der wahre Statthalter des poetischen Geistes auf Erden' ('the true representative of the poetic spirit on earth') in the *Athenaeum* in 1798.[1] What clearly separates Goethe from the later Romantics is that he was already a mature writer by the time of the French Revolution, whereas even for the older writers who made up the first Romantic circle in Jena – the Schlegel brothers, Hardenberg and Tieck – the French Revolution coincided with their coming of age and radically set their sense of the world they lived in. Rather than being a kind of interruption, or shift in the course of things, it opened the world into infinite possibility and, as was also the case for Wordsworth, seemed to beckon and demand a new beginning, new ways of thinking and writing and imagining, at precisely the moment they were beginning as writers themselves.

This still leaves the question of where to place Hölderlin. Born in 1770, he was of the Romantic generation, and in 1795 was attending Fichte's lectures in Jena, where he also met Hardenberg. His poetry seems at first sight to have little in common with the work of his immediate contemporaries, mainly for two (connected) reasons: it depends entirely on forms derived from classical Greek, and it looks back to Greece as a locus of past fulfilment and as an earnest of its future recovery in heightened, other form. While Greece did not have such potent significance for the Romantics, the pattern, which makes of the present a transitional period between a past plenitude and 'eine künftige Revolution der Gesinnungen und Vorstellungsarten, die alles bisherige schaamroth machen wird' ('a future revolution of ways of thinking and feeling that will make all we have had so far go red with shame' – Hölderlin to Ebel, 10 January 1797), a 'neue goldne Zeit' ('new golden age' – Hardenberg), an 'allgemeine Metamorphose' ('general metamorphosis' – Friedrich Schlegel), was common to the thinking of all of them.[2] The sense of living in an age of crisis or transition, a peculiarly open and promising world in which 'Spuren einer neuen Welt' ('traces of a new world' – Hardenberg) were already discernible (*jeder Augenblick trägt unendlich viel Zukunft in sich*' / '*every moment carries an infinite amount of future within it*' – Friedrich Schlegel), determined the way they wrote, and is probably the best ground for regarding them as a group and differentiating them from older writers such as Goethe, Schiller and Bürger.[3] A metaphor often used for the times (by Hölderlin and Hardenberg for example) was fermentation, an apparently chaotic process resulting in clarity. The clarity of the achieved poem, explicitly or not (and in Hölderlin it was explicit), pointed out beyond the complexity of the present as one of the 'hints' or 'traces' of 'einer höhern Epoche der Kultur' ('a higher epoch of civilisation' – Hardenberg), a kind of anticipation or glimpse of what was hoped for and devoutly believed in partly because belief in it, as the Romantics were well aware, was a necessary prerequisite to, and already part of, its realisation.[4] It is easier to see that Hölderlin is of the Romantic movement by looking at his thought than at his poetic practice, but the two are inseparable and there are many points of contact between his poetry and the work of the Romantics. It was also the Romantic writers, Brentano and Arnim especially, who first recognised Hölderlin's quality and saw him for what he was – the major lyric poet of the age; though they knew only parts of his work, in versions that had been modified and truncated. It has been convincingly argued that Friedrich Schlegel's ideal of *Transzendentalpoesie* (transcendental poetry or poesy) was fulfilled more completely by Hölderlin than by any of the Romantics 'proper'.[5]

In early Romanticism, especially in Friedrich Schlegel and Hardenberg (but also in Hölderlin), there is a tendency to use prose as a means of anticipating and uncovering the course of future poetry, as if defining the kind of poetry they wished to write might itself make it happen. But these formulations remain necessarily vague, and they are not, or only in a few rare cases, to do with the lyric as such. When the Romantics talk of *Poesie* they mean not so much lyric poetry as Romantic literature, an important aspect of which in both the theory and the practice was the mixing of genres. If *Poesie* is set against anything it is not prose but philosophy, as when Hardenberg calls *Poesie* 'der Schlüssel der Philosophie, ihr Zweck und ihre Bedeutung' ('the key to philosophy, its goal and meaning').[6] As this idea itself shows, in line with the Romantic project of connecting everything, of creating a dense and light network of interrelation, poetry and philosophy should ultimately be combined (Schlegel said as much). Such a combination occurs in what is the most important lyrical work of early Romanticism (if Hölderlin is excluded from this), Hardenberg's *Hymnen an die Nacht* (1800; *Hymns to Night*), which also combine poetry and prose: they are mostly written in rhythmical prose with concealed metrical patterns (a rhyming quatrain at one point), interspersed with other stanzaic forms in verse.

This formal joining of opposites corresponds to a joining and bringing into relation of all sorts of disparate spheres, making of the *Hymnen an die Nacht* a grand metaphor or place of transition, a Romantic space in which the fleeing, fragmented forms of human consciousness are pulled into a fluid constellation. Hölderlin thought that 'im übergehenden ist die Möglichkeit aller Beziehungen vorherrschend' ('in the transitional there is the possibility of all relations'), and Hardenberg, who himself noted that 'Nichts ist *poëtischer*, als alle *Übergänge* und heterogène Mischungen' ('nothing is more *poetic* than all *transitions* and heterogeneous mixtures'), explores that openness, dissolving the structures of the visible world to reassemble them in the ideal, inward form of the *Hymnen* themselves.[7] It is possible to think of the *Hymnen an die Nacht* as making a real gesture towards satisfying Friedrich Schlegel's programmatic claim that 'die romantische Poesie ist eine progressive Universalpoesie' ('Romantic poetry is a progressive universal poetry'), seeking to touch on and connect all areas of experience and so suggest a totality.[8]

The *Hymnen* effect a series of initiations, one of them being that of the reader. Addressed to night, the poems turn at first to daylight, which like the choice of prose can be understood as a move to offer readers a familiar world before drawing them almost unawares into the world of night and poetry that ensues. At the same time the rhythms, the diction, the incantatory tone of this opening section are the same as in the passages in praise of night, we are already being swept up by the poems' ecstatic mode, and the seemingly discrete realms of night and day are subtly connected. Thus when the voice of the poems turns to night, the transition has already begun, the whole sequence occupies a fluid interzone, what in the fourth hymn Hardenberg calls the 'Grenzgebürge der Welt' ('mountains that border the world'). Light is what permits distinction and measurement, it is the regulator of time, and thus belongs to the world of what Hardenberg in another poem calls 'Zahlen und Figuren' ('numbers and figures'), the world of the Enlightenment; whereas the 'neue, unergründliche Welt' ('new unfathomable world') he espouses comes pietistically 'unterm Herzen' ('from the heart'), revealed by 'die unendlichen Augen, die die Nacht in uns geöffnet' ('the infinite eyes that night opens within us'). In the interim it is sleep that reaches into the domain of the night, but sleep transmuted beyond the familiar into what dwells in wine and narcotics, in sexual love and in 'alte Geschichten' ('old stories'). 'Trägt nicht alles, was uns begeistert, die Farbe der Nacht? Sie trägt dich mütterlich und ihr verdankst du all deine Herrlichkeit. Du verflögst in dir selbst – in endlosen Raum zergingst du, wenn sie dich nicht hielte' ('Does not everything that inspires us bear the colour of night? It carries you [light] like a mother and to it you owe all your glory. You would diffuse in yourself, dissipate in endless space, if night did not hold you'). Yet as dark encloses day so night is defined by daylight, and the voice pledges to live to the full his life in the world, before 'die willkommenste aller Stunden hinunter ihn in den Brunnen der Quelle zieht' ('the most welcome of all hours draws him down into the wellspring'). After the central visionary experience of the sequence, recounted in the third hymn and close to a diary-entry made after Hardenberg visited the grave of his fiancée, he feels 'ewigen, unwandelbaren Glauben an den Himmel der Nacht und sein Licht, die Geliebte' ('eternal, unchanging faith in the heavens of night and their light, the beloved'). Thus initiated into night, living out life on the borderlands of longing, he has the strength 'zu bewohnen deine Welt, sie zu heiligen mit Liebe, daß sie ein ewig angeschautes Denkmal werde – zu bepflanzen mit unverwelklichen Blumen' ('to inhabit your [light's] world, consecrate it with love so that it may become a memorial to be looked on for ever – to plant it with unfading flowers'). This Romantic activity draws its sustenance from the proximity of life and death, fulfilment and longing, night and day the *Hymnen* have themselves negotiated, and they are the kind of 'unfading flowers' he has in mind.

The first two movements of the poem end here, at the close of the fourth hymn: 'Ich lebe bei Tage / Voll Glauben und Mut / Und sterbe die Nächte / In heiliger Glut' ('I live by day / Full of courage and faith / And by night die / In holy fire'). A general but personal experience of night is confirmed and deepened by the more particular experience at the graveside. The fifth hymn seeks to generalise this initiation and find a mythology to embody it. It takes the familiar mythologies of the ancient world and of Christianity and recasts them into a synoptic history of humankind's relationship with the divine, stepping on from references to Christ and the Cross introduced towards the end of the fourth hymn. Taking issue with Schiller's poem 'Die Götter Griechenlands' (1788; 'The Gods of Greece') Hardenberg elaborates his own broadly triadic system in which Christ, who is actually addressed as death, surpasses Greek religion by familiarising humanity with death and allowing a 'healthy' wholeness of life and death. As the beloved initiates the poet into night, so Christ initiates mankind into death, and the hitherto only germinal presence of death in night now comes into flower. But here it is clearer than anywhere, since there is a semblance of system, that sense is strictly subordinate to melos and rhythm and metaphorical necessity: nothing adds up except poetically – the system permits the sketching of a frame in which points of rebirth and renewal can be held out and dwelt on, in the hope that the poems themselves might initiate a 'new world'. That is the kind of new mythology the *Hymnen an die Nacht* offer. In their recasting of Christ's life he is born not in a manger but in 'der Armut dichterischer

Hütte' ('poverty's poetic hut'). Poetry, Hardenberg's, has engendered him, equating him with the beloved and with death. The singer who appears in the fifth hymn reminds us again that the poems are a source, 'zugleich Poesie und Poesie der Poesie' ('at once poetry and poetry of poetry' – Friedrich Schlegel).[9] They are concerned entirely with the workings of realisation, of bodying forth, not with interpretation of what already exists. Their language, liquid, respiring, gently unfolding, asks to be read as an emanation of night, not just referring to it and tracing its contours, but its actual manifestation, like Christ and the beloved an incarnation. Perhaps the last hymn, the only one wholly in verse – it is in the form of a church hymn – adopts this more public mode as a way of acknowledging the unsustainability and provisionality of the more inward and absolute voice that precedes it.

In 1804 Hölderlin published nine poems which in a letter he had called 'Nachtgesänge' ('Night Songs') – poems *of* rather than *to* the night, and night figures prominently in his thinking too. In the private mythology which is unfolded most clearly in the elegy 'Brot und Wein' ('Bread and Wine') night-time represents the godless present inaugurated by a syncretic figure combining Christ and Dionysus: 'Oder er kam auch selbst und nahm des Menschen Gestalt an / Und vollendet und schloß tröstend das himmlische Fest' ('Or he came himself and took on a human shape / And full of comfort brought to an end the celebrations of heaven'). It is likely that Hölderlin read Hardenberg's *Hymnen* in 1800 in the last issue of the *Athenaeum*, when he was working on 'Brot und Wein', and that he understood his poem to be part of the contemporary dialogue about the role of religion. The first strophe, which without Hölderlin's consent was published on its own in 1807 under the title 'Die Nacht' ('Night'), making a deep impression on Brentano, effects a transition from evening into night which is also a shift from the literal into the figurative as the familiarity of a busy town emptying at the end of the day, with the bells and the watchman keeping time, yields to a stranger realm of otherness and infinity:

> Jezt auch kommet ein Wehn und regt die Gipfel des Hains auf,
> Sieh! und das Schattenbild unserer Erde, der Mond
> Kommet geheim nun auch; die Schwärmerische, die Nacht kommt,
> Voll mit Sternen und wohl wenig bekümmert um uns,
> Glänzt die Erstaunende dort, die Fremdlingin unter den Menschen
> Über Gebirgeshöhn traurig und prächtig herauf.
>
> (ll. 13–18)[10]

> And now a breeze comes and stirs the tips of the trees,
> And look, the shadow of our earth, the moon
> Comes secretly too, the enthusing, ecstatic night comes

Full of stars and not much concerned about us,
Shining and astonishing there, a stranger among us all
Lifting in splendour and sadness over the mountain tops.

The elegy's opening movement is thus comparable to the beginning of the
Hymnen an die Nacht, and like them it goes on to explore and expand the
meaning of 'heilige Nacht' ('sacred night'), intimating a new epiphany.

Hölderlin's work played little role in the development of Romantic poetry
because it was hardly available at the time, but Hardenberg-Novalis, along
with Tieck, provided a fund of themes, attitudes and even images that almost
circumscribed what came later. Eichendorff later spoke disparagingly of
'Novalisieren' ('Novalicising') 'ohne den Tiefsinn und den dichterischen
Verstand von Novalis' ('without the depth and poetic sense of Novalis').[11]
Apart from the theoretical impulse (Friedrich Schlegel, Hardenberg) there
was also an important formal impulse to early Romanticism, mainly from
A. W. Schlegel, whom Heine backhandedly called 'der größte Metriker
Deutschlands' ('Germany's greatest metrician') in *Die romantische Schule*
(1832; *The Romantic School*).[12] Partly through translation he (re)intro-
duced a wealth of intricate Romance stanzaic forms including the gloss, the
madrigal, the sestina, the canzone and above all the sonnet, most of which,
against the dominance of classical metres such as the elegiac and hexameter
forms used by Goethe and Schiller (and Hölderlin), immediately established
themselves as Romantic. These short and often strictly defined forms also
suited the social versifying games which were part of a general Romantic
tendency to cultivate friendship and 'sociability'. Such games perhaps had
something to do with an important aspect of Romantic poetry: the ascen-
dance of sound over meaning and of form over content.

Much Romantic poetry has a weightlessness, an insubstantiality about
it that – though it can often seem a weakness – may be its saving grace.
Tieck introduces his poem 'Umgänglichkeit' (roughly, 'Circulating'), when it
occurs in his novel *Franz Sternbalds Wanderungen* (1798; *The Wanderings
of Franz Sternbald*), with the words 'warum soll eben Inhalt den Inhalt eines
Gedichts ausmachen?' ('just why does content have to be the content of
a poem?'),[13] and the poem itself contrasts the language of men with the
language of birds: whereas the birds' 'twittering and whistling' expresses a
freedom and a kind of democratic variousness which is also evident in their
restless flight and migratory movements over the 'round' earth, the 'verständlich' ('comprehensible') language of humans is instrumental and consists
in capturing and killing the birds. The poem puts itself on the side of the
birds, imitating their airy speech and their elusive, circling flights, winging
its way by playful association towards a final untranslatable joke about the

day of judgement that has little or nothing to do with its starting-point. In the middle of this quixotic, off-hand poem, whose tone is flippant and serious at the same time, comes a stanza that interprets that tone and reaches far forward into the development of the Romantic lyric. Of the birds of the air, the 'thrushes, bullfinches, swallows, starlings', it says:

> Sie wissen alle nicht, was sie meinen,
> Sie wissen's wohl und sagen's nicht,
> Und wenn sie auch zu reden scheinen,
> Ist ihr Gerede nicht von Gewicht.[14]

> Not one of them knows what it is they mean,
> Or perhaps they know and do not say,
> And even if they seem to speak,
> What they speak of has no weight.

That is, the birdsong the poem emulates, and the many voices of which it hints at in the alternatives of the first two lines, speaks and does not speak, it has no discoverable intention, it is pure sound, a kind of empty speech. While human language clearly cannot be like this (words have meanings which are always going to interfere), it can approach it, and Tieck's poems explore the possibility of writing about nothing. One of his best-known poems is 'Mondscheinlied' ('Moonshine Song'). It consists entirely of the evocation of mood. In its flitting, irregular progression, its refusal to decide what kind of poem it wants to be, it shifts through various possibilities, 'bald dunkel bald hell' ('now dark, now light'), and so can be seen to be about not a particular experience, but experience itself. Tieck seems to invent a kind of writing which almost all German Romantic poetry is inflected by. It is a style in which like in the birdsong of 'Umgänglichkeit' things are said with such inconsequentiality that they seem to have no specific content or necessity, as if they could equally be something else, or as if they were being enounced and taken back at the same time.

One can think of this style as a form of irony, where irony means precisely this avoidance of fixity and consequence. There is a link here to Keats's notion of 'Negative Capability' – 'when man is capable of being in uncertainties, Mysteries, doubts, without any irritable reaching after fact and reason' (letter to George and Thomas Keats, 21 December 1817).[15] This 'remaining Content with half knowledge', as Keats also calls it, allows dwelling among possibilities, a hovering over complexity which certitude would prevent. Keats characterises the disposition for which the style of much German Romantic poetry is an apt medium because it is content to enjoy a mode the subject of which tends to slip through the fingers of the mind (one would be hard put to say what most lyrics in Tieck's tradition are *about*). Hardenberg, writing about irony, says that it is 'nichts anders – als die Folge, der Charakter ... der wahrhaften Gegenwart des Geistes. Der Geist erscheint immer nur in *fremder, luftiger* Gestalt' ('nothing other than the consequence, the character ... of true presence of mind. The mind only ever appears in *unfamiliar, airy* form').[16] This permits thinking about irony as a manifestation of the mind (or, of spirit). Manfred Frank, who has written at length on Tieck's irony and 'grace', has suggested that we can understand it as the adequate expression of a notion of the self that was also being arrived at in contemporary philosophy. He quotes an extraordinary passage from Schelling's lectures in Erlangen in 1820–1: of subjectivity, Schelling says that it is '*durch alles durch gehen und nichts sein*, nämlich nicht so sein, daß es nicht auch anders sein könnte ... Es ist nicht das, was *frei* ist, Gestalt anzunehmen. Denn so würde die Freiheit als *Eigenschaft* erscheinen, die ein von ihr noch verschiedenes ... Subjekt voraussetzt – sondern die Freiheit ist das *Wesen* des Subjekts' ('*to go through everything and be nothing* [think of Keats's 'Negative Capability'], that is, not to be in such a way that it could not also be different ... It is not that which is *free* to take on shape. For if it were, freedom would appear as a *quality* that presupposes a subject distinct from itself – rather, freedom is the *essence* of the subject').[17] Irony, as a kind of saying that disconcerts itself and 'has no weight', is the literary mode of such freeness, the mode which, as Hardenberg intimates, allows the mind or the soul to appear: the lightness, the elusiveness, the transparency of the style, which can so easily be felt as a failing, emerges as the mode of being in the world, of exploring that world without being defined by it. The cultivation of this style coincides with a historic moment at which the world seemed unusually open, unsettled, possible, and though it is not the only one it is the main connecting strand in Romantic poetry until Heine, who in fact continues it but to more political ends.

One contemporary who objected to this style was Karoline von Günderrode. Her third collection of writings, *Melete*, which was in proof when she killed herself in 1806, contains a fictitious exchange of letters between Eusebio and an unnamed other who complains that modern poetry is 'Liniengestalten entweder, die körperlos hinaufstreben im unendlichen Raum zu zerfließen, oder bleiche, lichtscheue Erdgeister, die wir grübelnd aus der Tiefe unsers Wesens herauf beschwören; aber nirgends kräftige, markige Gestalten' ('either sketchy shapes that strive up disembodiedly to dissolve in infinite space, or pale earth-spirits afraid of the light whom we conjure up pensively from the depths of our beings – but no strong figures of flesh and blood').[18] Her own poems draw on all kinds of mythologies for their matter, on Ossian, and on Hardenberg, to whom, like most of the early

Romantics, she wrote poems after his death. 'Der Kuß im Traume' ('The Dreamt Kiss'), a sonnet, connects desire, night, dream and death in the manner of the *Hymnen an die Nacht*, but without the religious aspect. Love and death are Günderrode's main preoccupations, especially combined as erotic dying. In 'Liebe' ('Love'), a poem not unlike Brentano's better-known 'Über eine Skizze' ('On a Sketch'), love is 'lebendiger Tod' ('living death'). In 'Don Juan' the hero 'steigt ... freudig zu den Todten' ('rises joyfully to the dead'), safe in the memory of his last sweet conquest.[19] Günderrode writes nearly always in a male voice, or from a male perspective, and she published under the (male) pseudonym Tian. Her focus on love and death as transitions to immortality, and her eclectic interest in world mythology, lead her to ritual. One of her best poems, 'Die Malabarischen Witwen' ('The Widows of Malabar'), works because it fits the ritual it describes, the self-immolation of Hindu widows on their husbands' funeral-pyres, to the poetic ritual of the sonnet. 'Die Sitte hat der Liebe Sinn verstanden' ('Custom has understood the sense of love'), and the sonnet expounds this sense in its own consummation:

> Zur süßen Liebesfeyer wird der Tod,
> Vereinet die getrennten Elemente,
> Zum Lebensgipfel wird des Daseins Ende.
>> (ll. 12–14)[20]

> Death becomes a sweet ceremony of love,
> Conjoins the separated elements,
> The end of life becomes its crowning moment.

Günderrode's use of the Romance forms that A. W. Schlegel had encouraged marks her closeness to the Jena circle, but she was a close friend of Clemens Brentano and his sisters. She did not live to see what was probably the single most important event in the development of the Romantic lyric and symbolically the founding of its second phase, the publication of the first volume of *Des Knaben Wunderhorn* (*The Boy's Magic Horn*) by Brentano and Achim von Arnim in Heidelberg in 1806 (two more followed in 1808). Almost at a stroke this collection of songs altered the diction of German poetry. Shrewdly dedicated to Goethe, it earned a 'dankbar und läßlich' ('grateful and indulgent') response from him in a prompt review.[21] Goethe had collected folk-songs himself round Strasbourg in the early 1770s. But though commonly thought of as a gathering of folk-songs, *Des Knaben Wunderhorn* presents itself in its subtitle as 'Alte deutsche Lieder' ('Old German Songs'), and the songs are almost entirely based on written, very often literary, sources. Only a handful were collected from the lips of singers; many were baroque poems by writers such as Friedrich Spee, poets unread at the time. This antiquarian tendency, the recovery of lost poems from various kinds of past, is countered or realised by a modernising, inventive rewriting or adaptation of most texts to contemporary taste, though as a truly creative work it formed that taste rather than simply dishing up what was already in demand. With great flair and subtlety Arnim and Brentano shaped a new literary style, the famous *Volksliedton* (folk-song tone), casting a gauze of coherence over their very disparate material. Goethe, in his review, was quite aware of the restorative, synthetic, augmentative nature of their work, and saw it as intrinsic to the process of transmission. But he also expressed the hope that the songs might gradually 'return' to the people 'von dem sie zum Teil gewissermaßen ausgegangen' ('from whom in part, in a manner of speaking, they came').[22] This quickly happened. Whereas Goethe could pick up the various layers of what were palimpsest-like texts, almost everyone else fell for the composite tone without equivocation, and several songs rapidly became folk-songs in the way Goethe had hoped – by being sung and passed on orally. By the time of *Die romantische Schule* (1832) this process, for Heine, was complete: 'In diesen Liedern,' he wrote, 'fühlt man den Herzschlag des deutschen Volks' ('In these songs you can feel the heartbeat of the German people'). He likened attempts by poets to imitate 'diese Naturerzeugnisse' ('these natural products') to preparing 'künstliche Mineralwasser' ('artificial mineral water').[23] But in one of his favourite poems, 'Der Schweizer' ('The Switzer'), the parts he reserved for special praise were in fact those added by Brentano.

By presenting what was actually a new tone as 'old', *Des Knaben Wunderhorn* gave Tieck's light, inconsequential style a wide currency, and supplied it with a multiplicity of forms, a new loose syntax and a narrow but subtly variable compass of diction and imagery. At the heart of all this is repetition: these songs and the thousands that quickly derived from them can be seen as a particularly pure form of poetry in their total espousal of the basic poetic principle of repetition. Birdsong, as an approachable ideal of naturalness, is never far away, and the dream that the songs might seem the spontaneous voicing of the popular spirit. In reality, of course, the collection was the invention of a tradition and, like all the Romantic verse which fed into it and which it spawned, a highly conscious and subtle mixing of the naive and the artful. As with the discovery of the German landscape (Arnim and Brentano did for the Rhine valley what Wordsworth and others did for the Lake District) finding and making went hand in hand. This soon gained political implications, if it did not have them already.

The making of the *Wunderhorn* was Brentano's schooling. Poems of his written before work on the *Wunderhorn* began, such as 'Der Spinnerin Lied'

('Song of the Spinstress') and 'Zu Bacharach am Rheine' ('By Bacharach on the Rhine'), would not have seemed out of place in it. They are made of a small number of repeated words and unfold through abrupt, elliptical juxtapositions, leaving gaps in sense between the self-contained verses which, connected as they are chiefly by musicality and recurring motifs, are resonant in the way of litanies or chants. It is an unavoidable commonplace to associate Brentano's work with music. Glosses were written by many poets on a Tieck verse that opens with the lines 'Liebe denkt in süßen Tönen, / Denn Gedanken stehn zu fern' ('Love thinks in sweet tones, / For thoughts are too remote'), and musicality was a chief means of loosening words from their discursive sense and lifting them into the mode of weightlessness.[24] Brentano took this further than anyone else, and the acoustic assumes an importance for its own sake.

Many of his poems take the form of lullabies, often explicitly, and the lullaby fits perfectly his dwelling on euphonous sounds, dispensing him from the immediate claims of sense. The circling return of words and sounds dislocates them from any fixed meaning, they tend towards babble, towards a mode which can be felt to be both empty and replete: precisely because of its distance from accepted meaning it becomes open to a fullness of meanings, none of which definitively settles. One poem, sometimes known as 'Wiegenlied' ('Lullaby'), ends with a modulating sequence of onomatopoeic verbs: 'Summen, murmeln, flüstern, rieseln' ('Humming, murmuring, whispering, trickling').[25] Each one picks up an element earlier in the poem and so has its place, but the effect of running into sound like this is to move into the realm of invocation, and all Brentano's poems cherish the hope that like spells or charms they might, magically, effect some kind of transformation; they seem to implore the words to open out to something beyond them even as they bind themselves more firmly into the domain of words. And the lullaby, while being something approaching empty sound, is also a song with a purpose, which is to soothe to rest, a modest form of transformation. (One might compare the late poems written to Emilie Linder which as well as courting her seek to convert her.) The passing from waking to sleep that is the lullaby's endpoint can stand for the various fusings that Brentano's poems work. Inner and outer landscapes, the religious and the erotic, subject and object, time and space, colour and sound, they are all mixed and blended in the fluid, undelimited, bewitching, in the end mystical language of a poetry of mood. This is its aim, a positive bridging of division, but it needs to be seen as a reaction, summoning up all the means of art, against the brokenness of the world. A consciousness that the very potency of their language separates it from the world and so makes for rather than overcomes division prompts some poems to turn against themselves in violent rejection of the fact that they keep open, as much as mend, the 'bittre süße Wunde' ('bitter, sweet wound') of the self.[26] But most find ever more involved and enigmatic ways of spinning language into private, sensual, but rarely concrete webs of sound which can be thought of as a single continuous text.

Whereas Brentano's mode can be seen to approximate to the lullaby, Eichendorff's is a kind of muted reveille. 'Wünschelrute' ('Divining Rod') contains a Romantic poetics in miniature:

> Schläft ein Lied in allen Dingen,
> Die da träumen fort und fort,
> Und die Welt hebt an zu singen,
> Trifft du nur das Zauberwort.[27]

> A song's asleep in every thing
> That dreams and dozes in the world
> And it all begins to sing
> If you find the magic word.

Rather than incantation, poetry is here an act of divination: there is transformation, but through a finding of what is already there, a discovery that connects the slumbering disparateness of 'things' into an animate 'world'. This awakening into song, brought about by the poetic word, points again to an ideal of oneness between poetry and the world. Just as the poem sings through the correspondence of rhymes falling into place, it is the correspondence of all things that makes the world break into song. Rhyme is the animating substance of almost all Romantic lyric, but in Eichendorff its significance is deepened by being made to intimate, as agent and symbol, the hidden order of the world. A key word for Eichendorff is 'lauschen', meaning an intent, almost devout, listening, and it is answered by 'rauschen', a word that covers a greater range of sounds that any English word can, but denotes, as in the poem 'Lockung' ('Lure'),[28] the sensual rustling of the natural world. Despite the importance of these words, Eichendorff's poetry is above all visual, it attends to the visible surface of things, and orders the contours of the world in such a way that it becomes transparent to a transcendent one – he sometimes referred to the language of his poems as 'hieroglyphic', and what it sought to represent was 'des Lebens wahrhafte Geschichte' ('life's true story').[29] Eichendorff is a Christian poet, sometimes obtrusively so (see 'Der Wandrer'),[30] but often the world that shines through the landscape of a poem could just as well be an earthly paradise. The longing for home (*Heimat*) compounds the memory of Eichendorff's childhood in Silesia with the anticipation of being taken up into God, it looks both forward and back, which is to say that it inhabits the present of the poem.

Eichendorff thought of himself as a latecomer (he was born ten years after Brentano, and twenty after A. W. Schlegel). But he made his lateness into a constituent part of his poetics. The limited and now worn diction he inherited became an equivalent to the veil of familiarity and use estranging us from the world, and the minute variations and adjustments by which he succeeded in quickening word and image into new validity corresponded to and actually affected the process in which the poems' landscapes appeared instinct with promise while still remaining recognisable. Eichendorff's position as the 'last Romantic', as Tieck called him, also meant that he was able to recapitulate and to an extent combine the *Wunderhorn* tone, Tieck's irony, the religiosity of Hardenberg and the Romance forms of the Schlegels, all modulated by a new seriousness and clarity of purpose, and with a simplicity of focus that lends the scenes and actions of the poems an archetypal force. At the same time he distances himself from the extreme fusions of earlier Romanticism: the erotic and the religious are held apart, intensity is often mistrusted in favour of sobriety. But in the best of his poems this sobriety attains a lucid intensity in which the world appears inscrutable even as it is stripped down to a basic revealing pattern.

'Im Walde' ('In the Woods') shows some of this. The wedding-party with which it begins, travelling on out of sight, is a recurring motif and recalls many other figures who cross landscapes leaving no trace:

Es zog eine Hochzeit den Berg entlang,
Ich hörte die Vögel schlagen,
Es blitzten viel' Reiter, das Waldhorn klang,
Das war ein lustiges Jagen!

Und eh' ich's gedacht, war Alles verhallt,
Die Nacht bedecket die Runde,
Nur von den Bergen noch rauschet der Wald
Und mich schauert im Herzensgrunde.[31]

A wedding passed by along the hillside,
I heard the song of the birds,
The flash of the riders, the hunting horn's cry,
What a merry chase it was.

And at the mere thought it all echoed away
And night descends all round,
Only the wind still makes the trees sway
And I shudder deep in my heart.

The scene of the first verse is made up of separate elements held together by rhythm and rhyme but hardly by the extremely paratactic (folk-song) syntax – suggesting an arbitrary and uncertain connectedness which in the second verse is borne out as the image disintegrates. The apparition of the wedding-party, flaring up in a moment of heightened consciousness like an epiphany (the singing birds), seems an instant of poise and fullness (the German word for wedding, *Hochzeit*, is literally a 'high-time') which the words of the poem cannot quite grasp. The fourth line is an almost throw-away attempt to sum it up, happy to fail, a line of no import which could just as well say something else – a version of Tieck's weightless irony. But it is also *aptly* carefree, and at the same time disconcertingly serious: what is being hunted? Earlier poems ('Der irre Spielmann' or 'Glückliche Fahrt') had already asked whether huntsman and quarry could be told apart.[32] This merry chase dissolves into nothing, and after the fifth line, in which it has echoed away (not just it, everything), the I is left in the present tense and in a void. The vanity of life has passed away with, in this poem, no certainty that there is anything else. Even the rustling of the trees gives no comfort. The poem runs out into quiet terror and unconsoling transparency, finding a new use for the light, superficial tone by correcting it.

Eichendorff's lateness is thrown into relief by Heine, who published a first collection of poems in 1822, when Eichendorff still had more than thirty years' writing ahead of him. Despite this, Heine's own claim that with him 'the old German lyric school' ('die alte lyrische Schule der Deutschen') came to an end while at the same time he inaugurated 'the new school, the modern German lyric' ('die neue Schule, die moderne deutsche Lyrik') has much truth in it, though he remained in dialogue with Romanticism for the whole of his life and the process of perfecting and undermining the Romantic lyric was anticipated by others, especially Brentano.[33] The *Buch der Lieder* (*Book of Songs*) navigates between an affinity with the images and poetic language of Romanticism and the real-isation that they have become mere conventions, unable to get a purchase on the modern, historical world except when fractured or refracted by an often savage irony. Heine takes the diction, syntax and motifs of *Des Knaben Wunderhorn* and combines them with the manners and fashions of contemporary society, exposing the disjunction between the implicit values of a poetic style and the very different values driving into moder-nity. The first poem of the 'Lyrisches Intermezzo' section of the *Buch der Lieder* makes the self's response to May into an automatic, endlessly repeatable reaction, its very effortlessness implying that it is a purely lit-erary event. And the list that opens and closes the third poem ('Die Rose, die Lilie, die Taube, die Sonne' / 'The rose, the lily, the dove and the sun') is not the incantation of Brentano, just a mere listing, indicating exhaustion. Another poem, 'Wahrhaftig' ('Truly'), abruptly points out that such 'stuff' is a long way from 'making a world' ('So machts doch noch lang keine Welt').[34]

Heine's chief means is the breaking of style, tearing the beautifully woven fabric of a poem in a gesture that allows a glimpse through to the contradictory reality. Eichendorff said that most of Heine's poems ended in suicide.[35] But it is important not to forget that the characteristic twists and punchlines of the *Buch der Lieder* do not simply serve to destroy what has preceded them; rather, the contradiction expresses a tension which is truthful to the historical moment. Heine uses the language and forms of Romanticism as he later used the machinery of censorship: as a way of integrating into his writing the texture of his times. Revealing the conventions of the Romantic mode, Heine is also forced to acknowledge the conventionality of language *per se*, but the Romantic foil which he lays down with such virtuosity, and which cannot strictly be thought of as a foil at all, allows him to articulate in shifts and juxtapositions a new sense of self among the complexities and dissonances of the world he lived in. His poems are political in that they do not permit themselves to retreat into autonomy or unbroken harmony, though the temptation to do so is still very powerfully felt. The light, insubstantial mode that connects much Romantic lyric still lives on in early Heine, but its function alters: it expresses not so much the freedom of the self-as-subject, but the uncertainty and contradictoriness of the self's place in the world.

The weightlessness of the lyric appears also in its musicality, which itself is partly a result of the hollowing out of semantic meaning and the dependence on rhyme. Many Romantic poems were intended to be sung, and often were to existing tunes, in which form several, particularly by Eichendorff, passed into the popular repertoire and so gained an anonymity they seem intrinsically to be striving for. But the full realisation of the musical tendencies of the poems was the settings that turned them into *Lieder*. There the text often serves as an almost neutral vehicle for the music, which intensifies the weightlessness by drawing the words even further from their semantic ground and into the purely acoustic. The *Lied* can thus be seen as an almost natural extension of the Romantic lyric, and perhaps, in its fusion of poetry and music, as a fulfilment of the Romantic longing for an all-encompassing form of art.[36] It is tempting, and conveniently suggestive, to think of the Romantic lyric as being absorbed and transmuted into Heine on the one hand and the *Lied* on the other, where both Heine and the *Lied* can be seen as taking aspects of the lyric to their logical conclusion.

NOTES

1. Joseph von Eichendorff, *Werke*, ed. Wolfgang Frühwald, Brigitte Schillbach and Hartwig Schultz, 6 vols. (Frankfurt am Main: Deutscher Klassiker Verlag, 1985–93), vol. I, p. 814; *NS* II, p. 466.

2. Friedrich Hölderlin, *Sämtliche Werke*, ed. Friedrich Beissner and Adolf Beck, 8 vols. (Stuttgart: Kohlhammer, 1943–85), vol. VI, p. 229; *NS*, III, p. 519; *KFSA* II, p. 261.

3. *NS* III, p. 519; *KFSA* XVIII, p. 215.

4. *NS* III, p. 519.

5. Mark Grunert, *Die Poesie des Übergangs: Hölderlins späte Dichtung im Horizont von Friedrich Schlegels Konzept der 'Transzendentalpoesie'* (Tübingen: Niemeyer, 1995).

6. *NS* II, p. 533.

7. Hölderlin, *Sämtliche Werke*, vol. IV, p. 282; *NS* III, p. 587.

8. *KFSA* II, p. 182 (*Athenaeum-Fragment* 116).

9. *KFSA* II, p. 204 (*Athenaeum-Fragment* 238).

10. Hölderlin, *Sämtliche Werke*, vol. II, p. 90.

11. Eichendorff, *Werke*, vol. I, p. 863.

12. Heinrich Heine, *Historisch-kritische Gesamtausgabe der Werke*, ed. Manfred Windfuhr, 16 vols. (Hamburg: Hoffmann & Campe, 1973–97), vol. VIII, p. 168.

13. Ludwig Tieck, *Schriften*, eds. Manfred Frank *et al.*, 12 vols. (Frankfurt am Main: Deutscher Klassiker Verlag, 1985–), vol. VII, p. 729.

14. Ibid., p. 406.

15. *The Letters of John Keats*, ed. Maurice Buxton Forman (Oxford: Oxford University Press, 1952), p. 71.

16. *NS* II, p. 428.

17. Quoted in Manfred Frank, *Einführung in die frühromantische Ästhetik: Vorlesungen* (Frankfurt am Main: Suhrkamp, 1989), pp. 372–3. See the whole of Lecture 21.

18. Karoline von Günderrode, *Sämtliche Werke und ausgewählte Studien*, ed. Walter Morgenthaler, 3 vols. (Frankfurt am Main: Stroemfeld/Roter Stern, 1990–1), vol. I, p. 352.

19. Ibid., pp. 109, 79, 29.

20. Ibid., I, p. 325.

21. Johann Wolfgang Goethe, *Werke*, ed. Erich Trunz, 14 vols. (Munich: Beck, 1988), vol. XII, p. 284.

22. Ibid., p. 270.

23. Heine, *Werke*, vol. VIII, p. 202.

24. Wolfgang Frühwald gathers glosses and parodies of these lines by A. W. Schlegel, Friedrich Schlegel, Sophie Bernhardi-Tieck, Tieck himself and Uhland in his anthology *Gedichte der Romantik* (Stuttgart: Reclam, 1984).

25. Clemens Brentano, *Werke*, eds. Wolfgang Frühwald, Bernhard Gajek and Friedhelm Kemp, second edn, 4 vols. (Munich: Hanser, 1978), vol. I, p. 248.

26. Ibid., p. 364.

27. Eichendorff, *Werke*, vol. I, p. 328.

28. Ibid., pp. 308–9.

CHARLIE LOUTH

29. Ibid., p. 39.
30. Ibid., pp. 320–1.
31. Ibid., p. 329.
32. Ibid., pp. 232–3, 264–5.
33. Heine, *Werke*, vol. XV, p. 13.
34. Ibid., vol. I, pp. 135, 137, 113.
35. Eichendorff, *Werke*, vol. VI, p. 53.
36. See *The Penguin Book of Lieder*, ed. S. S. Prawer (Harmondsworth: Penguin, 1964), p. 15.

FURTHER READING

Adorno, Theodor W., 'Zum Gedächtnis Eichendorffs', in *Noten zur Literatur* (Frankfurt am Main: Suhrkamp, 1981), pp. 69–94
  'Die Wunde Heine', in *Noten zur Literatur* (Frankfurt am Main: Suhrkamp, 1981), pp. 95–100
Constantine, David, *Hölderlin* (Oxford University Press, 1988)
Enzensberger, Hans Magnus, *Brentanos Poetik* (Munich: Hanser, 1961)
Fetzer, John, 'Die romantische Lyrik', in *Romantik-Handbuch*, ed. Helmut Schanze, 2nd edn (Stuttgart: Kröner, 2003), pp. 312–36
Frühwald, Wolfgang (ed.), *Gedichte der Romantik* (Stuttgart: Reclam, 1984)
Hamburger, Michael, 'Novalis', in *Reason and Energy: Studies in German Literature* (London: Weidenfeld and Nicolson, 1970), pp. 66–100
Malinowski, Bernadette, 'German Romantic Poetry in Theory and Practice', in *The Literature of German Romanticism*, ed. Dennis F. Mahoney, The Camden House History of German Literature, vol. 8 (Rochester, N.Y.: Camden House, 2004), pp. 147–69
Rodger, Gillian, 'The Lyric', in *The Romantic Period in Germany*, ed. S. S. Prawer (London: Weidenfeld and Nicolson, 1970), pp. 147–72
Rölleke, Heinz, 'Nachwort', in *Des Knaben Wunderhorn: Alte deutsche Lieder, gesammelt von Achim von Arnim und Clemens Brentano*, ed. Heinz Rölleke, Kritische Ausgabe, 3 vols. (Stuttgart: Reclam, 1987), vol. III, pp. 557–81
Schultz, Hartwig, 'Eichendorffs Lyrik', in Joseph von Eichendorff, *Werke*, ed. Wolfgang Frühwald, Brigitte Schillbach and Hartwig Schultz, 6 vols. (Frankfurt am Main: Deutscher Klassiker Verlag, 1985–93), vol. I, pp. 715–800
Uerlings, Herbert, *Novalis* (Stuttgart: Reclam, 1998)

84

5

ROGER PAULIN

The Romantic drama

Much of German Romantic drama is experimental, eclectic and derivative. Often it seeks to embrace what in real, empirical terms is not accessible to the finite mind, and it fails aesthetically. Much of it is written or influenced by avid readers of the widest literary traditions who hope to see these fulfilled within the expanding and commodious bounds of a new dramatic form. It is nothing if not ambitious: it seeks to take over from where Schiller left off and has no doubts about its ability to compete with Goethe. In real terms, only its sole great dramatist, Heinrich von Kleist, and its other really interesting figure, Zacharias Werner, had any sense of the formal restraints needed to achieve a dramatic form that could submit to the restrictions of stage performance. The stage history of German Romanticism – an apt mixture of tragedy and farce – is briefly told, and even Kleist's reputation as a dramatist was not secure until the twentieth century.

Yet German Romanticism can claim for itself arguably the most influential work of drama criticism of the nineteenth century: August Wilhelm Schlegel's *Vorlesungen über dramatische Kunst und Literatur* (1809–11; *Lectures on Dramatic Art and Literature*), which brought the 'Classical' and the 'Romantic' into sharp formal and ideological opposition and enthroned Shakespeare and Calderón as the exemplars of the 'modern' and 'romantic'. This approach stressed formal diversity and experiment, not classical restraint; it called for the primacy of national and religious values. Ludwig Tieck's corpus of Shakespearean criticism sought to integrate Shakespeare into these patterns and it saw the drama and the theatre as the source of national revival.

Of equal influence on the Romantic drama were Friedrich Schlegel's notions of 'Roman' and 'Universalpoesie', which sought to free literature from the restraints of form and tradition and to open it up to every kind of discourse. The heady prospect of 'every verse form I could think of' (Tieck),[1] of dialogues with the traditions and figures of past, present and future (Arnim, Brentano) was hard to resist, and the resulting 'Großdramen' express more Romantic aspirations than their fulfilment. Yet Goethe's *Faust II* is part of their legacy, Richard Wagner's musical drama as well.

Fiercely ambitious and determined to take the stage by storm, Kleist and Werner carried on a persistent struggle to find the ideal form and subject for the drama that would herald that conquest. It meant an engagement with the plays that were appealing to the audiences of the day: knights-and-robbers drama ('Ritterstück'), neo-classical revivals, national and patriotic subjects. It also involved the subversion of the values of those traditions, the reversal of gender roles, upsetting the notions of honour and chivalry, unleashing emotions that neo-classicism had reined in. Werner's attempts became more and more frenzied and less and less appealing to the public. Kleist's defiant modernity denied him a place among his contemporaries.

General remarks

It has become almost a convention to begin accounts of German Romantic drama – of Romantic drama in general – with a statement of what it is not. It is not part of the history of the European theatre. It does not belong to the mainstream of European drama. It represents, in German terms, merely the gap between the 'real' theatre of Goethe and Schiller in the late eighteenth century and that of Grillparzer or Büchner in the 1820s or 1830s. It is largely unwieldy and for many unreadable. Major critics and commentators, such as Hegel, disliked it. Allowing for a few aberrant examples that disprove the generalisations, this is the commonly held view.

There is a hardly more auspicious consensus on what Romantic drama actually is. It is literary rather than poetic. It aspires after great models (Shakespeare or Calderón) but never attains to them. It is not truly tragic, so often ending in heaven or other places of apotheosis. It is the stillborn child of abstract theory.

Much of this is arguable and indeed it could apply equally to its other European manifestations, not just to works by Tieck, Arnim or Brentano. But this critique is only applicable if performability is the ultimate criterion (not always an indicator of quality) or if tragic satisfaction (in the Greek or Shakespearean sense) alone gives moral or aesthetic gratification. It would, in these terms, be manifestly unfair to Heinrich von Kleist, of the Romantic generation and sharing many of their aspirations. One cannot, of course, merely turn the argument and claim that Romantic drama is significant because Kleist is a Romantic. But for the very reason that Kleist can be aligned with them, their concerns, formal and theoretical, do also become his. All of them share in processes of defining and experimenting, intellectual and poetic ferment, that form part of the account of Romanticism; they display the manifestations that accompanied it, fullness, openness, universality, syncretism. In choosing the dramatic form, the Romantics opted for the highest form of art (as Schiller believed it to be, and after him Hegel, Wagner and Nietzsche). They examined its provenance, plotted its future course and used it for social, religious and political messages for their own times (post-revolutionary and Napoleonic), positing in dramatic form human situations hitherto thought unthinkable. Precisely because they were freed from the constraints of the conventional stage, they were able to link all forms of art in every conceivable combination and synthesis. In their deployment of music, they foreshadow the most radical development in dramatic art of the nineteenth century, Richard Wagner's opera, his *Gesamtkunstwerk*.

Yet the Romantics did not see themselves as mere experimenters or theorists, but as dramatists. This meant playing for the highest stakes. It could involve *tabula rasa* declarations, decreeing existing forms of theatre to be irrelevant or debased. But it also saw them seizing the initiative where the existing theatre permitted. On Schiller's death in 1805, Zacharias Werner spoke of the 'vacant throne'[2] that might one day be his; Heinrich von Kleist brushed aside Goethe's assertion that a theatre suited to his needs was 'yet to come'.[3] Goethe had a point. As director of the court theatre in Weimar, he had seen Romantic plays fail, amid confusion and scandal. Kleist and Werner are the two major Romantic dramatists who did accommodate to the formal needs of the theatre. Other Romantics were not deterred by such brakes on their ambition: Tieck wrote over forty plays, Arnim fifteen, Brentano seven, Eichendorff six, almost none of them ever performed.[4] In those terms, length need not be a problem. Tieck's programmatic *Leben und Tod der heiligen Genoveva* (1800; *Life and Death of Saint Genevieve*) has 6,500 verses, where *Hamlet*, Shakespeare's longest tragedy, has 3,500, Schiller's *Wallenstein* trilogy 7,600, and both parts of Goethe's *Faust* 12,000. Arnim's *Halle und Jerusalem* (1811; *Halle and Jerusalem*) runs to 250 pages in the standard edition and Brentano's *Die Gründung Prags* (1815; *The Founding of Prague*) extends to nearly 10,500 verses. Even their shorter plays, their comedies especially, were not prepared to make crucial concessions; or their authors were not willing to enter into a dialogue with the actors and producers of their day. Kleist and Werner excepted, they show a general disdain for such accommodations.

This practice has several reasons. There is the perception that contemporary taste is too debased and trivial (this is Tieck's position), the view that poetic texts – their own, but more especially the highest in the canon, Shakespeare's or Calderón's – cannot but lose in an encounter with the stage as it at present ordained. A poetic text like Shakespeare's is an organic whole that cannot be subjected to the truncations and indignities even of Goethe's

Weimar stage. Several Romantics – notably August Wilhelm Schlegel, Tieck, and Eichendorff – are also translators (of Shakespeare and Calderón). They have a highly developed historical sense: it is they who rediscover the German drama of the sixteenth and seventeenth centuries and restore the sense of the continuity of a national historical and poetic past. Arnim even considered it the right of the poet to renew older texts in combination with modern poetic invention, a view that was challenged by the purist Grimm brothers. Friedrich Schlegel believed that historic texts must be subjected to modern intellectual and critical scrutiny to bring out their universality ('Ganzes') and their never-ceasing self-reflexivity. All of this reflects a major corpus of theory and debate on the subject of drama and dramatic form, not easily separable from the business of writing plays itself.

Theory and practice

We see this reflected in a play which, on the surface, seems alien to theory and is generally disrespectful of anything approaching it: Tieck's *Der gestiefelte Kater* (1797; *Puss in Boots*).[5] Here, Tieck puts on the stage an audience attending a performance of a new play, 'Puss in Boots'. It is by an Author (who also appears) aware of his public's needs and prepared to acquiesce in them. What they want is the sentimental and superficial stuff of the day, melodrama, domestic drama ('Familiendrama'), fairy opera. On that basic level, it satirises theatrical taste and expectations around 1795. On another, it reminds its readers that a fairy story like *Puss in Boots* is part of a stratum of 'naive' poetry that needs to be tapped into anew, a link with the original sources of folk poetry now occluded by modern sophistication. But we are still on the surface. We, the readers, are not the audience present in the play; the Author is not the real poet; and the action is integrated into a multiform discourse between stage, auditorium and reader. We are, by analogy, in the world of *A Midsummer Night's Dream*, where court, mechanicals and actors all engage complicity with the audience, where each part of the action reflects upon itself. Closer to Tieck and broadly hinted at in the play's fictitious place of publication (Bergamo) is the *commedia dell'arte*, the stock characters of which appear in this and other satirical comedies of Tieck. The Fool is none other than Hanswurst, the old rude prankster of German comedy, now exiled in a more refined age as jester at a ludicrous court. There, he has ample opportunity to subvert good taste and decorum and the pursuit of knowledge. His anarchic presence is counterbalanced by the Ogre ('Popanz') whose name is 'Law' ('Gesetz'); when on stage the cat devours the Law changed into a mouse, lawlessness breaks out in the audience and in the text. The text overturns the claims, not only of the rules, but of *vraisemblance* itself, and blurs the demarcations between real and unreal. Where the stage may still subscribe to sham notions of order and self and dramatic illusion, the text prefers chaos and loss of identity.

This little comedy forms part of a much wider debate on the nature of comedy and indeed of poetry itself. It is not Tieck who formulates this, but Friedrich Schlegel. As early as 1794, in an essay on the Greeks' notions of comedy, Schlegel had identified the *parekbasis*, the device that breaks the dramatic illusion, as the main feature in Aristophanes. A play like Tieck's *Der gestiefelte Kater* might illustrate this through its constant interchange of play within play and its principle of 'disillusionment'. On a deeper level, however, one can relate these features to Schlegel's theory of Romantic irony, whereby the work of art undergoes a process of self-creation and self-destruction. In this way, both the abstract principle behind the work of art (the symbolic representation of the absolute) and its expression (the use of language and rhetorical figure) constantly interrelate.

This may seem a long way from Tieck or indeed any kind of dramatic practice. Yet Friedrich Schlegel is here enunciating general principles which are reflected in the choice of subject, the form chosen and the attitude to human situations in plays by major representatives of the Romantic movement. Thus, in his most experimental phase, as co-editor of the periodical *Athenaeum* (1798–1800), he sees the drama essentially as a component of the 'Roman', the self-conscious work of art which accommodates in free combination and association all manifestations of human expression, breaking down the artificial divisions of genres and art forms and embracing the fullest range of articulation and artifice. It is part of 'Universalpoesie', Schlegel's encompassing term for all past, present and future forms of poetry. It is also the vessel of mythology, the term that Schlegel uses to express what gives poetry its inner sense and an ideological justification in its own times. Applied specifically to drama, Schlegel's theory involves syncretisms, syntheses, combinations of the most disparate elements: prose and poetry, comedy and tragedy, mythology and history.

There are no models as such, but Shakespeare may stand as a supernal exemplar: objective and conscious on the one hand, dissolving into playfulness on the other, rhetorical but also lyrical, tightly organised but also episodic. These views on Shakespeare represent the consensus of critical remarks by both Schlegel brothers and by Tieck. Tieck's and August Wilhelm Schlegel's essays on the organisation and artificiality of Shakespeare's plays, comedies and tragedies alike, are one side. They inform Schlegel's practice as he produces the first substantial verse translation of Shakespeare into German (1797–1810), arguably the greatest achievement of Romantic dramatic endeavour. Behind it is Herder's principle of an organic 'whole', the integrity of which cannot be infringed. Yet Romantic theory also has a sense of Shakespeare's looseness and disjunction and draws special attention to an open structure as in *Pericles* or the Histories. Shakespeare is important, too, as the incarnation of a golden age of poetry, expressing national aspirations and achievements and recording its historical development. Thus Shakespeare confers dignity on the historical drama as a poetic vehicle for ideological awareness and proclamation.

If Shakespeare increasingly becomes the focus of hopes for the regeneration of national poetry, he emerges, by the same token, as hard, aristocratic, unsentimental, Nordic, above all, agnostic to Christianity. For the religious dimension that informs their notion of mythology, the Romantics turn southward to Calderón. Also the product of a golden age, Calderón stands for the world of the southern Renaissance: lyrical, sensuous, colourful, Catholic, imbued with Christian symbolism. Where Shakespeare is firmly rooted in the realities and limits of political power, Calderón points beyond the here and now to the eternal verities of heaven.

The Romantics, the Schlegel brothers especially, are here giving new significance to the eighteenth-century view that the English and Spanish theatres are especially related – in their disregard of classical conventions and their bold neglect of the unities. What is more, this poetry comes about at a time of transition, when the age of chivalry gives way to early national awakenings. All this confers on it the accolade of 'Romantic'. It informs the substance of August Wilhelm Schlegel's classic statement in the twenty-fifth of his *Vorlesungen über dramatische Kunst und Literatur*, his so-called Vienna Lectures. There, in a comparison of ancient and Romantic poetry, he identifies as the underlying principle of the Romantic its love of commingling the disparate, poetry and prose, the serious and the comic, the spiritual and the sensuous. It is never satisfied with completed states, but expresses itself in longings and intuitions of things as yet unfulfilled.

The drama of universal poetry: Tieck, Arnim, Brentano

When Schlegel formulated this in 1809 he was thinking in the diachronic and the synchronic mode, both as the recorder of historical developments and as the contemporary of poets seeking to renew or even emulate these principles. For him, Romantic drama was not to be merely a pretext for musicality and formlessness, lacking any foundation in the conventions of the theatre. Indeed the historical drama alone, treating the great themes of people and nation, had Romantic dignity. Yet perhaps he was acknowledging a Romantic drama already in existence that had had a pervasive influence: Tieck's *Genoveva*.[6] This drama appeared already as the Schlegel brothers were making their theoretical formulations in *Athenaeum* and indeed it is praised there. *Genoveva* was, however, not a mere realisation of principles enunciated in that periodical, and Tieck's play could be seen just as much as a religious extension of modern dramatic practice, Schiller's especially. The broad and multiform unfolding of verse, mainly Romance stanzas, that characterises *Genoveva* might appear as a partial response to Friedrich Schlegel's 'Universalpoesie'. It would also serve to remind that German drama, Klopstock's, Goethe's, Schiller's, had long since been experimenting with open forms, musical interludes and varieties of versification.

The play is indeed 'programmatic', but on various levels of sophistication. It seeks to align venerable religious devotion to modern sensitivity and awareness. Thus it records the collision of religions or mythologies (Charles Martel's Franks versus the Saracens) in the undifferentiated terms of old legend or romance and presents the saintly piety of St Genevieve in the language of a mystical devotion that recalls Calderón. It utilises the patterns of hagiography as a link between past and present. Using the chorus-like figure of St Boniface (the patron saint of the Germans) it postulates, not a return to the naive verities of centuries long buried in time, but the sense that national and religious values are indivisible and ever-relevant (cf. the prophecy of the Holy Roman Empire yet to come), that culture, in the widest sense, is borne by the sense of dependence that Schleiermacher had annexed for religion. The underlying antithesis of nature versus spirit is Calderonian: the tempter (Golo) seeks to win the saint (Genoveva). The subtitle, 'ein Trauerspiel', is consonant with baroque martyr tragedy and the superterrestrial triumphs it celebrates. All this is not without its tensions. The play draws on modern erotic subtleties for the account of Genoveva's accusation and wrongful condemnation. The formal components of the play, the sensuousness of the verse forms, the mingling of the senses, the quivering frissons, the swoonings and nervous figurations, all deliver a warning of the enticements of the aesthetic as a device in the loss of innocence. Nothing in this play is unconscious: it is always self-reflective and aware of the power of its own artistry.

Goethe listened spellbound to Tieck's reading of this play. It is one reminder among many that *Faust* is but one of several plays at the time cast on the widest scale and employing the broadest range of form. The salvation of Faust goes far beyond any categories enshrined in *Genoveva*, but both plays owe much in their respective – and very different – endings, to Calderón. Tieck later repudiated his 'programmatic' drama, noting its 'pernicious' influence on a younger generation of Romantics.

One of these was Achim von Arnim, and Tieck certainly meant his play *Halle und Jerusalem*. Arnim's play, in which Christ and the Devil, Napoleon and Goethe, not forgetting the Wandering Jew and the 1797 campaign in Syria, form the configurational framework, might seem to be making multiformity into a principle. Where *Genoveva* is a poetic enactment of legend and distant past, *Halle und Jerusalem* is a deliberate mixture of fiction and history and is informed by Arnim's own notions of religious renewal. What is more, its undisguised delight in mixing and commingling involves close interplay of disparate elements, the hieratic but also the grotesque, the hybrid juxtaposition of literary forms and traditions, the confrontation of a modern text with one drawn from the past, the widest unfolding of formal devices, narrative and lyrical, that subvert any notion of traditional drama. Through this intertextuality, this *bricolage*,[7] Arnim seeks to bring time (love and death in the university town of Halle) and eternity (the Holy Sepulchre at Jerusalem) into dialogue. The hero and heroine step out into the modern world of intellectual nihilism and sated passions (Halle) and embark on a pilgrimage of asceticism and penitence to find redemption (Jerusalem). For others, the Holy Land, in its turn, becomes the scene of real battles against the Napoleonic *Zeitgeist* and of symbolic resolves for a spiritual revival, a kind of prefigurement of the Holy Alliance. Arnim's mosaic of characters involves Ahasverus, the Wandering Jew. His appearances (and his improbable link with the hero) serve the function of Gothic mystification. More seriously, he represents Arnim's hope for a future conversion of the Jews in a union of Judaism and Christianity. This redemptive syncretism leads Arnim into darker and more sinister areas of social and religious comment also touched by Romanticism: anti-Semitism. Here, it addresses the issues raised in Arnim's own times, emancipation and assimilation in a society of shifting moral values (in these matters, Arnim is both radical and reactionary). But, as a Romantic text, *Halle und Jerusalem* also postulates a mythology for its own times that overrides past and present positions of belief, Judaic or Christian, and looks forward to a new, enhanced and doctrine-free Christianity of word and of deed.

Arnim's huge drama operates in a space where myth, poetry and historical time interact. This is also true of Brentano's operatic verse play *Die Gründung Prags*,[8] but with some crucial differences. Arnim's is prodigal with form, but Brentano's is the most extraordinary sustained piece of Romantic poetry that there is, a *tour de force* of sheer poetic invention. It is more theatrical than Arnim's, in the sense that its many choruses and musical interludes suggest a vast choral work like Schumann's *Szenen aus Goethes Faust* (1844–53; *Scenes from Faust*). Arnim uses poetry to reactivate timeless values in the here and now. Brentano consciously moves in an area between the times. The subtitle 'historisch-romantisches Drama' summons up poetry ('romantisch' essentially means 'poetic'). Poetry implies myth: in the primal, pre-historic state of human consciousness, now lost except in its intimations in poetry, religious notions and poetic myths coexisted as one. The art of the modern poet serves to restore these lost realities, a lost wholeness, a lost paradise. Thus the story of the founding of the city of Prague (the name itself means 'threshold') stands symbolically for processes of transition, from poetic and mythic deep time to the 'historical' component also enshrined in the title, and the play represents a rite of spring between the dark night of time and some future fruition. The characters mark the translation from the semi-divine and prophetic matriarchy of Libussa and her sisters to the patriarchal state represented by the peasant-king Primislaus. The grounding of the city-state brings with it an end to fragmentation, dissension and anarchy and the hope of settlement and stable civilisation and national, rather than personal, identity. Thus the play is not static but gives voice to the struggles and sacrifices, the acceptance of female passivity, that accompany the change from female to male order. Unlike Werner's *Wanda* and Kleist's *Penthesilea*, Brentano's play is less concerned with the real, personal conflicts this involves. Mythological change, from a cosmogony representing deities of darkness and light, to the proclamation of a future Christian order, is another aspect of the play's interim state. Brentano is able to bring these elements together and give them new sense.

Werner and Kleist

The transitional states – between mythologies, religions, political systems – that characterise *Die Gründung Prags* are not alien to Tieck and Arnim and indeed partly inform Romantic views of Shakespeare. The very dramatic form itself, tending towards music drama and opera, transgresses any fixed notions of poetic genre. Zacharias Werner and Heinrich von Kleist,[9] as the two writers of the Romantic generation who enjoyed or (in the case of Kleist) have subsequently enjoyed, success on the stage, share many of the presuppositions that their contemporaries demanded of drama. But their burning ambition for recognition in the theatre and their – very different – awareness of addressing the times in which they lived, set theirs aside from the sprawling works of Tieck, Arnim or Brentano. All of Werner's tragedies end on a note of proclamation, ushering in a new humanity, new dynasties, new religious revelations, all of which are being fulfilled in our own times. Kleist's last two plays, *Die Hermannsschlacht* (1808; *The Battle of Teutoburg Forest*) and *Prinz Friedrich von Homburg* (1810; *Prince Frederick of Homburg*), can be read on one level as political and patriotic messages. Crucially, they draw on what the contemporary stage can offer: hence both Werner and Kleist seek Goethe's protection and approach

Iffland, the best-known actor-producer of the day. Both assimilate Schiller, if in different ways; both know Shakespeare (Werner's first play fairly creaks with reminiscences); they are familiar with the theatre of their day and its many forms, musical or otherwise. Werner has a weakness for pageants and grand operatic conclusions; Kleist's endings, even when spectacular, are always problematic. Both cross between modes, genres, mentalities and genders and seek to synthesise or combine these in dramatic form. But there are formal differences. Werner is an enthusiastic and occasionally virtuosic exponent of verse forms. Kleist, on the other hand, is characterised by taut and energetic dramatic language that recalls the verse of Schiller or Schlegel's Shakespeare.

Werner constructed his own theory of the tragedy, one that became increasingly idiosyncratic after his conversion to Catholicism (his later calling as priest and preacher is for some the consummation of his career as a dramatist). Kleist is notoriously spare in his comments. Again, for some, his suicide in 1811 is evidence of a dichotomy between his all-consuming ambition and the indifference of his contemporaries. Werner shares with his Romantic contemporaries the belief that the work of art, the tragedy especially, must be religious, must impart a sense of the infinite and must mediate between humankind and the universe, the divine. On this, however, he imposes the constraints of reason, which allows the artist to give shape to the infinite and make it intelligible and accessible to the human faculties. Art is an intermediary; it requires symbols for its mediating function: love, death, martyrdom, all three, if need be. This assumes forms not envisaged by the Schlegel brothers or Tieck, and it is such fusions of erotic death-wishes in Werner that link him closest with one aspect of Kleist, manifest in his tragedy *Penthesilea*.

Kleist's early formulated urge to be Sophocles and Shakespeare in one (the fragment *Robert Guiskard* is the result) can be related to Romantic syncretism. Yet the evidence for Kleist as a receptive contemporary of the Romantics comes very largely from the texts themselves. Thus the verse comedy *Amphitryon* (1807), Kleist's homage to both Plautus and Molière, metamorphoses both of these traditions to produce its own synthesis of old and new. The reduction of the old myth (Jupiter visiting a mortal in human guise) to human dimensions is one effect. Investing Alkmene, the heroine, with a sensitivity that goes beyond mere appearances to ratify intuition, is another, and more significant one. At the end, amid the jubilation at the forthcoming 'advent' (in overtly Christian parody) of the son and heir Hercules whom Jupiter has sired in Amphitryon's guise, Alkmene is left uncertain in her feelings towards both god and husband (her famous final word, 'Ach!'). The play has clear elements of comedy but also of tragedy, not romantically 'synthesised' but in subtle interrelation. The very term comedy has become generically multi-faceted; it contains uncertainties, not the guarantee of a happy end.

This reading of *Amphitryon*[10] draws on textual inference and parallels with contemporary dramatic theory. There is perhaps, more justification in relating Kleist – and to some extent Werner – to his friend and collaborator Adam Müller, the formulator of a significant theory of the drama. Similarly, the Romantic speculative psychology of Gotthilf Heinrich Schubert's *Ansichten von der Nachtseite der Naturwissenschaft* (1808; *Views of the Dark Side of Natural Science*), is known to have influenced Kleist and aspects of his practice. Müller's lectures on the drama, published in 1808 in the periodical *Phöbus* together with the first versions of three of Kleist's own plays, contain two importantly relevant sections: on Shakespeare, and on the religious character of the Greek stage. In his analysis of Shakespeare's Histories, Müller went further than Schlegel's general advocacy of the historical drama. He extrapolated from them a pattern for the times: from the chaos of civil war and usurpation there emerges a strong kingship and an established dynasty. There is no direct link here with Kleist, except that his last two dramas proclaim a message against the Napoleonic *Zeitgeist* and envision a unity of purpose in a consolidated nation. Werner's plays, not conceived in a chronological order any more than were Shakespeare's, nevertheless present a sweep and progression of history: from the decline and fall of the Roman Empire (*Attila*), near-mythical confrontations of religions and cultures (*Das Kreuz an der Ostsee* [1805; *The Cross on the Baltic*], *Wanda*), the imperial Middle Ages (*Cunegunde*), the demise of chivalry and the emergence of personal monarchy (*Die Söhne des Tals* [1803–4; *The Sons of the Vale*]), the Reformation (*Martin Luther*), and divine grace triumphant over fate (*Der 24. Februar* [1809; *The Twenty-Fourth of February*]). Unlike Shakespeare's, all of these works celebrate forces that extend far beyond political concerns: a synthesis of religion and 'higher humanity'. For all their occasional messages for the times, they also represent the transitional states that, in different guise, were the sphere of action of Tieck's, Arnim's and Brentano's dramas.

Müller's notion of 'tragic experience' in Greek drama involves moments of awareness which lead, ladder-like, to a higher existence beyond death, a 'resurrection'. Romantic syncretism has, of course, no problems with fusions of ancient and modern, indeed Schlegel in his lectures had stressed that modern men and women must be satisfied with longings and intimations, not the religious notions that once were the foundation of Greek tragedy. Schubert's sense of higher adumbrations ('Ahndung') induced by somnambulic states between waking and sleeping, are symbolic of the transition over the threshold of one existence into the higher mysteries of another, as the soul is winged to new life.

There are echoes in Kleist's *Das Käthchen von Heilbronn* (1808; *Kate of Heilbronn*). The play becomes more than just the 'großes historisches Schauspiel' that its title ironically proclaims and allows for transgressions of traditional patterns. Käthchen, a girl, is placed in the centre of the male-dominated genre of the *Ritterstück*. It is she whose dreams, hypnotic states, faints and blushes symbolise awarenesses higher than of those around her. Inner experience and its higher truths are what count, not the pre-established roles of estates and genders. Kleist gives this play a happy ending. His other drama of intimation and transfiguration from the same year, *Penthesilea* (1808) is, however, bleakly tragic in its outcome.

Kleist's stern blank-verse tragedy *Penthesilea* and Werner's lush verse drama *Wanda, Königin der Sarmaten* (1809; *Wanda, Queen of the Sarmatians*) are the two plays by each writer that are closest to each other in theme and tone. Goethe had a version of *Wanda* performed in Weimar in 1808; for *Penthesilea* he had only revulsion. What do they have in common? Both Wanda and Penthesilea are caught in a web of mythology and religious tradition. Their queenship is girt around with priestly sanctions. Neither may love the man she chooses: Wanda's is an enemy of the Sarmatian people; Penthesilea, an Amazon, a daughter of Mars, is not even permitted tender feelings. Both choose self-induced deaths in an erotically charged *Liebestod*. Both use the image of the oak tree in the storm to stress the vulnerability of greatness.

Yet these parallels cannot hide the essential differences. To solve the conflicts induced by gender roles embedded in mythology, Werner has recourse to a typically Romantic synthesis. The mystical philosophy which the play propounds also resolves the dichotomies of existence: the physical and the spiritual, love and death, become united in the universe; the sacrifice of the body (Wanda's leap into the river Vistula – pure grand opera!) leads to a higher, androgynous resolution, the return to a united element of that which earthly life has forced apart.

The alternation of eroticism, Bacchic dissolution and anomie in *Wanda* is also recognisable in *Penthesilea*. Where, however, Werner superimposes a resolution through his doctrines of higher love and death, Kleist offers no such escape. Indeed the conflicting elements in the play are deliberately deployed so that the one subverts the other. The mixture of mentalities and mythologies never allows of a resolution. There is for a start Achilles, whose ambition is to carry off Penthesilea as a prize. He has elements of the post-Homeric macho, the Shakespearean homicide, but also the sighing lover of modern sensibility. What he understands as courtship, Penthesilea interprets as an affront to her inner feelings. But her inner emotions are an enigma to herself and all around her. Unfeeling priestly ordinances shore up an inhumane political and religious matriarchy that does not allow for 'normal' expressions of respect or affection. Amazon androgyny, with its denial of full womanhood, leads her to think rather in terms of hunt and quarry. This female hunting instinct is what Penthesilea invokes when she misreads Achilles's approach as a violation of her integrity and chastity. In the frenzy of frustrated emotions she enacts the most monstrous scene in all German drama: she sets her dogs on Achilles and herself joins them in an orgy of destruction. For all its echoes of Euripides's *Bacchae*, Kleist's tragedy is un-Greek. There cannot now be any belief in the gods, except, as in *King Lear*, 'they kill us for their sport'. The cause of her downfall is in her own heart: it recalls Racine's 'Venus, all attached to her prey' ('Vénus toute entière à sa proie attachée'),[11] where Venus stands for Phèdre's inner consuming passion, not a direct divine agency. The cruel subversion of Penthesilea's love reaches an end in a momentary vision at her imminent death, where she glimpses – a poetic fulfilment of Schubert or Adam Müller – some kind of resolution beyond the bleakness of existence. But Kleist is not Werner: all he grants is a fleeting intimation of harmony and knowledge amid the ruins of human fragility and frailty.

Both Werner's and Kleist's plays counter any Rousseauistic notion that women engage in acts of sacrifice or mediation to civilise male passion. In Kleist's *Die Hermannsschlacht* (1808) both sexes alike join in the brutal business of freeing Germany of Roman domination (Thusnelda enticing a Roman to a rendezvous with a she-bear). Again, unlike Tieck or Werner, Kleist is not content merely to confront one culture with another; his white-hot hatred of the French (Romans) does not blind him to the irresolution, mendacity and duplicity of both Roman (Napoleon) and Teuton (the confederation against him).

Prinz Friedrich von Homburg (1811), Kleist's last play, also involves political confrontations. On the surface, this is Kleist's great patriotic play: the setting, the Great Elector of Brandenburg's campaign against the Swedes, is updated to Napoleonic times. The story, the Elector passing sentence of death for insubordination on one of his generals, the young prince of Homburg, and his subsequent pardon amid national jubilation, suggests an idealised Prussia obedient to the heart as well as to the letter of the law. On that level, the play represents a contract between ruler and ruled (Elector and nobles), the surrender of the individual to a nation that in its turn stands for values of right and justice. That would, however, reduce the play to a mere pragmatic settlement of interests. Its moments of lyricism and visionary, dream-like qualities seem alien to that world of *Realpolitik*. The elements that make up the texture of the play, the rule of law versus the dictates of the heart, do not, however, stand irreconcilably apart, but each is in its way 'romanticised'. On a deeper level, therefore, both the Elector and the Prince, from different approaches, seek to find an accommodation for life that enables men (in the terms of the play) to explore humanity in its fullest sense. At first, they differ in their perceptions. The Elector cannot envisage humanity without the congruity of social coherence. The Prince dreams of realms of personal glory and heroic fulfilment that transcend mere abstract order. This he must learn to reconcile with the needs of the state, while the Elector must learn to temper justice with mercy. All of this could be achieved within the bounds of reality. Kleist, however, draws us out of that realm in the play's triumphant close. The Prince, expecting the death sentence, awakes instead to the whole panoply of victorious celebration. In human terms, this cannot be 'real'. It may represent a mutual acceptance of insights, the Elector's more abstract view, the Prince's more personal experience. But it can only be done through a vision, not in reality. The near-to-last line, 'what else but a dream?' ('ein Traum, was sonst?'), expresses longing and hope, beyond any tragic intervention, the essential stuff of Romantic drama.

NOTES

1. Ludwig Tieck, *Schriften*, 28 vols. (Berlin: Reimer, 1828–54), vol. I, p. xxxix.
2. *Briefe des Dichters Friedrich Ludwig Zacharias Werner*, ed. Oswald Floeck, 2 vols. (München: G. Müller, 1914), vol. I, p. 367.
3. Goethe to Kleist, 1 February 1808. In Heinrich von Kleist, *Sämtliche Werke und Briefe*, ed. Helmut Sembdner, 2 vols. (Munich: Hanser, 1961), vol. II, pp. 806f.
4. See R. Paulin, 'The Drama', in *The Romantic Period in Germany*, ed. S. Prawer (London: Weidenfeld and Nicolson, 1970), pp. 173–201; S. Scherer, *Witzige Spiegelgemälde: Tieck und das Drama der Romantik* (Berlin and New York: de Gruyter, 2003).
5. See J. Brummack, 'Narrenfiguren in der dramatischen Literatur der Romantik', in *Das romantische Drama: Synthese Zwischen Tradition und Innovation*, eds. Uwe Japp, Stefan Scherer and Claudia Stockinger, pp. 45–64.
6. See C. Stockinger, 'Ludwig Tiecks *Leben und Tod der heiligen Genoveva*: Konzept und Struktur im Kontext des frühromatischen Diskurses', in Japp *et al.*(eds.), *Das romantische Drama*, pp. 89–118; Scherer, *Witzige Spiegelgemälde*, pp. 344–63.
7. D. Kremer, 'Durch die Wüste: Achim von Arnims uferloses Drama *Halle und Jerusalem*', in Japp *et al.* (eds.), *Das romantische Drama*, pp. 137–57; U. Ricklefs, '"Ahasvers Sohn": Arnims Städtedrama *Halle und Jerusalem*', in *Universelle Entwürfe – Integration – Rückzug: Arnims Berliner Zeit (1809–1814)*, ed. U. Ricklefs (Tübingen: Niemeyer, 2000), pp. 143–244.
8. U. Ricklefs, 'Objektive Poesie und Polarität Gesetz und Gnade: Brentanos *Die Gründung Prags* und Grillparzers *Libussa*', in *Germanistik in Erlangen*, ed. G.-D. Peschel, (Erlangen: Universitätsbund, 1983), pp. 239–69; J. F. Fetzer, 'Clemens Brentano: Die Schwelle als Schwäche oder Stärke des romantischen Dramas?', in Japp *et al.*(eds.), *Das romantische Drama*, pp. 119–36.

9. See A. Menhennet, *The Romantic Movement* (London: Croom Helm, 1981), pp. 108–50.
10. H. J. Kreutzer, 'Zeitgenossenschaft: Kleists *Amphitryon, ein romantisches Drama*', in Japp *et al.*(eds.), *Das romantische Drama*, pp. 227–39.
11. Act I, Scene 3.

FURTHER READING

Cox, J. N., *In the Shadows of Romance: Romantic Drama in Germany, England, and France* (Athens: Ohio University Press, 1987)

Gillespie, Gerald (ed.), *Romantic Drama* (Amsterdam and Philadelphia: Benjamin, 1994)

Hardy, Swana L., *Goethe, Calderón und die romantische Theorie des Dramas* (Heidelberg: Winter 1965)

Kluge, Gerhard, 'Das romantische Drama', in *Handbuch des deutschen Dramas,* ed. Walter Hinck (Düsseldorf: Bagel, 1980), pp. 186–99

Schulz, Gerhard, 'Das romantische Drama: Befragung eines Begriffes', in *Das romantische Drama: Synthese zwischen Tradition und Innovation*, eds. Uwe Japp, Stefan Scherer and Claudia Stockinger (Tübingen: Niemeyer, 2000), pp. 1–19

Ulshöfer, Robert, *Die Theorie des Dramas in der deutschen Romantik* (Berlin: Junker & Dünnhaupt, 1935)

6

JOHN A. MCCARTHY

Forms and objectives of Romantic criticism

Origins, contours, markers

In his *Kritische Fragmente* (1797; *Critical Fragments*) Friedrich Schlegel famously remarked that the literary critic is just a reader who chews the cud. Hence he needs more than one stomach. Schlegel also asserted that modern poetry is a running commentary on the short philosophical proposition: 'All the arts should become science, and all science should become like the arts.' Thus the arts and sciences are inherently related.[1] These two aphorisms encapsulate our core argument. The sciences and the arts were not only intimately interrelated for Romanticism, but their seemingly heterogeneous methods of inquiry – and by extension the art of criticism and its public dissemination – were also inseparable. Thus not only the critic, but also the reader, is best served by having more than one stomach, the better to digest such diverse fare.

These aphorisms of course foreshadow Schlegel's even more famous *Athenaeum Fragment* No. 116 on the nature of *Universalpoesie*, which he characterises as a state of eternal becoming that can never be exhausted by theory and the inner essence of which can be accessed only by 'eine divinatorische Kritik' ('a divinatory criticism', Firchow, p.175; *KFSA* II, pp.182–3). This perception in turn lies behind his later, self-reflective judgement in the essay 'Über die Unverständlichkeit' (1800; 'On Incomprehensibility') on the forms and possibility of genuine communication between author and critic, text and reader. There he claims that his is a 'Zeitalter der Tendenzen' ('Age of Tendencies'), that is, an era in which all ideas and projects are best understood as constitutionally incomplete, caught up in an on-going dialectic that allows only preliminary conclusions. The search for knowledge and understanding is no temporary venture. The new age, itself quick-footed and nimble, requires a quick and nimble reader (Firchow, pp. 264, 268; *KFSA* II, pp. 367, 370).

In a less-famous statement, Joseph Görres (1776–1848) – Romantic critic, essayist, political activist and editor of the *Rheinischer Merkur*

(*Rhenish Mercury*) – reinforced the point in a variation of the earlier *Querelle des anciens et modernes* when he wrote in *Aurora* in 1804 that 'Der Charakter des Antiken ist Poesie, selbst in der Philosophie, der des Modernen Philosophie, selbst in der Poesie ... ungestüme Kraftergüsse, wildes Gegeneinandertreiben entgegengesetzter Tendenzen' ('the character of antiquity is poetry even in philosophical works, whereas the character of modernity is philosophy, even in poetry itself ... uncouth antagonism of opposing tendencies').[2] In his announcement of lectures at the University of Heidelberg on the nexus of philosophy and physiology in November 1806, Görres speaks of philosophy as pansophy, religion as theosophy, and physiology as the revelatory signature of a once vital spirit (Görres, *Ausgewählte Werke* I, pp. 138–42). Criticism and publicity were part and parcel of the era, an age which is the 'Collisionspunkt andrer Zeitalter' ('point of collision of bygone ages')[3] and hence in several ways revolutionary. Görres refers to a broad revolution in philosophy, poesy, and politics, each independent of the others, each the result of different causes, yet each related through underlying principles and parallel in its development.[4] The intermingling of incisive critique and literary flourish characterised to a significant extent the verbal outpourings of the Schlegel brothers, Joseph Görres, Friedrich von Hardenberg (Novalis), Ludwig Tieck and other Romantics. They drew the logical consequences of the previous Age of Critique, the Enlightenment, although, like any new school of thought, they insisted upon their own innovations and distinct identity.

Scholarly assessments of Romantic criticism have by no means overlooked its socio-political connotations. Jochen Schulte-Sasse, for instance, discusses three takes on the Romantic critique of society.[5] The three critiques analysed are 1. an enlightened leftist-rationalist perspective; 2. a leftist-liberal, system-theoretical standpoint; 3. a deconstructive-anarchic position. The first impugns what it views as an escapist attitude that undermines the reforming function of literature and art. The second discerns in Romantic criticism and art a humane element of self-realisation that can impact on society through the individual's involvement. However, it assumes that a clear division is drawn between the autonomous world of art and the practical world of quotidian existence. The third sees an emancipatory element in Romantic art and criticism that loosens constrictions and unleashes energy for social and political intervention.[6] While this Romantic critique of society is not unrelated to our cognitive interest, the present focus shall be limited to the school's understanding of criticism without the broader socio-political implications.

The critic and academician Adam Müller is symptomatic of the Romantic position. His Dresden lectures on science and literature (1806) – many of them, like Görres's, gems of essayistic writing – are exemplary for their inter-mingling of science, literature and literary criticism. Expanding the concept of literature beyond its narrow sense of rule-governed and genre-specific writing (which he sees as exemplified by French literature), Müller argues that every language or literature possesses natural universalising tenden-cies and pursues them via acts of critique within the broad public sphere.[7] Genuine criticism promotes the concept of the totality of literature so that the literary domain is conceivable only as endlessly expanding (Müller I, p. 48). Arguing that critique in this sense of the word does not yet exist in German lands, he cites Lessing and Friedrich Schlegel as critics and publi-cists who have shown the way. He also cites literary journals such as the Jena *Allgemeine Literatur-Zeitung* (*General Literary Gazette*) as having recently adopted this mode of mediatory criticism ('vermittelnde Kritik'), which is logically necessary to realise the overall objective (Müller I, p. 53). The goal is to replace the Enlightenment figure of the critic-tyrant who dictates taste to an unduly compliant reader ('Tyrann des sklavischen Lesers') with an experimenter-cum-negotiator figure who gleefully probes the limits of dis-ciplines and categories (Müller I, p. 74). The attitude of mediation confers on German literature and criticism a distinct advantage over the hegemonic French model (Müller I, p. 53). Whilst also citing contesting forces as the true character of the era, Müller nonetheless proposes that there is a unify-ing bond underlying the antagonistic trends (Müller I, p. 73).

Two standpoints seemingly most opposed are those of the humanities and the natural sciences or ethics and physics. Yet they share common ground: the realm of law (or the idea) is for Müller at bottom one with the realm of nature or the concrete (Müller I, p. 75). Remarking upon the history of progress in the human and natural sciences since the mid-eighteenth century, Müller opines that, in their pure form, the humanities are not reducible to a process of absolute invention ('Erfinden'). Nor are the natural sciences engaged in mere discovery ('Entdecken'; Müller I, p. 76). On the contrary, both branches of inquiry participate in a reinvention ('Wiedererfinden') of the unity of the one, animated, albeit agonistic organism that constitutes the whole. All phenomena and processes are signs of the interconnection between organic and inorganic nature. As signifiers, all manifestations act as so many 'letters' and prove essential to the combinatory process of inter-pretation. This is true of our interpretations of both written texts and the 'inscriptions' of nature.

Müller shared this view with Görres, Friedrich Schlegel (who utilised the language of chemistry in promoting his own poetics), Schelling (who theo-rised aesthetics in understanding nature as the continually emergent 'I') and Hardenberg (who first proposed an authentically scientific poetry and an aestheticisation of science). They, in turn, were inspired by Leibniz, who had proposed the idea a century earlier in his *Monadology* (1711), by Spinoza, who in his pansophy had conflated nature with the Divine, and by Robert Boyle, Isaac Newton, and Antoine-Laurent Lavoisier, who sought to explain the basic building blocks of nature with their mechanical or alphabetic models of chemistry respectively.

Thus, everything spiritual and moral Müller considered a proper object of study for the natural scientist, while everything real and physical fell for him within the domain of the humanist (Müller I, pp. 77–81). That, of course, was the argument of Schelling's *Ideen zu einer Philosophie der Natur* (1797; *Ideas for a Philosophy of Nature*) and *Von der Weltseele* (1798; *On the World-Soul*), which insisted that only through aesthetic cognition could one grasp the unity of agonistic forces in nature as 'both blind mechanism *and* teleological purposefulness, unconscious and conscious productivity, necessity and freedom'.[8]

Hence Müller's lectures can be regarded as an application of Schelling's *Naturphilosophie* to the study of culture. In Lecture 8, moreover, Müller contends that the realms of ethics and physics extend, in altered form, as far as history and political science. Together with nature and law they comprise what he labels the 'holy family' (Müller I, pp. 82, 86). Thus, for Müller, the tracing of history in its broad sense can even reconcile diverse events and phenomena. Like so many 'letters' or signs in a text, historical events invite interpretation and promote critique. No wonder that he equates the genuine mode of scientific inquiry with evolutionary organic processes themselves. Nothing stands still; nothing is embedded in stone. For his part, Friedrich Schlegel spoke of the 'chemical' nature of the era ('ein chemisches Zeitalter') because – like chemically induced change – the moral, intellectual, and political worlds experience constant alteration or revolution (*Athenaeum* I, p. 310).[9]

The literary text in this wider understanding is open, expandable and constitutive of the project of criticism. Müller designates this approach somewhat confusingly as 'dramatic' (Müller I, p. 155). In truth, his theory is a variation of Friedrich Schlegel's adage that asserts: because it is equally fatal for the mind to have a system and to have none, the two states will simply have to be combined in an uneasy and seemingly paradoxical unity (*Athenaeum Fragment* No. 53; Firchow, p. 167; *KFSA* II, p. 173). That insight led to Schlegel's suggestion of contriving a 'symphilosophy' or a 'sympoetry' by combining 'several complementary minds' in creating communal works of art.[10] Drawing upon dramatic moments of the 'Chemical Revolution' that occurred around 1800, Michel Chaouli notes the aptness of the new heterogeneous view of the essential elements of nature as an allegorical description of the verbal arts.[11] Natural signs are considered to be analogous to letters of the alphabet or words in a language that achieve meaning through combination and recombination.

That being so, it is not surprising that scholars have always recognised the unique signature of Romantic criticism amongst the turbulent political, scientific, intellectual and aesthetic discourses dominating the literary scene around 1800. Ernst Behler, for instance, designated the emergence of early Romantic literary theory as a 'decisive turning point in the history of criticism ... that differed sharply from the dominant classicist understanding of aesthetics and poetics'.[12] Jochen Schulte-Sasse emphasised the Romantics' anti-capitalism and rejection of bourgeois values in their polemical insistence on the autonomy of art (pp. 99–101). Others, such as René Wellek, Silvio Vietta and Matthew Bell, while acknowledging the characteristic signature of German Romanticism, have however also noted that the movement is inextricably embedded in the aesthetic and philosophical developments of the preceding century.[13] To an extent this is so. From a European perspective, German Romanticism did not represent a rupture in the great tradition of critical ideas (Goethe's Faust, for example, appears as the quintessentially divided Romantic protagonist). But Romanticism did signify a distinct shift in emphasis.

To discern both continuity and rupture we must rethink our received notions of the contrariness of Enlightenment and Romanticism. This dichotomy, based as it is on a misreading of the preceding epoch as a 'one-dimensional and undialectical mode of thought' (Vietta, Literarische Frühromantik, p. 12), is false. At the very least, the relationship between late Enlightenment and early Romanticism is one of tension between convergence and divergence. This is especially evident in their attitudes toward the foremost representatives of 'the age of criticism': Lessing, Kant, Goethe and Schiller.[14] While it is demonstrably true that both Schlegels also learned as critics from Lessing, who was justly lauded as the intellectual 'Niesewurz' ('snuff') of his era (Müller I, p. 121) and as 'Prometheus der deutschen Prosa' ('Prometheus of German prose'; F. Schlegel, 'Forster', KFSA II, p. 92), their entwinement with the past also involves the much older and broader tradition of rhetoric (with its affective and performative categories of probare, conciliare, delectare, docere, movere) and the rise of dialogic, 'dramatic' and essayistic writing in the eighteenth century.[15]

By the same token the Romantics' predilection for founding literary journals (Athenaeum, Aurora, Phöbus, Berliner Abendblätter [Berlin Evening Gazette], Zeitung für Einsiedler [Tidings for Hermits]) belongs in the context of the media landscape expansion in the last third of the eighteenth and early nineteenth centuries. That said, whilst this chapter seeks to convey the essence of Romantic critique, the reader should not expect smooth compartmentalisations. For one thing, that is precisely the kind of pedantry the Romantics railed against. For another, the spectrum of their concerns and applications is too vast for adequate treatment in a limited format. While specialists of the German scene around 1800 distinguish between Classicism, late Enlightenment and early Romanticism, comparatists viewing the literary landscape from outside do not categorise so discretely. They are happy to lump the literary giants who gathered in Weimar and Jena together as 'Romantics'.

Yet in spite of common roots there are agreed distinguishing characteristics of German Romanticism that can guide us in what follows, even if they prove to consist in somewhat elusive 'modes of representation' such as allegory, irony, catachresis, metalepsis and ellipsis.[16] The first and most important is the Romantics' deeply self-conscious understanding of their imaginative work as part of an ongoing Platonic process of 're-membering', that is, restoring the parts that have been torn asunder by abstract analysis and the operations of time and space.[17] This distanced self-understanding led to a number of developments. First is 'Romantic irony', a well-known attribute of the first phase of Romanticism (the Schlegels, Hardenberg, Tieck). Second is the subjectivist embrace of fantasy that was more typical of the second phase of Romanticism (Hoffmann, Eichendorff). Third is the use of perspectivism to relativise and historicise narrated reality. This strategy foregrounded the stark contrast between the world of the imagination and everyday life. Fourth, the idea of nature as animate and autopoietic process (*natura naturans*) was emphasised. This provided the foundation for an interactive concept of mimesis that dissolved the boundaries between product and process.

Fifth, Romantic critical theory drew heavily on Greek antiquity, although – like Wieland before them – the Romantics did not idealise Greek art in neo-classicist fashion as the objective and changeless prototype of even modern art. Rather, the Greek 'ideal' was viewed as an invitation for moderns to experiment with the received canon and compete with the original on contemporary terms.[18] Hence the Greek influence was augmented by other literary forerunners, especially Dante, Boccaccio, Calderón, Cervantes, Shakespeare and Goethe. Like the Ancients, these moderns captured the vibrancy of life itself. Art history and music (treated elsewhere in this volume) also had their impact. Related to the notion of an universal ideal of perfection that functions as a catalyst for change are the repeated attempts throughout time and place to measure up to the ideal (or *an* ideal). Hence, a sixth major mark of Romantic critique is the concept of infinite perfectibility. For that reason, the Romantics embraced all forms of revolution: political, social and aesthetic. They saw these revolutions as characterising equally the physical and moral realms and as emanating from the laws governing each realm. Both worlds are continuously evolving; they are caught up in an eternal becoming.

A seventh trait of the Romantic aesthetic is the mingling of genres and styles, the conjoining of poetry and philosophy, spontaneity and reflection. 'If we adopt this model', Behler muses, 'we transcend the dominance of one single principle (reason or imagination, theory or creation, classicism or Romanticism) in favour of a pluralistic movement of counteractive and interactive principles that seem to oppose, but in their interaction actually generate and maintain each other' (Behler, *Theory*, p. 5; cf. Urban, p. 152). Part of the essential tension in this process is the non-closure in rational understanding, the gaps in logic. Thus, an eighth trait, incomprehensibility, emerges as a feature of the Romantic programme. Lack of understanding is not seen as something to be resolved, but as a state to be affirmed as inherent in an existence that is on the one hand concretely fixed and iterative and on the other elusively imprecise in its unexpected twists and turns.

Romantics preferred the essay and expressly dialogical forms of publicity because they make manifest the continuous, open-ended – fragmentary – essence of the thought process. Their ideal of epistemological openness prepared the way for reflection which takes place in an aesthetic mode yet transcends the traditional bounds of the aesthetic. Thus no ultimate theory of the Romantic aesthetic can be formulated in traditional axiomatic terms. Essentially, the Romantic concept of critique could not by definition evolve into a system per se – at least not in the normal sense of an ordered system. Its aesthetic is eternally emergent. We do well to adopt this term from contemporary science debates on the nature of the creative universe to describe its operations. Complexity is its very nature.

The spirit of process: publicity and the objectives of criticism

In 1799 Johann Adam Bergk published a timely assessment of the contemporary state of communication in the public sphere, *Die Kunst Bücher zu lesen* (*The Art of Reading Books*). His stated purpose was to analyse print culture – books and periodical literature – as a *Bildungsanstalt* (institute of education) intended to lead readers to autonomy, develop character and promote critical independence of thought.[19] His statement of purpose was symptomatic of the role assigned to authors and readers by popular writers of the era. Whereas some authors were straightforward in their reader directives, others were more subtle. A new, anonymous and expanding reading public had a wide range of publications to choose from. In this context, the Romantics of course had their own objectives and such favoured forms as: the letter, dialogue, treatise, essay, review, character sketch and the profusely decorated arabesque.

A wide range of journals dominated the general literary scene before the Romantics emerged as an independent force. All sought to elevate readers' level of taste, awareness and critical thinking. The more significant included the *Bibliothek der schönen Wissenschaften und der Freyen Künste* (*Library of Aesthetics and Liberal Arts*), *Briefe, die neueste Litteratur betreffend* (*Letters Concerning Contemporary Literature*), *Frankfurter gelehrte Anzeigen* (*Frankfurt Learned Gazette*), *Allgemeine Deutsche Bibliothek* (*General German Library*), *Deutsches Museum* (*German Museum*), *Der teutsche Merkur* (*The German Mercury*), *Berlinische Monatsschrift* (*Berlin Monthly*), *Journal des Luxus und der Moden* (*Journal of Luxury and Fashions*) and the *Allgemeine Literatur-Zeitung*.[20] Strikingly, three of the last four of these long-lived journals were edited and published in Weimar or Jena (the others appeared in Berlin), and the early Romantics published in them. More narrowly focused (and shorter-lived) periodicals that also appeared in these two intellectual centres were Goethe's *Propyläen* (*Gateway*), Schiller's *Horen* (*The Hours*), Wieland's *Attisches Museum* (*Attic Museum*) and the Schlegels' *Athenaeum*. More esoteric in style and objectives, these journals could nonetheless not have existed without the spade work done by the more popular and encyclopedic endeavours. The very fact that the Schlegels founded the *Athenaeum* in 1798 in direct opposition to the successful and influential *Allgemeine Literatur-Zeitung* (*ALZ*) and polemicised against Schiller's *Horen* and Wieland's *Teutscher Merkur* underscores the continuity within the apparent divergence. (A. W. Schlegel had almost single-handedly filled the belletristic columns of the *ALZ* from 1796 to 1799.) They drew the full consequence of the older generations' insistence on independence of thought and character by emphasising the individual and characteristic.

But they define popular style differently from their Enlightenment predecessors. They do not mean the broadest public appeal through the use of common language and uncomplicated reasoning, but rather an emotionally modulated style that combines 'anschauliche Darstellung' ('vivid depiction'), 'schöne Diktion' ('refined diction') and the association of ideas in an act of 'kritischer Mimus' ('critical mime') that can alternately – or simultaneously – be dogmatic, sceptical or philosophical.[21] This agility of style appeals to the reader's imagination, emotions and reason. Friedrich Schlegel defines genuinely popular writing in his essay on Georg Forster in precisely these terms, as addressing 'den ganzen Menschen' ('the whole person') with all his or her mental, affective and creative powers (Schlegel, 'Forster', *KFSA* II, p. 82; cf. also *Athenaeum*, *KFSA* XVI, p. 139, No. 638).

As the allusion to Goethe's theory of aesthetic education in *Wilhelm Meister* suggests, the art of criticism assumes the function of the traditional systematic theory of aesthetics. Popularity in this refined sense is commensurate with the variable thought and stylistic processes used to judge and describe an object of study in this mimetic manner. The reading public's often puzzled reaction to the *Athenaeum* style bore witness to the need for a new critical mode of reading to comprehend the new art of criticism. Friedrich Schlegel's *Kritisches Fragment* No. 85 formulates his view of the author/reader relationship with a signal lack of hermeneutic sympathy: 'Every honest author writes for nobody or everybody. Whoever writes for some particular group does not deserve to be read' (Firchow, p. 153). Later he defines the desired reviewing mode pithily: 'A real review should be the solution of a critical equation, the result and description of a philological experiment and a literary investigation' (*Athenaeum Fragment* No. 403; Firchow, p. 228). Hermeneutics were at the core of the Romantics' new concept of criticism.

The first numbers of *Athenaeum*, signed by both Schlegels, August Wilhelm's unsigned introductory commentary to *Beyträge zur Kritik der neuesten Litteratur* (*Contributions to Criticism of New Writing*) (*Athenaeum* I, pp. 141–9), his unsigned introduction to the *Notizen* (*Notes*) (*Athenaeum* I, pp. 285–8), his review of *Litterarischer Reichsanzeiger oder Archiv der Zeit und ihres Geschmacks* (*Imperial Literary Gazette, or Archive of the Age and Its Taste*) (*Athenaeum* II, pp. 328–30), and his proposal for a 'new' kind of journal in his 'Entwurf zu einem kritischen Institute'[22] – all these texts point to the need for a critical approach commensurate with the demands of a new era. From the outset, the Schlegels make clear their intent to publish a journal characterised by an easy manner of presentation ('im Vortrag nach der freyesten Mittheilung') in the form of treatises, letters, rhapsodic observations and aphoristic fragments. Their aim was to educate the reader. Everything that deals with art and philosophy broadly understood can be found in these pages (I, i). They aim at entertaining the reader by writing animated and attractive prose whilst demanding independence of thought and undermining preconceived notions (I, ii).

This initial characterisation of the *Athenaeum*'s style and character is further explored in the prefatory remarks to the 'Beyträge' (1799), where A. W. Schlegel offers his 'Privatansichten' ('personal views') as an interested observer of the contemporary literary scene (*Athenaeum* I, p. 147). The era, he comments, is marked by such a flood of print that reviewing books has become a necessary evil. The book-fair catalogues themselves, he notes ironically, would appear to be the best review organs: they essentially summarise the books they announce, slavishly reproducing the very physiognomy of the original. As a consequence, critic and reader are offered no real guide to the value of the book announced. Moreover, existing review journals offer little help, because they endeavour to cover all branches of knowledge and treat everything indiscriminately. Specialist journals, on the other hand, go to the opposite extreme: they tend to be too esoteric and inaccessible to the general reader. This is true, he laments, even of journals devoted to literature and the humanities.

What Schlegel therefore envisions is a review journal that focuses only on those works which exude a sense of vitality. Why strive for complete coverage, he asks, when so many works amount to literary waste paper ('litterarische Makulatur'; *Athenaeum* I, p. 148)? Instead, the criterion of inclusion for Schlegel and all the Romantics is the degree to which a work might be considered 'alive'. Every living organism is interconnected with its environment to such an extent that one need not worry about canvassing everything or digressing in a commentary: 'And yet only the letters of a book can be enclosed between the covers of a volume. In as far as the book is alive, that is, has spark and content, it exists simultaneously as product and as impulse in multilayered contexts' ('Und doch lassen sich nur die Buchstaben eines Buches in die Scheidewände des Bandes einschließen: in so fern es lebt, einen Geist und einen Gehalt hat, steht es als Wirkung und wiederum wirkend in mannichfaltigen Beziehungen').[23] Clearly audible here is the echo of Lessing's classic distinction between spirit and letter that drew upon a Pauline tradition of biblical hermeneutics and was to resound throughout the rest of the century.[24] For Lessing the desirable characteristic of the written word is its ability to emit sufficient intellectual sparks to stir the reader to reflection and/or concrete action. The ability to recognise 'vital signs' and the concomitant potential to revolutionise thought is also the mark of a genuinely 'classic' work or author. This explains the Romantics' preference for character portraits such as A. W. Schlegel's critical (if appreciative) review of Gottfried August Bürger's significance for German literature (1800; *AWS* VIII, pp. 64–139), his brother's fragmentary 'Charakteristik' of Georg Forster (*Lyceum*, 1797) or Adam Müller's 'Fragmente über William Shakespeare' in *Phöbus* (1808; Müller I, pp. 158–204).

In such texts they laud as present or lament as absent the interconnections between author and world which aim at progressive development of the individual. They discover in such works infinitely many depths, subterfuges and intentions. In his Forster essay Friedrich Schlegel identified this kind of writing as central to the goals of Romanticism, calling it 'cosmopolitan and social'.[25] He captured that essential nexus in a one-liner from the 'Ideen': 'Der Mensch ist ein schaffender Rückblick der Natur auf sich selbst' ('Man is nature's creative reflection back upon itself'; *Athenaeum* III, p. 8).

The preferred kind of writing is the Fragment which sees human history as part of the dialectic of individual and nature. In addition to the view of humankind as caught up in feedback loops with creative nature, Schlegel also foregrounds the intrinsic character, poetry and uniqueness of each individual ('Gespräch über die Poesie', *Athenaeum* III, p. 58). He asserts tellingly that humankind is inherently linked to the creative forces of the earth, which he calls a divine poem: 'das eine Gedicht der Gottheit, dessen Theil und Blüthe auch wir sind – die Erde' ('the one poem of divinity, whose part and bloom we too are – earth').[26] It is in this context that we should understand Hardenberg's aphorism that our calling is to contribute to the earth's development: 'Wir sind auf einer Mißion: zur Bildung der Erde sind wir berufen' ('We are on an mission: we are called to the formation of the world').[27] Each individual is called to seek his full potential by acting in concert with the living organism of the earth and thereby participating in its development. Leibniz's idea that competing ideas can harmoniously coexist in so far as they do not immediately contradict each other (the compossible) is audible here as is Spinoza's concept of nature evolving (*natura naturans*).

Friedrich Schlegel's 'Rede über die Mythologie' ('Address on Mythology') develops this concept of integrative action. The mythology of the ancients, in which gods personify universal forces of nature, no longer obtains. A new mythological framework must arise from the depths of the human spirit ('aus der tieffsten Tiefe des Geistes'). This, by contrast, will be the most self-consciously artful of art works, the purest expression of the signature phenomenon of the age: idealism (*Athenaeum* III, p. 96). The connection between earth and the human spirit is nonetheless underscored when Schlegel remarks that modern idealism expressed itself first in physics, and only later in philosophy and art (III, p. 97). But essentially, every successful mythology is nothing more than a hieroglyphic rendition of nature (III, p. 101). The chief characteristic of the new mythology is self-constitutively to represent nature through ever-changing, continuously creative feedback loops of imagery. Hence – now drawing on Spinoza – Schlegel suggests that even the new mythology is in the end also nothing less than the direct expression of nature's artistic energy. Once humankind begins to understand that it is caught up in 'a grand process of universal rejuvenation', once it comprehends that nature abides by principles of 'eternal revolution', then it will be able genuinely to grasp the meaning of the earth and the sun as mutually interdependent (*Athenaeum* III, p. 105). Philosophy, poetry and physical interaction animate and form one other. Thinking is itself a divinatory event. In light of this newly defined intimacy of thought, critical reflection and endogenous natural processes, humankind can truly be said to stand on the threshold of a new era. Just how foundational this prophetic insight is in the Romantics' art of criticism and their modes of publicity is clear from echoes of it in commentaries by A. W. Schlegel, Görres, Müller, Hardenberg and others. But there is no space to pursue those echoes here.

The object of critique is normally accepted to be an established fact. The investigation of that fact and the result of the inquiry themselves attain the status of a fact. Yet for the Romantics, these 'facts reconstitute themselves as experiments and approximations. A. W. Schlegel's view on this illuminates the early Romantics' art of criticism, for he labels research 'an historical experiment' that deals with and results in facts so that each fact is marked simultaneously by a unique individuality ('strenge Individualität') and a quality both mysterious and experimental ('zugleich ein Geheimniß und ein Experiment'). Hence, it is linked to the evolving qualities of nature itself ('nämlich ein Experiment der bildenden Natur'; *Athenaeum* II, p. 311).

Similarly, he defines an idea as the complete, ironic unity of absolutely antithetical thoughts that produce their own creative energy (*Athenaeum* I, p. 207). Hence a fragment assumes the character of a hedgehog: apart and rebarbatively complete unto itself (p. 230). Thus, the fragment appears as the purest form of universal philosophy (p. 248) and as one link in the chain of verbal exchanges we call dialogue (p. 126). A longer chain of such exchanges constitutes the epistle, while memoirs amount to 'a system of fragments' (p. 126: 'System von Fragmenten'). The linking of these verbal forms together into larger units recalls the combinatory principle of chemical compounds, the 'letters' of the material world that result in the 'book of Nature' which requires constant scrutiny to decipher its meaning. As synecdoche (the part standing for the whole), the fragment is in equal measure subjective and individual and objective; it is a necessary ingredient of all disciplinary systems of thought (p.126). In this light, as medium for the reconciliation of opposites, we can appreciate Friedrich Schlegel's assertion of the three main tendencies of his turbulent era as a list of such complementary opposites: in the sociopolitical realm, the French Revolution; in philosophy and science, Fichte's *Wissenschaftslehre*; in literature, Goethe's novel *Wilhelm Meisters Lehrjahre* (p. 232). What unites them is the energy they draw from the life of the earth and the life they breathe into abstract thought – precisely the qualities Georg Forster possessed as scientist and author.[28] In the same collection Schlegel apotheosises the French Revolution analogically as a gigantic earthquake, as the mother of all revolutions (as 'ein fast universelles Erdbeben ... oder als ein Urbild der Revoluzionen, als die Revoluzion schlechthin'; *KFSA* I, p. 309).

A. W. Schlegel's 'Entwurf zu einem kritischen Institute' (1800; 'Proposal for an Institute of Criticism') maps out the means for revolutionising thought by using the medium of periodicals. Rejecting the practice common in review journals to canvass as many publications as possible in monthly or quarterly segments as superficial and mechanical, he paradoxically suggests taking a longer view of things and, at the same time, a more limited one. In place of the journal – a term that evokes a sense of the events of the day – he proposes yearbooks that would appear only with each book fair (that external marker of the rhythm of literary life). The greater time lapse before publication would allow for more intense examination of truly deserving works. 'Wissenschaft und Kunst' would replace the usual rubric 'Literatur', a designation that he considers to be limited and imprecise. While not all books would or could be reviewed, those that deal with human values and concerns would be foregrounded. The natural sciences would not be excluded, because they seek to understand the laws of nature, and human life is embedded in nature (*AWS* VIII, p. 52). In as far as they belong to the history of humanity, the categories of history and art history would be included. Other rubrics of the proposed 'Institute of Criticism' are mathematics, philology, theory and practice of the fine arts, poetry and *belles lettres*. He even includes those branches of theology, jurisprudence and medicine that shed light on the nature of the human being (*AWS* VIII, p. 53). The reviews would be undertaken by a small group of collaborators who, thanks to their contrasting individualities and broad intellectual interests, would both create a synergy and communicate it to readers, animating them to become active participants in the constant commerce of criticism (p. 54).

Like the chemist in his lab, then, the editor is not manager but investigator and facilitator. The preferred forms of criticism (epistle, dialogue, aphorism, treatise, essay and notice) would be enlivened by wit and insight (pp. 55–6). There would of course also be a rubric for 'Kritik der Kritik' (p. 56). Schlegel's 'Entwurf eines kritischen Instituts' thus bears an obvious resemblance to chemistry-inspired concepts of inorganic and organic nature and of *progressive Universalpoesie* as emergent phenomena. In sum, the art of Romantic criticism acts like *fermenta cognitionis* to counteract mental rot (*Athenaeum* I, p. 248) and further progressive development.

The Schlegels even utilised the form of a journal itself as a vehicle of their reviewing practice (Urban, pp. 151, 161). Their journal envisioned its task to be the 're-presenting of presentation', a critical recasting of knowledge and art 'in terms of their present or modern configuration' (Seyhan, p. 2). This move thus appropriates for the journal the unique feature of essayism as a mode of expression which deploys both medium and message. The reviewer, the main actor in the new journal form, has to be hermeneutic interpreter, critic and translator rolled into one (Urban, 178). In his tribute to Lessing, whom he views as a highly complex and revolutionary spirit,

Friedrich Schlegel emphasises that the hermeneutics we associate with him should be considered to be the genuine business and inner essence of criticism (*KFSA* II, pp. 100–8, 112). That business is most aptly performed through implication, the trace, the partially formulated sign. Indeed, the Romantics all argued that the reviewer must become one with the book to be reviewed, seek to understand it as the author intended; not simply to summarise the argument, but to translate it for the reader, make the argument 'come alive' by recasting it and recombining its constitutive elements. 'Über die Unverständlichkeit' was penned in response to complaints of unintelligibility levelled at the *Athenaeum* and is, essentially, a defence of the method of his Fragments, which was to suggest that thoughts are always preliminary, interpretations never finished and indeterminacy a fundamental aspect of the chaos which envelops us. Truth is paradox, knowledge exegesis, language symbolic signs requiring interpretation, and irony the medium of true understanding.

Genuinely new in this stance is Schlegel's insistence that incomprehensibility be raised to the level of a decisive principle. Complaining – like many critics before him – that readers have not yet learned to read critically, he reconstructs the model reader who is willing to become a partner with the author/critic in experimenting with meaning and who acknowledges that reading can prove to be a dangerous game because of the dislocations it occasions. That is also the point of Hardenberg's comment on the nature of the genuine reader as an extension of the author: 'Der wahre Leser muß der erweiterte Autor seyn' (*Vermischte Bemerkungen*; *NS* II, p. 470, No. 125). His entire world view is marked by a tension between fragment and whole, between the desire for closure and the essential resistance to it, whether in the events of the empirical world or in the process of remembering.[29]

Common to all discussions of the Romantics' art of criticism is the insistence on its open-ended, fragmentary nature that requires a proactive reader. What they essentially describe is known in genre theory as essayism. It can serve as an overarching term that includes what has variously been called 'dramatic', 'dialogic' or fragmentary. It is mimetic in Friedrich Schlegel's sense of 'mimetischer Modus'. The essayistic attitude thus forms a fourth generic category alongside the classical triad: epic, dramatic and lyric. Hitherto, scholars have not generally recognised the relevance of essayism – this unique form of 'poetic interaction'[30]– for situating the typical reflective stance of the Romantic school. Chaouli does not. It is, nonetheless, the kind of writing that occupies the middle ground between historical narrative, philosophical explanation and scientific exploration and does so by combining all three modes into one. Reaching back at least as far as Montaigne, essayism predates a chemical model of the Romantic verbal arts around

1800 by several hundred years. It has the advantage of not prioritising scientific models over humanistic ones (cf. Chaouli, pp. 208–14). Perhaps the Chemical Revolution is itself the result of a deeper lying impulse of inquiry that could explain the striking similarities in dialogical, dialectical, combinatory practice? In any event the art of Romantic critique is aimed at drawing out tendencies and not producing hard facts.

NOTES

1. *KFSA* II, pp. 149, 161, Nos. 27 and 115: for English translations see *Friedrich Schlegel's Lucinde and the Fragments*, trans. Peter Firchow (Minneapolis: University of Minnesota Press, 1971), pp. 145, 157 (hereafter Firchow).
2. Joseph Görres, 'Der Charakter des Antiken', *Aurora, eine Zeitschrift aus dem südlichen Deutschland*, No. 17 (13 June 1804), pp. 282–3; reprinted in Joseph Görres, *Ausgewählte Werke*, ed. Wolfgang Frühwald, 2 vols. (Freiburg im Breisgau, Basel and Vienna: Herder, 1978), vol. I, pp. 97–103, here p. 97.
3. *Athenaeum: Ein Zeitschrift*, ed. August Wilhelm Schlegel and Friedrich Schlegel, facsimile edition, ed. Ernst Behler, 3 vols. (Darmstadt: Wissenschaftliche Buchgesellschaft, 1992), vol. 1, p. 311.
4. Görres, 'Korruskationen', in Görres, *Ausgewählte Werke*, vol. I, pp. 113–17.
5. Jochen Schulte-Sasse, 'The Concept of Literary Criticism in German Romanticism, 1795–1810', in *A History of German Literary Criticism, 1730–1980*, ed. Peter Uwe Hohendahl (Lincoln and London: University of Nebraska Press, 1988), pp. 99–177, here p. 114.
6. Theodore Ziolkowski, *German Romanticism and its Institutions* (Princeton, N.J.: Princeton University Press, 1990) examines the romantic inwardness against the actual political and social background of the era. He concludes that the 'Romantic writer stood *between* reality and the ideal' (p. 17).
7. Adam Müller, 'Vorlesungen über die deutsche Wissenschaft und Literatur', in *Kritische, ästhetische und philosophische Schriften*, ed. Walter Schroeder and Werner Siebert, 2 vols. (Neuwied and Berlin: Luchterhand, 1967), vol. I, p. 17. Hereafter cited by volume and page number. Müller develops his anti-French theory before the rise of German patriotic fervour 1806–15.
8. Nicholas Saul, 'The Pursuit of the Subject: Literature as Critic and Perfecter of Philosophy 1790–1830,' in *Philosophy and German Literature, 1700–1990*, ed. Nicholas Saul (Cambridge: Cambridge University Press, 2002), pp. 57–101, here p. 81.
9. Compare Müller, 'Vorlesungen': 'Das Leben schauend und das Leben bildend, oder wissend und handelnd zugleich, schreitet die echte Wissenschaft fort: Was ist nun das Leben selbst anderes als diese Wissenschaft?' (vol. I, p. 78). On the scientific foundations of the romantic conception of life see Robert J. Richards, *The Romantic Conception of Life: Science and Philosophy in the Age of Goethe* (Chicago and London: University of Chicago Press, 2002), esp. pp. 207–321, and Michel Chaouli, *The Laboratory of Poetry: Chemistry and Poetics in the Work of Friedrich Schlegel* (Baltimore and London: The Johns Hopkins University Press, 2002), esp. pp. 91–145. Rapid advances in chemistry and their impact on Romantic theory are explored.

10. *Athenaeum Fragment* No. 125, pp. 177–8; *KFSA* II, p. 185. Schlegel labels this unifying method of analysis 'kombinatorische Kunst': *Athenaeum Fragment* No. 220 (*KFSA* II, p. 200).
11. Chaouli, *The Laboratory of Poetry*, p. 103.
12. Ernst Behler, *German Romantic Literary Theory* (Cambridge: Cambridge University Press, 1993), p. 1.
13. See René Wellek, *A History of Modern Criticism 1750–1950*, vol. II: *The Romantic Age* (Cambridge: Cambridge University Press, 1981), p. 2; Silvio Vietta, *Literarische Phantasie: Theorie und Geschichte: Barock und Aufklärung* (Stuttgart: Metzler, 1986), pp. 241–69, and *Die Literarische Frühromantik* (Göttingen: Vandenhoeck & Ruprecht, 1983), pp. 208–20; Matthew Bell, *The German Tradition of Psychology in Literature and Thought, 1700–1840* (Cambridge: Cambridge University Press, 2005), pp. 143–207.
14. Astrid Urban, *Kunst der Kritik: Die Gattungsgeschichte der Rezension von der Spätaufklärung bis zur Romantik* (Heidelberg: Winter, 2004), p. 54.
15. See John A. McCarthy, *Crossing Boundaries: A Theory and History of Essay Writing in German, 1680–1815* (Philadelphia: University of Pennsylvania Press, 1989), pp. 298–307, and Peter D. Krause, *Unbestimmte Rhetorik: Friedrich Schlegel und die Redekunst um 1800* (Tübingen: Niemeyer, 2001).
16. Azade Seyhan, *Representation and Its Discontents: The Critical Legacy of German Romanticism* (Berkeley, Los Angeles and Oxford: University of California Press, 1992), p. 71. An allegory is a visible symbol representing an abstract idea; irony is a trope that involves incongruity between what is expected and what is said; catachresis is the paradoxical use of words either erroneously or intentionally; metalepsis is the substitution of one figurative sense of a thing for another figurative sense of a thing; ellipsis is the omission of words or sentences designed to cause reflection on what or why something has been left out.
17. See Vietta, *Literarische Phantasie*, p. 248; Alice Kuzniar, *Delayed Endings: Nonclosure in Novalis and Hölderlin* (Athens: University of Georgia Press, 1987), p. 48.
18. See Müller, *Schriften*, vol. I, pp. 205–48; also John A. McCarthy, 'Klassisch Lesen: Weimarer Klassik, Wirkungsästhetik und Wieland', in *Jahrbuch der Deutschen Schillergesellschaft*, 36 (1992), pp. 414–32, and Peter Schnyder, *Die Magie der Rhetorik: Poesie, Philosophie und Politik in Friedrich Schlegels Frühwerk* (Paderborn, Munich, Vienna, Zürich: Schöningh, 1998).
19. J. A. Bergk, *Die Kunst Bücher zu lesen: Nebst Bemerkungen über Schriften und Schriftsteller* (Jena: Hempelsche Buchhandlung, 1799), pp. vii–viii.
20. See Werner Faulstich, *Die bürgerliche Mediengesellschaft (1700–1830)* (Göttingen: Vandenhoeck & Ruprecht, 2002), and Ernst Fischer, Wilhelm Haefs and York-Gothart Mix (eds.), *Von Almanach bis Zeitung: Ein Handbuch der Medien in Deutschland 1700–1800* (Munich: Beck, 1999).
21. Willy Michel, *Ästhetische Hermeneutik und frühromantische Kritik* (Göttingen: Vandenhoeck & Ruprecht, 1982), pp. 56–83.
22. August Wilhelm Schlegel, *Sämmtliche Werke*, facsimile reprint of the Leipzig 1846 edition, ed. Eduard Böcking, 30 vols. (Hildesheim and New York: Olms, 1971), vol. VIII, pp. 50–7. Hereafter cited as *AWS*.

23. *Athenaeum,* vol. I, p. 149; See also Schlegel, 'Gespräch über die Poesie' (*Athenaeum,* vol. III, p. 67) and his review of Fritz Jacobi's *Waldemar* (*KFSA* II, pp. 58, 69–71).

24. Jeffrey Librett, *The Rhetoric of Cultural Dialogue: Jews and Germans from Moses Mendelssohn to Richard Wagner and Beyond* (Palo Alto, Calif.: Stanford University Press, 2000) follows this motif from the mid-eighteenth century, while Ulrike Zeuch, *Das Unendliche – Höchste Fülle oder Nichts? Zur Problematik von Friedrich Schlegels Geist-Begriff und dessen geistesgeschichtlichen Voraussetzungen* (Würzburg: Königshausen & Neumann, 1991) traces the deep roots of Friedrich Schlegel's use of the concept 'spirit'.

25. Schlegel, 'Forster' (*KFSA* II, p. 91). The full text reads: 'Weltbürgerliche, gesellschaftliche Schriften sind also ein ebenso unentbehrliches Mittel und Bedingnis der fortschreitenden Bildung, als eigentlich wissenschaftliche und künstlerische. Sie sind die echten Prosaisten.'

26. 'Gespräch über die Poesie', *Athenaeum,* vol. III, 1, p. 59. Schlegel repeats the argument in 'Forster' where he calls for the 'unbedingt notwendige Wiedervereinigung aller der Grundkräfte des Menschen, welche in Urquell, Endziel und Wesen eins und unteilbar, doch verschieden erscheinen, und getrennt wirken und sich bilden müssen' (*KFSA* II, p. 91). Adam Müller echoes the sentiment in his essays 'Vom Organismus in Natur und Kunst' (1808) and 'Vom Antorganismus' (1808) (*Kritische Schriften,* vol. II, pp. 266–75).

27. *Athenaeum* I, p. 80. Hardenberg's work contains numerous allusions to these interconnections.

28. In his essay on Forster, Schlegel lauds the Forster's 'Geist freier Fortschreitung' that exudes the sense of an invigorating walk in the fresh open air, captures the 'unendliche Lebenskraft der allerzeugenden und allnährenden Natur', reveals traces of the *telos* of universal wisdom ('Spuren von dem Endzweck einer allgütigen Weisheit'), animates the reader to critical reflection ('Selbstdenken') and brings together all branches of knowledge into a single, inseparable totality ('Die Wiedervereinigung endlich aller wesentlich zusammenhängenden … wenngleich jetzt getrennten und zerstückelten Wissenschaften … zu einem einzigen unteilbaren Ganzen'). That assessment more or less sums up the Romantics' ideal of criticism (*KFSA* II, pp. 80–1, 85, 99).

29. See Laurie Ruth Johnson, *The Art of Recollection in Jena Romanticism: Memory, History, Fiction, and Fragmentation in Texts by Friedrich Schlegel and Novalis* (Tübingen: Niemeyer, 2002), p. 139.

30. John McCumber, *Poetic Interaction: Language, Freedom, Reason* (Chicago: University of Chicago Press, 1989), pp. 379, 383–4.

FURTHER READING

Brown, Marshall, *The Shape of German Romanticism* (Ithaca, N.Y.: Cornell University Press, 1979)

De Man, Paul, *The Rhetoric of Romanticism* (New York: Columbia University Press, 1984)

Engell, James, *The Creative Imagination: Enlightenment to Romanticism* (Cambridge, Mass.: Harvard University Press, 1981)

Gorman, David, 'A Bibliography of German Romantic Literary Criticism and Theory in English', *Style* (Winter 1994) (FindArticles.com, accessed 12 August 2007. http://www.engl.niu.edu/style/)

McGann, Jerome J., *The Romantic Ideology: A Critical Investigation* (Chicago: University of Chicago Press, 1983)

7

JANE K. BROWN

Romanticism and Classicism

Broadly conceived, European Romanticism designates a period of 100 years extending from Rousseau to Baudelaire, and in painting and music it follows Classicism. German literary history not only uses the term more narrowly, as this volume demonstrates, but it also distinguishes between contemporaneous movements called Romanticism and Classicism. In the context of European comparative scholarship Johann Wolfgang Goethe (1749–1832) and Friedrich Schiller (1759–1805) are Germany's greatest Romantics, but for German scholars they embody the movement called German or Weimar Classicism, which is cast variably as the enemy, diametric opposite, or complement of Romanticism. Scholars today no longer universally accept the distinction between Romanticism and Classicism, nor do they even argue much whether it should be drawn, since proponents of both sides consider the question settled. A frequent compromise has been to speak of a *Goethezeit* (Age of Goethe), which can then be divided into Classicism and Romanticism or not as one chooses. This essay describes the historical details of the connections between the groups, their intellectual commonalities and differences and what might properly be called Goethe's role in German Romanticism; then it considers briefly the history and function of the distinction.

As the canon of German literary history crystallised in the late nineteenth century, Classicism often included in addition to Goethe, Schiller and Wilhelm von Humboldt (1767–1835) the older dramatist and theorist Gotthold Ephraim Lessing (1729–81) and the poet Christoph Martin Wieland (1733–1813), tutor to the Duke of Weimar and Goethe's respected associate. The rest of the canonical figures of the era were Romantics, except for a swing group consisting of Jean Paul (1763–1825), Friedrich Hölderlin (1770–1843) and Heinrich von Kleist (1777–1811). Jean Paul's stylistic allegiance remained with Laurence Sterne and the generation of sensibility that peaked in Germany in the 1770s and 1780s, but continued to be popular in the 1790s. Hölderlin wrote in classical forms and used classical mythology originally in the style of Schiller's poetry, and so seemed to belong to the Classicists; Kleist, similarly, seemed to be Schiller's successor as an author of blank verse historical dramas. None of the three successfully established a close bond with either Goethe or Schiller, and the last two belonged to the generation of and were friends with other Romantics. If Romanticism was diseased, as Goethe famously once said, then the madman Hölderlin and the paranoiac suicide Kleist were more representative than the reactionary Catholic convert Friedrich Schlegel or the diligent Prussian administrator Joseph von Eichendorff.

While Germany lacked the centralised metropolitan culture of Britain or France in the late eighteenth century, its intellectual community was small and intricately bound by ties of friendship, kinship and marriage. The German Classicists and Romanticists knew one another, rather better than, say, the Lake Poets did Keats, Shelley or Byron. Indeed, they knew each other often all too well, so that their relationships are coloured by age differences, specific friendships and constellations of personalities. The best way to illustrate these intricate relations is to consider the close association of the first group of Romantics with the university town that gave them their name.

Jena drew the first generation of modern German intellectuals for one simple reason: Goethe's presence.[1] After achieving world fame as the author of *Die Leiden des jungen Werthers* (1774; *The Sorrows of Young Werther*), Goethe moved to Weimar in 1775 at the invitation of its young duke, who had sought the poet's acquaintance while on his educational grand tour. Once there, Goethe took on an active role in the administration of the tiny duchy, which consisted primarily of the towns Weimar and Jena, only about twenty kilometres apart. He devoted himself to the court and the government for twelve years – among his many responsibilities was the university in Jena – until he fled on his famous journey to Italy, from which he returned as a public intellectual, but with a greatly reduced role in the state. He remained, however, deeply engaged with the theatre, art collections, museums, libraries and university, where he influenced academic appointments in virtually all fields. The two most important for the rise of the Jena Romantics were those of Schiller as professor of history in 1789 and Johann Gottlieb Fichte (1762–1814) as professor of philosophy in 1794. Schiller became Goethe's closest literary associate and fellow Classicist, while Fichte became the philosophical heart of the Romantic movement; the reputations of both, along with that of Goethe himself, drew most of the German intellectual vanguard to Weimar or Jena in the late 1790s.

Jena was a bastion of German Idealism. Even before the arrival of Fichte, Carl Leonhard Reinhold (1758–1823), a literary associate and son-in-law of Wieland but also an enthusiastic admirer of Kant, served as professor of philosophy from 1787–94. Schiller, too, had become an enthusiastic Kantian by the early 1790s. As a result of Goethe's efforts, Friedrich Wilhelm Joseph Schelling (1775–1854) joined the faculty in 1798 and remained until 1803. Friedrich Daniel Ernst Schleiermacher (1768–1834) contributed at Goethe's request to the Jena *Allgemeine Literaturzeitung* (*General Literary Gazette*), although he did not actually spend time there. Georg Wilhelm Friedrich Hegel (1770–1831) became a *Privatdozent* (non-stipendiary lecturer) for philosophy in Jena in 1801 and remained there until 1807 (during the last two years as unpaid, so-called *professor extraordinarius*). Because Goethe was famously hostile to abstraction he is generally assumed to have had no real interest in Idealist philosophy, but this record of appointments shows otherwise. Furthermore, he is known to have studied at least Kant's *Kritik der Urteilskraft* (1790; *Critique of Judgement*) with great care.[2] Goethe remained in contact with both Hegel and especially Schelling until the end of his life. At the high point of Jena Romanticism Goethe spent almost half his time in Jena, visiting Schiller, writing and participating in the on-going literary and philosophical discussions. Goethe's closest intellectual contacts in the 1790s were with Kantians, and the core of the second generation of German Idealism spent its formative years in Jena in regular contact with Schiller and Goethe.

The Schlegel brothers formed an equally important part of this coterie. August Wilhelm (1767–1845) spent most of 1796 to mid-1797 in Jena, then settled there officially as *professor extraordinarius* for aesthetics and literature in 1798; Friedrich (1772–1829) joined him for most of his first stay there, and lived there again from 1799 to 1801. Goethe socialised with both and shared their – for the times – loose social morals. Goethe lived with his common-law wife Christiane Vulpius, Friedrich with his, Dorothea Mendelssohn (daughter of the philosopher Moses Mendelssohn), who had left her husband, Simon Veit, to follow Schlegel to Jena, and August Wilhelm was married to the rather notorious revolutionary Caroline Böhmer, whom Goethe had first met years before as the daughter of the famous Göttingen Orientalist J. D. Michaelis. Goethe helped her obtain a divorce when she left Schlegel for Schelling in 1803; he also facilitated the abandoned husband's introduction to his next companion, Madame de Staël. August Wilhelm Schlegel introduced Georg Friedrich Philipp von Hardenberg (Novalis, 1772–1801) to both Goethe and Schiller in March 1798 and brought him again in the summer of 1799. He also introduced Ludwig Tieck (1773–1853) in 1799. Tieck's friend Wilhelm Heinrich Wackenroder (1773–98) had already died before this meeting. Goethe and Tieck met several times during the latter's lengthy stay in Jena and thereafter

Tieck visited Goethe about once a decade. Tieck was a great admirer of Goethe before they met; while Goethe was only moderately enthusiastic about Tieck's poetic work, he had great respect for his scholarly writing on Elizabethan drama as well as for his translations of Shakespeare and Cervantes. The Schlegels reviewed Goethe's works with enthusiasm; August Wilhelm contributed to Goethe's journals; Goethe staged their plays and August Wilhelm's translations of Calderón and Shakespeare, for which he had high praise. It is clear that he found both brothers stimulating in their different ways, although he found much not to admire personally, especially in the socially rather inept Friedrich.

Although Schiller was generally more outgoing than Goethe, he was less diplomatic and willing to compromise. He wooed August Wilhelm to contribute to his journal, Die Horen (The Hours), but took an instantaneous dislike to Friedrich, from whom he refused and even ignored contributions. He reserved a special dislike for Caroline, whom he called 'Lady Lucifer'. In a classic study of the relations between the Schlegels and Goethe, Josef Körner traced in detail the day-to-day fluctuations of mood and attitude in this complicated set of relationships.[3] Goethe and the Schlegels supported one another in different ways at different times without there ever being the strong bond of affection and respect that existed between Goethe and Schiller. When the increasingly prickly relations between Friedrich Schlegel and Schiller erupted in Schlegel's hostile and insulting review of Die Horen in May 1796 in Deutschland, a politically liberal journal edited by Goethe's former friend but now opponent, Johann Friedrich Reichardt, Goethe found himself in an awkward position and spent several years mediating in vain. As Friedrich Schlegel drifted toward Catholicism after 1805, Goethe, always a resolute secularist, reached the limits of his patience for this difficult connection, and he in turn expressed himself openly with some hostility. Yet in the 1820s there was a partial rapprochement with both brothers. With a different chemistry between Schiller and the Schlegels, we might not speak of German Classicism.

Because Schiller died in 1805, he had no connections to the younger, so-called 'Heidelberg' Romantics, but Goethe had almost paternal connections to many of them. In the 1770s Goethe had been friends with Clemens Brentano's (1778–1842) grandmother, the novelist Sophie La Roche (1731–1807) and also somewhat in love with his mother, Maximiliane La Roche Brentano (1756–93); he maintained an interest in several of Maximiliane's twelve children. Clemens had a few cordial visits with Goethe and admired him. His brother-in-law, Achim von Arnim (1781–1831), was rather closer to Goethe, whom he first met independently in 1801 in Göttingen, where Arnim staged an homage to the visiting celebrity. In return Goethe visited him and T. F. A. Kestner, fifth son of Charlotte Buff (1753–1828), another early beloved of Goethe and the model for the heroine of *Werther*. Goethe responded cordially to Arnim's and Brentano's folk-song collection, *Des Knaben Wunderhorn* (1805; *The Boy's Magic Horn*), and Arnim visited him several times until his wife, Bettine (1785–1859), another of Maximiliane's children, was so rude to Christiane that Goethe had nothing more to do with the couple, and politely resisted Bettine's efforts to re-establish relations in the 1820s. Bettine had long adulated Goethe and pumped his mother for stories about him, material that Goethe later used in his autobiography. She and two of her sisters first visited him in Weimar in 1807, at which time she was sure she had won his heart; in 1835 she established her literary claim to fame by publishing her much rewritten correspondence with him under the title *Goethe's Briefwechsel mit einem Kinde* (1835; *Goethe's Correspondence with a Child*). He did take some sympathetic interest in her friend, Karoline von Günderrode (1780–1806), but mentions her only after her death. Of the remaining second generation of Romantics only Eichendorff and E. T. A. Hoffmann did not actually meet Goethe; their work, Hoffmann's better known to Goethe than Eichendorff's, seems to have remained essentially beyond his comprehension.

Finally, there are the three swing figures, Jean Paul, Hölderlin, Kleist, and the most visible Romantic dramatist, Zacharias Werner (1768–1823). Jean Paul visited Weimar in 1796 and lived there from 1798 to 1801; despite efforts on both his and Goethe's part to develop a connection, he interacted more comfortably with the older Weimar generation associated with Goethe's youth (Wieland, Herder and the Dowager Duchess Anna Amalia), while the mature Goethe was deeply engaged with the generation that came after him. Hölderlin, the friend of Hegel and Schelling from the time they shared lodgings at the Tübinger Stift, served through Schiller's mediation as tutor in the household of Charlotte von Kalb in Jena 1794–5. He admired Schiller but remained intimidated by Goethe, who had limited sympathy for his apparent lack of emotional discipline. Kleist's well-known resentment of the failure of his comedy *Der zerbrochne Krug* (*The Broken Jug*) on the Weimar stage in 1808 is generally attributed to Goethe's insistence on staging the play in three acts and to the inappropriateness of the Weimar declamation style to Kleist's dialogue; but the break had as much to do with Goethe's cool response to eight scenes of *Penthesilea* and to an invitation to contribute to Kleist's journal *Phöbus* sent while the production was in preparation. Goethe had had similar unfortunate failures of some of his own verse plays at their first performances in Weimar, most notably among them his *Iphigenie auf Tauris* (1788; *Iphigenia in Tauris*). Whether or not he knew that Kleist was a friend of Wieland's son, he seems to have read with care at least four of his plays and the novella *Michael Kohlhaas*; the material mostly came to him from Kleist's friend Adam Müller, who was courting Goethe to contribute to their journal.

Indeed, the Weimar stage was an influential showcase under Goethe's directorship, and his willingness to stage plays by promising dramatic talents about whom he had some personal reservations is actually rather striking. Notable in this connection is Zacharias Werner, childhood friend of E. T. A. Hoffmann and considered in the first decade of the nineteenth century to be Schiller's probable successor as leading German dramatist. Despite strong reservations about Werner's religious enthusiasm, Goethe engaged in long discussions about religion with him, was inspired by him to write sonnets and mounted inaugural performances of two of his plays in Weimar, *Wanda* (1808) and *Der 24. Februar* (1809; *The Twenty-Fourth of February*). The second, especially, was extremely successful and influential. Goethe broke with him only after Werner converted to Catholicism and became a monk.

The biographical details demonstrate the constant interaction between the groups we call Classic and those we call Romantic. They were all in the same place at the same time with largely overlapping circles of friends, acquaintances, relatives and quasi-relatives. Goethe was eighteen years older than the eldest of the Romantic circle, August Wilhelm Schlegel, and Schiller eight. Both had also made their literary mark twenty to ten years before any in the Romantic circle began to publish, and Goethe knew their parents or even grandparents, or had met them as children. The Weimar poets were the older generation, both admired and also looked to for encouragement and support. But there was not so much distance between them and the Romantics that daily issues of personality, compatibility and varying moods did not play a role in their relations. Goethe had little use for emotionalism or exaggeration in personal relations. Since it took him seven years to warm up even to the devoted Schiller, it is hardly surprising that Friedrich Schlegel, Hölderlin, Kleist or Bettina von Arnim did not appeal to him.

I turn now to the substance of the various positions. Especially since the massive Friedrich Schlegel edition of Ernst Behler and Hans Eichner, which began to appear in 1958[4] and has clarified the elusive and often cryptic Schlegel's philosophical and aesthetic development, scholars on both sides of the Romantic–Classical divide have demonstrated conclusively that Goethe, Schiller and the Jena Romantics held essentially the identical philosophical positions in the 1790s with regard to epistemology and aesthetics.[5] These recent analyses flesh out an argument originally made by Josef Körner, the first to work with the Schlegel manuscripts, that their positions overlapped (*Romantiker und Klassiker*, pp. 141f.) and that Schiller's essay *Über naive und sentimentalische Dichtung* (1796; *On Naive and Sentimental Literature*) was the decisive influence in making Friedrich Schlegel into a Romantic (*Romantiker und Klassiker*, p. 33). Friedrich Schlegel first introduced the opposition Classical–Romantic as the distinction between Classical and Modern, that is, between the literature of Greek and Roman antiquity and that of Europe from the Middle Ages to the present. The terms referred to historical categories, not to different modes of thought or positions on the political, social, epistemological or ontological status of literature. Even long after their break, in 1810 Schlegel characterised Schiller as the ultimate modern (Romantic) German dramatist, in preference to Werner (*Romantiker und Klassiker*, p. 157) and the following year listed as members of the Romantic generation Schiller, Jean Paul and August von Kotzebue (a popular dramatist from Weimar who, however, had no connections to the circles under discussion; *Romantiker und Klassiker*, pp. 158–9). In both Schiller's essay on naive and sentimental poetry and Schlegel's thought Goethe holds a middle position as the connector or mediator between the Classical and the Romantic (*Romantiker und Klassiker*, p. 97).

To be sure, Schlegel was mercurial, partly as a matter of policy, partly as his personal relations to Goethe and Schiller fluctuated. The same can be said for Schiller's and especially Goethe's attitudes toward both brothers. Nevertheless these variations must not obscure the fact that virtually all of the Romantics came to Weimar originally as admirers of Goethe or as seekers of his protection, or both. Led by Friedrich Schlegel, the Jena Romantics recognised the greatness of Goethe's *Bildungsroman, Wilhelm Meisters Lehrjahre* (1795–6; *Wilhelm Meister's Apprenticeship*). Schlegel's essay of 1798, 'Über Goethes *Meister*', remains one of the most important documents in the novel's reception; all the novelists in the Romantic group were deeply influenced by *Wilhelm Meister,* even as some, like Hardenberg, reacted against it. Indeed, Goethe's works after *Werther* – his great classical plays like *Iphigenie, Tasso* and *Egmont* – had not received much critical acclaim, and outside the Romantic circle *Wilhelm Meister* and Goethe's great Roman elegies of 1795 were considered immoral. Even the publication of a fragment of *Faust* in 1790 evoked little response outside the Jena circle, where it was discussed as the paradigmatic modern tragedy. Whatever the differences between them, the two sides needed one another.

Another way to think about the connection between the two movements is to consider the common categories invoked to describe Romanticism in its relation to Classicism. I will take as representative a cogent overview of the period by T. J. Reed. Beginning from 'release from an allegiance to reality' as 'the central feature and the central problem of Romanticism',[6] Reed frames a series of categories widely accepted as characteristic of Romanticism. He begins with the Romantic preference for allegory over the symbol preferred by Classicism; yet by all accounts *Faust II* was the culminating allegorical work of the century,[7] begun during Schiller's lifetime though completed only shortly before Goethe's death in 1832. Reed's next identifier is the Romantic priority placed on aesthetics, writing about art; yet Schiller and even Goethe wrote extensively on aesthetics in the 1790s, indeed often in dialogue with the Romantics. The cultivation of fairy tale (*Märchen*) is a third category; yet Goethe's 'Märchen' at the end of his *Unterhaltungen deutscher Ausgewanderten* (1795; *Conversations of German Refugees*), his response to the French Revolution, set the paradigm for the Romantic mix of the marvellous and the quotidian, 'the primitive and the sophisticated' ('Goethezeit', p. 517), the pre-rational and the allegorical. A fourth category, mysticism and religious feeling, best exemplified in Hardenberg's *Hymnen an die Nacht* (1800; *Hymns to Night*), would seem to be antithetical to Goethe's firmly anti-Christian views and commitment to nature; yet, as Reed himself points out, Hardenberg's hymns owe some of their language to Goethe's rhapsodic hymns of the 1770s. If Goethe was beyond rhapsody in the 1790s, he was certainly not beyond mystical identification of the religious in nature, as his continuation of Mozart's *Die Zauberflöte* (1801; *The Magic Flute*) demonstrates, nor was he beyond explorations of religious mysticism, as both the story of Mignon in the last book of *Wilhelm Meister* and the treatment of Ottilie in *Die Wahlverwandtschaften* (1809–10; *Elective Affinities*) reveal. Serious historical interest in folk poetry is the next category, but Goethe, again, helped Herder to set this paradigm with his justly famous early efforts at collecting and imitating folk songs in the 1770s. While the Grimm brothers set a new standard of historical scholarship in this area, Goethe was at least as important a contributor to the historical approach to all cultural phenomena, both with his history of the theory of colour and as author of the first autobiography that addressed the author's times as well as his life. Reed mentions paradox in passing with regard to folk song ('Goethezeit', p. 520), but in connection with Schlegel's irony it is actually a central category for the Romantics. Yet Goethe was the greatest ironist of the time, in the spirit of German Idealism, which focused on the need to unite oppositions that were by nature antithetical. 'Harmony' is the term for this generally associated with Classicism, rather than 'paradox', but both terms come together in the musical mysticism associated with the irony of Mozart and Schumann, with the musician figures in the writings of Wackenroder and Hoffmann, with the operatic choruses and gestures in the plays of Goethe and Schiller, with the musical acting style Goethe cultivated on the Weimar stage, and the preoccupation in both groups with metrical form and with song. Thus there is far more commonality than the usual schematisms admit.

If these standard categories for distinguishing Romanticism from Classicism do not hold up, there are two more about which Goethe expressed himself with notorious hostility, medievalism and the 'night side of nature' exemplified most obviously in E. T. A. Hoffmann, whose tales Goethe found distasteful. Yet both warrant further scrutiny. Goethe repeatedly attacked the Nazarene school of German painting, which had established itself in Rome in 1810, for what he considered its hypocritical piety and its neo-Catholicism. Yet at the same time he maintained a cordial friendship with Sulpiz Boisserée (1783–1854), a leading collector of medieval German and Netherlandish art. Boisserée had become interested in medieval art under the influence of Friedrich Schlegel, with whom he shared lodgings in Paris in 1803–4. He first approached Goethe by letter to enlist his support for completing Cologne cathedral, a project which was not one of Goethe's priorities; nevertheless, the two soon became friends. Boisserée showed Goethe his fine collection of medieval painting (now the heart of the collection in the Alte Pinakothek in Munich) and stimulated the poet's sympathetic interest in it, though Goethe continued to prefer the classical and Renaissance/Baroque traditions he had always championed. Friedrich Schlegel had failed to arouse Goethe's interest in Gothic art years before and was jealous when his 'student' Boisserée succeeded. Goethe's position on art was thus not a rigid opposition on principle to medieval art, but rather a lack of sympathy that could be overcome by appropriate tact and maturity.

The issue of the 'night side of nature'[8] is more complex. It refers initially to the horror tales of Hoffmann with their focus on the dark side of human nature, the irrational and what we now call the subconscious. Goethe read Hoffmann and, agreeing with Walter Scott's critique, dismissed what he read as essentially the products of mental illness.[9] Yet it was Goethe himself who, in the wake of Rousseau, had set loose in Germany the fascination with the darker passions. Werther's violent suicide had made a profound impression all over Europe in the 1770s. While the psychology of Goethe's novel was largely rationalist, it opened the door to the exploration of powerful and not fully comprehended feelings, most notably by characterising its virtuous heroine, Lotte, as a seductive mermaid, precisely the figure that became a central representation of the dangerous unconscious in so many Romantic tales, including Hoffmann's fairy-tale opera *Undine*.[10] Goethe's objections to the sickness of Romanticism must be understood in the context of his life-long irritability at being known as the author of *Werther* and of his initial refusal to deal with Schiller, whom he first knew as the author of violent Storm and Stress plays brought into fashion and then rejected by Goethe. Ultimately Goethe's own literary innovations had opened the door to such deplorable developments and he protested perhaps too much against them.

The gap between Classicists and Romanticists was thus largely a matter of degree rather than of substance, and the tolerable amount of difference was often determined, as always in human relations, by personality, mood and circumstance. The least negotiable issue seems to have been religion. The more the individuals, the more the school moved toward Catholicism, the less sympathetic Goethe became. His disliked the Nazarenes for their catholicising more than for their medievalising, and he was disgusted by the conversions of Werner and Friedrich Schlegel. When the Schlegel brothers began publishing on Indian religion and culture in the 1820s, however, he read the work with interest and was willing to resume correspondence with them. Goethe was hardly a religious bigot, but as 'the great heathen'[11] he was resented equally by the Catholic and Protestant establishments in the nineteenth century. Indeed, Goethe himself sometimes turned to extreme Catholic imagery, particularly in *Wilhelm Meister* and in the last scene of *Faust II*. What does it mean, then, that religion became such a point of friction between Classicism and Romanticism, indeed for Goethe a betrayal?

There are many possibilities. When Goethe returned from Italy in 1789 he finished off the complete edition of his works that had been appearing, and then for a while he appeared to tread water. His attempts to write about the French Revolution in the early 1790s were largely unsuccessful and he was getting nowhere with the first version of *Wilhelm Meister*. The revival of his creativity and excitement is associated with his growing friendship with Schiller, as their correspondence amply testifies. But the Jena Romantics certainly provided substantial additional stimulation to what became the single most creative and productive decade of Goethe's life. There they were living an exciting intellectual and indeed Bohemian life, buoyant and optimistic about the new age coming into being, all in rather joyous hostility to those contemporaries who refused to transcend Enlightenment normativity. Friedrich Schlegel proclaimed the three most important events of the century to be the French Revolution, Fichte's *Wissenschaftslehre* (theory of knowledge) and *Wilhelm Meister* (*Athenaeum Fragment* No. 216). The person who turned against this programme was not Goethe, but, from his point of view, the Romantics. To give up their little Bohemia in Jena in favour of the extreme piety of Restoration Catholicism betrayed the whole programme of ushering in a new age. It betrayed the commitment to developing the individualism and subjectivity uncovered by the Enlightenment into a force for a new moral freedom.

In the context of the Revolution, the Schlegels' conversion was not only a betrayal, but an act of cowardice as well. Goethe had never been an enthusiast for the French Revolution, not so much because of its programme, as on account of its chaotic destructiveness. He admired Napoleon's ability to control the forces it unleashed, a task of which the German princes had shown themselves to be incapable. The changes in the political system were not welcome to him, but they seemed inevitable, and he was deeply committed to living forward in time and adapting to historical change. But now the Romantics, harbingers of the great future, were scuttling back into the orthodox establishment. In a certain sense, those who could face up to the Revolution stayed Protestant, and those who couldn't became Catholic.

Finally, there was a betrayal in yet another sense, a betrayal of the Kantian aesthetic principle that had in effect brought them all together. For the common ground of their aesthetics was the principle of the disinterested pleasure evoked by the work of art, enunciated by Kant in the *Kritik der Urteilskraft*. This principle underlay Goethe's and also Schiller's insistence on the absolute autonomy of the work of art, and it underlay Friedrich Schlegel's call for a new mythology. Once again, Goethe led the way when he used Catholicism to remove the mysterious Mignon from the real world and make her an aesthetic being, a personification of art. Catholic Baroque imagery serves the same purpose in the last scene of *Faust II*. But for the Romantics who converted to Catholicism their religion was no longer a mythology; instead, it was the truth. Goethe knew the intelligence of these men and women too well to doubt their ability to distinguish the literal from the figurative; by taking religion literally they disrupted the balance of ideal and real that underlay their common aesthetic programme. Had Goethe not preferred to leave the term Romantic to the intellectual companions about whom he was so ambivalent, we would have to call him the only one who remained faithful to the Romantic cause, the paradigmatic Romantic.

Of course, Goethe and Schiller had never signed up to Friedrich Schlegel's use of the term 'Romantic' to identify all non-classical European literature beginning in the Middle Ages, and as the Romantics increasingly made the Catholic Middle Ages their model for the revitalisation of contemporary literature, 'Romantic' became an ever-more negative term for them. By the 1820s the terms identified the camps which preferred either Goethe and Schiller, on the one hand, or the figures known today as Romantics on the other. In a substantial essay of 1833, *Die romantische Schule* (*The Romantic School*), Heinrich Heine characterised the groups as 'schools'. By nature a biting wit and deeply committed to the liberal and anti-clerical political position, Heine skewered the Romantics with a great deal of personal gossip and ironic praise. Even so he intelligently described many aspects of their work and set most of the categories still applied. Heine's problem in the essay was that he was ambivalent about Goethe and had previously expressed himself with hostility. Now, partly because of tensions with his own contemporaries and partly because he disliked the Romantics even more than he did Goethe, he played up Goethe's Classicism as a foil to them. The essay remained very influential also in England and France throughout the century, and thus has always coloured perceptions of Romanticism in Germany. By the end of the century the dichotomy between the 'schools' had solidified into periods with fixed and opposing qualities and the most recent history of German literature in English devotes separate volumes to them.[12] By this point the term Classicism had taken on several overlapping and mutually reinforcing meanings, as Dieter Borchmeyer has helpfully pointed out,[13] for it refers to a historical period (classical antiquity), to a norm of perfection, to a style cultivated by Goethe and Schiller (nominally related to a style cultivated by earlier French neo-classicists like Racine), and to particular historical epochs in France, England and then Germany that do not entirely overlap in time or ideology.

In one respect Heine was trapped by his own ambivalence, for his attempt to set Classicism up as the liberal tradition in Germany failed miserably. The newly re-established German Empire adopted Goethe and his Classicism as its cultural paternity in the 1870s, and Goethe and Schiller's 'humanity' was made the figurehead for German imperialism and eventually for Nazism. What interested their exploiters was the ever-creative expansiveness of Goethe's Faustian vision – perhaps Goethe at his most Romantic. And indeed these same periods did see a revival of interest in the Romantic group. Nevertheless Heine correctly intuited (or perhaps created) the continuing importance Goethe's and Schiller's Classicism could have for representing Germany, for all succeeding German states continued to used them as banner-carriers for their more and less republican and liberal ideals as well. Here the various meanings of 'Classicism' come freely into play: through their adulation of Goethe and their learning from him, as well as in the context of Germany's complicated politics for the last two centuries, the Romantics, by constituting themselves as a school, created German Classicism.

NOTES

1. Information about Goethe's interactions with his contemporaries is most readily available in summary form in Gero von Wilpert, *Goethe-Lexikon* (Stuttgart: Kröner, 1998).
2. The evidence was established by Géza von Molnár in *Goethes Kantstudien: Eine Zusammenstellung nach Eintragungen in seinen Handexemplaren der 'Kritik der reinen Vernunft' und der 'Kritik der Urteilskraft'* (Weimar: Hermann Böhlaus Nachfolger, 1994) and the implications for understanding Goethe's works of the 1790s by Nicholas Boyle in *Goethe: The Poet and the Age*, vol. II (Oxford: Clarendon Press, 2000), *passim*.
3. Josef Körner, *Romantiker und Klassiker: Die Brüder Schlegel in ihren Beziehungen zu Schiller und Goethe* (Darmstadt: Wissenschaftliche Buchgesellschaft, 1971).

4. *KFSA.*
5. Ernst Behler lays out the essential closeness of the positions and draws out the finely nuanced distinctions in 'Die Wirkung Goethes und Schillers auf die Brüder Schlegel', in *Unser Commercium: Goethes und Schillers Literaturpolitik*, ed. Wilfried Barner, Eberhard Lämmert and Norbert Oellers (Stuttgart: Cotta, 1984), pp. 559–83.
6. T. J. Reed, 'The "Goethezeit" and its Aftermath', in *Germany: A Companion to German Studies*, ed. Malcolm Pasley (London: Methuen, 1972), p. 517.
7. See, for example, Jane K. Brown, *Goethe's 'Faust': The German Tragedy* (Ithaca, N.Y.: Cornell University Press, 1986), pp. 135–249, esp. pp. 142–4.
8. See Jürgen Barkhoff's essay in this volume.
9. In a review of *Foreign Quarterly Review*, in *Goethe's Werke*, 143 vols. (Weimar: Böhlau, 1887–1919), Section I, vol. XLII. 2, p. 87.
10. Elaborated in detail in Jane K. Brown, ' "Es singen wohl die Nixen": *Werther* and the Romantic Tale', in *Rereading Romanticism*, ed. Martha Helfer (Amsterdam: Rodopi, 2000), pp. 11–25.
11. The expression gained its currency from Heinrich Heine in *Die romantische Schule*, in *Historische-kritische Gesamtausgabe der Werke*, vol. VIII/1, ed. Manfred Windfuhr (Hamburg: Hoffmann und Campe, 1979), p. 155.
12. The classic examples are Fritz Strich's *Deutsche Klassik und Romantik, oder Vollendung und Unendlichkeit* (Bern: Francke, 1962), and Hermann August Korff's *Geist der Goethezeit: Versuch einer ideellen Entwicklung der klassisch-romantischen Literaturgeschichte* (Darmstadt: Wissenschaftliche Buchgesellschaft, 1979). The recent example is the *Camden House History of German Literature*, 10 vols. (Rochester, N.Y.: Camden House, 2001–6), which devotes vol. VII to Classicism and vol. VIII to Romanticism.
13. In the first chapter of *Camden House History of German Literature*, vol. VII, ed. Simon Richter (Columbia, S.C.: Camden House, 2005), pp. 55–61.

FURTHER READING

Behler, Ernst, 'Die Wirkung Goethes und Schillers auf die Brüder Schlegel', in *Unser Commercium: Goethes und Schillers Literaturpolitik*, ed. Wilfried Barner, Eberhard Lämmert, and Norbert Oellers (Stuttgart: Cotta, 1984), pp. 559–83

Borchmeyer, Dieter, 'What Is Classicism?', in *The Literature of Weimar Classicism*, ed. Simon Richter (Rochester, N.Y.: Camden House, 2005), pp. 44–61

Boyle, Nicholas, *Goethe: The Poet and the Age*, vol. II (Oxford: Clarendon Press, 2000)

Guilloton, Doris Starr, 'Schiller and Friedrich Schlegel: Their Controversial Relationship', in *Friedrich von Schiller and the Drama of Human Existence*, eds. Alexej Ugrinsky and Wolfgang Wittkowski (New York: Greenwood, 1988), pp. 149–54

Körner, Josef, *Romantiker und Klassiker: Die Brüder Schlegel in ihren Beziehungen zu Schiller und Goethe* (Berlin: Askanischer Verlag, 1924)

Kunisch, Hermann, 'Friedrich Schlegel und Goethe', in *Kleine Schriften* (Berlin: Duncker & Humblot, 1968), pp. 189–204

8

GESA DANE

Women writers and Romanticism

Anyone concerned to discover the truth about women writers in Germany around 1800 needs to resolve some thorny problems of literary historiography. If, for example, one takes the five women portrayed by Margarete Susman in her influential volume *Schriftstellerinnen der Romantik* (1929; *Women Writers of Romanticism*) – Caroline Schlegel (1763–1805), Dorothea Schlegel (1763–1839), Rahel Varnhagen (1771–1833), Karoline von Günderrode (1780–1806) and Bettine von Arnim (1785–1859) – there is no doubt that they have many features in common. All five were born within twenty years of one another, and their careers more or less overlapped with those of the male Romantics. But these women, unlike the men, belonged to no school or group with a defined literary programme. Nor did they think of themselves in that way. Although all these women were linked with the leading literary circles of the day, their actual relationships were wholly individual, mainly of a deeply personal character, and only rarely did they include the literary activities of the other women. Some were linked by friendship, like Bettine von Arnim and Karoline von Günderrode or Dorothea Schlegel, Henriette Herz and Rahel Varnhagen. But some were bound only by critical distance or even total rejection.

If one then includes other women writers and publicists around 1800 – Benedikte Naubert (1756–1819), Philippine Gatterer (1756–1831), Henriette Herz (1764–1847), Therese Huber (1764–1828), Margarete Forkel (1765–1856), Johanna Schopenhauer (1766–1838), Sophie Mereau (1770–1806), Caroline de la Motte-Fouqué (1773–1831) and Wilhelmine von Chézy (1783–1856) – the picture becomes still more confusing, and attempts to discern meaningful groupings still more problematic. What, other than their female sex and the circumstance that each in her own way participated in the literary life of the age, do these women writers have in common? In fact there was one thing. All of them belonged to the still young – third-generation – tradition of writing women in eighteenth-century Germany, even if not all explicitly thought of themselves as woman writers, authors or poets. Their family histories hint at the importance of genealogy here. Helmina von Chézy was the granddaughter of the poet Anna Louisa Karsch (1722–91), and Bettine von Arnim of Sophie von La Roche (1730–1807). The women of 1800, therefore, had predecessors and models stretching back to the Enlightenment.[1] Without this pre-history it is doubtful whether these writers, with their characteristically intensive participation in the literary life of the day, would ever have made their appearance on the public stage.

Many of them became 'women of the Romantic School' only thanks to the constructions of literary historians 100 years later. Their contemporary Heinrich Heine recognizes no such grouping. In his *Die romantische Schule* (1832; *The Romantic School*) he mentions only one text by a woman, Dorothea Schlegel's novel *Florentin* (1801).[2] Even in Rudolf Haym's massive eponymous study women play only bit parts.[3] The literary histories of the nineteenth century tell the same story: if these women played any role at all, then it was only insofar as they were linked with a well-known man, as, for example, were the women of the Jena Romantic circle or those around Goethe. It was Ricarda Huch's studies in Romanticism which changed the picture. Her *Die Romantik* (1899–1902, *Romanticism*) is packed with information about women such as Caroline Schlegel, Bettine von Arnim and Dorothea Schlegel. She specifically foregrounds both their intellectual achievement and links with Romanticism.[4] For Huch Romanticism is an attitude of mind and a *Weltanschauung*, registered seismographically in literature and philosophy. As an 'intellectual orientation' Romanticism is for her anti-naturalistic and cerebral, in that it seeks to penetrate beyond mere appearance. Huch gives special weight to the movement's modernity as a foil to the aspirituality and technocentrism of her own day. After the 'wholesale rejection' of Romanticism in the first half of the nineteenth century Huch hoped that Romanticism would be regenerated in her own time.[5]

Susman's *Frauen der Romantik* of 1929 carries on in many respects where Huch's work left off, as when she notes the tense relationship of the present time with Romanticism. She views early Romanticism as the first phase of a comprehensive renewal of German intellectual culture, particularly with regard to the existential problems posed by religion, death and love in their personal dimension. Early Romanticism, for her, is a particular form of self-understanding, of creatively intensified self-consciousness, which in the last analysis paradoxically cannot help us live our lives. The women writers of Romanticism, she says, sought with vital intensity and in many individual variations to live this unliveable ideal, transformed it into a typical style and at last made it practicable: 'The greatness of Romantic Woman lies in the fact that while opening herself wholly to the spirit she nevertheless did not succumb.'[6] In five, chronologically sequenced chapters, 'Caroline', 'Dorothea', 'Rahel', 'Bettine' and 'Karoline von Günderrode', she paints portraits of these select women, classifying them according to the *Gestalt* typology used by the circle around Stefan George, to which she belonged. Thus Caroline Schlegel was the woman of history, Dorothea a woman unsure of her religion, Rahel Levin the problematic woman, Bettine the creative woman and Günderrode the woman of antiquity. Today such a typology fails to convince. It overlooks the intricate overlapping of qualities as much as the contingencies and ruptures of real life. Furthermore Susman, who liked to ascribe 'male' attributes to Rahel and 'female' ones to Dorothea, fails to recognise to what extent rigid gender stereotypes were being questioned around 1800[7] – even if many women in everyday life still had to conform to received expectations in performing their role. But Susman takes credit as the first to see these women as a group, to grasp the differentiation of female biographies of the day, and set them in the context of intellectual history. Indeed, her sensitivity to the significance of love, death and religion in the life of these women adumbrates themes which today are in the forefront of scholarly inquiry.

In the last thirty years scholarly attention has focused on the social and gender questions overlooked by Susman. Extensive research has been conducted into the position of women around 1800, and biographies or literary-historical studies exist of most of these women writers.[8] In her *Schriftstellerinnen der Romantik* (2000; *Women Writers of Romanticism*) Barbara Becker-Cantarino has produced a literary handbook which draws the sum of research in this area to date. Following her work on women writers and poets in Germany from 1500, she retraces the women's steps on 'the long road to equality' and authorship.[9] She traces the social context of epistolary culture and the literary salon, and offers model analyses of four women writers' work, notably Therese Huber's novel *Die Familie Seldorf* (1795–6; *The Seldorf Family*) and Dorothea Schlegel's *Florentin*. Günderrode is examined in the context of her importance for poetry and mythology, Bettine von Arnim in the context of her book on Günderrode and its poetics. Becker-Cantarino then tracks the reception of these women in the twentieth century, for example in Hanna Arendt's *Rahel Varnhagen* (195–9) and Christa Wolf's *Kein Ort: Nirgends* (1979; *No Place on Earth*). As the chronology which concludes her volume suggests, 'women writers of Romanticism' were active from 1762 until 1840, from the year of the Enlightenment writer Luise Gottsched's death to the year in which Bettine von Arnim's *Die Günderrode* appeared. As this synopsis makes clear, the women writers of Romanticism need to be assessed in a far broader context of cultural history if we are truly to understand the particular quality of their literary activities. We should however orientate ourselves far less than Becker-Cantarino around received concepts of literary genre. To focus exclusively on the lyric and the novel, for example, marginalises writers of 1800 like Rahel Varnhagen, Caroline Schlegel and Henriette Herz, those 'women writers without an *oeuvre*'.[10] What they record in letters, conversations and journals reveals much about the tension between tradition and modernity which defines their experience. For example, Rahel Varnhagen's letters, quite apart from their pragmatic informativeness about her contemporaries, enable us to reconstruct the mentality of an entire epoch as mirrored in their self-reflexive, playful, experimental trains of thought. Her letters also give us insight into the conditions under which a Jewish woman had to live around the turn of the eighteenth century in a markedly Christian society – what it meant to be perceived as Jewish and to be confronted with a whole range of preconceptions and prejudices.[11] Something similar is true of Dorothea Schlegel's letters. Amongst many other things, they disclose the private motivations of her inner, religious development, which was in no sense prompted by external considerations.

The letters and journals edited over the last decade are more than mere ego documents or sources for the literary life of the age. Read correctly, they reveal the conditions under which these women become authors qualified to participate in literary life. The formula 'Romantic women' we should understand as a tendentially open concept, connoting the commonly shared and changed conditions of literary life and not strictly the intellectual sense of conforming to a like 'attitude of mind'.

The work of these writing women is difficult to fit into the context of genre-centred literary history. Work in genres such as the lyric, the drama, the novel and smaller epic forms such as the fairy tale does exist, but what claims our attention are primarily letters, correspondence and journals. On the one hand, we find Günderrode's lyric poems, which follow classical models and forms, and her drama *Mahomet* (1803), which is indebted to the Orientalist fashion. Or we find Therese Huber's narratives, which delineate the shapes and foreground the conflicts of women's lives.[12] Both women follow completely different notions of writing and literature. On the other hand we find epistolary novels by Bettine von Arnim such as *Goethe's Briefwechsel mit einem Kinde* (1835; *Goethe's Correspondence with a Child*), *Günderrode* and *Clemens Brentanos Frühlingskranz* (1844; *A Vernal Wreath for Clemens Brentano*), in all of which she interweaves authentic letters with fiction. These contrast with *Dies Buch gehört dem König* (1843; *This Book Belongs to the King*), a committed socio-political tract directed at King William IV of Prussia. The 'Romantic' Bettine von Arnim is the prime example of the difficult relation between Romanticism and late Romanticism, since she in no way shares the fundamentally conservative attitude of the late Romantics, and with her democratic convictions in many respects ought to be categorized with the *Vormärz* (the radical epoch preceding March 1848).[13]

This contradictory outcome, both in respect of the genres deployed by women and of their 'attitude of mind', points to further problems in the literary historiography of women, which can only be resolved by examining our multi-faceted concept of Romanticism in the light of recent debates on the relation between gender and canonicity.[14] The women authors of the epoch around 1800 by no means always appeared before the public under their own name (if indeed they risked such a step at all). Dorothea Schlegel, for example, chose to publish anonymously. So, for a time, did Therese Huber, who published under a very rare type of pseudonym, that of her second husband, the well-known writer Ludwig Ferdinand Huber. Sophie Mereau published her first novel, *Das Blüthenalter der Empfindung* (1794; *The Flowering of Sentiment*), anonymously. Thereafter, however, she used her real name in full. Johanna Schopenhauer and Bettine von Arnim only ever published work under their own names. Whilst Günderrode published her first volume *Gedichte und Phantasien* (1804; *Poems and Fantasias*) under the pseudonym 'Tian', Bettine von Arnim published *Die Günderrode* thirty-six years later under her own name. It still remains to be explained from case to case why some women renounced the possibility of publishing under their own name. The frequent changes of name occasioned by marriage, remarriage after divorce or death or the assumption of a Christian name, in fact conceal fractured life paths, and these in turn disclose women's true state between conformity and transgression. Many marriages were arranged between friends or neighbours of a family on the basis of 'enlightened barter of females'. The first change of name followed that.

Gender and, in the wider sense, educational factors are important in one further respect in the lives of the women writers treated here. Their careers and writing activities are inconceivable without the intellectual and literary inspiration they received in different measure either in the parental home, in a foundation for well-born spinsters (Günderrode's case), or through a grandmother (Sophie von La Roche in Bettine von Arnim's case). The increasing participation of the middle class in cultural and literary affairs and public discussion in the second half of the eighteenth century is nowhere more evident than in its daughters, precisely because they had no access to the official education in the grammar school, university and academy. In the eighteenth century it was the Protestant Pastor's household which permitted access to education and sophisticated language for a significant number of sons who went on to write, but not for their daughters.[15] Since women had no right of entry to educational institutions, they received their education through private tutors or resorted to alternatives.

The lyric poet Philippine Gatterer, for example, had by her own account, as far as poetry was concerned, grown up 'wie ein wilder Baum ohne Pflege' ('like a tree in nature, without training').[16] But this should be taken as a stylisation which runs through her entire oeuvre. In his letters Gottfried August Bürger would attempt to lecture her on taste, and she presents herself in her responses as a woman poet following her poetic vein only under pressure. Nonetheless the beginnings of an independent notion of poetry can be discerned. The antique dactylic hexameters of her short lyric 'An die Muse' ('To the Muse'), for example, begin with an invocation of the Muses' support, and end:

> Verlängern die Parzen mir nur, mit ihren oft drohenden Händen
> Den Faden des Lebens, der kaum erst entstand;
> So tret' ich, voll Schüchternheit, einst zur hohen Versammlung der Dichter;
> Und weihe den fühlenden Schwestern mein Lied.[17]

> If only the Fates, with their so frequently ominous hands
> Do lengthen the thread of my life, so recently spun out,
> Then of modesty full shall I rise to that high convention of poets;
> And to feeling sisters dedicate my song

The modesty *topos* here evident, which dominates both the lyric and autobiographical testimony of this writer, in fact conceals that she was both a learned and skilled woman poet who confidently exploited the possibilities of the classical metres introduced into German by Klopstock – even if she lacked the classical education which her famous male peers in the Göttinger Hain School had been privileged to enjoy.

Intertextual readings allow us to reconstruct precisely which literary models made their way into the novel production of women authors. Margareta Forkel's *Maria* (1782)[18] can serve as the example. Forkel, probably the youngest debutant women novelist in German literature, published this multi-perspectival epistolary novel in her eighteenth year. Georg Christoph Lichtenberg commented: 'Eine Gans unsrer Stadt, die Frau des Musik Director Forkel hat einen Roman ... drucken lassen'[19] ('A silly young goose from our city, the wife of Music Director Forkel, has published ... a novel'). This novel reveals its author's close familiarity with the contemporary fashion of the letter novel, from Samuel Richardson to Sophie von La Roche's *Das Fräulein von Sternheim* (1769; *Lady Sternheim*) and Goethe's *Werther* (1774). The particular fascination of her novel lies in how a mere girl of eighteen writes in enlightened and sentimental style *against* the excesses of sentimentality, against what was then known as the *Werther* fever. Individual letters contain extensive reflections on the education of small children and girls, the relations of the sexes and the balance of reason and emotion. That said, the novel's unfolding plot leaves no doubt as to the different destinies of women and men in society. Woman's domain is the home: weddings, wedlock and family. Should that mechanism fail, she may become an educator of her own sex. The sphere of professional activity is left to men. Margareta Forkel was also a spirited and witty contributor to contemporary debates on literature and music. Johann Heinrich Voß had in the course of the translation of Homer arrived at the conclusion that the Greek letter ε ('eta') should be pronounced not as 'eh' but as 'aay', a view which launched a heated controversy. Forkel comments by putting this into the mouth of a character in *Maria*: 'Lustig, diesen gelehrten Streitigkeiten beizuwohnen und zu sehen, wie sich diese Leute mit den wichtigsten Mienen der Welt über Kleinigkeiten zanken, die anderen nicht einmal der Rede werth scheinen'[20] ('Amusing to witness these scholarly disputes and see how people quarrel so pompously about trivia which others deem unworthy of a word').

Dorothea Schlegel's *Florentin*, by contrast, is cast in the mould of early Romantic poetics and displays many and various intertextual nods to models of the Romantic literary canon such as Cervantes's *Don Quixote* or Goethe's *Wilhelm Meisters Lehrjahre*. *Florentin* mixes diverse literary genres such as the dialogue and song, and presents the life-story of the central figure over several chapters as an autobiographical confession. As an artist's novel with a painter hero, it is full of self-reflexive passages on art, literature and painting.

Private letters too are a significant resource, both for identifying the reading material of women writers and as documents of cultural history. Caroline Michaelis (later the wife of A. W. Schlegel and subsequently Schelling) has become justly renowned for the influence of her correspondence, letters which reveal an intuitive skill in her deployment of both French and German. Her letters also document her reading, which includes everything of contemporary repute in German, English or French literature, especially anything by Goethe. She comments on Goethe's play *Die Geschwister* (1776; *Brother and Sister*): 'Schade daß Goethe, der so ganz herrlich so ganz hinreißend schreibt, so sonderbare Gegenstände hat; und doch kan ich weder seinen Werther, noch Stella noch die Geschwister unnatürlich nennen, es ist so romanhaft, und liegt doch auch so ganz in der Natur, wenn man sich nur mit ein bischen Einbildungskraft hineinphantasirt'[21] ('A pity that Goethe, who writes so absolutely delightfully and so absolutely compellingly, chooses such peculiar subjects; and yet I can call neither his Werther nor his Stella nor his Brother and Sister unnatural, it is all so novelistic and yet so well founded in nature, if only one feels one's way into it with a little imagination'). Caroline Michaelis's letters also shed much light on her self-understanding: 'Ich bin,' she writes as a fifteen-year-old Göttingen professor's daughter, 'keine Schwärmerin, keine Enthousiastinn, meine Gedanken sind das Resultat von meiner, wenn möglich ist, kalten Überlegung'[22] ('I am no zealot, no enthusiast, my thoughts are the result of my own, where possible, cold reflection'). Enthusiasm and zealotry are key concepts of the contemporary discussion on enlightenment and sentimentality. Another is friendship, which crops up again and again in her letters without ever descending into the lurid friendship cult of the *Sturm und Drang* or the sentimentality of writers like Gleim: 'Vielleicht sind meine Begriffe von der Freundschaft zu ausgedehnt, und ich begreife die Liebe mit drunter, doch wirklich verlieben werde ich mich gewiß nie (denn was ich bisher dafür hielt, war nur Täuschung meiner selbst, ich entsagte diesen Hirngespinsten mit so weniger Mühe)'[23] ('Perhaps my notions of friendship are too broad, and I include love in them, yet I will certainly never fall in love (what I had till now thought it to be was but self-delusion, I abandoned those frenetic delusions with so little effort')). Elsewhere she says she has tasted 'alle Freuden eines glücklichen Bewußtseyns' ('all the joys of a happy state of mind') and adds: 'Noch erwarten mich gute Tage, schöne mannig-fache Auftritte von Glück'[24] ('Good days, many fine scenes of happiness, are still to come'). From such passages in the letters one can see that exemplary expressions of what has often, over-hastily, been categorized as 'Romantic' in fact presupposes Enlightenment – in the shape of the rational analysis of sentiment and its translation into what is here called a 'state of mind'. Precisely these women writers reveal that the so-called Romantics are still bound by many ties to the Protestant Enlightenment, which by 1794 are only beginning to be loosened.[25]

Before her marriage to Huber, the then Therese Heyne also confesses that from an early age she read everything which came into her hands. Her father, the renowned classical philologist Christian Gottlob Heyne, even asked her to write literary critiques. Once, the young poet Friedrich von Ramdohr had sent her father his tragedy *Otto III*, with a request for a thorough review. In a letter of 1782 to her friend Luise Mejer, Therese Heyne relates what then transpired: 'Papa konte nicht. Mama wolte nicht. Ich habs Gelesen, einen ganzen Bogen voll geschrieben, an Critik, Papa traut meinem Urtheil genug, sich ganz danach zu richten ... Man wird mich nicht nennen ... aber es ist herrliche Uebung und meines Vaters Zutraun schmeichelhaft; daß ich das Urtheil gemacht darf keiner wißen'[26] ('Papa couldn't do it. Mama didn't want to do it. I read it through, wrote pages and pages of criticism, Papa trusts my judgement enough to follow it completely ... I shall not be named ... but it is splendid practice and my father's trust flatters me; none may know that I wrote this opinion'). Thus she speaks in her father's name and he acknowledges her literary judgement as his own. Here, as if under experimental conditions, one sees how the literary socialisation of young women authors became possible in professorial households. Small wonder that Goethe's *Werther* or *Götz von Berlichingen* failed to please Therese Heyne. She was concerned about their moral effect on her peers: 'Ich sah die Menschen thörigt drum werden, las es fand die nachteiligen Sachen und blieb unbethört' ('I saw people deluding themselves with them, read them [,] found the matter suspect and remained undeluded'). In this same letter she describes how she heard of and was made familiar with the various disciplines in her professorial home. Looking back over her early reading, she notes that it even included theology: 'Ich las freigeisterische Schriften, ich las dogmatische ohne Glaubenszweifel, ohne Kirchenglauben, Gott, Unsterblichkeit, Pflichterfüllung fand ich überall wo gebildete Menschheit war'[27] ('I read freethinking works, I read dogmatic ones with no hint of doubt, [and] no faith in the Church[;] God, immortality, fulfilment of duty I found wherever educated persons dwelt').

Those who examine the participation of Romantic women writers in literary life around 1800 find them positioned at the margin of a society in flux. The women who took part in literary societies, circles and salons came from very different backgrounds: Christian and Jewish, aristocratic and middle-class. And there they met men of very different origins: literati, officials, military, aristocracy. Social exchange such as this, transcending sex and class, was something new and broke convention. Barely fifty years before no woman had taken part in the famous Wednesday Club meetings in Berlin with Gotthold Ephraim Lessing, Moses Mendelssohn and Friedrich Nicolai. But even around 1800 the social and legal position of women was marked by inequality. Hence it is revealing that in the wide-ranging debate of the day on the anthropological status of women the aim was less to remove inequalities than renew them on foot of the cultural practices allegedly demanded by women's biology. Claudia Honegger has argued that this debate, which covered pedagogy, philosophy and anthropology, and was one of the widest-ranging controversies of the eighteenth century, is ultimately centred on the issue of the 'order of the sexes'.[28] It gives the context in which many women had to search for self-understanding as both woman and author. It echoes throughout this letter from Dorothea Schlözer to another girl, Luise Michaelis: 'Liebes Mädchen, ich will Dir Vieles beichten, was wir 15jährigen Mädchen sonst in der Welt nie so früh erfahren, und auch in keinem Buche steht, was ich aber schon seit mehreren Jahren unter vier Augen von guter Hand habe: Weiber sind nicht in der Welt, blos um Männer zu amüsieren. Weiber sind Menschen wie Männer'[29] ('Dear girl, I have much to confess that we fifteen-year-old girls normally do not soon discover in the world, and which is also not in any book, but which I received several years ago in confidence from a good source: women are not in the world simply to amuse men. Women are people as much as men'). In one fell swoop these lines make plain just how unorthodox the insight, that 'women are people as much as men', was at the end of the eighteenth century. Years later, Luise Michaelis (the younger sister of Caroline Schlegel) was to recall this letter, alluding in her memoirs to 'einen sehr merkwürdigen Brief' ('a very remarkable letter'), which expressed so many things in such a fashion that 'ich mich schämte, den Brief zu zeigen' ('I was ashamed to show it to anyone else').[30]

But the relation of the sexes around this time cannot adequately be described as repression or subjugation – even if the signs of inequality are everywhere. Even if some women, mindful of what was held to be 'masculine' or 'feminine', did share the traditional perspectives and opinions, we cannot always call this the mere internalisation of norms. Irrespective of the gender debates which seek for theoretical clarity, the relationship of the sexes is informed by complex a priori stances and attitudes which are best studied as a phenomenon *de longue durée* in the history of mentalities. This becomes clear in exemplary fashion in a letter of Therese Huber thanking her father for his friendly verdict on one of her works: 'Das gütige Urtheil welches Sie über mein Talent als Autor fällen, hat mich weinen machen, wie im achtzehnten Jahre ... Weiblicher ging wohl nie ein Weib von der, ihrem Geschlechte vorgeschriebenen, und es allein beglückenden Bahn ab; als ich'[31] ('The kind judgement you pass on my talent as an author made me weep like a girl of eighteen. No woman ever yet left the path prescribed for her sex as the sole way to happiness in a more womanly fashion; than I'). Therese Huber's view of her role circumscribes the horizon of her age. Care for the family is 'feminine', is her 'prescribed path'. She can only justify her writing to her father – and herself – because she wrote and published in order to care for the material well-being of the family. Following Huber's death in 1804, her publications remained mainly anonymous. Only after 1811 did she write under her own name.[32]

A more detailed look at the concrete relationships of the sexes uncovers a telling comparison between Therese Huber and Karoline von Günderrode. In Günderrode's correspondence with the philologist Friedrich Creuzer on their respective literary productions, we find from her discussions both of her poetic works and confessions of affection and yearning. She asks him only to correct her work and give scholarly advice. He, however, the scholar by profession, requires for *his* work both an intellectual response from her God-given understanding ('aus dem ewigen Verstehen das Dir ein Gott gegeben Erkenntnis u Licht für mich zu schöpfen' ['from the eternal understanding given you by God to acquire knowledge & light for me'])[33] *and* sympathy. That scholarship is connoted 'masculine' by both Creuzer and Günderrrode is unsurprising. Here, then, we have an exchange between equal intellectual and even emotional partners. Therese Huber, by contrast, always (at least during her husband's life) saw herself as the one who provided work for him, who attempted to insert her writing into *his* oeuvre.

The last word may be given to Friedrich Schlegel, who wrote this about his later sister-in-law, Caroline Böhmer (née Michaelis): 'Die Überlegenheit ihres Verstandes [sc.: über den meinigen] habe ich sehr frühe gefühlt. Es ist mir aber noch zu fremd zu unbegreiflich, daß ein *Weib* so sein kann, als daß ich an ihre Offenheit, Freiheit von Kunst recht fest glauben könnte'[34] ('The superiority of her intellect [sc.: to mine] was soon palpable. But it is still too strange, too incomprehensible for me that a *female* can be thus[,] so that I cannot yet firmly accept her openness, her freedom from artifice'). Here the astonishment these women of letters occasioned in their masculine peers is still obvious. The received notions of 'masculine' and 'feminine' are questioned, and in response men are compelled to register the insecurity of their own role.

NOTES

1. Any literary-historical account of women authors would have to begin with Hrosvitha von Gandersheim and include women authors from 1400 to 1700. It would, however, encounter one major difficulty: the lack of intra-literary connections between these writers. Compare Barbara Becker-Cantarino, *Der lange Weg zur Mündigkeit: Frauen und Literatur in Deutschland von 1500 bis 1800* (Munich: dtv, 1987).

2. See Heine, *Die romantische Schule*, in *Werke und Briefe*, ed. Hans Kaufmann, 10 vols. (Berlin: Aufbau, 1961), vol. VII, p. 64.

3. See Rudolf Haym, *Die Romantische Schule: Ein Beitrag zur Geschichte des Deutschen Geistes* (Hildesheim: Olms, 1961; 1st edn, Berlin 1870).

4. See Ricarda Huch, *Romantik*, in *Gesammelte Werke*, ed. Wilhelm Emrich, 11 vols. (Cologne: Kiepenhauer und Witsch, 1969), vol. VI: *Literaturgeschichte und Literaturkritik*, pp. 17–646, esp. pp. 45f.

5. All references: ibid., p. 21.

6. See Margarete Susmann, *Frauen der Romantik*, ed. Barbara Hahn (Frankfurt am Main: Suhrkamp, 1996), p. 10.

7. See, for example, ibid., pp. 64–98.

8. On this: Barbara Becker-Cantarino, *Schriftstellerinnen der Romantik: Epoche – Werk – Wirkung* (Munich: Beck, 2000), pp. 19–42.

9. Compare Becker-Cantarino, *Der lange Weg zur Mündigkeit*.

10. The phrase is Barbara Hahn's. See *Von Berlin nach Krakau: Zur Wiederentdeckung von Rahel Levin Varnhagens Korrespondenz* (Berlin: Zentraleinrichtung von Frauenstudien und Frauenforschung an der Freien Universität Berlin, 1989), p. 3.

11. See Heidi Thomann Tewarson, 'Jüdinsein um 1800: Bemerkungen zum Selbstverständnis der ersten Generation assimilierter Berliner Jüdinnen', in *Von einer Welt in die andere: Jüdinnen im 19. und 20. Jahrhundert*, eds. Jutta Dick and Barbara Hahn (Vienna: Christian Brandstätter, 1993), pp. 47–70.

12. Huber, while she argues that men are in any case unsuitable for the role of chief protagonist in a novel, is also persuaded that no woman could possibly describe the passions which drive the male. See Huber, 'Kann eine Romandichterin Männer schildern, und ist ein Mann zum Romanhelden zu brauchen?', in *Die reinste Freiheitsliebe, die reinste Männerliebe: Ein Lebensbild in Briefen und Erzählungen*, ed. Andrea Hahn (Berlin: Henssel, 1989), pp. 213–16, here p. 215.

13. Compare Hartwig Schultz's article 'Arnim, Bettine von', in *Literaturlexikon: Autoren und Werke deutscher Sprache*, ed. Walter Killy, 12 vols. (Gütersloh: Bertelsmann, 1988–92), vol. I, pp. 214–16, here p. 215.

14. See Renate von Heydebrandt, Simone Winko, 'Arbeit am Kanon: Geschlechterdifferenz in Rezeption und Wertung von Literatur', in *Genus: Zur Geschlechterdifferenz in den Kulturwissenschaften*, eds. Hadumond Bußman and Renate Hof (Stuttgart: Kröner, 1995), pp. 206–61.

15. Compare the tradition of pastors' sons in German literary history after the seventeenth century as reconstructed by Albrecht Schöne, *Säkularisation als sprachbildende Kraft: Studien zur Dichtung deutscher Pfarrersöhne*, 2nd edn (Göttingen: Vandenhoeck & Ruprecht, 1968; 1st edn 1958).

16. Philippine Gatterer to Gottfried August Bürger, 13 September 1777, in *Gottfried August Bürger und Philippine Gatterer: Ein Briefwechsel aus Göttingens empfindsamer Zeit*, ed. Erich Ebstein (Leipzig: Dieterichsche Verlagsbuchhandlung, 1921), p. 35.

17. Philippine Gatterer, *An die Muse*, in *Gedichte von Philippine Gatterer*, vol. I (Vienna and Prague: Hass, n.d.), pp. 49–52, here p. 51.

18. [Margareta Forkel,] *Maria: Eine Geschichte in Briefen* (Leipzig: Weidmann und Reich, 1782).

19. Georg Christoph Lichtenberg to Friedrich Nicolai, 20 March 1785, in Georg Christoph Lichtenberg, *Briefwechsel*, eds. Ulrich Joost and Albrecht Schöne, 4 vols. (Munich: Beck, 1990), vol. III: *1785–1792*, p. 69.

20. Forkel, *Maria*, p. 45.

21. Caroline Michaelis to Luise Gotter, end of October 1781, in Caroline Schlegel, *Briefe aus der Frühromantik*, ed. Erich Schmidt, 2 vols. (Berne: Herbert Lang, 1970), vol. I, p. 56.

22. Caroline Michaelis to Luise Stieler, 7 October 1778, ibid., p. 7.

23. Caroline Michaelis to Luise Gotter, 1 November 1781, ibid., p. 57.

24. Caroline Michaelis to Luise Gotter, 23 October 1782, ibid., p. 67.

25. Compare Ulrich Barth, 'Ästhetisierung der Religion – Sakralisierung der Kunst: Wackenroders Konzept der Kunstandacht', in *Aufgeklärter Protestantismus* (Tübingen: Mohr und Siebeck, 2004), pp. 225–56.

26. Therese Heyne to Luise Mejer, 4 November 1782, in Therese Huber, *Briefe*, ed. Magdalena Heuser, 5 vols. (Tübingen: Niemeyer, 1999–2005), vol. I, p. 49.

27. Therese Heyne to Karl August Böttiger, 10 January 1816, in *Briefe*, vol. IV, p. 94.

28. See Claudia Honegger, *Die Ordnung der Geschlechter: Die Wissenschaften vom Menschen und das Weib 1750–1850* (Munich: dtv, 1996; 1st edn 1991).
29. See Leopold von Schlözer, *Dorothea von Schlözer: Ein deutsches Frauenleben um die Jahrhundertwende 1770–1825* (Göttingen: Deuerlichsche Verlagsbuchhandlung, 1937), pp. 107–09, here p.108; Dorothea Schlözer was the first woman to have a doctoral dissertation accepted by the Faculty of Philosophy at a German university.
30. See the *Erinnerungen von Luise Wiedemann geb. Michaelis, der Schwester Carolinens*, ed. Julius Steinberger (Göttingen: n.p., 1929), p. 8.
31. Therese Huber to Christian Gottlob Heyne (23–8 August 1810), in Huber, *Briefe*, vol. IV, p. 194.
32. See Becker-Cantarino, *Schriftstellerinnen der Romantik*, p. 19.
33. Friedrich Creuzer to Karoline von Günderrode, 18 May 1806, in Karoline von Günderrode, *Sämtliche Werke und ausgewählte Studien*, ed. Walter Morgenthaler, 3 vols. (Frankfurt am Main: Roter Stern, 2006; 1st edn 1990–1) vol. III, p. 247.
34. Friedrich Schlegel to August Wilhelm Schlegel, 21 August 1793, in *KFSA* III/23, p. 121.

FURTHER READING

Bock, Gisela, *Frauen in der europäischen Geschichte: Vom Mittelalter bis zur Gegenwart* (Munich: Beck, 2000)

Bovenschen, Silvia, *Die imaginierte Weiblichkeit: Exemplarische Untersuchungen zu kulturgeschichtlichen literarischen Präsentationsformen des Weiblichen* (Frankfurt am Main: Suhrkamp, 1979)

Brinker-Gabler, Gisela (ed.), *Deutsche Literatur von Frauen* (Munich: Beck, 1988)

Dawson, Ruth P., 'Im Reifrock den Parnaß besteigen: Die Rezeption von Dichterinnen im 18. Jahrhundert', in *Frauensprache–Frauenliteratur? Für und wider eine Psychoanalyse literarischer Werke*, ed. Inge Stephan and Carl Pietzcker (Tübingen: Niemeyer, 1986), pp.24–9 [=*Akten des VII. Internationalen Germanisten-Kongresses Göttingen 1985*, ed. Albrecht Schöne, 11 vols. (Tübingen: Niemeyer, 1986), vol. VI].

Frevert, Ute, '*Mann und Weib, und Weib und Mann*'. *Geschlechterdifferenzen in der Moderne* (Munich: Beck, 1995)

Gallas, Helga and Magdalena Heuser (eds.), *Untersuchungen zum Roman von Frauen um 1800* (Tübingen: Niemeyer, 1990)

Gerhard, Ute (ed.), *Frauen in der Geschichte des Rechts* (Munich: Beck, 1997)

Hahn, Barbara, *Unter falschem Namen: Von der schwierigen Autorschaft der Frauen* (Frankfurt am Main: Suhrkamp, 1991)

'Der Mythos vom Salon: Rahels "Dachstube" als historische Fiktion', in *Salons der Romantik: Beiträge eines Wiepersdorfer Kolloquiums zu Theorie und Geschichte des Salons*, ed. Hartwig Schultz (Berlin, New York: de Gruyter 1997), pp.213–34.

Hechtfischer, Ute *et al.* (eds.), *Metzler Autorinnen Lexikon* (Stuttgart and Weimar: Metzler, 1998)

Heipcke, Corinna, *Autorhetorik: Zur Konstruktion weiblicher Autorschaft im ausgehenden 18. Jahrhundert* (Frankfurt am Main: Peter Lang, 2002)

Köhler, Astrid, *Salonkultur im klassischen Weimar: Geselligkeit als Lebensform und literarisches Konzept* (Stuttgart: Metzler, 1996)

Kontje, Todd, *Women, the Novel, and the German Nation 1771–1871* (Cambridge: Cambridge University Press, 1998)

Kord, Susanne, *Ein Blick hinter die Kulissen: Deutschsprachige Dramatikerinnen im 18. und 19. Jahrhundert* (Stuttgart: Metzler, 1992)

Loster-Schneider, Gudrun, and Gaby Pailer (eds.), *Lexikon deutschsprachiger Epik und Dramatik von Autorinnen (1730–1900)* (Tübingen and Basel: Francke, 2006)

Runge, Anita, *Literarische Praxis von Frauen um 1800: Briefroman, Autobiographie, Märchen* (Hildesheim: Olms, 1997)

Varnhagen, Rahel Levin, *Briefwechsel mit Pauline Wiesel*, ed. Barbara Hahn (Munich: Beck, 1997)

9

CARL NIEKERK

The Romantics and other cultures

Isaiah Berlin has argued that Johann Gottfried Herder (1744–1803) introduced a notion of pluralism into German intellectual and cultural history that was profoundly innovative and of great consequence for later generations, in particular the Romantics. Berlin defines Herder's concept of pluralism as not only the belief in the 'multiplicity', but in the 'incommensurability, of the values of different cultures and societies, and in addition, in the incompatibility of equally valid ideals'.[1] Following Herder's trajectory, the Romantics rejected what they perceived as the Enlightenment's outdated emphasis on universalism to embrace a notion of alterity that, at least on the surface, seemed to be more open to 'irrational' elements in the world views and belief systems of other cultures. Berlin's assessment has found widespread support and in fact, one could argue, the idea that cultural pluralism is a counter-Enlightenment phenomenon represents the consensus of the field. This chapter will revisit the issue of Romantic pluralism and revise Berlin's theories. One problem is that Berlin, and many other scholars after him, highlights the importance of Herder's 1774 essay *Auch eine Philosophie der Geschichte zur Bildung der Menschheit* (*Another Philosophy of History for the Cultivation of Humanity*), with its emphasis on the incompatibility of cultures and the significance of cultural differences, but neglects the importance of Herder's four-volume *Ideen zur Philosophie der Geschichte der Menschheit* (1784–91; *Ideas on the Philosophy of History of Humanity*).

Both *Auch eine Philosophie* and the *Ideen* reflect the introduction of a temporal element into natural history and anthropology that in the eighteenth century was promoted by anthropologists like George-Louis Leclerc de Buffon (1707–88), Petrus Camper (1722–89), and Johann Friedrich Blumenbach (1752–1840). Between 1771 and 1774 a very popular translation of Buffon's *Histoire naturelle* had appeared in Germany. *Auch eine Philosophie* can be understood as a philosophical response to Buffon's text that seeks to reflect the consequences of a radically developmental view of life for the Enlightenment's programme. As such, the text functions as a conservative critique of the Enlightenment. The Enlightenment believed it could dictate development, where in reality mankind's advancement is beyond rational control. Herder's text questions the West's ability to understand other cultures; cultures need to be understood on their own terms.[2] In practice, the Enlightenment prolongs abusive routines: Under the spell of reason, Europeans 'subjugate' and 'pillage' ('unterjochen' / 'plündern') other parts of the world (p. 100).

Herder views this differently in his *Ideen*, published a decade later. In contrast to *Auch eine Philosophie*, the *Ideen* articulate a world view that is remarkably friendly toward the Enlightenment. In this respect the text is clearly influenced by Johann Friedrich Blumenbach's *De generis humani varietate nativa* (1776; *On the Native Variety of the Human Species*), also highly dependent on Buffon, but more ambitious in its attempt to explain all varieties of mankind through a theory of climate. For Herder too, biological and cultural differences are the result of, or at least strongly influenced by, climate.[3] That customs are rooted in geography and climate explains how different cultures develop divergent forms of rational behaviour; nevertheless, all humans are reasonable and strive to improve civilisation (*Ideen*, pp. 116f. and 187f.). By assuming a common origin of all human life in spite of its manifest varieties (*Ideen*, p. 251), Herder successfully combines notions of universalism *and* cultural relativism, identity *and* difference. Like the anthropological models of Buffon, Camper and Blumenbach before him, Herder's deliberations can be understood as attempts to understand other cultures as rational; the world outside of Europe is no longer populated by imaginary creatures, but by humans who attempt to be rational in their own ways. In the history of the perception of other cultures, this meant clear progress, and yet also posed a serious problem for the Romantics who did not strictly believe in rationality. But did they then revert to a pre-modern view of the world that was more interested in stereotypes than in understanding the other?

Romantic travel narratives

Romantic travel literature suggests the answer to this question is a clear 'no'. The prototypical Romantic explorer is doubtless Alexander von Humboldt (1769–1859), who is in particular known for his travels through South America from 1799 to 1804. Humboldt had studied with Blumenbach in Göttingen, and his concept of science is highly indebted to Blumenbach's thinking. For Humboldt, culture is an extension of nature; it is the result of geographical and climatological factors. Humboldt does not develop an independent anthropology; humans are part of nature and their development is steered by climate and geography.[4] In general, he starts out his travel reports with a description of an area's geographical location, climate, landscape, natural resources, flora and fauna; only then does he attempt an anthropological description of the cultures of the inhabitants. Such descriptions emphasise other cultures' relative autonomy. His portrayal of the culture of the Chaymas, who lived in the inlands of Venezuela, at the time called New-Andalusia ('Neu-Andalusien'), around Caripe, for instance, is full of respect for their cultural achievements.[5] The Chaymas live together in communities, they practise diverse forms of agriculture, and did so before the Europeans arrived (II, pp. 179, 180). Native Americans in general are characterised by a 'moral rigour' ('moralische Unbiegsamkeit' II, p. 185). Above all, they seek to maintain their own language and culture (II, pp. 203, 204).

One could conclude from this that Humboldt attempts to understand other cultures on their own terms, and not by thoughtlessly applying European standards. On the other hand, he certainly did not idealise native cultures (their level of civilisation depends on the local climate) and also assumed a clear civilatory mission for the Europeans.[6] He acknowledges that their role is not always a positive one. The second volume of the *Reise in die Aequinoctial-Gegenden des neuen Continents* (*Journey to the Equatorial Regions of the New Continent*), containing the description of New-Andalusia, starts with an unequivocal condemnation of the slave trade in this area, motivated by material gain and religious bigotry (II, pp. 2, 3). In spite of his strong stance against colonial abuse and the fact that he published the majority of his writings not in German, but French, Alexander von Humboldt's name and reputation were later used to legitimate German nationalist and colonial ambitions.[7] Humboldt's work certainly contributed much to an awareness of global diversity, but his idea that trade would be followed by freedom[8] may strike us as rather naive today.

Humboldt explicitly refused to call the Chaymas 'savages' ('*Wilde*') (II, p. 179) – an attitude that is mirrored in other Romantic travel narratives, for instance Adelbert von Chamisso's *Reise um die Welt mit der Romanoffischen Entdeckungs-Expedition in den Jahren 1815–18* (1836; *Journey around the World with Romanov's Expedition in the Years 1815–18*).[9] In spite of the fact that the title of Chamisso's book is a clear reference to Georg Forster's classical *Reise um die Welt* (first published in English in 1777; *Journey around the World*), Humboldt's and Chamisso's aversion to seeing the non-European as 'savage' is a unambiguous break with the eighteenth-century idea of the 'noble savage' as a model of alterity. In general, the importance and popularity of the type of exploratory travel literature produced by, for instance, Forster, started to wane and it was replaced by newer forms of travel writing with different interests.

In an exemplary way this newer model is represented by Heinrich Heine's *Reisebilder* (*Pictures from my Travels*). Volumes III and IV, first published in 1830–1 and containing his travels through Italy in the year 1828, are clearly documents of early tourism; while Goethe in his *Italienische Reise* (1816–17) made his travels (1786–8) into highly individual experiences, Heine emphasises that it is hard to get away from fellow travellers, and their response to the 'other' culture is a significant part of his own report. The attitude Heine himself develops stands in stark contrast to the attitudes of the (German and British) visitors of, for instance, the German-style hotel run by a German patron in Milan.[10] They combine a desire to live like at home with a very negative view of Italians in general. Heine himself is not free of stereotypes either, but he does attempt to explain his observations. Italian culture is in decline, he observes many times; but that can be explained: the country suffers from the dominion of foreign powers (p. 273). Italy's Catholicism plays a major role in Heine's *Reisebilder*. Heine makes no mystery of his own fierce anti-Catholicism. And yet, he does much to relativise his own attitude. That a cathedral can be a pleasant refuge from the brutal heat is something that Germans from the Protestant north do not realise (p. 263). The encounter with a poorly dressed monk who consoles the sick and teaches children to pray, with an occasional piece of bread as reward, leads him to the resolution not to write anything against this man and to the insight that German priests and monks are but poor copies of their Italian colleagues (pp. 435, 436). In the end, Heine feels a greater affinity with his Italian friend's devotion to the holy cross than with his British friend's cynicism (p. 466). The realisation that religion is culturally determined, and is experienced differently within different national and historical contexts, also explains the many digressions in the *Reisebilder* in which Heine reflects upon his own Jewishness and the treatment of Jews in societies in general.

While there are many continuities between Enlightenment and Romanticism (not least Heine himself), it is correct to say that the Romantics displayed more openness toward other cultures. Travel literature of the Romantic era also showed more awareness of the fact that images of other cultures are constructions and highly dependent on one's own perspective. Simultaneously, though, the Romantics also establish a new normativity in particular in their theorising about cultural difference.

Theoretical approaches to cultural difference after Herder

It is remarkable that Hegel in his *Vorlesungen über die Philosophie der Weltgeschichte* (1822–3; *Lectures on the Philosophy of World History*) not only starts his geographical overview with the Orient (to be followed by the Greek, Roman and Germanic worlds), but also dedicates far more space to the Orient (194 pages) than to any other area.[11] This is indicative of a broader trend: the Orient fascinates Romanticism, much as the Pacific functioned as a key location a generation earlier in the imagination of late-Enlightenment intellectuals.[12] There exists a hunger for factual knowledge about the Orient, its inhabitants, their histories and their cultures. But this fascination is more than a desire to document knowledge about Oriental culture. For the Romantics, Orientalism turns into a model for understanding other cultures in general, and, in consequence, also one's own culture.

In 1808 Friedrich Schlegel published *Über die Sprache und Weisheit der Indier* (*On the Language and Wisdom of the Indians*), a text of which it can be said that it shaped Western Orientalism, far beyond the German borders. Schlegel builds on Herder's work, according to which human civilisation started in Asia (*Ideen,* 386, 390). Schlegel attempts to give a more precise foundation to this idea through what are meant to be precise linguistic and cultural observations. His main thesis is that the old Indian language Sanskrit is related to Persian, ancient Greek, Latin and the Germanic languages, and that this points to a developmental relationship.[13] The origins of Germanic culture, in other words, are to be found in India. While Herder believed in one single source from which all civilisations originated (*Ideen,* pp. 390–7), Schlegel in contrast emphasises the existence of competing language and cultural traditions that originated independently of each other, even though they did have considerable influence on each other (pp. 161, 163). Interestingly, Schlegel's argument forces him to distinguish between competing models of the Orient – a highly significant move for the history of German thinking about non-European others. One Oriental tradition, says Schlegel, is based in India, closely related to the Germanic tradition, and will therefore be called by future scholars 'Indo-European' or 'Indo-Germanic'. An alternative Oriental tradition which includes Tibet, China, Arabia and, to some extent, the Jewish cultural tradition is seen as fundamentally different from this 'Indo-Germanic' model (pp. 115, 297, 299). While Schlegel emphasises that all these traditions are legitimate in their own ways (p. 163), there can be no doubt (for the attentive reader) that he sees the 'Indo-Germanic' tradition as superior.

Goethe and Heine read *Über die Sprache und Weisheit der Indier* as Schlegel's tribute to the Catholic Church.[14] (Schlegel had converted to Catholicism around the time that the book was published.) In view of the way in which Schlegel discusses religious matters in the last chapter of his book (pp. 295–317), this is understandable, but Goethe's and Heine's observations also point to a broader issue. In his genealogical search, Schlegel is interested in establishing one central trajectory for Germanic culture, and he has a rather negative view of the interactions among divergent traditions that are an unavoidable part of any cultural history. This is precisely the issue Goethe addresses in the second text of the period that had a paradigmatic function for the understanding of other cultures. His *West-östlicher Divan* (*West-Eastern Divan*) is a collection of poems based primarily on the four-teenth-century Persian court poetry of Hafis, and accompanied by a lengthy essay with the title *Noten und Abhandlungen zu besserem Verständnis des West-östlichen Divans* (*Notes and Treatises to Further the Understanding of the West-Eastern Divan*). It was first published in 1819, roughly a decade after Schlegel's text, and clearly had a polemical function.[15] It is significant that at the very start of his commentary Goethe emphasises how different East and West are. He wants to be seen as a traveller who does his best to adapt to the 'unfamiliar way of life' ('fremde Landsart'), but also realises such attempts can only be successful up to a point, that he would be recog-nised by his 'peculiar accent' ('eignen Akzent') as a stranger ('Fremdling').[16] Furthermore Goethe's view of the Orient, in contrast to Schlegel's, is highly inclusive and heterogeneous. Once he describes Oriental culture as a 'mix-ture' ('Gemisch', p. 142; see also p. 150); Hebrews, Arabs, Persians and Christians are all part of Goethe's Orient, and while Goethe has his pref-erences among these cultures, he, like Herder, conceives of their relations primarily in developmental terms, not hierarchically. Only after we rea-lise the fundamental differences between East and West do we start to see similarities between East and West, between Horace and Hafis (p. 183). Goethe does not intend to collapse the differences between East and West but rather to accept the East and what it stands for as part of his own self-image. Only if we acknowledge the fundamental otherness of the East does the provocation of Goethe's statement that 'what we Germans call *Spirit*' ('was wir Deutsche *Geist* nennen', p. 165) can be found in *Oriental* poetry become clear. In an age in which the Napoleonic wars were a recent mem-ory and nationalism was rampant, Goethe reminded his fellow Germans to look elsewhere.

To consider Goethe a proponent of Romanticism is in some respects problematic. While the Romantics saw Goethe in some respects as a model, and contacts between Goethe and individual Romantic authors, among them the Schlegels, existed, Goethe in general kept his distance, personally and ideologically. And yet his sensitivity toward other cultures in the *West-östlicher Divan* is a genuine legacy of Romanticism. For Goethe, in contrast to Schlegel, the Orient represented the other side of the West – of Western rationality – but he wanted this other side also to be part of the West. The Orient allows the West to get back in touch with its repressed other. Thus he envisions a dialogue that moves beyond geographical and language borders. Even though he did much to counter stereotypes about the Orient, in particular its alleged despotic character, Goethe's view of the Orient is of course not without Orientalist clichés.[17] In the end Goethe's Orientalism too is a form of Western self-reflection; the East is instrumentalised on behalf of the West's self-improvement. But the polemical potential of such a model in the early nineteenth century is considerable.

Jews and Gypsies as 'outsiders' in Romantic texts

Romantics made possible a new, constructive understanding of alterity. Nonetheless their kind of understanding rests on a premise that hinders the appreciation of certain kinds of difference, in particular the difference represented by 'outsiders'. In the early nineteenth century, Jews and Gypsies are not seen as part of European (or German) culture, but as such 'outsiders'. Herder's negative view of the European Jews can be explained by the fact that they are a people without a territory (*Ideen*, p. 702). The same can be said for Gypsies. Following the theories of a Göttingen scholar, Heinrich Grellmann, who in 1783 had published a path-breaking monograph on Gypsies, Herder assumes that they are originally from India, but were expelled from there. He characterises them as a 'multitudinous, alien, pagan, subterranean people' ('zahlreiches, fremdes, heidnisches, unterirdisches Volk') and sees assimilation, by forcing them into the military, as their only road to the future (*Ideen*, p. 703).

Not all Romantic texts see it that way. A remarkable text, in this respect, is Achim von Arnim's *Isabella von Ägypten: Kaiser Karl des Fünften erste Jugendliebe* (1812; *Isabella of Egypt: The First Love of Emperor Charles V's Youth*). The text is a love story, mixing fairy-tale elements and historical reality, involving a Gypsy girl, Isabella or Bella, and Charles V (1500–58). The fictional plot is set in what is known today as Flanders and around 1515, just before Charles V became Holy Roman Emperor. By choosing this historical setting, it reminds its Romantic audiences of a time in which the attitude toward Gypsies was 'an open and inquiring one' and their political leaders 'could negotiate with kings and bishops' – an image that starts to change between 1530 and 1550[18] – even though Arnim's text itself makes very clear that violence against Gypsies was, also at this time, rampant. By claiming that Gypsies originated in Egypt but chose to go into exile as a form of self-imposed punishment for having rejected Mary, Joseph and Jesus, Arnim chooses a genealogy that is not in line with the latest theory, but relies on older, mythical and Gypsy-authored sources.[19] By pointing out that Gypsies had lost touch with their native territory, the text, in spite of its Christian imagery, addresses a key issue in Herder's theory of alterity: cultural difference is unproblematic as long as it is tied to a territory to which that culture is native, but it turns problematic when such a territory is abandoned or lost.

From the start the text problematises European generalisations about Gypsies: Bella's father is hanged, not because of something he did himself, but because of the crime of another Gypsy in a group he accompanies.[20] While Bella's father is a Gypsy king, her mother, who is already dead when the story starts, was Flemish (p. 628). That makes Bella into a cultural hybrid, who is strongly attached to her father's culture, about which she knows little, but also able to speak and read Flemish. Precisely this hybridity, her ability to function within European culture, combined with a strong desire to know more about Gypsy culture, enable her to achieve what her father could not: to return the Gypsies to their fatherland (Egypt). In order to do so, she is told, she needs to have a child with Charles so that he will guarantee the Gypsies a safe return home. In the end, Bella overcomes all obstacles placed in her way and accomplishes what she set out to accomplish. In doing so, the text makes clear that she is Charles's moral superior. In spite of this seemingly happy outcome, the text is, however, ambiguous about the exact role of Gypsies in Europe. The text certainly makes the case for a more humane treatment of Gypsies, Charles gives them freedom and allows them to pursue employment, but this is only meant as a temporary solution until they will leave for their homeland (p. 723). Charles, in spite of his love for Bella, does not want to marry her because of her Egyptian background (pp. 722, 723). In the end, the crucial separation of these different cultural spheres has been reaffirmed; with that, the text confirms the territorial principle underlying Herder's anthropology.

While the image of Gypsies is in principle positive but also ambiguous – they are well-meaning, but not part of European culture – Jews have a predominantly negative image in *Isabella von Ägypten*. Here Arnim reproduces a version of Schlegel's theory of competing models of Orientalism.[21] Gypsies are persecuted, we are told by the narrator, because Jews in European societies pretended to be Gypsies to avoid expulsion (p. 624). Jews are also responsible for one of the main obstacles that prevent Charles from finding (the real) Bella. A Jew fabricates a Golem, a life-like clay figure that closely resembles Bella (p. 688), and thereby confuses Charles, who, in spite of her very different (hollow) character, assumes she really is Bella. But while in the case of the Gypsies the transgression of boundaries, geographical and cultural, is tolerated under the condition that it is reversed, no such scenario is envisioned for the European Jews. It is possible to read *Isabella von Ägypten* as a manifesto calling for more tolerance toward minorities, and yet 'tolerance' and 'intolerance' are closely intertwined in this text. The status of Jews is highly ambiguous in Romanticism. On an institutional level, the Romantic period is the era of the great literary salons of Henriette Herz, Sarah Levy and Rahel Varnhagen – all of Jewish descent. The importance of these salons in particular for the dissemination of Goethe's works and Romantic texts is considerable. And yet, there is also a counter-movement. Arnim and Brentano were members of the so-called Christlich-Teutsche Tischgesellschaft (Christian-German Dining Club), a nationalist, religious and explicitly anti-Semitic group of intellectuals established in 1811.[22] Its founding marked the transition from a salon culture in which Jewish women played a prominent role to a café culture in which men dominated.[23] Exemplary for the anti-Jewish feelings in this group is Clemens Brentano's *Der Philister vor, in und nach der Geschichte* (*The Philistine before, in and after History*) which was intended to be a 'Humorous Essay' ('Scherzhafte Abhandlung')[24] and presented in March 1811 to the Christlich-Teutsche Tischgesellschaft, to be followed later that year by speeches by Achim von Arnim and Adam Müller on the same topic. For the Romantics, the 'Philister' ('Philistine') is an exemplary counter-figure. In Brentano's view, Philistine and Jew are linked: Jew and Philistine relate to each other like seed and full-grown plant (p. 963). Brentano's essay is notoriously vague and also often self-contradictory, but one could interpret this as an indication that Brentano sees Jews as the source of a problem that is much more common in German society. The Philistine has no ideas, no enthusiasm, no genius and no creativity (p. 967). The Philistine talks a lot about patriotic themes, but does not understand what they mean; he is like the cuckoo that colonises strange nests (p. 998). This last point picks up on Herder's theory that Jews are without their territory, and therefore only can partake superficially in others' cultures. Consequently, Brentano does not want Jews (or Philistines) as members of the Christlich-Teutsche Tischgesellschaft (1002).

Scholarship has shown that Brentano's text is by no means unique, but part of a broader movement of anti-Semitic defamation in which certainly not all Romantics participated, but that nevertheless was a powerful subcurrent in Romanticism.[25] It is remarkable how self-contradictory Romantic texts sometimes are in their attitude toward Jews. At the centre of Brentano's fairy tale *Gockel und Hinkel* (1815–16; *Gockel and Hinkel*) is a magic ring, attributed to the biblical King Solomon, that fulfils all of the proprietor's wishes instantly. It allows the three main characters – Gockel, Hinkel and Gackeleia – to live a life of incredible wealth. There is, however, also a problem. The ring is also claimed and eventually stolen from him by three Jews. The imagery related to Judaism in *Gockel und Hinkel* is characterised by a profound ambiguity. On the one hand, Brentano's fairy tale associates

Jewish culture with wisdom and wealth for those who possess this wisdom and know how to use it; on the other hand, it associates Jewishness with greed and dishonesty. This same dualism can already be found in Herder. Herder respects the ancient Hebrews who have not lost touch with their culture (and 'native' territory), but has little respect for contemporary European Jews, compared by him to a 'parasitical plant' ('parasitische Pflanze') (*Ideen*, p. 702; also pp. 483–92).

Negative stereotypes about Jews proliferated during the Romantic period. Cultural history has ignored or downplayed them for a long time, although there is a clear connection between these stereotypes and the anti-Semitic imagery of, for instance, Wagner or the Third Reich. Even contemporaries did not seem to take them too seriously. In his overview of German Romantic Literature, Heinrich Heine dedicates several pages, an unusual amount of space, to *Isabella von Ägypten*, and in particular lauds Arnim's compassionate attitude toward Gypsies, but wastes no words on the text's Jewish stereotypes (pp. 117–20).[26] There were also developments that pointed to positive changes. Legal reforms were under way to make the position of Jews equal to that of all other citizens (anti-Semitic discourse responded to this by focusing on Jews' social acceptability instead of on the legal issue).[27] In spite of the very violent anti-Jewish incidents in 1819 in a number of German cities, the so-called Hep-Hep riots,[28] in particular in Berlin, Jews throughout the period played an important economic and cultural role.[29] None of this should detract from the insight, however, that anti-Jewish attitudes were not incidental, but represented the other, negative side of a discourse about otherness that had deep roots in German intellectual history.

Nationalism and alterity

It is one of the paradoxes of Romanticism that the movement is perceived simultaneously as committed to pluralism and yet also as the birthplace of modern German nationalism. This ambiguity is already visible in Herder, who promoted pluralism, but also advocated a (re)turn to Germany's own tradition of folk literature in order to reinforce German national self-awareness and self-consciousness. This coexistence of nationalism and pluralism is the logical consequence of a notion of alterity that is based on territoriality; one could speak of a mutual reinforcement of the two.

A concurrent interest in alterity and nationalism can be seen, for instance, in *Des Knaben Wunderhorn* (1806–8; *The Boy's Magic Horn*), three volumes of collected folk-songs published by Arnim and Brentano. The first includes an essay by Arnim that explains the editors' intentions. Paradoxically, travel is for Arnim a necessary condition of the type of folk literature he is interested in. He specifically mentions Gypsies, journeymen, soldiers and (travelling) students as possessing a form of knowledge which for him is a key feature.[30] Mobility, in other words, is a prerequisite of folk literature. Even so, at the end of his essay the author speaks of the collection as a 'general monument for the greatest of the newer nations, the Germans' ('allgemeinen Denkmahle des größten neueren Volkes, der Deutschen'), and there is no doubt that he sees the songs as a means to create such a new community (*Wunderhorn* I, pp. 413, 414). From something very concrete at the beginning of the essay, 'Volk' has turned into an abstract entity. But do the individual poems in *Des Knaben Wunderhorn* add up to a nationalist agenda? While this is certainly what the editors had in mind, it is also possible to look at them as anthropological material that tells its readers something about reigning attitudes in Germany, but is primarily descriptive and not prescriptive. Some of the poems are certainly anti-Semitic[31] or intolerant in other ways. In spite of the fact that the editors often took great liberties in 'editing' the individual poems, some of them are remarkably subversive. One could think in this context of one of the best-known songs from *Des Knaben Wunderhorn*, the 'Lied des Verfolgten im Turm' ('Song of the Persecuted Man in the Tower'; III, pp. 43–5) with its chorus 'Thoughts are free' ('Die Gedanken sind frey'), later set to music by Gustav Mahler.

The novellas of Heinrich von Kleist also demonstrate that nationalism in the early nineteenth century does not necessarily exclude cultural pluralism. There is no doubt that his novella 'Die Verlobung in St Domingo' (1811; 'The Betrothal in St Domingo'), for example, can be read as an anti-colonial pamphlet,[32] but what exactly is at the root of Kleist's anti-colonialism? The historical context for the plot of the novella is the island Haiti in the year 1803, when black slaves had mounted a successful revolt against their French oppressors. The two protagonists of the story are on opposite sides of the conflict. Gustav von der Ried is a Swiss officer, working for the French army, who attempts to bring his family to the relative safety of Port au Prince, which is still in the hands of the French. Toni, of mixed racial heritage, is the adopted daughter of one of the leaders of the revolt, Congo Hoango. Because of her pale, yellowish skin colour, her mother uses her to trick fleeing Whites into Congo Hoango's house, only to have them murdered as soon as the owner has returned. Defying her mother's orders, Toni decides to help Gustav and his family, but is shot and killed by Gustav, who does not understand her intention (and subsequently takes his own life). The surviving Europeans return to Switzerland, and we are left with the image of a monument dedicated to Toni and Gustav in the garden of the property they have bought with the money left over from their colonial adventure.[33] But why did Kleist write a text about such a distant conflict? It may have interested Kleist, a former officer in the Prussian army, that while large parts of Germany suffered under French occupation, the slaves of Haiti had found successful ways to fight the French. Europe is on Kleist's mind. The text is a powerful argument against the different forms of chaos that ensue when people do not remain inside their 'native' territory – in particular the French. With that, the text is a powerful argument for Herder's theory of territoriality: cultures develop in their own geographical context, and this principle needs to be respected. Nationalism in Europe translates into anti-colonialism outside of Europe.

Conclusion

At the core of the Romantics' conceptualisation of other cultures, there is a fundamental ambiguity. It is correct to say that the Romantics possess a concept of alterity that goes beyond that of the Enlightenment and is more open toward the otherness of other cultures. In spite of a trend toward a Euro- or Germanocentric outlook on other cultures (F. Schlegel), Romantic texts also manifest genuine attempts to come to an adequate understanding of other cultures. Furthermore, there also exist attempts to construct a genuine transcultural discourse (Goethe). This transcultural discourse, however, has its limits. One can of course question whether there actually existed an intercultural dialogue – a dialogue between equal partners – within Romantic literature. But beyond that, there is also a virulent anti-Semitic trend within the Romantic movement. I hope to have shown that it is important to see Romantic attitudes toward Jews and Gypsies in the context of a broader Romantic theory of alterity. The intolerant side of Romanticism is not an aberration, but rather closely linked to a concept of alterity that could also be progressive and liberating. The Romantics' conceptualisation of other cultures is multi-functional. An argument that can be used to support nationalism can at the same time also be used to attack colonialism (Kleist). From our contemporary point of view, the Romantics' discourse on alterity is also often inconsistent: while Gypsies are, to some extent, idealised, Jews are vilified, sometimes in the same text (Arnim). Romantic texts introduced the idea of different Orients – a good and a bad Orient.

The fundamental ambiguity in the Romantics' relationship to other cultures has had far-reaching consequences for Germans' perception of cultural difference. This ambiguity is reflected in the movement's reception history. Within German cultural history, Romanticism was a highly influential movement. Its impact can be seen in Wagner's *Parsifal*, but also in Mahler's *Lied von der Erde* (*Song of the Earth*); in the works of the arch-conservative

Ernst Jünger, but also in the texts of the hippy-idol Hermann Hesse. Only if we keep in mind the ambiguity at its root will we be able to understand the true complexity of the Romantic thinking.

NOTES

1. Isaiah Berlin, *Three Critics of the Enlightenment: Vico, Hamann, Herder*, ed. Henry Hardy (Princeton, N.J., and Oxford: Princeton University Press, 2000), p. 176.
2. See Johann Gottfried Herder, *Auch eine Philosophie der Geschichte zur Bildung der Menschheit*, in *Werke*, eds. Günter Arnold *et al.*, 10 vols. (Frankfurt am Main: Deutscher Klassiker Verlag, 1985–2000), vol. IV (1994), p. 39.
3. See Johann Gottfried Herder, *Ideen zur Philosophie der Geschichte der Menschheit*, in *Werke*, vol. VI (1989), in particular book 7 of volume I, pp. 251–85. (Quoted hereafter as *Ideen*.)
4. See Alexander von Humboldt, 'Einleitung', in Alexander von Humboldt and A. Bonplandt, *Reise in die Aequinoctial-Gegenden des neuen Continents in den Jahren 1799, 1800, 1801, 1802, 1803 und 1804*, vol. I (Stuttgart and Tübingen: Cotta, 1815), p. 16.
5. Humboldt and Bonplandt, *Reise*, vol. II, chapter 9, pp. 176–255.
6. See Mary Louise Pratt, *Imperial Eyes: Travel Writing and Transculturation* (London, New York: Routledge, 1992), p. 140.
7. Susanne Zantop, *Colonial Fantasies: Conquest, Family, and Nation in Precolonial Germany, 1770–1870* (Durham, N.C., and London: Duke University Press, 1997), p. 170.
8. Ottmar Ette, *Weltbewußtsein. Alexander von Humboldt und das unvollendete Projekt einer anderen Moderne* (Weilerswist: Velbrück, 2002), p. 62.
9. Adelbert von Chamisso, *Reise um die Welt mit der Romanzoffischen Entdeckungs-Expedition in den Jahren 1815–18 auf der Brigg Rurik*, in *Werke*, vol. I (Leipzig: Weidmann, 1836), p. 119.
10. Heinrich Heine, *Reisebilder* (Zurich: Diogenes, 1993), pp. 294f.
11. Georg Wilhelm Friedrich Hegel, *Vorlesungen über die Philosophie der Weltgeschichte, Vorlesungen: Ausgewählte Nachschriften*, eds. Karl Heinz Ilting, Karl Brehmer and Hoo Nam Seelmann, vol. XII (Hamburg: Meiner, 1996).
12. See Todd Kontje, *German Orientalisms* (Ann Arbor: University of Michigan Press, 2004), p. 67.
13. Friedrich Schlegel, *Über die Sprache und Weisheit der Indier*, in *KFSA* VIII, pp. 105–380, here p. 115.
14. Ursula Struc-Oppenberg, 'Einleitung: Über die Sprache und Weisheit der Indier', *KFSA* VIII, pp. ccxxvii, ccxxviii.
15. See Kontje, *German Orientalisms*, pp. 121–4.
16. Johann Wolfgang von Goethe, *West-östlicher Divan*, in *Werke*, ed. Erich Trunz, vol. II (Munich: Beck, 1994), p. 127.
17. Kontje, *German Orientalisms*, p. 119.
18. Thomas Acton, 'Modernity, Culture and Gypsies: Is There a Meta-Scientific Method for Understanding the Representation of "Gypsies"? And Do the Dutch Really Exist?', in *The Role of the Romanies: Images and Counter-Images*

of 'Gypsies' / Romanies in European Cultures, eds. Nicholas Saul and Susan Tebbutt (Liverpool: Liverpool University Press, 2004), pp. 98–116, here p. 106.

19. See Claudia Breger, Ortlosigkeit des Fremden: 'Zigeunerinnen' und 'Zigeuner' in der deutschsprachigen Literatur um 1800 (Cologne: Böhlau, 1998), p. 274.

20. Achim von Arnim, Isabella von Ägypten, in Werke, vol. III, ed. Renate Moering (Frankfurt am Main: Deutscher Klassiker Verlag, 1990), p. 625.

21. See Breger, Ortlosigkeit, pp. 294–9.

22. For an overview of the history of the Christlich-Teutsche Tischgesellschaft see Heinz Härtl, 'Romantischer Antisemitismus: Arnim und die "Tischgesellschaft"', Weimarer Beiträge, 33 (1987), pp. 1159–73, here pp. 1160–64, and Stefan Nienhaus, Geschichte der deutschen Tischgesellschaft (Tübingen: Niemeyer, 2003).

23. See Günter Oesterle, 'Juden, Philister und romantische Intellektuelle: Überlegungen zum Antisemitismus in der Romantik', Athenäum, vol. II (1992), pp. 55–89, here p. 78. See also Wolfgang Frühwald, 'Antijudaismus in der Zeit der deutschen Romantik', in Conditio Judaica: Judentum, Antisemitismus und deutschsprachige Literatur vom 18. Jahrhundert bis zum Ersten Weltkrieg, eds. Hans Otto Horch and Horst Denkler, vol. II (Tübingen: Niemeyer, 1989), pp. 72–91, here p. 87.

24. Clemens Brentano, Der Philister vor, in und nach der Geschichte: Scherzhafte Abhandlung, in Werke, ed. Friedhelm Kemp, vol. II (Munich: Hanser, 1963), pp. 959–1016.

25. See Oesterle, 'Juden, Philister und romantische Intellektuelle'.

26. Heinrich Heine, Die romantische Schule, critical edition, ed. Helga Weidmann (Stuttgart: Reclam, 2002), pp. 117–20.

27. See Oesterle, 'Juden, Philister und romantische Intellektuelle', pp. 68, 69. Jews briefly enjoyed equal rights in Prussia, but these were revoked as part of the post-Napoleonic Restoration (see Frühwald, 'Antijudaismus', p. 75).

28. See Stefi Jersch-Wenzel, 'Legal Status and Emancipation', in German-Jewish History in Modern Times, vol. II: Emancipation and Acculturation 1780–1871, eds. Michael Brenner, Stefi Jersch-Wenzel and Michael A. Meyer (New York and Chichester: Columbia University Press, 1997), pp. 7–49, here pp. 36–8.

29. See Frühwald, 'Antijudaismus', pp. 89 and 87.

30. Achim von Arnim and Clemens Brentano, Des Knaben Wunderhorn: Alte deutsche Lieder, ed. Heinz Rölleke, vol. I (Stuttgart: Reclam, 1987), pp. 393, 394.

31. Martina Vordermayer, Antisemitismus und Judentum (Frankfurt am Main: Lang, 1999), pp. 135–41.

32. Zantop, Colonial Fantasies, pp. 154–9.

33. Heinrich von Kleist, 'Die Verlobung in St Domingo', in Sämtliche Werke und Briefe, ed. Helmut Sembdner, vol. II (Munich; dtv, 1987), pp. 160–95, here p. 195.

FURTHER READING

Berman, R.A., Enlightenment or Empire: Colonial Discourse in German Culture (Lincoln and London: Nebraska University Press, 1998)

Bormann, A. von (ed.), Volk – Nation – Europa: Zur Romantisierung und Entromantisierung politischer Begriffe (Würzburg: Königshausen & Neumann, 1998).

Dougherty, F.W.P., *Gesammelte Aufsätze zu Themen der klassischen Periode der Naturgeschichte / Collected Essays on Themes from the Classical Period of Natural History* (Göttingen: Norbert Klatt, 1996)

Eigen, S. and M. Larrimore (eds.), *The German Invention of Race* (Albany: State University of New York Press, 2006)

Fischer, B., *Das Eigene und das Eigentliche: Klopstock, Herder, Fichte, Kleist: Episoden aus der Konstruktionsgeschichte nationaler Intentionalitäten* (Berlin: Erich Schmidt, 1995)

Herrmann, H.P., H.-M. Blitz, and S. Moßmann, *Machtphantasie Deutschland: Nationalismus, Männlichkeit und Fremdenhaß im Vaterlandsdiskurs deutscher Schriftsteller des 18. Jahrhunderts* (Frankfurt am Main : Suhrkamp, 1996)

Lepenies, *Das Ende der Naturgeschichte: Wandel kultureller Selbstverständlichkeiten in den Wissenschaften des 18. und 19. Jahrhunderts* (Munich and Vienna: Hanser, 1976)

Librett, J.S., *The Rhetoric of Cultural Dialogue: Jews and Germans from Moses Mendelssohn to Richard Wagner and Beyond* (Palo Alto, Calif.: Stanford University Press, 2000)

Seyhan, A., *Representation and Its Discontents: The Critical Legacy of German Romanticism* (Berkeley, Los Angeles and Oxford: University of California Press, 1992)

Zammito, J.H., *Kant, Herder, and the Birth of Anthropology* (Chicago and London: University of Chicago Press, 2002)

10

NICHOLAS SAUL

Love, death and *Liebestod* in German Romanticism

In this essay I shall argue something infrequently heard in modern academic discourse: that we need to turn the clock back a little in the scholarship of German Romanticism (if only to go forward the more progressively). It used to be commonplace to link German Romanticism intrinsically with a suspect ideology of love and death, and in especial with the erotic death cult most prominently exemplified by the *Liebestod* of Richard Wagner's doomed Tristan and Isolde. But scholarship in recent decades has turned away from that preoccupation. With some justification, it is true, other themes have come to the fore. Romanticism is (for example) now no longer thought of as an aggressively irrationalist and obscurantist phenomenon. Instead, its anti-Enlightenment polemic is understood as the expression of a pioneering critique of abstract rationalism very much within the utopian tradition of the project of Enlightenment.[1] Similarly, the engagement of Romantic thinkers with the political sphere is now recognised to be much more complex than the received scheme of conservatism and reaction used to suggest. And analogous corrections of our historical understanding have been made across virtually the entire spectrum of Romanticism's thematic preoccupations.

This is true in some sense of the traditional identification of Romanticism with morbidity and perverse love. Thomas Mann's early novella *Tristan* (1902)[2] well represents what we used to think. This bleak allegorical analysis of the sickness afflicting art, life and modern culture certainly foregrounds and criticises a pessimistic ideology of love and death. In a sanatorium around 1900 the beautiful, yet mortally ill Gabriele Klöterjahn encounters a minor aestheticist poet, Detlef Spinell. In the absence of her merchant husband, they recognise an aestheticist affinity and fall in love. That the illicit affair is doomed is symbolised by their wilful self-dissolution into the love-death music from the second and third acts of Wagner's *Tristan und Isolde* (1865), which Gabriele plays one gloomy February afternoon. The escape into the dream-world of beautiful, yet dead, art is cruelly exposed for what it is by the return of Klöterjahn, a vigorous and enterprising man who personifies appetite for life. Spinell has written him a contemptuous letter, in which the aesthete imagines he is striking a blow for love and art by revealing how he, the poet, has recognised and released an inner beauty in Gabriele forever beyond the reach of the merchant's banal consciousness. Unfortunately Klöterjahn's spluttering, incoherent, yet powerful retort, to his face leaves the effete Spinell crushed. As news reaches them of Gabriele's, final agonies, Klöterjahn rushes to confront death at his wife's side. Spinell for his part takes flight, only to meet his nemesis in the shape of the infant Anton Klöterjahn in the garden. As if intuitively aware of the situation, yet blithely unconcerned by his mother's fate, Anton is seized at the sight of Spinell by an unstoppable, positively jovial fit of lustful and vigorous mirth, which administers the final defeat and closes the tale. Thus the life principle, symbolised by the Klöterjahn males (dislikeable in many ways as they are), vanquishes the aesthetic, which is associated with a sterile, vacuously spiri-tualised form of love incapable of survival and inexorably associated with morbid acquiescence in dissolution.

Now Thomas Mann's initial target here is obviously Wagner, who is sub-jected to a familiar Nietzschean critique as producer of a kind of overwhelm-ing, yet precisely thereby life-denying, art. But another target – *the* target – is of course Romanticism. Wagner's libretto is itself suffused with intended allusions to an earlier version of lovers who perversely yearn for death: Hardenberg-Novalis's *Hymnen an die Nacht* (1800; *Hymns to Night*), with their poetic derivation from Hardenberg's biographical yearning for union with his dead fiancée. Mann's superlative transmedial rendering of the music in words makes this genealogy clear.[3] The definitive identification of this kind of art with Romanticism is however Gabriele. On her first appearance and again during the central *Tristan* episode she wears a dress covered with opulent, embossed velvet arabesques (pp. 172, 191), which – if Klöterjahn is life – reveal her to be nothing less than the Romantic muse – death – personified. The arabesque, we know, is the Romantics' favoured aesthetic means ironically to encompass the infinite in the finite, and as such the sig-nature par excellence of the Romantic world view, encompassing the unity of love, life and death. Friedrich Schlegel's novel *Lucinde* (1799) is in formal terms the very paradigm of the arabesque. Its advocacy of Romantic suicide makes it also the very paradigm of that apparently morbid world view.[4] *This*, then, is what Gabriele, arabesque incarnate, embodies.[5] As Mann's sly allusions to the Darwinian doctrine of his first novel *Buddenbrooks* (1901; *The Buddenbrooks*) make clear (the aesthetic Gabriele is last in the degen-erating line of a once-vigorous Bremen merchant dynasty), he is suggesting that this kind of art – *Romantic* art, if not necessarily the art of Thomas

Mann – is intrinsically morbid, linked with decay and best kept behind the walls of the sanatorium (which indeed seems to be Spinell's natural habitat). Clearly Mann is in one of his more Goethean moods here, and *Tristan* is not only a rewriting of Nietzsche but also of Goethe's notorious dictum: 'Das Klassische nenne ich das Gesunde und das Romantische das Kranke' ('I call the Classical the healthy and the Romantic the sick') – an intimidatingly authoritative view which dominated the reception of German Romanticism until well after the end of the Second World War.[6]

Thus *Tristan* is simply one example. Mann repeated the substance of this critique in the Pfitzner passages of his *Betrachtungen eines Unpolitischen* (1918; *Reflections of an Unpolitical Man*), which go so far as to characterise the creativity of the German soul as being rooted paradoxically in a Romantic sympathy with death. Ricarda Huch, the doyenne of German Romantic scholarship around 1900 and author of a classic work on it (structured, of course, on the model of organic growth and decay), devoted an entire chapter of her first volume to death. Walther Rehm in 1928 devoted the longest (and last) chapter of his important study of the theme of death in German literature to Romanticism. And the association of Romanticism, love and death was equally firm outside of Germany. Mario Praz's peerless *Romantic Agony* (1933), with its revelation that Romanticism propagated the perverse as well as the ethereal understanding of beauty, established for decades the normal paradigm of scholarship outside germanophone lands. It was in this tradition that Siegbert Prawer in 1952 wrote a memorable invective against Hardenberg-Novalis's 'dangerous' yearning for the love-death. More recently, Philippe Ariès, in his standard cultural history of death (1978), still associates Romanticism with an erotic death cult around 1800.[7]

That said, with the arrival of an age of anti-ideology in the 1950s and epoch-making new historical-critical editions of Hardenberg's and Friedrich Schlegel's works, a revisionist trend subtly yet silently shifted the focus of Romantic studies. The standard introductions to Romanticism of Ernst Behler and Lothar Pikulik (both 1992)[8] barely give death (or life, or love) a mention, preferring to talk of 'Religion' or 'Erotik'. Pikulik, having briskly asserted that early Romanticism accounts for the entire inventory of conceptual innovation in the Romantic movement as a whole, lists wit, experimentation, hypothetical speculation, irony, analogy, the encyclopaedia and the *Fragment* as key indicators of the Romantic mentality, but not death. More recent work has, it is true, noted the (decidedly Goethean) affinity for *life* connotated by the (decidedly un-Goethean) Romantic engagement with death, at least in Hardenberg's case.[9] Otherwise – strikingly in view of the great recent popularity of death as a theme in cultural history (which in addition to Ariès has produced distinguished work by Elisabeth Bronfen and Jonathan Dollimore) – there has in recent decades reigned almost complete silence on the theme of death (and love) in German Romanticism.[10]

And yet if we take Hardenberg (together with Friedrich Schlegel) as the representative thinker of the movement, we find a man who emphatically asserts of Romanticisation (surely the key word in the movement's conceptuality) this: 'Der Tod ist das romantisirende Princip unsers Lebens. Der Tod ist das – das Leben das + . Durch den Tod wird das Leben verstärkt' ('Death is the romanticising principle of our life. Death is the negative, life the positive. Life is reinforced by death', *NS* III, p. 559, No. 30). In Schelling – perhaps even more than Fichte *the* philosopher of German Romanticism – we find the paradoxical view that sickness itself, as part of the process of negation and synthesis which enacts becoming, is but another form of life, and conversely that life itself is merely one form of illness, from which death represents recovery and redemption.[11] Both statements suggest that the Romantic attitude to death is on one hand less morbid than Thomas Mann and the older tradition of scholarship believe and on the other more significant than the newer tradition of scholarship yet acknowledges. In what follows therefore I shall briefly sketch the significance of death in selected texts of German Romanticism as part of my case to return to the theme of death as a central focus of Romantic thought.

What did the Romantics think of death existentially, outside of the aesthetic sphere? As a cultural movement situated on the cusp of the transition from tradition to modernity, their attitudes characteristically exhibit both pre-modern and modern features. The young Hardenberg, for example – very much an Enlightenment thinker and devotee of neologistic theology in the style of Johann Joachim Spalding – in 1788 wrote an elegiac poem in remembrance of the popular Leipzig preacher Johann Georg Zollikofer (*NS* I, p. 459), which offers comfort to the mourners through an appeal to ancient physiognomic and metaphysical tradition: by recognising in the smile on the face of his human remains the consoling physical trace of Zollikofer's first, blissful encounter with immortality (rather than extinction). August Klingemann's marvellously sceptical *Nachtwachen* (1805; *Nightwatches*)[12] trump this in their first major scene. Here at dead of night we met a dedicated freethinker, who is being harassed on his deathbed by a (clearly Roman Catholic) priest. This priest, as he bellows ruthless exhortations to repent into the ear of the (now to all intents and purposes lifeless) remains, exemplifies belief in another surviving popular tradition, that life still dwells in the material body until the process of decay sets in,[13] and that the sense of hearing is the last to dull. The nightwatchman is much less sure. As he observes the body displayed in death (*Nachtwachen*, p. 15), he, like the young Hardenberg before Zollikofer, notices the smile on its face. But he is unable to decide on the meaning of this semblance of life: is it the expression of the freethinker's satisfaction that his infidelity has been validated, or the opposite, the smile of one who has reawakened in the beyond and can only signal ironic amusement at his own earthly foolishness?

The nightwatchman will later decide his view, but undecidability on the question and (so to speak) positive indifference is in fact characteristic of the early Romantic position on death. Friedrich Daniel Ernst Schleiermacher's *Über die Religion: Reden an die Gebildeten unter ihren Verächtern* (1799; *On Religion: Addresses to its Cultivated Despisers*)[14] are of course the Romantic counterblast to ecclesiastical or rationalistic orthodoxy of any colour in an age of rapid secularisation. Schleiermacher's desire both to restore the place of religion in modern consciousness and to overcome the contradictions of existing positive systems leads him, we know, to identify a particular domain of human consciousness as properly religious and to define that domain reductively as the site for the imaginative intuition of the infinite. That in turn is for Schleiermacher the source of the quintessentially religious feeling of absolute dependence and nothing less than the common denominator of religious experience across all systematised expressions of positive religious belief. This move however privileges subjectivity. It makes subjective choice decisive in modern religious experience, privileges the individual virtuosi of religion (and creators of new positive religions), and collapses any meaningful distinction between competing doctrines. This anti-dogmatic streak thus makes it for Schleiermacher finally a matter of indifference whether the divine is worshipped as a personal or impersonal deity and positively dangerous to seek God through a dogmatic faith in personal immortality. Instead, unity with the infinite – and that means dissolution of the self – is the way (*Reden*, p. 246). What the Romantics preferred, then, to dogmatic faith – or sceptical disbelief – in the story of the things that may follow death was imaginative experience by the privileged subject of the infinite in *this*, the finite realm – a sort of secularised version of Lutheran *gratia praeveniens* (pre-emptive grace). From this perspective a theological reading of (for example) the epiphanic temporal structure of Hardenberg's *Heinrich von Ofterdingen* (1800–2) as its pilgrim hero makes his way to a new Jerusalem becomes possible.[15]

The latitudinarian stance of modern Romantic religion – accepting the fact of death, indifferent to the dogma of afterlife, yet insistent upon experience of the boundless presence of the infinite in order to overcome death – also underlies the allegedly morbid Romantic attitude to suicide. The Romantics abhorred the orthodox (Augustinian) Christian condemnation of suicide and offered an (in their sense) religious version of the tolerant antique or Enlightenment views. Friedrich Schlegel's *Lucinde* gives the definitive theoretical account of Romantic suicide, which differs not only from *Werther* but also from the self-evidently morbid, denunciatory variants of Wagner or Thomas Mann with which we began our meditation. Here Lucinde's lover Julius asserts that she would indeed, like a Hindu widow, serenely choose to follow him into death. But this serenely willed (rather than impassioned) act of Romantic suicide is not a Wagnerian love-death in the sense of a statement of positive belief in the subsequent metaphysical union of souls, an affirmation of illusion or impassioned denial of life. The emphasis lies rather on the finite side of the equation, for we should recognise that Lucinde's putative suicide is a carefully constructed, simultaneously *ethical* and *aesthetic* act: the wilful foreshortening of the narrative thread of her biography. This act does not so much deny life as aestheticise it: transform her earthly existence into the ultimate Romantic *Fragment*. As such it symbolises the subject's paradoxical encapsulation of the infinite in the finite, performs the sovereign triumph of love over death, and affirms the absoluteness of her love. Even the cynical nightwatchman – if only for a moment – alludes admiringly to this theory (*Nachtwachen*, p. 9). Karoline von Günderrode echoes it in 'Die malabarischen Witwen' (1805; 'The Widows of Malabar'), and her *Briefe zweier Freunde* (1805; *Letters of Two Friends*) qualify the outcome of the love-death as the union not of souls, but of ultimate elements of the self which evince affinity with the beloved other. They will eventually (in the Schellingian cycle of life) be reborn in the world in some new, higher combination.

This is also the sense in which the arch-Romantic Hardenberg saw death as the Romanticising principle of life. The evidence of this is his deployment of the antique analogy of sleep and death. Reintroduced by Lessing into the modern discourse of death in *Wie die Alten den Tod gebildet* (1767; *How the Ancients Pictured Death*), the analogy was the favourite instrument of Enlightenment philosophers for managing the fear of death, then particularly heightened thanks to the process of secularisation. If Lessing had argued that the seductive equation of sleep and death, figured as a beautiful youth and his mirror image rather than the gruesome skeleton or hooded scytheman of later Christian epochs, might picture the human encounter with mortality less terrifyingly for us moderns, and Schiller had echoed both wish and image in his sentimental elegy 'Die Götter Griechenlands' (1788; 'The Gods of Greece'), Hardenberg – provoked perhaps by Herder's attack on the image's underlying euphemistic quality – attempted in the *Hymnen* to show how the living Christ might be identified with *this* god of antiquity and so made newly plausible to the secularised mind. The *Hymnen* of course famously show how the resurrection – Christ stepping from the grave – might be rendered as the beautiful youth of antiquity physically stepping forth Pygmalion-like from the gravestone and becoming flesh. Thus the underlying continuity of Greek and Christian religion is established à la Schleiermacher. Both Christ and the beautiful Greek youth may be construed as intuitions of the infinite. More significantly, one is richer than the other. In Christ's person the realms of life *and* death are (aesthetically) demonstrated to be united. In this way the encounter with death is paradoxically *also* an encounter with the hidden principle of life, so that the apparently morbid fascination with death turns out for Hardenberg to be a revelation and the transcendental aesthetic therapy for the sickness of the age (its failure to understand death): 'Im Tode ward das ewge Leben kund, / Du bist der Tod und machst uns erst gesund' (*NS* I, p. 147; 'In death eternal life was made known, / You are death and you alone restore our health').

Thus even if it ultimately signifies renewed commitment to life, there *is* something fundamental for the Romantic mentality about the confrontation with death. This harsh and today unfashionable truth – despite all other commonalities[16] – ought to relativise our judgement of Goethe's hostility to the movement. Goethe was from this standpoint both right and wrong. His novel *Die Wahlverwandtschaften* (1809–10; *Elective Affinities*) contains a virulent attack on the Romantic fascination with death. The lovers Eduard and Ottilie are not merely potentialised versions of Werther and Lotte. They are also, as revealed by their sense of predestination, obsession with animal magnetism, androgynous complementarity, mutual mimicry and suicidal willingness to follow each other into death, Goethe's citation of the fundamental Romantic idea as set out in *Lucinde*. The evidently Romantic quality of the lovers is reinforced by the sacral aura which the narrator inscribes around the person of Ottilie, which suggests her sanctification and transfiguration after death and so might seem to valorise the suicide in typically Romantic style. However, Goethe's drastic foregrounding of the narrator's increasingly biased sympathy with Ottilie simultaneously undermines that strategy of representation, and suggests conversely that Ottilie, whilst a tragic and sympathetic figure, is for Goethe (rather than his narrator) in truth a pathological case who simply starves herself to death. But if this is Goethe's verdict on Romanticism, it is clear from the aforegoing analysis of *Lucinde* how foreshortened his interpretation of *Lucinde* in fact is, and how emphatic the vitalism is that underlies it.

Now, having sought to re-establish the Romantic preoccupation with death and revalorise it as paradoxically serving the purpose of life, it must still be acknowledged that German Romanticism conceals ethically suspect and macabre elements. Zacharias Werner (1768–1823), one of the most prominent yet rarely treated writers of the second Romantic generation, is a case in point. His writings push the Romantic will to confront death to the level of systematic obsession and belong to those which most pungently offended Goethe's taste. If Friedrich Schlegel's notion of Romantic suicide involves a lover's serene and sovereign choice to take poison, and Hardenberg permits himself occasional allusions to the yearning for death, Werner's dramatic works (at least prior to his conversion in 1810 and ordination in 1814) modulate the self-sacrifice of the beloved – almost always the female – into a ritualised necessity of self-slaughter, which (by contrast to the austere classicism in this regard of Schlegel and Hardenberg) is habitually presented in its full, grisly and garish, anti-classical plasticity.[17] If after his conversion Werner attempts to minimise the sexual aspects of his presentation of death, he nevertheless continues compulsively to foreground its manneristic, stomach-turning physicality.

Of this Werner's aptly named 'Der Sieg des Todes' (1813–14; 'The Triumph of Death'),[18] a mediaevalising ballad derived directly from Italian experiences, is a good example. In a note, Werner informs the reader that the poem is inspired by an encounter in Pisa at the Camposanto with a fourteenth-century fresco *Il trionfo della morte* (1334–42; *The Triumph of Death*) by the Florentine master 'Andreas Orgagna'.[19] Werner's horrific tale is ostensibly a *memento mori* for the secularised modern age. Closely following the narrative of the painting, it tells of the adventure which befalls a hunting party organised by Luccan nobility for their guests when they tire of the pleasures of music. On the forest path, as the crowned heads vaingloriously celebrate their elevated role in life and its apparent promise of eternity, they unexpectedly encounter in open coffins the corpses of three apparently murdered tyrant kings, presented by the narrator as justly punished for their crimes. Words fail the living regents at this repellent vision of divine judgement. Queen Mechtildis cries tears of sympathy symbolic of the visceral mode of cognition for which Werner clearly strives. But only awesome Saint Macarius, witnessing the scene from his mountain-top hermitage, finds the appropriate text: '"Ihr, gewogen und zu leicht befunden, / Bebt!"' ('"You, who have been weighed and found wanting, / Tremble!"'; Werner, p. 97). As the vision fades, the sobered kings move on, along the same path, with death now waving his banner in triumph over them. Their subsequent fate is not known, although Mechtildis heeds the warning, takes the veil, and prays on each All Soul's Day that the Princes may grow wise.

In truth this ballad is however in the technical sense over-determined, and the over-determination reveals the latent meaning to be other than the manifest homiletic lesson. Nearly a third of Werner's text is devoted to a set-piece lurid description of the three corpses in carefully graduated stages of decomposition, and here the moral commentary by the narrator for the secular modern mind takes second place to the gleeful evocation of dripping gore, rotten flesh, distended bellies, noxious vapours, a tongue erect in rigor mortis, a grinning skull and squirming serpents. Certainly the passage can also be legitimated by the requirement of ekphrastic correspondence. And Werner does render pretty well in words what 'Orgagna' (Buffalmacco) painted. But the exaggeration is palpable. Werner's secular sermon in fact derives a perverse (manneristic) pleasure from dwelling on the depiction of the unbeautiful which its high moral tone merely veils. The triumph of death is not just a timely corrective reminder of the inevitable but also – as the erect tongue suggests to our Freud-schooled vision – the indicator of death's perverse colonisation of Werner's excited fantasy. Elsewhere, Werner links this sexually charged morbidity both with a certain misogyny (he celebrates the creation of new life through a male act of necrophilia) and the Romantic belief that the essence of life (evidenced by phosphorescence) escapes from living matter in the process of decay.[20]

The nightwatchman, as ever the welcome corrective to Romantic over-determinations, satirises such things in his last chapter, when, in his final search for the remains of his father in the cemetery, he encounters a strange young man haunting the graves. This person, clearly a Romantic lover modelled on Hardenberg and Hardenberg's less philosophical imitators, is gifted with a sixth sense permitting him to recognise the shapes of those buried in the earth with clarity in inverse proportion to the degree of the body's decomposition (*Nachtwachen*, pp. 179ff.). The nightwatchman abandons him just as he pathetically embraces the almost completely decayed form of his beloved, before she finally vanishes. *This*, then, is the aspect of Romanticism which Thomas Mann means to emphasise when he has the beardless and sterile Detlef Spinell, lover of the arabesque Gabriele, bear the sobriquet 'der verweste Säugling' ('the decayed baby'; *Tristan*, p. 176), and quake at the final confrontation with the rather more vital child Anton. But *Lucinde* is the wrong victim of this satire. Moreover, even if there *does*, undeniably, exist such a streak of sadistically eroticised thanatology in *some* Romantic writers, why do we think differently of Heinrich von Kleist? In Kleist a baby's brains are spilled against a cathedral wall by a flailing fundamentalist, a man's corpse has a scroll rammed into its mouth, a woman feeds greedily on blood at the breast of a man just slaughtered by her dogs, a raped girl's body is cut into segments and distributed as mementos to the tribes of Germany, a man swallows the barrel of a pistol, shoots out the back of his head and splatters the wall behind.

It is unnecessary to dwell on the deep structures possibly implicit in the possible over-determinations of Kleist's imagery.[21] But the point is clear. Romanticism *does* have a fundamental relation with death. However, that relation with death in the most sophisticated proponents of the idea is placed at the service of life. Moreover Romanticism is not alone in that preoccupation. In truth, of course, both Goethe and the Romantics *and* Kleist share a fascination with death which self-evidently haunts Goethe's pages even without the need to polemicise against Romanticism. The fascination with death, as Hardenberg so clearly diagnosed, is in fact a signature feature of the literature of the age, and it is no longer acceptable to espouse Goethe's one-sided judgements on Romantic thanatocentrism as canonical and authoritative. The silencing of scholarly interest even today on the the theme of death in Romanticism is surely one last consequence of that superannuated anathema. That mutual concern with death today merits treatment systematically and in unprejudiced fashion in terms of the new scholarly thanatology. Romanticism's breaking of the death taboo,[22] the treatment of mourning in *Heinrich von Ofterdingen, Godwi* or *Die Wahlverwandtschaften*, the problem of Romantic suicide, the problem of death's place in that central Romantic concept, the theory of the growing and decaying organism, the relation of physical decay with spiritual becoming,[23] the relation of Romantic subjectivism with the otherness of death and *other* othernesses:[24] all these aspects await the gaze of tomorrow's researchers.

NOTES

1. See Andrew Bowie, *From Romanticism to Critical Theory. The Philosophy of German Literary Theory* (London and New York: Routledge, 1997); also Manfred Frank, '"Intellektuale Anschauung": Drei Stellungnahmen zu einem Deutungsversuch von Selbstbewußtsein: Kant, Fichte, Hölderlin/Novalis', in *Die Aktualität der Frühromantik*, eds. Ernst Behler and Jochen Hörisch (Paderborn, Munich, Vienna, Zurich: Schöningh, 1987), pp. 96–126.
2. Citations are from Thomas Mann, *Sämtliche Erzählungen* (Frankfurt am Main: Fischer, 1963), pp. 170–206. Henceforth cited as *Tristan*.
3. Compare 'Wer liebend des Todes Nacht und ihr süßes Geheimnis erschaute, dem blieb im Wahn des Lichtes ein einzig Sehnen, die Sehnsucht hin zur heiligen Nacht, der ewigen, wahren, der einsmachenden' (*Tristan*, p. 193) with the rhetoric of Hardenberg's first and fourth *Hymnen*.
4. See on this Nicholas Saul, 'Morbid? Suicide, Freedom, Human Dignity and the German Romantic Yearning for Death', in *Historical Reflections / Réflexions historiques* (2006), pp. 579–99.
5. Compare the classic essay of Wolfdietrich Rasch: 'Thomas Manns *Tristan*', in *Zur deutschen Literatur der Jahrhundertwende: Gesammelte Aufsätze* (Stuttgart: Metzler, 1967), pp. 146–85.
6. See Goethe's conversations with Eckermann, 2 April 1829. On this Nicholas Saul, 'The Reception of German Romanticism in the Twentieth Century', in Dennis F. Mahoney (ed.), *The Literature of German Romanticism* (Rochester, N.Y.: Camden House, 2004), pp. 327–59.

7. See Ricarda Huch, *Die Romantik: Blüthezeit der Romantik: Ausbreitung in Verfall*, 2 vols., 3rd edn (Leipzig: Haessel, 1908–12); Walther Rehm, *Der Todesgedanke in der deutschen Dichtung* (Halle: Niemeyer, 1928), pp. 358–473; Mario Praz, *The Romantic Agony* (Oxford University Press, 1970; 1st edn, 1933); Siegbert Prawer, 'Novalis: "Sehnsucht nach dem Tode"', in *German Lyric Poetry: A Critical Analysis of Selected Poems from Klopstock to Rilke* (London: Routledge and Kegan Paul, 1952), pp. 112–20; Philippe Ariès, *The Hour of Our Death*, trans. Helen Weaver (London: Allen Lane, 1981; 1st edn, Paris 1978).

8. See Ernst Behler, *Frühromantik* (Berlin and New York: de Gruyter, 1992); Lothar Pikulik, *Frühromantik: Epoche – Werk – Wirkung* (Munich: Beck, 1992). Compare in the anglophone tradition Glyn Tegai Hughes, *Romantic German Literature* (London: Arnold, 1979); Alan Menhennet, *The Romantic Movement* (London: Croom Helm, 1981); Dennis F. Mahoney (ed.), *The Literature of German Romanticism* (Rochester, N.Y.: Camden House, 2004), where indexes record sporadic, decreasing and finally no references to death.

9. Herbert Uerlings, *Novalis* (Stuttgart: Reclam, 1998), pp. 148ff. See also Saul, 'Morbid?'.

10. Elisabeth Bronfen, *Over Her Dead Body: Death, Femininity and the Aesthetic* (Manchester: Manchester University Press, 1992); Jonathan Dollimore, *Death, Desire and Loss in Western Culture* (London: Allen Lane, 1998). The exception of course is the gender dimension of research in Romanticism, where however (as in Bronfen) the emphasis is on the mortification of the female rather than the ontological problem of death itself.

11. F. W. J. Schelling, *Erster Entwurf eines Systems der Naturphilosophie*, in *Schriften von 1799–1801* (Darmstadt: Wissenschaftliche Buchgesellschaft, 1975), pp. 1–269, here pp. 222f.

12. *Nachtwachen von Bonaventura*, ed. Wolfgang Pfeiffer–Belli (Coberg: Winkler, 1947).

13. See Ariès, *The Hour of Our Death*.

14. F. D. E. Schleiermacher, *Über die Religion: Reden an die Gebildeten unter ihren Verächtern* (1799), in *Kritische Gesamtausgabe*, eds. Hans-Joachim Birkner *et al.* (Berlin and New York: de Gruyter, 1984–), Section 1: *Schriften und Entwürfe*, vol. II: *Schriften und Entwürfe aus der Berliner Zeit 1796–1799*, ed. Günter Meckenstock (1984), pp. 185–326.

15. See Anthony Phelan's essay in this volume.

16. See Jane Brown's essay in this volume.

17. See Nicholas Saul, 'The Body, Death, Mutilation and Decay in Zacharias Werner', in *German Life and Letters*, n. s. 52 (1999), pp. 255–70.

18. In Zacharias Werner, *Ausgewählte Werke*, 15 vols. (Grimma: Verlags-Comptoir, 1840–1), vol. II, pp. 3–7.

19. Correctly: Andrea Orcagna (1308–c.68). The work is now thought to be by Buffalmacco (Buonamico di Martino, active 1315–36). See Alexander Perrig, 'Malerei und Skulptur des Spätmittelalters', in Rolf Toman (ed.), *Die Kunst der italienischen Renaissance: Architektur, Skulptur, Malerei, Zeichnung* (Cologne: Könemann, 1994), pp. 36–95, esp. pp. 76f.

20. See Saul, 'The Body'.

21. Compare Gerhard Schulz, 'Todeslust bei Kleist und einigen seiner Zeitgenossen', in *Kleist-Jahrbuch* (1990), pp. 113–25.
22. See on more contemporary aspects of this Kate Berridge, *Vigor Mortis: The End of the Death Taboo* (London: Profile, 2001).
23. A good beginning on the *Naturphilosophie* of this has been made by Stefan Graetzel, *Die philosophische Entdeckung des Leibes* (Stuttgart: Steiner, 1989), pp. 88–97.
24. See Zygmund Bauman, *Mortality, Immortality and Other Life Strategies* (London: Polity, 1992); also Emmanuel Lévinas, most easily accessible in Seán Hand (ed.), *The Lévinas Reader* (Oxford: Blackwell, 1989).

FURTHER READING

Alvarez, A., *The Savage God: A Study of Suicide* (Harmondsworth: Penguin, 1971)

Améry, Jean, *Hand an sich legen: Diskurs über den Freitod* (Stuttgart: Klett-Cotta, 1976)

Anz, Thomas, 'Der schöne und der häßliche Tod: Klassische und moderne Normen literarischer Diskurse über den Tod', in *Klassik und Moderne: Die Weimarer Klassik als historisches Ereignis und Herausforderung im kulturgeschichtlichen Prozeß: Walter Müller-Seidel zum 65. Geburtstag*, eds. Karl Richter and Jörg Schönert (Stuttgart: Metzler, 1983), pp. 409–32

Freud, Sigmund, *Jenseits des Lustprinzips*, in *Studienausgabe*, ed. Alexander Mitscherlich *et al.*, 14 vols. (Frankfurt am Main: Suhrkamp, 1982), vol. III, pp. 217–72

Das Unbehagen in der Kultur, in *Studienausgabe*, vol. IX, pp. 191–270

Minois, Georges, *History of Suicide: Voluntary Death in Western Culture*, trans. Lydia G. Cochrane (Baltimore and London: Johns Hopkins University Press, 1999; 1st edn, Paris: Fayard, 1995)

Wöbkemeier, Rita, *Erzählte Krankheit: Medizinische und literarische Phantasien um 1800* (Stuttgart: Metzler, 1990)

II

ANDREW BOWIE

Romantic philosophy and religion

Philosophical definitions

'Romanticism' has often been regarded as being impossible to define in a clear manner, and there is very little agreement on what characterises philosophers who, even just in a German context, can be specifically termed 'Romantic'. Some commentators restrict the term 'Romantic philosophy' to the 'early German', 'Jena' Romantics, Friedrich Schlegel and Friedrich von Hardenberg (Novalis) and, sometimes, F. D. E. Schleiermacher and K. W. F. Solger, whereas others include Immanuel Kant, G. W. F. Hegel, Arthur Schopenhauer, Friedrich Nietzsche and others. If we look at a characteristically provocative remark by a philosopher and writer who helped to bring the term Romantic into common usage, we can both elucidate the issue of definitions and get a sense of how one self-styled Romantic philosopher regards the task of philosophy. Friedrich Schlegel talks of the 'Ungeheurer Irrthum, daß von jedem Begriff nur *Eine* Definition möglich sei' ('Massive mistake, that only *One* definition is possible of every concept'), and he suggests that we should rather seek 'Unendlich viele ... reale synthetische' ('infinitely many ... real synthetic [definitions]').[1]

In the *Kritik der reinen Vernunft* (1781, second, expanded edition 1787; *Critique of Pure Reason*) Kant is also overtly suspicious of the idea that concepts can be strictly defined. He claims that definition is really only possible for mathematical axioms, and that 'meine Erklärung kann besser eine Deklaration (meines Projekts) als Definition eines Gegenstandes heißen' ('my explanation [of a concept] can better be termed a declaration (of my project) than a definition of an object').[2] Explaining a concept is thus inseparable from inquiry into what that concept applies to. Both Kant's and Schlegel's approaches to defining concepts point to a direction in philosophy which questions some key assumptions about the nature of language and thought that are still widely held in significant parts of philosophy today.

The direction in question is perhaps most familiar from the later Wittgenstein's approach to language. Wittgenstein understood words as tools that can be used for different purposes, so that they need not be regarded primarily in terms of a definition of their meaning. Such an approach already started to emerge in the work of J. G. Hamann and J. G. Herder in the second half of the eighteenth century, who moved away from the idea that the primary function of language is to 'represent' already constituted objects, towards the idea that language helps to *constitute* what things are. Hamann and Herder were interested in the fact that things can be seen in a whole variety of ways, depending on what they are used for, which aspect of them is picked out by the words used in relation to them, etc. The questioning of 'representationalism' as a theory of language is part of what I want to claim can be justifiably termed 'Romantic'.[3] A Romantic position is, in these terms, one which questions whether a definitive philosophical account can be given of the relationship between what is subjective and what is objective. Hardenberg puts this in terms of both a picture and the original not being fixed quantities: a picture can, for example, enable one to see something in new ways, which would not be possible if it merely re-presented, in the sense of 'presented again what is already there', what it depicts.

How, then, is thought to be determinate at all if, as Schlegel contends, it is supposed to keep producing new 'synthetic' definitions, i.e. definitions which arise from new combinations of terms? The seventeenth-century rationalist philosopher Baruch Spinoza contended that one can only define what something is by saying what it is not, so that 'all determination is negation'. Defining red, for instance, cannot be achieved by appealing to an intrinsic attribute 'red' that is known independently of all the relationships of red to other things. When defining red (as opposed to just pointing to an example of it) we can only contrast red with other attributes, showing that it is not orange, yellow, green, etc., and that it is also not a geometrical shape, and so on.[4] If we wanted definitively to say what something is, we would therefore have to go through the rest of the universe. This seems to lead to the impossibility of conclusively defining anything. On the other hand – and this is Schlegel's point – the more we are able to relate something to the relevant things that it is not, the richer our sense of how to characterise the thing can become, even though there may be no end to that characterisation. Any characterisation may also change over time, as new relations become more relevant than the relations which preceded them.

Such an approach is more commonly associated with artistic responses to the world, but it is not incompatible with doing natural science. The widely held idea that Romantic philosophy should be understood as rejecting the results of the modern natural sciences, because they somehow alienate us from the natural world, is generally mistaken. (The issue is more complex with regard to Romantic literature, especially in Britain.) Many German Romantic thinkers, like Hardenberg's friend Johann Wilhelm Ritter, who discovered ultraviolet light, were seriously involved in scientific research. The real point of Romantic philosophical questioning of the sciences is to explore how what can be explained scientifically fits in with aspects of human existence which resist law-bound, causal explanation. This questioning can, as it often does in Ritter – and in F. W. J. Schelling – lead to problematic speculation, based on analogies rather than on precise observation, but it is also able to suggest perspectives on how we relate to the natural world which a conventionally scientific approach may obscure.

The conceptual structures which inform the philosophy of the Romantic period are inherent in the issue of definition, and can be further specified by distinguishing two differing ideas of 'infinity'. If definition takes place within a closed system like geometry, the totality of relations that would make a definition complete can be spelt out, and infinity would be determinate. A point located in an enclosed space will relate to an infinity of other points in that space, but these will all be locatable via their relations to each other within the space. If, in contrast, what is in question cannot legitimately be *proven* to be closed, because we have no way of characterising it as a whole, the totality of relations becomes impossible to describe. Each element therefore stands in an indeterminate series of relations to every other element, and infinity becomes indeterminate, even if we still assume that there is a totality of elements. If we think of Spinoza's rationalist view as implying that reality itself functions like a geometrical system, the questioning of rationalism in the Romantic period can be seen as involving doubts about whether we can positively claim that reality is a closed system of this kind. Two figures in particular are vital in the genesis of Romantic ideas from these issues, the first is Kant, and the second is F. H. Jacobi, the writer, philosopher and friend of Goethe.[5]

Both Kant and Jacobi are concerned with the question of what it means for something to be a 'condition' (*Bedingung*) of something else. For Kant the world of the laws of nature is a world of 'conditions', in which the explanation of a phenomenon depends upon seeking its condition. Each particular thing in the world is conditioned by other things which are in turn conditioned by other things, and so on. This chain of conditions therefore leads to something analogous to the problem of attempting to give a complete definition of something. Any particular judgement of how it is that something is the way it is seems to be reliant upon an endless series of prior conditions.

This situation leads to one of Kant's main ideas. He locates the 'conditions of possibility' of knowledge – the prior general forms of thought without which specific phenomena would not be intelligible – in our thinking, rather than in 'things in themselves'. He does so precisely in order to avoid the regress that results from attempting to trace all the conditions of a specific state of affairs in the world. Kant uses the idea of 'the unconditioned' in relation to the notion of the world of conditions. He maintains that 'reason' – the faculty which unifies the rules of thought into the idea of a coherent system – must hypothesise the existence of the '*Unbedingte* ... in den Dingen an sich selbst ... zu allem Bedingten, und dadurch die Reihe der Bedingungen als vollendet' ('*unconditioned* ... in all things in themselves for everything conditioned, so that the series of conditions should thus become complete').[6] Reason has to do this because we can only *know* particular things that are conditioned by other things. Knowledge can only be of 'appearances' given to perception, not of 'things in themselves'. Seeking to know the unconditioned involves a misapprehension of what is it to know: knowledge is the result of the search for the conditions that explain natural phenomena. Hardenberg offers an interpretation of what is implied by Kant when he says, playing on the etymology of the German word for condition: 'Wir suchen überall das Unbedingte, und finden immer nur Dinge' ('We everywhere seek the unconditioned, and always only find things'; *NS* II, p. 412, No. 1). The consequences of this view of the inaccessibility of the unconditioned, or what is also called 'the absolute', will be apparent in the next section, when we contrast German Romantic with German Idealist philosophy.

Kant makes his claims because the world given in 'intuition', '*Anschauung*' (perception), is never exactly the same at any two different moments. Knowledge relies on establishing identities between things, so the sameness of things must be located in the categories of thinking in the 'understanding', not in 'things in themselves', because the appearances to which the latter give rise are never identical at all.[7] We therefore cannot *know* things in themselves, because we only know via the capacity of thinking to subsume different appearances under the same concept. However, thinking still leads for Kant to the idea of the totality of conditions. The whole of nature must be unconditioned, because otherwise it would have to have a condition, whose condition would in turn have to be sought, and so on.

Kant's view of the limits of human knowledge relates to two important ways of thinking about the unconditioned. For Spinoza the unconditioned is to be considered as God, who is that which is cause of itself, rather than, like everything else, being caused by its conditions. Such a characterisation of God was, though, highly controversial, not just in Spinoza's time, but also in the Romantic period and since. This is because for Spinoza God is no longer seen as a personal, providential creator of the universe, who is in some sense outside of His creation (and so does not suffer from its imperfections). The other way of thinking about what is unconditioned emerges because Kant realises that if the world consisted of nothing but chains of conditions, there would be no place for human freedom: our actions would be dictated by the laws of nature.

Kant maintains that our 'spontaneity', the capacity to act in terms of moral maxims which go against our causally determined inclinations, means that our reason can determine our will via a 'causality through freedom'. The term 'spontaneity' is another way of referring to that which is 'cause of itself', rather than being caused by something else. However, Kant does not only regard our will as spontaneous: the understanding is also spontaneous. This is because the universe could just have existed, without knowledge of it occurring at all. Causal processes in material nature are of a different order from the subject's thinking when it understands causes *as* causes. Thinking about causes undoubtedly does rely on causal processes in the brain, but these do not constitute an explanation of the content of thoughts. The status of the subject, which is the basis of both knowing and willing, is a central concern of Romantic philosophy. On the one hand, the subject is an embodied part of physical nature, and, on the other, it appears to exist in a manner which is separate from nature, so that it seems to be inherently divided. The question is whether this division can be overcome, and, if not, how we should respond to the impossibility of overcoming it.

The startling conjunction of the idea of an unconditioned core of subjectivity and the idea of God as the unconditioned suggests a tension between the growing power of the self-determining 'bourgeois' subject, who is being liberated from traditional theological and other constraints, and the sense that this power may be deeply problematic. The success of modern science can be seen as resulting from its ability to *exclude* subjective perspectives from the ways in which nature is understood. This ability is, however, inseparable from the *subject*'s ability to control and manipulate nature, including its own nature. The exclusion of subjective perspectives suggests to some scientists and philosophers that subjectivity itself must be causally explicable, so that the brain, for example, is regarded as essentially just a computer, and the self and its ideas are a mere product of the brain's causally governed processes. This conception echoes vital aspects of what Jacobi finds problematic in Spinoza.

In Jacobi's terms the wholly causal conception has no way of accounting for human goals based on the meanings that arise in the social world. Such meanings are not just based on natural instincts, because they are constituted through language and other forms of social interaction. Furthermore, the reasons for wishing to understand the workings of nature in the first place are not something which science itself can explain in a non-circular manner. There can be no 'science of science': what would decide which aspects of science legislated over the rest of science, apart from another science of science, and so on? The questionable aspects of a reductive scientific approach that are apparent here relate to the reasons why Kant both sets limits on what can be objectively known and yet does not reject the idea of there being aspects of existence which cannot be known. For Kant, if there were no subject to find out how nature works, there would be no *objective* world, though there could be a world 'in itself'.

The problem which ensues from this is how to know about the subject in objective terms. The explanation must come about by the subject's explaining itself, and this would seem to leave what produces the account outside of the account. Hardenberg sometimes uses the image of a painter to show the problem. In a painting in which the painter includes themself as painter of the picture within the picture, they remind the viewer that without them there would be no painting. At the same time, however, the painter appears as an objective image *within* the painting, thus inverting the real state of affairs, which is that the image depends on the painter as creative subject.

The problem of describing spontaneous subjectivity in objective terms leads J. G. Fichte, in the *Wissenschaftslehre* (1794; *Theory of Knowledge*) and other texts, to intensify the Kantian view of the ineliminable role of the subject in the constitution even of the objective world of nature into the idea that the activity of the subject is therefore the basis of the world's being intelligible at all. The tension between the objectivism of the scientific view that is implicit in certain interpretations of Spinoza, and the subjectivism of Fichte's intensification of the Kantian view is the matrix from which Romantic philosophy emerges. It is Jacobi who first reveals problems with both the Fichtean and the Spinozist positions.[8]

The 'Pantheism Controversy', via which Spinoza's work came to public attention in Germany, was occasioned by G. E. Lessing's claim in 1783 to Jacobi that he was a Spinozist, a claim which was tantamount to a declaration of atheism. This led to a bitter and influential dispute between Moses Mendelssohn, the Berlin Enlightenment philosopher, and Jacobi. Jacobi's objection to Spinoza's world of 'conditions of conditions' is that everything that happens would be merely mechanical and devoid of meaning. Thinking therefore has no creative role, of the kind Jacobi regards as essential to what makes even causally based scientific research a part of humanity's 'revelation of existence' in art and science. Our ability to explain in terms of conditions cannot itself be explained in such terms. If one thinks solely in terms of conditions, thinking just regresses into an 'abyss' ('*Abgrund*'), because it cannot reach the unconditioned that would be its basis. Jacobi wishes to prevent this regress by showing the necessity for '*Glaube*', which can mean 'belief' or 'faith'. For him this necessity leads to the idea of God as what prevents the regress of conditions: faith in God is the basis of the inexplicable sense of truth required for anything to be intelligible at all. God therefore cannot be explained. The non-theological version of this idea is that truth cannot be explained because any explanation of it must already presuppose an understanding of truth, otherwise there has to be an explanation of why the explanation of truth is true, etc.

Jacobi's underlying fear is of 'nihilism', which results when the ground of existence is interpreted deterministically. It might seem that he would therefore be enthusiastic about Fichte's grounding of philosophy in the self-determining activity of the subject. Jacobi, however, regards Fichte's elevation of the subject to the founding principle of philosophy as equally prone to nihilism. This is because he is suspicious of any systematic *philosophical* attempt to account for the nature of existence. Knowing the answers in philosophy would render each new piece of knowledge merely the result of a new combination of elements within a game with only a finite number of possibilities. Fichte's I, which grounds intelligibility in human reason, is therefore essentially narcissistic, only seeing what it itself produces. Jacobi thinks that both the Spinozist interpretation of the truth of the world as a rational system of conditioned conditions and the Fichtean interpretation of that truth as the result of the activity of the I are in effect the same, because both seek to explain everything via an abstract philosophical foundation which conjures away the endless diversity of concrete existence. The questioning of Spinozist and Fichtean 'foundationalism' also plays a key role in Romantic philosophy.

Romanticism and German Idealism

Many accounts of German Romantic philosophy (e.g. Berlin, *The Roots of Romanticism*) regard Fichte's idealist claim that the intelligible world is a product of the activity of the I as the core of that philosophy. This is simply mistaken. To explain why, it is important to make a distinction here which was first adumbrated by Walter Benjamin in his dissertation on Romantic criticism in 1919 (Benjamin, *Begriff der Kunstkritik*). This is the distinction between 'German Idealism', which does have to do with Fichte's aim of establishing a foundation for philosophy in subjectivity, and 'early German Romantic philosophy', which came to question a grounding of philosophy in this manner. The problem is that interpretations of German Idealism remain highly contested, it not being clear which philosophers come under the heading.

Philosophical idealism is generally characterised by Bishop Berkeley's claim that 'being is perceiving'. Berkeley's idea is that things exist solely as perceptions – how else, after all, do we *know* that they exist? This is not an easy view to refute. Even Kant thinks that being 'real' means being able to be perceived. German Idealism should, though, not be assumed to be simply another form of Berkeleyan idealism. Its main representatives, Fichte, Schelling and Hegel, regard Kant as the source of their approach, and Kant rejects Berkeley's idealism. Kant's claim to refute idealism is, however, not wholly persuasive, as Salomon Maimon (1753?–1800) demonstrated, so opening the way for Fichte's new version of idealism.[9]

German Idealism is concerned with the relationship between what the subject contributes to the world's intelligibility and what the world contributes. Even though the resistance of the objective world may feel to us like the prior reality, there could be no such resistance without a prior subjective principle that could feel it *as* resistance. The fact that there is an *objective* world entails something subjective which is logically prior to that world if the world is to be manifest *as* objective at all.[10] Something can, in these terms, only be an object, a '*Gegen-stand*', if it 'stands against' what it is not, namely the subject. In Fichte's extreme version of this position the 'absolute I' (not the relative I of any thinking individual) therefore produces the objective world by 'inhibiting' itself, by making itself relative to itself, splitting into objects which are defined by their not being other objects. These objects are not absolute, because they condition each other; the activity of the I, on the other hand, is absolute because it is self-caused, and so is always driven beyond any particular objectification. The essential insight of philosophy for Fichte is consequently into the I as the living principle out of which the world of finite particulars is generated.

During the 1790s Friedrich Hölderlin, Jacobi, Friedrich Schlegel, Hardenberg and Schleiermacher all question Fichte's position in related ways.[11] In his *Über die Religion: Reden an die Gebildeten unter ihren Verächtern* (1799; *On Religion: Addresses to its Cultivated Despisers*), Schleiermacher sums up some of the concern about Fichte's kind of transcendental philosophy: 'Ich frage Euch also: was tut Euere Transzendentalphilosophie? Sie ... entspinnet aus sich selbst die Realität der Welt und ihre Gesetze' ('I ask you, then: what does your ... transcendental philosophy do? It ... spins from itself the reality of the world and its laws').[12] For Schleiermacher transcendental philosophy fails to take account of the fact that our primary relations to the world are not generated by systematic thought, but rather by 'feeling'. This is the basis of his very influential account of religious consciousness as consisting in a sense of the unity of the universe. In the same year Jacobi ironically suggests that the absolute I in Fichte's system is actually like a sock: a sock consists of one thing, the single thread of which it is made, that turns back on itself in complex ways, in order to form itself into something. In both Schleiermacher and Jacobi, Fichte's kind of idealism is regarded as not being open to what cannot be generated by the presuppositions of his system.

Hölderlin already questions Fichte's referring to the absolute as 'I' in 1795. The relationship between subject and object cannot, he thinks, be conceived of from the subjective side alone, and so presupposes a whole which includes both subject and object. This whole cannot be termed an absolute 'I', because an I must be relative to a not-I. Hölderlin therefore terms the whole '*being*', as that within which subject/object, I/not-I relationships take place. For Hardenberg, writing at much the same time, philosophy becomes a 'striving' to think an absolute 'basis' ('*Grund*') that would enable it to be complete by explicating the relationship between subject and object. Hardenberg's position is summed up in the claim: 'Dies uns gegebne Absolute läßt sich nur negativ erkennen, indem wir handelnd finden, daß durch kein Handeln das erreicht wird, was wir suchen' ('The absolute which is given to us can only be recognised negatively by acting and finding that what we are seeking is not reached by any action'; NS II, p. 289, No. 648), and he relies on the paradoxical principle that philosophy is systemlessness ('Systemlosigkeit') brought into a system (NS II, p. 270, No. 566).

The critics of Fichte share the sense that the Idealist philosophical project, which is meant to demonstrate that the structures of thought are isomorphic with the structures of reality, puts the relationship between thinking and being the wrong way round. Schelling, who sometimes argues in an idealist manner, often also insists that, because the 'productivity' of nature which gives rise to living organisms is the prior condition of human existence and human thought, thought cannot fully grasp its own basis, and is 'unconsciously' produced. This sense of our dependence on our natural being will lead him, from the late 1820s onwards, to argue in Romantic fashion against the most impressive attempt at an idealist system, that of Hegel. The argument is that Idealism takes 'predicates' – concepts – as the real subject of being; instead of concepts being what can be predicated of being, they become the prior reality.[13] Romantic philosophy insists, in contrast, on the primacy of being before consciousness and so assumes that being always transcends the way we conceptualise it, which makes a complete system of philosophy impossible. Importantly, this impossibility does not obviate a sense of lack that results from the awareness of the impossibility.

A positive statement of a Romantic position of this kind is, however, open to the objection to any attempt to assert anything general about 'being' made by Hegel in his *Wissenchaft der Logik* (1812–16; *Science of Logic*), where he argues that 'being' is in fact nothing without the conceptual articulation of the ways in which it becomes something. The difference between the Hegelian and the Romantic position has paradigmatic significance for modern philosophy. Hegel contends that nothing is 'immediate', in the sense of 'intelligible independently of its relations to other things'. He attempts to get beyond Fichte by developing a method which would overcome the regresses of foundationalism by not seeking to establish a foundation at the beginning of philosophy. Instead he looks at how knowledge is concretely generated in history. Knowledge comes about, he claims, by truths being refuted, not by positive claims being definitively established. Whereas for many philosophers this would lead to a sceptical attitude, in which certain knowledge is impossible, Hegel thinks that the process of refutation is itself the manifestation of truth.

The final, positive truth is that, by understanding how each particular truth will always be negated by subsequent truths, philosophy can reach a position which overcomes that negativity. Hegel calls this the 'absolute idea', in which each negated truth is also preserved in the higher truth that it makes possible. Ptolemaic astronomy, for instance, is a condition of Galilean astronomy: without an initial 'mediated' view of the working of the heavens that is more than just a mere series of random data, the improved view could not come into being. Gaining access to truths that are available outside such a process is unthinkable, because that would involve relying on something 'immediate', and truth must always be 'mediated'. Philosophy's task is therefore to describe the dynamic structures which mediate particulars by relating them to other particulars. There is for Hegel nothing outside of these structures that could be rationally articulated. This is why he thinks claims about being's transcending of concepts are empty. Exactly how Hegel is to be interpreted remains controversial. His manner of seeking to avoid foundationalism actually comes close to Romantic philosophy, but there is a crucial difference.

The idea that truth cannot be grounded on an initial positive foundation was already sketched by Friedrich Schlegel in lectures which Hegel may have attended in 1801. Schlegel claims that 'Die Wahrheit entsteht, wenn entgegengesetzte Irrthümer sich neutralisiren' ('Truth arises when opposed errors neutralise each other'), but he includes an important proviso: 'Wenn die absolute Wahrheit gefunden wäre, so wäre damit das Geschäft des Geistes vollendet, und er müßte aufhören zu seyn, da er nur in der Thätigkeit existirt' ('If absolute truth were found then the business of spirit would be completed and it would have to cease to be, since it only exists in activity').[14] Elsewhere he makes the suggestion that 'Wahrlich, es würde euch bange werden, wenn die ganze Welt, wie ihr es fodert, einmal im Ernst durchaus verständlich würde' ('In truth you would be distressed if the whole world, as you demand, were for once seriously to become completely comprehensible').[15] What is at issue here is the very status of philosophy and the claims it can make.

Whereas philosophy even today is seen by many people as the search for ultimate truth, Romantic philosophy wants to ask whether this aim is necessarily the most advantageous aim in terms of human flourishing. We have already seen how Hardenberg thinks that the ground philosophy seeks is an 'idea' the concrete realisation of which seems to be impossible. If one does not accept Hegel's treatment of the question of being, which excludes the non-conceptual, the question is what philosophy can say about what is conceptually inaccessible. One response is to claim that the Romantic alternative to Hegel is a mystical surrender of reason before 'the unsayable'. There is a mystical dimension to some of Hardenberg's and Schlegel's thought, but the surrender of conscious thought characteristic of many kinds of mysticism does not square with a concern with Schlegel's idea of 'infinitely many ... real synthetic [definitions]' of concepts. Hardenberg makes it clear that he also has an emphatic sense of the need for rationality, even as he questions the limits of philosophy: 'Ich bin überzeugt, daß man durch kalten, technischen Verstand, und ruhigen, moralischen Sinn eher zu *wahren Offenbarungen* gelangt, als durch Fantasie, die uns blos ins Gespensterreich, diesem Antipoden des wahren Himmels, zu leiten scheint' ('I am convinced that one achieves *true revelations* rather by cold, technical understanding and calm moral sense than by fantasy, which just seems to lead us into the realm of ghosts, this antipode of the true heaven'; NS III, p. 578, No. 182). To see how the concern with the non-conceptual in fact affects the perception of philosophy in Romanticism we need to contrast the relationship between art and philosophy in Hegel and in the early Romantics.

Art and philosophy

Hegel famously announces the 'end of art' in his *Vorlesungen über die Ästhetik* (1820–29; *Lectures on Aesthetics*), because he thinks that the role for art exemplified by Greek tragedy's place in Athenian culture is impossible in modernity. In consequence, 'Die *Wissenschaft* der Kunst ist darum in unserer Zeit noch viel mehr Bedürfnis als zu den Zeiten, in welchen die Kunst für sich als Kunst schon volle Befriedigung gewährte' ('The *science* of art is thus in our time much more necessary than in times in which art for itself as art provided complete satisfaction').[16] The reason is that art is tied to 'sensuous particularity': the truth of a painting depends on presenting a particular thing or scene, of a novel on its individualising social issues in particular characters. For the full truth about an issue to emerge one needs a greater degree of abstraction, which philosophy is supposed to provide. The ultimate insight of philosophy for Hegel is, as we saw, into the finitude of everything particular. The Romantic position is significantly different from Hegel's. Whereas Hegel's position can be seen as contributing to the demythologisation of the world characteristic of modernity, the Romantics think that what gives rise to mythology has not been overcome by modernity, because most people think in sensuous, concrete terms, not abstract theoretical ones. The call for a 'new mythology', which would link the theoretical notions of philosophy and science to sensuous experience, in the form of images and stories, is therefore crucial to Romantic thinking.[17] The problem, they suggest, is that modern art lacks a 'centre', of the kind that mythology represented for ancient cultures, from which to derive collectively binding images and symbols. The question for philosophy is, and remains even today, as the widespread revival of dogmatic religion suggests, how to respond to this situation.

Both the Hegelian and the Romantic positions are 'ironic': in them any positive truth claim is bound eventually to be rescinded. In Hegel's case, however, the irony ceases at the end of the system, because negativity is the path to the Truth. It is not, of course, that we are therefore supposed to know everything concretely. Hegel thinks, rather, that he has shown how appeals to anything that resists conceptualisation involve a failure to understand the real nature of thinking. Romantic irony, on the other hand, does not come to an end, and the sense that we can never rest with a final certainty becomes the essential fact about our existence. Romantic irony is, then, an attitude which tries to find a response to the finitude of individual human existence which is not a positive, philosophical explanation of finitude. This is why art, which emerges from mythology, is assessed differently from the way Hegel assesses it.

In Hegel's system each thing is 'reflected' in all other things. Even before Hegel formulates his key ideas, Schlegel denies that reflection can achieve a total account of thought's relationship to things, and this leads him towards his conception of the philosophical importance of art. He maintains that 'Die Unmöglichkeit das *Höchste* durch Reflexion positiv zu erreichen führt zur Allegorie' ('The impossibility of positively reaching the Highest by reflection leads to allegory').[18] Allegory, which Schlegel associates with modernity, in contrast to symbol, which he associates with older cultures, where God or the Gods can be positively represented, is related to irony because it is a form in which what is represented is not what is meant. The image or story as which the allegory appears is negated, but it is not the case that what the allegory stands for then appears in positive form. Instead Romantic allegory generates a sense of an absence that always points beyond what appears. This results in the feeling that Schlegel calls 'longing'. Longing is not an indeterminate wish for something inaccessible, because it goes together with the understanding, the capacity for knowledge. The point is that the knowledge produced by the understanding needs to be complemented by something else. Schlegel attributes considerable importance, for instance, to forms like music, which resist being converted into conceptual terms and so manifest what is meant by longing.[19]

There are two main ways of seeing the sense of inherent lack that informs Romantic philosophy: one is in terms of the idea that complete knowledge of anything is impossible, which means that we need philosophical ways of responding to cognitive limits. These ways form the basis of what Hegel seeks to do by showing how thought goes beyond the conditioned to the absolute idea. The other is in terms of the idea that relating to the world in a purely cognitive way entails an impoverishment of human existence. The sense of incompletion which goes along with our sense of finitude leads to the need for other kinds of response. Hardenberg sums this up in his suggestion that philosophy is 'eigentlich Heimweh – *Trieb überall zu Hause zu seyn*' ('really homesickness – *drive to be at home everywhere*'; NS III, p. 434, No. 857), and he claims that music, the art in which time plays a constitutive role, enables the mind to be 'auf diese kurzen Augenblicke in seiner irdischen Heymath' ('for short moments in its earthly home'; NS III, p. 283, No. 245). Philosophy, then, cannot enable us to be at home, being only the 'drive' that generates the feeling of lack. The problem with philosophical expressions of the absolute is that they ultimately come down to saying 'A=A', in that the truth of the world is supposed to be repeated in thought. The philosophical demand for a totally articulated, transparent system can be construed in these terms as leading to empty abstraction, whereas art's resistance to being definitively interpreted and the constant demand for innovation inherent in modern art make possible a more diverse and open relationship to the world.

Schlegel's stance is not a precursor of later, Nietzsche-derived, postmodern scepticism, which seeks to subvert truth by revealing its basis in something else, such as power, but it also does not adopt Hegel's totalising answer to the sceptic. His point is that the search for truth need not just be a philosophical task, but will involve all the expressive and other means available, which are likely to be paradoxical and contradictory. What, though, does this sort of philosophical approach mean in concrete social and political terms, if it is seen in the light of the subsequent technological application of the sciences and the modern development of the state in often repressive forms?

Hegel's appraisal of art's diminishing role in modernity seems more justified than the Romantic elevation of art in relation to philosophy. The fact is that the versions of Romantic philosophy offered by Hardenberg, Schlegel and Schleiermacher[20] do not have a major historical influence on other philosophers.[21] Schopenhauer takes up the idea of art's importance for philosophy, but he just makes art a temporary respite from the torment of the Will, rather than regarding art, as Schlegel does, as a means of seeing things anew. Nietzsche at his best is an heir of Romantic philosophy, his rhetorical verve and fondness for paradox sometimes echoing Schlegel, but he gives up the Romantic sense that art is a resource for truth in favour of the idea that art is the source of necessary illusions. Later, the growing dominance of the natural sciences leads many philosophers, particularly in the Anglo-American analytical tradition, to conceive of their task almost exclusively in relation to the sciences. The growth of what Max Weber termed 'disenchantment' in modernity has not, then, been favourable to Romantic philosophy's desire for an appropriate modern combination of rationality and imagination.

However, despite their marginal status in relation to much of mainstream modern Western philosophy, Romantic ideas remain alive. This is now not least because philosophical positions for which only scientifically warrantable assertions are candidates for truth have increasingly come to be seen as culturally damaging. They neglect the diverse ways in which truth functions in everyday communication and in differing cultural practices. As a consequence, versions of anti-representationalism have increasingly come to the fore as a reaction against the limiting of philosophical understanding of language to its referential role. Recent research (e.g. Cavell, *Must We Mean*; Eldridge, *Living a Human Life*; Bowie, *Music*) has, for example, begun to demonstrate how far Wittgenstein can be regarded as an heir to Romanticism, as, in certain respects, can Heidegger, Adorno and deconstruction.[22] The most significant representative of contemporary pragmatism, Richard Rorty, regards philosophy, in a manner that echoes Hardenberg and Schlegel, as a kind of 'literature', thus as a way of telling stories about who we are, rather than as the source of eternal truths. The fact that important trends in contemporary philosophy have begun to revive ideas from Romantic philosophy suggests that its significance may lie as much in its future as in its past.[23]

NOTES

1. Friedrich Schlegel, *Kritische Schriften und Fragmente*, 6 vols., eds. Ernst Behler and Hans Eichner (Paderborn, Munich, Vienna, Zurich: Schöningh, 1988), vol. V, p. 29. All translations are my own.
2. Immanuel Kant, *Kritik der reinen Vernunft*, in *Werkausgabe*, ed. Wilhelm Weischedel, 10 vols. (Frankfurt am Main: Suhrkamp, 1968), vols. III, IV. Here: B IV, p. 757, A IV, p. 729.
3. See Charles Taylor, *Human Agency and Language* (Cambridge: Cambridge University Press, 1985), and Andrew Bowie, *From Romanticism to Critical Theory* (London and New York: Routledge, 1997).
4. This idea is the basis of Saussure's theory of the signifier, where 'cat' gains its identity by not being 'mat', 'hat', etc.
5. There are, of course, a great many other thinkers involved. For the detailed story, see Manfred Frank, '*Unendliche Annäherung': Die Anfänge der philosophischen Frühromantik* (Frankfurt am Main: Suhrkamp, 1997).
6. Kant, *Kritik der reinen Vernunft* B, *Werkausgabe* III, p. 27.
7. How things in themselves give rise to appearances is one of the most problematic issues in Kant, as Jacobi points out in 1784. Kant says things in themselves cause appearances, but causal relations are supposed to pertain only to relations *between* appearances. There is therefore no way to *know* that things in themselves are the source of appearances.
8. See Bowie, *From Romanticism*, Frank, *Unendliche Annäherung*.
9. See Frank, *Unendliche Annäherung*, Andrew Bowie, *Introduction to German Philosophy from Kant to Habermas* (Cambridge: Polity, 2003).
10. See Dieter Henrich, *Fichtes ursprüngliche Einsicht* (Frankfurt am Main: Suhrkamp, 1967).
11. See Frank, *Unendliche Annäherung*, Andrew Bowie, *Aesthetics and Subjectivity: From Kant to Nietzsche* (Manchester: Manchester University Press, 2003).
12. F. D. E. Schleiermacher, *Über die Religion: Reden an die Gebildeten unter ihren Verächtern* (Hamburg: Felix Meiner, 1958), p. 25. Such claims notoriously allow him to assert that a religion without God can be better than one with God.
13. This conception is adopted by both Ludwig Feuerbach and Marx in their critiques of Hegel.
14. Friedrich Schlegel, *Transcendentalphilosophie*, ed. Michael Elsässer (Hamburg: Meiner, 1991), p. 93.
15. Schlegel, *Kritische Schriften und Fragmente*, vol. II, 2, p. 240.
16. G. W. F. Hegel, *Vorlesungen über die Ästhetik*, 2 vols., ed. Friedrich Bassenge (Berlin and Weimar: Aufbau, 1965), vol. I, p. 21.
17. See Manfred Frank, *Der kommende Gott: Vorlesung über die neue Mythologie I*, Bohrer, *Mythos und Moderne*.
18. Schlegel, *Kritische Schriften und Fragmente*, vol. V, p. 105.
19. Schlegel, *Kritische Schriften und Fragmente*, vol. VI, p. 12.
20. Solger essentially offers a theologically tinged elaboration of Schlegel's account of art, longing, irony and temporality.

21. This is also because many of the most interesting texts were either not published at the time, or were regarded as beyond the pale. Schleiermacher's working out of less provocative formulations of Romantic ideas tended to be published too late to have a major effect.
22. See Bowie, *From Romanticism* and *Aesthetics*.
23. This essay was written with the support of a Major Research Fellowship from the Leverhulme Foundation.

FURTHER READING

Benjamin, Walter, *Der Begriff der Kunstkritik in der deutschen Romantik*, ed. Hermann Schweppenhäuser (Frankfurt: Suhrkamp, 1973; 1st edn, 1920)

Berlin, Isaiah, *The Roots of Romanticism* (London: Chatto and Windus, 1999)

Bohrer, Karl, *Heinz, Mythos und Moderne: Begriff und Bild einer Rekonstruktion* (Frankfurt am Main : Suhrkamp, 1983)

Bowie, Andrew, *Schelling and Modern European Philosophy* (London and New York: Routledge, 1993)

From Romanticism to Critical Theory (London and New York: Routledge, 1997)

Introduction to German Philosophy from Kant to Habermas (Cambridge: Polity, 2003)

Aesthetics and Subjectivity: From Kant to Nietzsche (Manchester: Manchester University Press, 2003)

Music, Philosophy, and Modernity (Cambridge: Cambridge University Press, 2007)

Brandom, Robert, *Making It Explicit* (Cambridge, Mass. and London: Harvard University Press, 1994)

Tales of the Mighty Dead (Cambridge, Mass. and London: Harvard University Press, 2002)

Cavell, Stanley, *Must We Mean What We Say?* (Cambridge: Cambridge University Press, 1976)

Eldridge, Richard, *Living a Human Life: Wittgenstein, Intentionality, and Romanticism* (Chicago: University of Chicago Press, 1997)

Frank, Manfred, *Der kommende Gott: Vorlesung über die neue Mythologie I* (Frankfurt: Suhrkamp, 1982)

Die Hauptschriften zum Pantheismusstreit zwischen Jacobi und Mendelssohn, ed. Heinrich Scholz (Berlin: Reuther & Reichard, 1916)

Henrich, Dieter, *Fichtes ursprüngliche Einsicht* (Frankfurt: Suhrkamp, 1967)

Hölderlin, Friedrich, *Werke, Briefe, Dokumente*, ed. Pierre Bertaux (Munich: Winkler, 1963)

Jacobi, Friedrich Heinrich, *Jacobi an Fichte* (Hamburg: Friedrich Perthes, 1799)

Kant, Immanuel, *Kritik der praktischen Vernunft: Grundlegung der Metaphysik der Sitten, in Werkausgabe*, ed. Wilhelm Weischedel, 10 vols. (Frankfurt: Suhrkamp, 1968), vol. VII

Schelling, F. W. J., *Sämmtliche Werke*, ed. K. F. A. Schelling, section 1, vols. I–X, section 2, vols. I–IV (Stuttgart: Cotta, 1856–61)

Taylor, Charles, *Human Agency and Language* (Cambridge: Cambridge University Press, 1985)

12

ETHEL MATALA DE MAZZA

Romantic politics and society

Tendencies of an age

'Die Französische Revolution, Fichtes Wissenschaftslehre, und Goethes Meister sind die größten Tendenzen des Zeitalters' ('The French Revolution, Fichte's *Theory of Knowledge*, and Goethe's *Wilhelm Meister* are the three greatest tendencies of the age'), Friedrich Schlegel remarks in a famous Fragment (No. 216) published in *Athenaeum* in 1798. According to Schlegel, it was but a small step from the mass revolt in France to the treatise of a German professor and then to the latest novel of a bestselling author. But in this unusual juxtaposition of events, which followed both *on* and *from* each other, the Revolution, en route to Germany, went politically adrift. The event was repeated on paper, in books designed to educate readers rather than in actions dethroning monarchs. These writings, as we shall see, shifted the uprising from politics to philosophy and literature.

Many authors of the Romantic generation – poets and philosophers as well as publishers, literary critics and political thinkers – followed the same path around 1800. The events in France, which most of them, like Schlegel himself, knew only at second hand through newspapers, books and word of mouth, provided both an impetus and an object of criticism for their political thought. Sobered by the increasingly radical 'tendencies' of the revolutionaries and the dramatic escalation of the Revolution, the authors engaged in a heated debate about the notions of state and society, nation and *Volk*. In theoretical sketches and practical experiments, they developed models designed to be understood not only as more convincing alternatives to the French revolutionary state, but also as counter-concepts drawing their social meaning from home-grown traditions.

All these debates turned on the question of how Germans might conceive an authentic national culture of their own, precisely because the political situation in Germany at the close of the eighteenth century was hardly comparable to the French. A German state, in the sense of a homogeneous, centralised political entity, did not exist. What remained of the 'Heiliges Römisches Reich deutscher Nation' ('Holy Roman Empire of the German Nation') was dispersed over a fragmented landscape of larger and smaller territories, some of which barely qualified as states. But this made the demands arising from the Romantics' reflections all the more ambitious. On the one hand they formulated political ideals and social *fictions* in the utopian 'as if' mode of literature. On the other hand they intended their texts to perform pragmatically as *interventions* that would produce the desired community by literary means, and, through a dialogue with the reading public, generate the 'We' in whose name they pre-emptively spoke. The social models of the Romantics were aesthetic constructs in the most precise sense: they grounded their postulate of togetherness on the imaginative 'evidence' of aesthetic experience.

The most important of these constructs will be discussed in this chapter, in which it will become apparent that shifts in emphasis occurred as time passed. While the earlier conceptions insisted on the importance of explicit dialogue and communication, the later ones emphasised a sense of agreement, a 'feeling' of communal identity. Where the earlier, anticipatory models of togetherness – 'a "Fragment aus der Zukunft"' ('Fragment of the future'),[1] as Schlegel called them – necessarily remained ideas and projections aiming at innovation, the later ones were devoted to the (re-)construction of a buried past.

Critique of the existing order

In the last decade of the eighteenth century, the German Romantics were neither the first nor the only thinkers to distance themselves critically from the French Revolution. In 1790, soon after the outbreak of the Revolution, Edmund Burke's polemical *Reflections on the Revolution in France* harshly condemned the French monarchy's destruction. His apology for the Ancien Régime insists not only on the need for continuity in politics but also on the indispensability of a culture of beautiful illusions. In a bygone 'age of chivalry', recalls Burke, virtues such as dignity, noble-mindedness and 'subordination of the heart' would compensate for the dependencies and hierarchies of the time. He contrasts this heart-warming 'drapery' of gallantries with the social coldness of a rationality that recognises only stark formal obligation and the rigour of law. He concludes that reason alone has no binding force. Its principles cannot produce any emotional bonds – either with one's neighbour or with one's nation. A state that lacks aesthetic charm and 'pleasing illusions'[2] cannot win over its citizens; it must enforce respect; it must compel obedience by imposing obligations on its citizens, by monitoring, prosecuting, punishing and – at worst – eliminating them.

When Burke's *Reflections* appeared in England, they were ahead of their time: there were as yet few signs of the murderous fervour with which the Revolution would overwhelm France. Hence the determination to bring reason to political fruition and ground the state in a constitution aroused great sympathy for the French revolutionaries in Germany, particularly among those writers and philosophers who would later criticise the Revolution. Both Johann Gottlieb Fichte and Friedrich Schlegel composed passionate defences of the Revolution in this phase. But with the translation of Burke's *Reflections* in 1793, German enthusiasm became ambivalence. In the meantime, events in France had unfolded rapidly. As the Jacobin Terror turned on enemies within the republic, the new state revealed the despotic side of its rationality, a move that made the Romantics receptive to Burke's case. They reacted to the totalitarianism of the rule of law with a political critique that cast fundamental doubts on the cohesive power of law and the social contract and called for less rigid forms of social integration.

Liberal opinions voiced in the 1770s by Freemasons and Illuminati with the aim of 'counteracting the inevitable evils of the [absolutist] state'[3] – albeit without undermining the existing order as such – thereby acquired a new tenor. Some thinkers went as far as to reject any monopoly of governance, monarchic or republican, and thus questioned the very idea of a state. Fichte, in his *Vorlesungen über die Bestimmung des Gelehrten* (1794; *Lectures on the Destiny of the Scholar*), defines the state's sole purpose to be the preparation of a 'vollkommere ... Gesellschaft' ('perfect society') which would *'render governance superfluous'*.[4] Schiller, in his *Über die ästhetische Erziehung des Menschen* (1795; *On the Aesthetic Education of Humankind*), outlines a cultural programme that would mitigate the 'Uhrwerk' ('mechanism') of the modern state, which has become 'a stranger to its citizens'.[5] The so-called *Ältestes Systemprogramm des deutschen Idealismus* (1797; *Earliest System Programme of German Idealism*), a collaborative manifesto (probably) by Hegel, Schelling and Hölderlin, demands that the 'whole wretched human artifact of state, constitution, regime, legal system' be dismantled *'bis auf die Haut'* (*'stripped to the skin'*).[6]

Significantly, at this early point in the Romantic discourse, the 'Other' of the state was exposed through the metaphorical recognition of a 'naked', carnal substrate, which revealed the nature of the body politic under a different aspect. Henceforth Romantic conceptions of society consistently emphasised this metaphor. In particular, they propagated the notion of the state as a body that conserved the fabric of society and could best be grasped with what had previously seemed primitive instruments of cognition: feelings and reflexes, passions and inclinations.

The tradition of the body politic

Since Aristotle drew an analogy between *polis* (polity) and *soma* (body) in his *Politics*, the 'body politic' has been a socio-philosophical topos in Western thought. The image of the congregation as a spiritual body and as a community in Christ dates back to St Paul. His model – conceiving of the *ecclesia* (church) as a mystical body of Christ uniting the multitude of believers – became the principle of both the institutional history of the Catholic Church and the theological foundations of secular law in the Middle Ages. Following the doctrine that evolved from the concept of the body of Christ, English jurists ascribed to the king two bodies: one 'natural' and mortal, the other 'mystical' and immortal: the second guaranteed the eternity of royal authority.[7] Similarly, early modern political philosophy developed an image of the state that transcended its subjects as an 'artificial man' and transformed them into a unity by incorporating them in the body politic of the Leviathan.[8]

However, the social models of the Romantics modified this basic paradigm. Instead of considering the body politic as the product of a legal construct – a contract of submission, for instance, as Hobbes presumed – they saw it as the premise of all social interaction. They were interested in the physical body as an elemental and ever-present substance from which society drew its vital energies and out of which its natural bonds grew, independently of any individual action. The Romantics defended such theories by citing the latest discoveries in medical-scientific knowledge of the human body. In the last third of the eighteenth century, the humanities and natural philosophies developed a new understanding of the body, which was no longer regarded as a sort of hydraulic machine set in motion by the ebb and flow of 'humours', but as a living organism governed endogenously by its own neuro-sensory system. Its life processes should no longer be described in terms of mechanistic principles of action and reaction, matter and motion. Rather, they manifested themselves as the results of physiological processes governed from within by a complex rhythm of stimulus and (sensitive or irritable) response. To the extent that the nervous system acquired a central role as the mediating instance between the brain and other organs and ensured intra-corporeal communication between the physical and the intellectual, the received categorical distinction of body and soul was abandoned. The border established in the old model between spiritual and corporeal realms became porous, and emphasis shifted from their differences to their reciprocal influence. Thus it became plausible also to think of the forms of intersubjective communication as extensions of this kind of organic interplay. Stimulating conversations, inspiring ideas, infectious enthusiasms, electrifying impulses could be seen as analogies of nervous stimulus-response reflexes. The old Christian notion of a collective corporeal unity gained new relevance. The Romantics hoped to make people experience this bodily oneness of the social or political community through the senses, and they chose aesthetic discourse as one of their chief means to achieve that goal.

Reforming society from within

One of the earliest and most pertinent examples of this is *Glauben und Liebe* (1798; *Faith and Love*), a marvellously intricate collection of aphorisms by Friedrich von Hardenberg (Novalis). On the accession of a new, young and widely admired King and Queen of Prussia Hardenberg challenges the royal pair to embody his Romantic ideal of government. Hence, rather than plead for the destruction of the existing state (a kind of rationalised monarchy), he advocates a political reform from within the given structure designed to create a quite new state with no significant distinction of public and private, individual and polity, reality and poesy, indeed, even monarchy and republic. In this, so-called 'poetic state'[9] all relationships will be founded in the deepest emotional bond of love (marital and parental love, the rulers' love of their subjects, the subjects' love of their rulers). This will guarantee the intimate and enduring interconnectedness of individual and collective in every dimension, so that the ideal community is manifest in every real relationship in the state. Thus Hardenberg advances a programme to (re) generate the Prussian body politic by medical analogy, through the most diverse communicative 'stimulations' between centre and parts of a body he sees as disjointed and dysfunctional. Apart from concrete measures, such as improving social hygiene and accelerating the flow of capital into concrete projects, this programme is thus also intended to be implemented pragmatically by the rhetorical functioning of the lyric aphorisms themselves. These insist at the level of content on a wholly novel representative role of the royal couple King Frederick William III and Queen Luisa, not as absolute monarchs by divine right or paper contract, but as the absolute incarnation of divine love – of each other, and of their subjects. At the level of form, the invocation of this ideal is couched in a self-consciously indeterminate 'mystischer Ausdruck' ('mystical expression'), which is cunningly designed to serve as 'Gedankenreiz' ('intellectual stimulus'), provoke the creative intellect of the reader to (re)construct in himself what is merely implied, and so finally, in this indirect way, arouse 'lebhafteste Regungen' ('liveliest stirrings') of love and loyalty for the absolute love concealed in the 'mystical expression'. Thus the ideal is *aesthetically* made present and realized in each individual. In the royal pair – who paradoxically embody bourgeois virtues and values *par excellence* – every citizen (not subject) is empowered to recognise and love the ideal self-image.

Not for nothing did Hardenberg applaud Burke's *Reflections* as a 'revoluzionäres Buch gegen die Revoluzion' ('revolutionary book against the Revolution').[10] His aphorisms take the philosopher's appeal at its word and seek the political in beauty – in this case the beauty of the royal familial idyll – in order to move the heart and exploit the cohesive power of shared emotion. Strange as the appeal to 'stimulus' may seem today, Hardenberg's highly original, aesthetic-rhetorical move is based on solid knowledge and creative application of contemporary physiological science – in particular the theory of the then famous Scottish neuropathologist John Brown, who constructed his diagnostic model of health and ill-health on the notion of equilibrium in the body between stimulus and response through (active) irritability or (passive) sensation. Hardenberg's therapy of poetic stimulation, prescribed for a social body diagnosed by him as suffering from the lack of 'excitability' (Brown), aims at promoting harmony among the loving citizens by increasing their capacity actively to respond. Once this equilibrium is attained, the 'Buchstabe' ('letter') of the 'constitution' is obsolete; Prussia can spontaneously secure its political togetherness without further written guarantees; the 'papierne[r] Kitt' ('papier mâché')[11] of law can be dispensed with, and the rule of the merely arbitrary signs of a paper document – an empire to which, in the end, even literature itself belongs – will be over.

Friedrich Schleiermacher's *Versuch einer Theorie des geselligen Betragens* (1799; *Essay on a Theory of Social Conduct*) offers a different model, founded on conversational exchange. After a discussion of aesthetic topics it develops a theory of socialisation that focuses not on the state, but on the social 'circle', which, as a third space between the public and private spheres, is characteristically free of formalities and restrictions. Where labour binds the communicative spirit to external ends, and family restricts free communication to a handful of people, the open, non-instrumental sphere of sociality – a sphere 'not dominated by any law' – allows the individual to abandon himself to the 'freie[s] Spiel' ('free play') of forces. Of course, sociality is based on the experience of difference in the conflict between contrary positions. For Schleiermacher, conversational exchange provides just such an experience of difference, insofar as speakers continually encounter new asymmetries of self and other. But as long as speakers engage in the process of discursive mediation, no shared outcome or final agreement is needed to make their communication socially productive. On the contrary: the more diverse the participants and opinions are, the more intensive their negotiation of differences can be. 'Reciprocity' ('Wechselwirkung')[12] is Schleiermacher's term for a dynamic of discussion that can be regarded as a model of social self-regulation, because the unceasing hermeneutic commitment creates a loose yet foundational commonality between speakers. What makes Schleiermacher's theory challenging is that it presupposes disagreement as a premise of social interaction and turns the processing of differences into a practice of integration. Unanimity, in this sense, would mean paradoxically a tearing apart of social bonds.

Another Utopian vision, realised through written exchange rather than dialogue, is developed in Friedrich Schlegel's novel *Lucinde* (1799). *Lucinde* unfolds this model – partly by means of recognisable biographical parallels between the eponymous heroine and Dorothea Veit, Schlegel's own lover – from the happy union of the sexes. At its narrative centre this union constitutes, first, the goal of an embedded *Bildungsroman*. Julius, a dilettante painter, undergoes 'Lehrjahre der Männlichkeit' (an 'apprenticeship in manhood') in preparation for encountering his erotic and intellectual equal in Lucinde. However, the identity-in-difference of the loving couple is also mirrored in the highly diverse short prose pieces that ring the central *Bildungsroman*. The union of sexual opposites resonates in the union of different textual genres. The novel *Lucinde* can therefore be read as both an erotic and an aesthetic manifesto. It also, however, provides a miniature example of a vast project Schlegel had sketched out a year before in his *Ideen* Fragments: the 'absolute book'. This book, also called the 'new Bible', is theorised by Schlegel as a book *of* books, one in which 'alle Bücher' are 'nur Ein Buch' ('all books are simply One Book'), the totality of what is printed and possible. This notion of the new Bible or 'ewig werdendes Buch' ('eternally nascent book')[13] attracted Schlegel not only through its unity-in-diversity but also its ability to catalyse the formation of a new community – of writers and readers. But if *Lucinde*, with its synthesis of many and one, represents a poetic matrix of the 'unendliches Buch' ('infinite book'), its fertility in the reproduction of literature still had to be proven.

Each of these models – Hardenberg's poetic state, Schleiermacher's sociality and Schlegel's new Bible – imagines an intensive form of reciprocal interaction which is catalysed and governed by literature. Each also, let us note, exploits despite its visionary character an empirical model from which it derives its Utopian ideal. Hardenberg conceives of his poetic state, in a comparatively conventional manner, as a multiplicity of bourgeois marriages. Schleiermacher and Schlegel have in mind the more Bohemian Jena circle to which they – and Hardenberg – belonged. The principle of collective writing ('sympoesy') and collective philosophising ('symphilosophy'), as well as the erotic libertinism of some of the members, left their traces in the concept of a society engaged in free communication.

In reality, the sociality of the Jena circle lasted only a year (1798). Even in this small group the interplay designed to guarantee the constant self-regeneration of sociality proved highly unstable. Nonetheless, their experiment inspired several other literary collectives. One of the best-known is the so-called 'Serapion Brotherhood', a fraternity of intellectuals centred on E. T. A. Hoffmann in legitimist Restoration Berlin after 1816. In the work bearing that name, published by Hoffmann 1819–21, the anthology of stories is framed by the provocative and provoked exchanges of the group. However, for political Romanticism the Heidelberg circle, which comprised Achim von Arnim, Bettine von Arnim, Clemens Brentano, Sophie Mereau, Karoline von Günderrode, Joseph von Eichendorff, Joseph Görres and Friedrich Creuzer, was more important. Apart from literary concerns, the Heidelberg Romantics shared an interest in historical studies and in the collecting of forgotten stories, songs, fairy tales and myths. In the early nineteenth century, they exemplified the widespread German desire for national and cultural reassurance, which grew in proportion as German political circumstances worsened, and Napoleon extended his hegemony over Europe. Many writers felt moved to engage in patriotic declarations and initiatives. The political thought of Romantics now focused specifically on questions of national identity.

The invention of tradition

Initially, the search for identity turned to the past. In 1806 and 1808, Achim von Arnim and Clemens Brentano published a collection of half-forgotten, half-invented folk-songs entitled *Des Knaben Wunderhorn* (*The Boy's Magic Horn*). In 1807 Joseph Görres's survey *Die teutschen Volksbücher* (*German Chapbooks*) appeared. There followed in 1812 and 1815 the Grimm Brothers' *Kinder und Hausmärchen* (*Fairy Tales for Household and Nursery*). With a little help from the modern imagination, all these projects sought to rescue a threatened oral culture. The preservation of a native culture thus went hand in hand with its (re)invention. The intention was to recover an originary common property that could be claimed as the cultural inheritance of the nation and thus as a guarantee of national identity. 'Once we have acknowledged that an inner spirit lives … in every class', Joseph Görres wrote in the introduction to his *Volksbücher*, 'we will also become more familiar with the idea that the lowest regions can also mean, and count for, something in the collective world of thought, and that the great Literary State has a House of Commons in which the nation directly represents itself'. Unlike the writings of named authors, the stories and songs of the oral tradition belonged to everyone and no one. The people, among whom they circulated, were the origin, reservoir and vehicle of transmission of a poetic treasure in which – supposedly – an archaic dawn of culture was preserved. For political Romanticism, this mobilisation of a *Volk* and its originary 'Stimme' ('voice') was significant, since these German authors appropriated the term claimed by the French revolutionaries for their new sovereign but endowed it with a different meaning. In place of a *politically empowered* people, the source of identity appeared in the form of a *poetically productive Volk*.

The early Romantic social Utopias were not interested in this *Volk*. In projecting their ideals of revitalising intellectual stimuli, free sociality and the infinite book, they assumed a standard of education that few could reach in the early nineteenth century. This standard was now abandoned or questioned. As Arnim's essay 'Von Volksliedern' ('On Folk-songs') in the *Wunderhorn* argues, education, as the privilege of the elite, had lost political credit. The voice whose songs, poems and stories the Heidelberg Romantics recorded belonged to people from the simplest, mostly illiterate social strata. Such people, as Görres said, live 'the spreading, dreamlike, somnolent life of a plant; their mind is cultivated only seldom and modestly, and can only bask in the rays of the higher universal forces; while its flowers draw everything down into the roots beneath the earth, where they produce edible tubers which, like potatoes, never see the sunlight'.[14]

The philologist Jacob Grimm and the jurist Friedrich Carl von Savigny emphasise that the authentically German legal traditions also have their roots in this poetic soil. Starting from the proposition that 'law and poetry grow up together from a single bed', Grimm, in his essay 'Von der Poesie im Recht' (1815; 'On the Poesy in Law'), outlines a programme for the historical study of law founded primarily on language – vocabulary, metaphors, rhetorical formulas and idiomatic expressions – with the aim of unearthing the oldest legal norms embedded in it. He regards above all analogies as important indicators of the close relationship between early law and poetry, for instance when he demonstrates that old German used 'for the very same words or names the ideas of law and of poetry' (e.g. calling both the judge and the poet a *'finder'*); or when he cites the frequency of alliterations and periods structured in triads in medieval legal formulations to prove that legal norms were, initially, 'nichts anders wie sagen und geschichten, metrisch in lieder gebunden' ('metrically bound in songs, not unlike sagas and stories'). In these features Grimm also claims to discern an intrinsically poetic quality of German legal talk, manifest both in its inclination towards almost-pleonastic 'tautology',[15] – more accurately, the figure of *hendiadys* (as in German *'Haus und Hof'*, *'Kind und Kegel'*, *'Mann und Maus'* – or English 'to have and to hold', 'sound and fury', 'rain and weather') – and in a pristine 'sensual element'[16] of German legal maxims, symbols and rituals, whose power lies 'not in dead books and formulas', but 'in the mouth and the heart'.[17] The critical distance of folk-song collectors from the achievements of high culture resurfaces in Grimm's research into legal history in the form of an aversion to the effete written style of codification – a late echo of Burke – as well as an example of the general distaste for the dominance of Roman over German law.

In Savigny's epoch-making *Vom Beruf unsrer Zeit für Gesetzgebung und Rechtswissenschaft* (1814; *On the Vocation of our Age for Legislation and Jurisprudence*), a treatise that inspired Grimm, the resistance to foreign domination finds a new opponent in the *Code Napoléon* that had been introduced in virtually all the German states. Like Grimm, Savigny argues for a return to history as source of authority. In a detailed response to the proposal of his colleague Anton Thibaut that a common code of law for the German states be introduced, Savigny identifies the double risk that such a construct would hold: mechanising the practice of law – which could be 'overwhelmed by mere texts' – and weakening the constitution's authority. Authority, he continues, derives from something not made by men, but which has grown and, like religion, is born of spirit. Thus Savigny appeals to the German sensibility for the 'natural development of communities and constitutions'; he insists on the 'indissoluble organic connection of generations and ages; between which only development, and no absolute end or beginning, is conceivable'; and he recommends that jurisprudence follow a 'strenge historische Methode' ('strict historical method') that would trace every given matter to its roots in order to 'discover an organic principle, whereby that which still has life may be separated from that which has died and only belongs to history'. While not using the term *Volksgeist* (national spirit) – which Savigny employs only much later, in his *System des heutigen römischen Rechts* (1840; *System of Contemporary Roman Law*) – the early essay on the *Beruf unsrer Zeit* already assumes popular belief, custom and habit to be the only legitimate sources of law. The reconstruction of these customs and beliefs is delegated to meticulous philological work on 'material at hand'. For the constitution to become 'common to the whole nation', jurisprudence should not only transmit 'den ganzen Reichthum der vergangenen Geschlechter' ('the whole intellectual wealth of past generations'), but also impart to juridical language the 'frische, ursprüngliche Lebenskraft' ('freshness and primitive vigour')[18] which will preserve it from death in a grave of letters.

Defensive measures

The historical search for traces of the originary *Volk* and its spirit distinguishes the juridical and poetic enterprises of these writers from the numerous contributions of philosophers and poets such as Johann Gottlieb Fichte, Heinrich von Kleist and Adam Müller who championed the Prussian cause. The debates they joined were about urgent defensive measures rather than the archaeology of a national culture. After the heavy defeat inflicted by Napoleon's troops on the Prussian army at Jena-Auerstedt in 1806, ministers and generals hastened to consolidate the Prussian state, which was now under Napoleon's rule, from within. Their military reforms were followed by reforms in administration, education and civil rights. In speeches, plays and the manifestos of newly founded literary associations, the authors of this period echoed these efforts. At the same time they developed highly emphatic ideas of the community of the *Volk*, in particular of the sacrifices it might legitimately demand and the wars that were to be fought in its name.

Kleist's play *Die Hermannsschlacht* (1809; *The Battle of Teutoburg Forest*), for example, anticipates the national uprising against Napoleon. It portrays a partisan war of the colonised Germanic peoples fuelled by hatred of the colonisers, albeit a war which aimed not at the recovery of freedom, but rather at blind, raging destruction of the Roman (i.e. French) enemy. It is the 'Pflicht jedes Einzelnen' ('duty of each individual'), Kleist writes explicitly in the *Katechismus der Deutschen* (1808; *Catechism of the Germans*), 'zu den Waffen zu greifen, den Anderen ... ein Beispiel zu geben, und die Franzosen, wo sie angetroffen werden mögen, zu erschlagen' ('to take up arms, to be an example ... to others, and to defeat the French wherever they can be confronted').[19] In Kleist's play the hero Hermann justifies this war of annihilation as a 'cleansing service' for the national body: 'Die ganze Brut, die in den Leib Germaniens / Sich eingefilzt, wie ein Insektenschwarm, / Muß durch das Schwert der Rache jetzo sterben' ('The entire brood that has infiltrated / The body of Germania like a swarm of insects / Must now perish beneath the sword of revenge').[20]

In contrast, Adam Müller's *Zwölf Reden über die Beredsamkeit und ihren Verfall in Deutschland* (*Twelve Addresses on Eloquence and its Decline in Germany*) recommended a national 'Waffenübung der Seele' ('mobilisation of the soul').[21] These speeches self-consciously rely on the force of sublime oratory to elevate their listeners and readers. However, while Fichte, in his patriotic *Reden an die deutsche Nation* (1807–8; *Addresses to the German Nation*), demands the extension of 'die neue Bildung' 'an alles ohne Ausnahme, was deutsch ist …, so daß dieselbe nicht als Bildung eines besonderen Stands, so daß sie Bildung der Nation schlechthin als solcher … werde' ('the new education to every German without exception, so that it becomes not the education of a single class, but the education of a nation'),[22] Müller invokes the universal comprehensibility of the spoken words of the mother tongue and the 'unmittelbare Gewalt der Töne' ('immediate power of sounds').[23] Eloquence is to be as much the instrument of a 'military' as of an aesthetic education. It should produce an inner movement from which a mature 'Nationalselbstgefühl' ('national self-assurance')[24] might grow, which would confront the external enemy with internal resistance.

In this way the *Reden über die Beredsamkeit* fulfil the demand raised by Müller in his *Elemente der Staatskunst* (1808–9; *Elements of Statecraft*). According to the theory developed here of the state as organism, the 'nature of the state' evolves in response to 'heftige *Bewegungen*' ('violent *movements*'), which are most likely to emerge during revolutions and wars. While the internal antagonisms of city and country, aristocracy and bourgeoisie, man and woman account for these violent movements, the *Addresses* give the argument a rhetorical turn. They stress the psychological dynamics of the passions and identify the rhetoric of the statesman as a means of unleashing surges of patriotic feeling. While in Hardenberg's aphorisms poetry strives to secure the propagation of faith and love through the life of the royal couple, in Müller's *Addresses* it is the statesman who must function as an artist, deploying his power as an orator and infusing the masses with faith and love for an organic state. The body remains the 'nächste und schönste Muster aller Vereinigungen und Körperschaften' ('closest and most beautiful archetype of all unions and corporations') in an organic state – an 'innige, gewaltige Verbindung' ('intimate, powerful bond') which we feel 'in jedem Lebens-Moment am unmittelbarsten' ('most immediately at every moment in life').[25]

Political experiments

These few examples hint at the immense spectrum of Romantic political thought. Reflections on innovative governmental politics are accompanied by those on the liberalisation of intellectual and erotic interaction, Utopian projects by patient historical research, scholarly endeavours by chauvinistic agitations and civil education programmes by military mobilisation. In their heterogeneous morphology, Romantic concepts of the state and society, nation and *Volk* are symptomatic of the openness and questionability of what can count as political fact, the business of everybody, *res publica* in the literal sense. The French Revolution made this question acute by challenging the legitimacy of the Ancien Régime and denying the king the right and monopoly of acting in the name of his subjects. Since then, not only have the foundations of all political authority been contested, but politics as such have become a topic about which there can hardly be any agreement, because its definition always depends on the variable concepts that allocate a place to it.[26] Even though the Romantics distanced themselves from the constitutional form in which the revolutionaries in France framed the political, their own reflections are still marked by the innovative thought of the Revolution. The monarchy propounded by Hardenberg is different from that of the Ancien Régime, and the bestial methods with which Kleist's Hermann stokes his Germanic tribesmen's hatred of Rome are dictated by Napoleon's own armies. In inciting the Germanic peoples to fight a battle in which victory is not a matter of professional obligation but of patriotic ardour, Hermann steals the secret of the French troops' success in order to deploy it *against* them. The Romantics thus reproduce that for which the Revolution had set a precedent. This explains why in the case of most German Romantic authors both sympathy with and hostility to French modernity are so close together. It also explains why even the conservative approaches manifest themselves with the aplomb of innovation and why, conversely, even the most daring Utopias are infused with a longing for the return to a buried origin.

Scholars have tended to overlook this paradox in Romantic thought by separating a 'progressive' early Romanticism from a 'reactionary' late Romanticism and explicitly privileging the former. By devaluing the later Romantics modern scholars were reacting not least against the reception of the term *Volk* by the National Socialists, who transformed the political body into a crudely biological substance. Identified with the Germanic race, the *Volk* was bred, 'veredelt' ('purified') and protected against corruption by foreign 'Schädlinge' ('vermin'). The 'Religion des Blutes' ('religion of blood') proclaimed by Alfred Rosenberg as the *Mythus des 20. Jahrhunderts* (1930; *Myth of the Twentieth Century*) sought to topple the gods of the universalist religions – Catholicism and Enlightenment faith in humanity – and to replace them with the particular Germanic values that would triumph in the historical struggle for survival.[27] We know the ultimate, murderous consequences of the delusion over race. The roots of such bio-political deliriums can indeed be detected in some Romantic concepts of the organic community, for example in Kleist's metaphor of – French – parasites in the body of Germania. Rosenberg, in his turn, places his history of the Germanic race and culture explicitly within Romantic – but also, it should be said, Classical – German traditions.

Nonetheless, it would be short-sighted to denounce the Romantic concepts of politics and society as precursors of National Socialist ideology. In their search for political models beyond any possible polity, in their ceaseless efforts to escape the artificiality of legal constructs, the projects of Romantic authors are, if anything, political experiments in the laboratory of post-Revolutionary modernity, aimed at simultaneously explaining and contesting the social order. The extent to which Romantic concepts affirm the contingency of social relations – through their very faith in the integrative power of poetry, literature, ordinary speech, the performance of legal ritual, and rhetoric – was precisely described by the philosopher Carl Schmitt in his polemical critique of the movement, *Politische Romantik* (1919; *Political Romanticism*).[28] Schmitt attacked Romantic thought as lacking commitment. Later he developed a 'decisionistic' concept of the political that rejected the ambivalence of Romanticism and set out clear distinctions between friend and foe. It is not chance that Schmitt formulated his critique at a time when Germans had yet to accept the outcomes of the First World War in the Treaty of Versailles. In a Germany that only grudgingly tolerated the Weimar Republic, Romanticism experienced a new boom. Ferdinand Tönnies's sociological classic *Gemeinschaft und Gesellschaft* (*Community and Society*), which appeared for the first time in 1887 but was not widely read until the Weimar Republic, was perhaps the most important book to spread Romantic ideas into German political thought of the 1920s. The abundance of studies, new editions and collections of Romantic literature that emerged in the years between the wars, among them Jakob Baxa's anthology *Gesellschaft und Staat im Spiegel deutscher Romantik* (1924; *Society and State in the Mirror of German Romanticism*), bears witness to this renaissance.

If political Romanticism is today again attracting attention, it owes that to the very traits Carl Schmitt condemned. Niklas Luhmann's systems theory, which derives its foundational principle from the requirement to manage contingency, paves the way for the re-emergence of the concept of the organism as 'system' or functionally differentiated structure. Other recent adaptations of – in this case early – Romantic thought can be found in models of community developed during the last few decades in France. Taking their cues from the philosophy of thinkers like Jacques Derrida, Jean-Luc Nancy and Philippe Lacoue-Labarthe, these models point towards a community in the making ('communauté désœuvrée'),[29] a community that constitutes itself in its lack of unity and in the experience of its own lack of integrity.

Translated by Julia Ng and Ladislaus Löb

NOTES

1. In *KFSA* II, p. 198, No. 216, and p. 168, No. 22. The translation is from Friedrich Schlegel, *Dialogue on Poetry and Literary Aphorisms*, trans. and eds. Ernst Behler and Roman Struc (University Park and London: Pennsylvania State University Press, 1968), pp. 143 and 134. All translations, save where acknowledgement is made, are my own.
2. See *The Writings and Speeches of Edmund Burke*, eds. L. G. Mitchell and W. B. Todd, 12 vols. (Oxford: Clarendon Press, 1989), vol. VIII, p. 128.
3. The citation is from Gotthold Ephraim Lessing, 'Ernst und Falk: Gespräche für Freimaurer', in *Werke*, ed. H. G. Göpfert, 8 vols. (Darmstadt: Wissenschaftliche Buchgesellschaft, 1996), vol. VIII, pp. 467 and 469. See *Philosophical and Theological Writings*, trans. H. B. Nisbet (Cambridge: Cambridge University Press, 2005), pp. 198–9 (quotation modified).
4. Johann Gottlieb Fichte, *Einige Vorlesungen über die Bestimmung des Gelehrten*, in *Gesamtausgabe der Bayerischen Akademie der Wissenschaften*, eds. R. Lauth and H. Jacob, 34 vols. (Stuttgart and Bad Cannstatt: Frommann-Verlag, 1966), section 1, vol. III, p. 37.
5. Friedrich Schiller, *Über die ästhetische Erziehung des Menschen in einer Reihe von Briefen'*, in *Sämtliche Werke*, eds. G. Fricke and H. G. Göpfert, 5 vols. (Darmstadt: Wissenschaftliche Buchgesellschaft, 1993), vol. V, pp. 584–5. See *On the Aesthetic Education of Man, in a Series of Letters*, eds. and trans. Elizabeth M. Wilkinson and L. A. Willoughby (Oxford: Clarendon Press, 1967), p. 35.
6. In *Materialien zu Schellings philosophischen Anfängen*, eds. M. Frank and G. Kurz (Frankfurt am Main: Suhrkamp, 1975), p. 110f. Compare *Miscellaneous Writings of G. W. F. Hegel*, ed. J. Stewart (Evanston: Northwestern University Press, 2002), p. 111.
7. Ernst H. Kantorowicz, *The King's Two Bodies: A Study in Mediaeval Political Theology* (Princeton, N.J.: Princeton University Press, 1957).
8. Thomas Hobbes, *Leviathan, or The Matter, Forme, & Power of A Common-wealth Ecclesiasticall and Civill*, ed. M. Oakeshott (Oxford: Basil Blackwell, 1960), p. 5.
9. Friedrich von Hardenberg, 'Vermischte Bemerkungen', in *NS* II, p. 468, No. 122.
10. See Friedrich von Hardenberg, 'Glauben und Liebe', *NS* II, p. 485, No. 3, p. 488, No. 17, and p. 500, No. 53, and 'Blüthenstaub', *NS* II, p. 459, No. 104. Translations are from *Pollen and Fragments: Selected Poetry and Prose of Novalis*, trans. A. Versluis (Grand Rapids, Miss.: Phanes, 1989), p. 41, No. 89, pp. 43–4, No. 100, p. 47, No. 113 (translation modified) and p. 37, No. 67.
11. Hardenberg, 'Glauben und Liebe', p. 487, No. 15, and p. 488, No. 16.

12. See Friedrich Schleiermacher, 'Versuch einer Theorie des geselligen Betragens', in *Philosophische Schriften*, ed. J. Rachold (Berlin: Union Verlag, 1984), pp. 41, 47.

13. Friedrich Schlegel, 'Ideen', *KFSA*, II, p. 265, No. 95.

14. Joseph Görres, 'Die teutschen Volksbücher', in *Gesammelte Schriften*, ed. Wilhelm Schellberg, 18 vols. (Cologne: Gilde-Verlag, 1926–), vol. III, pp. 176, 174.

15. Jacob Grimm, 'Von der Poesie im Recht', in *Kleinere Schriften*, 8 vols. (Berlin: Dümmerl, 1882), vol. VI, pp. 153, 158, 159.

16. See Jacob Grimm, *Deutsche Rechtsalterthümer*, 2 vols. (Darmstadt: Wissenschaftliche Buchgesellschaft, 1955), vol. I, p. vii.

17. Ibid., p. 179.

18. Carl von Savigny, *Vom Beruf unsrer Zeit für Gesetzgebung und Rechtswissenschaft* (Hildesheim: Olms, 1967), pp. 24, 43f., 4, 113, 117f., 161, 113, 52. Translations are from *Of the Vocation of our Age for Legislation and Jurisprudence*, trans. A. Hayward (Kitchener: Batoche, 1999), pp. 25, 35, 14, 67, 69, 92, 67, 39 (translations slightly modified).

19. Heinrich von Kleist, 'Katechismus der Deutschen', in *Sämtliche Werke und Briefe*, ed. H. Sembdner, 2 vols. (Munich: dtv, 1984), vol. II, p. 358.

20. Heinrich von Kleist, *Die Hermannsschlacht*, in *Sämtliche Werke und Briefe*, vol. I, p. 593 (v. 1681–3).

21. Adam Müller, *Zwölf Reden über die Beredsamkeit und ihren Verfall in Deutschland*, in *Kritische, ästhetische und philosophische Schriften*, eds. Walter Schroeder and Werner Siebert, 2 vols. (Neuwied and Berlin: Luchterhand, 1967), vol. I, p. 372. Translations, sometimes modified, are from *Adam Müller's Twelve Lectures on Rhetoric: A Translation Followed by a Critical Essay*, trans. Dennis Bormann and Elisabeth Leinfellner (Ann Arbor: University of Nebraska Press/ University Microfilms International, 1978), p. 181.

22. J. G. Fichte, *Reden an die deutsche Nation*, ed. R. Lauth (Hamburg: Meiner, 1978), p. 24. The English is from *Addresses to the German Nation*, trans. R. F. Jones and G. H. Turnbull (Chicago and London: Open Court, 1922), p. 15.

23. Adam Müller, *Reden*, p. 331 (*Lectures on Rhetoric*, p. 142 – translation modified).

24. Adam Müller, *Ueber König Friedrich II. und die Natur, Würde und Bestimmung der preussischen Monarchie* (Berlin: Sander, 1810), p. 17.

25. Adam Müller, *Die Elemente der Staatskunst*, ed. J. Baxa, 2 vols. (Jena: Fischer, 1922), vol. I, pp. 5, 324.

26. *Gemeinschaften: Positionen zu einer Philosophie des Politischen*, ed. J. Vogl (Frankfurt am Main: Suhrkamp, 1994); *Metamorphosen des Politischen: Grundfragen politischer Einheitsbildung seit den 20er Jahren*, ed. A. Göbel, (Berlin: Akademie, 1995); *Das Politische: Figurenlehren des sozialen Körpers nach der Romantik*, eds. U. Hebekus, E. Matala de Mazza and A. Koschorke (Munich: Fink, 2003).

27. Alfred Rosenberg, *Der Mythus des 20. Jahrhunderts: Eine Wertung der seelisch-geistigen Gestaltenkämpfe unserer Zeit* (Munich: Hoheneichen, 1930).

28. Carl Schmitt, *Politische Romantik* (Berlin: Duncker & Humblot, 1998).

29. Jean-Luc Nancy, *La Communauté désœuvrée* (Paris: Bourgois, 1986).

FURTHER READING

Anderson, Benedict, *Imagined Communities: Reflections on the Origin and Spread of Nationalism*, 2nd edn (London: Verso, 1991)

Balke, Friedrich, *Der Staat nach seinem Ende: Die Versuchung Carl Schmitts* (Munich: Fink, 1996)

Beiser, Frederick C. (ed.), *The Early Political Writings of the German Romantics* (Cambridge: Cambridge University Press, 1996)

Epstein, Klaus, *Die Ursprünge des Konservativismus in Deutschland: Der Ausgangspunkt: Die Herausforderung durch die Französische Revolution 1770–1806* (Frankfurt and Berlin: Propyläen, 1973)

Gaus, Detlef, *Geselligkeit und Gesellige: Bildung, Bürgertum und bildungsbürgerliche Kultur um 1800* (Stuttgart: Metzler, 1998)

Hobsbawm, Eric J., *Nations and Nationalism since 1780: Programme, Myth, Reality* (Cambridge: Cambridge University Press, 1992)

Kaiser, Gerhard, *Pietismus und Patriotismus im literarischen Deutschland: Ein Beitrag zum Problem der Säkularisation*, 2nd edn (Frankfurt: Athenäum, 1973)

Kittler, Wolf, *Die Geburt des Partisanen aus dem Geist der Poesie: Heinrich von Kleist und die Strategie der Befreiungskriege* (Freiburg: Rombach Verlag, 1987)

Kohn, Hans, *Prelude to Nation-States: The French and German Experience, 1789–1815* (Princeton: Van Nostrand, 1967)

Matala de Mazza, Ethel, *Der verfaßte Körper: Zum Projekt einer organischen Gemeinschaft in der Politischen Romantik* (Freiburg: Rombach Verlag, 1999)

Plessner, Helmuth, *Die verspätete Nation: Über die politische Verführbarkeit bürgerlichen Geistes*, 5th edn (Frankfurt am Main: Suhrkamp, 1994)

Redfield, Marc, *The Politics of Aesthetics: Nationalism, Gender, Romanticism* (Palo Alto, Calif.: Stanford University Press, 2003)

Vogl, Joseph (ed.), *Gemeinschaften. Positionen zu einer Philosophie des Politischen* (Frankfurt am Main: Suhrkamp, 1994)

13

JÜRGEN BARKHOFF

Romantic science and psychology

Paradigms of Romantic science

Romantic science and psychology are an integral and essential part of the great Romantic project towards a new synthesis, and, as such, they are intimately linked to other central aspects of German Romanticism such as art and philosophy. Indeed the conviction that only a synthetic perspective, encompassing all human abilities and attributes, could lead to an adequate understanding of nature, is a central tenet of Romantic science. The Romantics saw the methodological restrictions which characterise positivistic modern science as a dangerous reductionism. In their view this dissecting, mechanical approach treated nature's manifestations as dead objects without any meaning, destroying the integrity of nature and reducing it to the status of 'a ruin'.[1] Against such fragmented knowledge, they provocatively posited a unifying perspective on nature, achievable only through a higher synthesis of exact knowledge and speculation, scientific experiment and intuition or, ultimately, science and art.

Overall Romantic science is a highly ambitious attempt to counter some of the defining features of modernity that evolved during the Scientific Revolution of the seventeenth century and the Enlightenment of the eighteenth century and culminated in the saddle epoch around 1800; a threshold period that straddled old and new, the Ancien Régime and the modern world. Romantic science sought to offer an alternative to three underlying trends. The first is secularisation, the loss of religion as the unifying world view, with the consequence that neither knowledge nor meaning, neither the structure of the cosmos nor the dignity of nature could be guaranteed by the authority of a divine force. The second and related trend is the differentiation in the spheres of knowledge with its vast gains in empirical knowledge and an ever-increasing speed in its accumulation. This necessitated more and more specialisation, the emergence of the multitude of modern academic disciplines, the divide between the natural sciences and the humanities, and that between knowledge and understanding. The third is the Cartesian dualism of subject and object or mind and matter. For the immensely influential seventeenth-century philosopher René Descartes objective truth could only be attained by pure thought and mathematics. For reasons of scientific objectivity he thus categorically separated the material world from the operations of mind, so that any subjective influence (such as the feelings or expectations of the researcher) would be eliminated from the process of finding 'pure', experimental knowledge.

It must be noted, however, that Romantic scientists were in no way opposed to rigorous scientific experiment and made a number of valuable, still valid discoveries. They believed, however, that their results had to be integrated into a wider metaphysical perspective. It was the highest aspiration of Romantic science to find the unifying principle in nature, to falsify the Cartesian subject–object divide and to overcome the alienation between man and his environment which modernity, and in particular modern science, had caused.

Romantic science was a complex and by no means uniform movement that flourished during a relatively short period between the late 1790s and 1830, with a climax around 1815. Despite its diversity, it was overall deeply influenced by Friedrich Wilhelm Joseph Schelling's speculative philosophy of nature as laid down in *Von der Weltseele* (1798; *On the World Soul*) and *Erster Entwurf eines Systems der Naturphilosophie* (1799; *First Outline of a System of a Philosophy of Nature*). His fundamental assumption, the existence of a monistic, spiritual 'world soul', which encompasses the physical and the metaphysical, the object world and the human spirit, body and mind, informed most Romantics' scientific theorising. The movement's experimental and philosophical obsession with forces such as magnetism, electricity and galvanism, so called imponderables that were invisible and could not be measured with technical instruments, but could be observed in their effects, is testimony to this. The Romantic scientists hoped to be able to present experiential proof for the existence of such an all-pervading life-force.

In the medium of such a unifying force, matter and consciousness were seen as ultimately identical. For Schelling and the Romantic scientists, the manifestations of the natural world and the structures and concepts of the human mind correspond harmoniously, as they are governed by the same, unifying, monistic metaphysical principle. To postulate such an identity invites the speculative, philosophical and even imaginative poetic enquiry into nature as the discovery of analogies and correspondences between man and nature. Such a methodology is in direct opposition to the approach of dualistic subject philosophy, which saw the investigation of nature as the imposition of necessarily alien, human categories onto the non-human world. For the Romantics, nature is the outer, visible side of the spirit, and human consciousness is the highest form of nature. This implies that the discovery of nature in its parts and as a whole is necessarily also a journey of self-discovery, one in which self-knowledge and the understanding of nature mutually condition and support each other. This is paradigmatically expressed by the Romantic scientist Henrik Steffens: 'Willst du die Natur erkennen? Wirf einen Blick in dein Inneres, und in den Stufen geistiger Bildung mag es dir vergönnt seyn die Entwicklungsstufen der Natur zu schauen. Willst du dich selber erkennen? Forsch' in der Natur und ihre Thaten sind die des nämlichen Geistes' ('Do you want to investigate nature? Then cast a glance inwards and in the stages of spiritual formation it may be granted to you to see the stages of natural development. Do you want to know yourself? Investigate nature and your actions are those of the Spirit there').[2] This presumed identity of spiritualised nature and a so-to-speak naturalised human spirit explains why at no point in German cultural history were science and psychology as closely related as during Romanticism.

Thinking in polarities, analogies, potentialisations and metamorphoses is characteristic of Romantic science and nature philosophy. The effects of this schematising were often formalistic and to us today may seem forced or even arbitrary, but especially the use of analogy provided a plausible tool to re-emphasise the intimate bonds between humans and the world. Ritter, for example, when talking about the increased inclination in nature for fusion under the influence of heat, paralleled this physical phenomenon to the psychological observation that awareness and insight are often fuelled by enthusiasm: 'So also it is with us. The warmer we are, the more we can understand and comprehend; we thaw.'[3]

If enthusiasm, empathy and inspiration are at least as important for the understanding of nature as empirical knowledge and philosophical reasoning, then it is not surprising that for the Romantics no one is better equipped to re-establish the ontological connection between man and nature than the artist. Imagination is even better suited than speculative philosophy to unlock the hidden symbolism of nature as a well-ordered whole, to transcend the isolated phenomena of natural science and to synthesise them into a higher, meaningful symbolic order. Ritter explicitly likens the harmonious structure of nature and the meaningful beauty of a work of art, born out of artistic ingenuity: 'Anyone who finds in infinite nature nothing but one whole, one complete poem, in every word, every syllable of which, the harmony of the whole rings out and nothing destroys it, has won the highest prize of all.'[4] This analogy refers back to pre-modern, alchemistic, magical and mystical concepts of a language of nature, which, to the initiated, conveys the hidden sympathies between all that exists, the correspondences between the macrocosm of nature and man as its microcosm.

It is one consequence of such thinking that Romantic science rejected a systematic and objectifying treatment of its findings and instead opted for essayistic, aphoristic and programmatically unsystematic ways of presenting its ideas; experimental forms of knowledge based on imaginative associations and unexpected combinations. The poet-philosopher Friedrich von Hardenberg (Novalis) for example, one of the central protagonists of early Romanticism, was working on a universal encyclopaedia as the most daring utopian Romantic project. Based on aesthetic principles like symbolism, analogy and associative combination, this encyclopaedia was meant to synthesise science and poetry, knowledge and inspiration, physics and metaphysics, philosophy and psychology into a work of learned art which would encompass all knowledge and understanding in a new, daring and revelatory way.

Ultimately, the philosophical and even more so the poetical consciousness inspired by nature becomes the highest form of nature's self-knowledge and as such the 'redeemer' of nature under the conditions of modern reflexivity. In this vein, Hardenberg, who was also a fully trained and practising mining engineer, educated at the most advanced technical university of his time, the Mining Academy at Freiberg (Saxony), elevates the poet to the position of 'transscendentale[r] Arzt' ('transcendental physician', *NS* II, p. 535, No. 42), destined to overcome the modern divisions within the individual and even to heal the ailments of his age.

The history of the Romantic project of course tells us that such an aspiration overburdened the autonomous artist. Later Romantics revealed the unsustainable ambition or even hubris of early Romanticism by focusing especially on the precarious psychological dimensions of this project.

Romantic medicine

To see the poet as transcendental healer of humanity is indicative of the central position medicine occupied within the Romantic system of knowledge. For Schelling medicine was the queen of sciences, since it combined knowledge of the interaction between body, mind and the soul of nature's noblest creation, the pinnacle of its self-expression, humankind.

Schelling and Hardenberg subscribed to the medical theory of the Scottish physician John Brown, which appealed to the Romantic fascination both with polarities and ephemeral life-forces. His stimulation theory explained all illness as either a dearth or an excess of electrical stimulation in the nervous system. According to Brown and his followers such 'sthenic' or 'asthenic' pathological states could be cured or at least mitigated by an appropriate diet and regimen of activity which would increase or decrease the level of stimulation back to healthy levels. Brown's theory combined some well-established dietetic regulations for a healthy lifestyle with a bipolar philosophical framework which ultimately encompassed the physical, psychological and metaphysical health of the individual. Hardenberg, however, was particularly attracted by the possible extension of Brownianism to the whole of society. He diagnosed his own age as asthenic, that is, fundamentally weakened and hence over-stimulated and hypersensitive. He saw the artist as archetypal representative of this condition, nervous, prone to abstraction, alienated from nature. Precisely this symptomatic pathology also predestined him to offer both the most fitting diagnosis and, in his art, a possible cure for his time. Already here, in early Romanticism, we can see the interest in the abnormal and extreme as a heightened, privileged state of awareness, which in late Romanticism becomes so important.

Mesmerism

By far the most widespread, influential and therapeutically relevant variant of Romantic medicine and psychology was animal magnetism or mesmerism. Its originator, the late Enlightenment medical doctor Franz Anton Mesmer, discovered the cathartic and calming influence of his famous 'magnetic' passes along the body of his patients during experiments with the healing power of magnets. From 1774 on, he developed his theory of animal magnetism, explaining his experiences as a charismatic healer in terms of a speculative cosmological fluid theory. He saw his cures of mostly nervous complaints (and mostly in women) as effected through the workings of an ephemeral universal fluid, pervading the cosmos and the human body alike. The blockage or lack of this fluid in the nerves was the cause of all illness. A magnetiser, saturated with the magnetic fluid and empowered by nature to share it, could remedy this by administering magnetic strokes, as the positive pole pouring his excess of magnetic fluid into the needy patient, the negative pole, thus re-establishing (usually) her relation with cosmic harmony. Mesmer called this force animal magnetism by analogy with other imponderables pervading the nerves like electricity and galvanism. The term mesmerism was later introduced by his Romantic followers. Mesmer himself was a materialist, saw himself as a man of the Enlightenment, formulated his theory in the mechanistic terminology of his time and invoked Newton and Descartes as authorities. However, as he had been educated at the Jesuit university at Dillingen prior to studying medicine in Vienna, pre-modern, hermetic theories of magical healing by such as Paracelsus,

Athanasius Kircher and van Helmont were a much stronger influence on his thinking. Additionally, his immodest claim to have found in animal magnetism the panacea, the alchemists' dream, and even more so his healing methods by touch and gaze reminded his medical colleagues of the magic-magnetic cures of Baroque medicine, which modern medicine as a science was just in the process of debunking. It also brought him uncomfortably close to the countless quacks and charlatans who threatened the professionalism of enlightened medicine.

In Vienna and after 1778 in pre-revolutionary France, Mesmer and his controversial cures created a veritable mesmeric craze and were hotly debated in salons, medical circles and academic societies alike, especially since one of his French followers, the Marquis de Puységur in 1784, induced a somnambulist trance in one of his patients. This produced an array of astounding and unexplainable phenomena bordering on the paranormal, such as telepathy and clairvoyance. In contrast to Mesmer, who saw the manipulations of the magnetiser as directed towards the body, Puységur understood them as affecting the psyche; this paved the way for our modern post-Freudian understanding of mesmerism as an early form of hypnosis or suggestion. The magnetic trance opened a way into the unconscious; today Mesmer is acknowledged as an important predecessor of Freud, and mesmerism has a central place within the history of the discovery of the unconscious. The scientific establishment of the Enlightenment, of course, rejected Mesmer's theory as pure speculation and viewed his practice as fraud or at best as the result of an over-excited imagination. As a practice, animal magnetism posed a considerable threat to two cornerstones of the enlightened world view: the optimism that the inner workings of nature could be objectified, and the belief in the ultimate superiority of reason over the unconscious.

It is easy to see why the Romantics were so attracted to mesmerism. It provided an irresistible synthesis of many of their major preoccupations: its theory and practice fused the philosophy of nature and medical anthropology with psychology and metaphysics, but also integrated the realm of the aesthetic. As the Romantics reinterpreted Mesmer's most subtle material fluid as a spiritual force, the transgressive phenomena of somnambulist trances could be taken as empirical evidence for the workings of Schelling's world soul. They also offered ample opportunity to explore what Jean Paul famously called 'das ungeheure Reich des Unbewußten, dieses wahre innere Afrika' ('the enormous realm of the unconscious, this true inner Africa').[5] Thus between 1808 and the late 1830s, for Romantic philosophers of nature like Schelling and his student Gotthilf Heinrich Schubert, for key figures of Romantic medicine like Christoph Wilhelm Hufeland, Karl Christian

Wolfart or Carl August von Eschenmayer, and for most Romantic writers mesmerism became, as Nicholas Saul so aptly put it, 'the most Romantic of all sciences'.[6]

Romantic mesmerism had many propagators among doctors, philosophers and artists, and there are dozens of theoretical treatises which try to explain mesmerism in the context of Romantic nature philosophy, but the two most influential contributions to the theoretical debate were from the Berlin medical doctor Carl Alexander Ferdinand Kluge and the aforementioned medical doctor, nature philosopher and cultural historian Schubert. Though not a Romantic in the strict sense, Kluge in 1811 published the standard reference work on animal magnetism *Versuch einer Darstellung des animalischen Magnetismus als Heilmittel* (1811; *Essay at an Account of Animal Magnetism as a Remedy*). It systematised the manifold phenomena of so-called magnetic 'disorganisation' in six gradations and gave special attention to the three 'higher' states of magnetic sleep in which individual sense perception was reduced or completely shut down and replaced by a heightened sense of commonality (*Gemeingefühl*). To explain this Kluge applied Johann Christian Reil's influential bipolar model of the unconscious. According to Reil, two antagonistic nervous systems are simultaneously at work in our body. The cerebral system with the brain as its centre dominates during our waking hours, clearly differentiating between individual senses, coordinating perception and guaranteeing overall rational control. During sleep and related states like the magnetic trance, however, the other, so-called ganglionic system with the solar plexus as its centre takes over, subdues the individual senses and mobilises a synthetic sixth sense, not controlled by reason, but led by intuition and seen as particularly receptive to the overall harmony of the world soul. As a medical doctor Kluge placed particular emphasis on the therapeutic potential of the higher gradations of magnetic sleep, especially the seeming ability to diagnose one's own illness and propose suitable cures. The philosophical potential of the magnetic sleep, however, is of course also immense. The ability to perceive and interpret the workings of one's inner body seemed proof that the magnetic medium could overcome the mind–body divide. Furthermore, the gift of some somnambulists to predict the further development of their cure, to divine the right therapy and to read their magnetiser's thoughts suggested that this universal force could effectively transcend time and space and (re-)connect everything with everything.

On a psychological level extensive case histories on magnetic cures, which often continued with daily sessions over months or even years, document how in this setting the reduced rational control and the patients' heightened awareness for their condition and needs allowed for constructive therapeutic insights. The majority of magnetised were young adolescent women on the threshold of physiological and social womanhood, and some of their psychosomatic complaints and the interpretations they themselves offered reveal anxieties around this transition process. Magnetisers who saw their own role as philosophical doctors in psychological terms took the self-perceptions of the magnetised seriously and used the intimate bond between magnetiser and patient, the so-called 'rapport', for cautious therapeutic interventions, in some cases effectively achieving pre-Freudian 'talking cures'.

Arguably these magnetic cures were the most advanced psychological treatments of their time, while psychiatry as an official discipline, as it established itself mainly through Johann Christian Reil's influential *Rhapsodieen über die Anwendung der psychischen Kurmethode auf Geisteszerrüttungen* (1803; *Rhapsodies on the Application of the Psychological Method for Healing Mental Disturbances*) and his subsequent reforms of mental asylums, displayed an attitude much less receptive than that of the Romantics to the inside perspective of the mentally disturbed.

On the other side of the spectrum we find Gotthilf Heinrich Schubert, the most important populariser of nature philosophy and an ardent proponent of animal magnetism. His tremendously influential *Ansichten von der Nachtseite der Naturwissenschaft* (1808; *Views of the Dark Side of Natural Science*) set out to explore those aspects of natural history and anthropology which elude the reductive methodology of the 'positivistic' sciences. Animal magnetism is, of course, a prime example of those, and Schubert takes its transgressive somnambulist phenomena as empirical evidence for man's ability to communicate with the whole of nature in the medium of an all-pervading 'life soul'. For him the magnetic trance as well as dreams, religious ecstasy, artistic inspiration, illness and even madness represent privileged states of awareness which allow us to achieve the highest goals of Romantic science and nature philosophy: to access the essential being of nature and even catch a glimpse of the afterlife.

Literary mesmerism

In his *Die Symbolik des Traumes* (1814; *Symbolism of Dream*) Schubert calls the intuitive sensorium our inner 'versteckte[r] Poet' ('hidden poet'),[7] thus stressing once more the intimate relationship between psychology and art in Romanticism. Mesmerism is a prime example of their fruitful interaction, as its most sophisticated explorations are not to be found in speculative treatises, but in literature. Especially the authors of high and late Romanticism were deeply fascinated by the phenomenon and used it as a central motif in many of their texts. Most of them had read Schubert's works and many knew other specialist literature. Many Romantics – Hardenberg, Jean Paul, Bettina von Arnim, Friedrich Schlegel – were practising magnetisers. Their most productive mesmerist activity, however, was writing. Three tendencies in particular rewrote and radicalised the mesmerist discourse.

The first concerns balance of power in the mesmeric relation. E. T. A. Hoffmann's 'Der unheimliche Gast' (1818; 'The Uncanny Guest') and even more so his 'Der Magnetiseur' (1814; 'The Magnetiser') portray mesmeric communication not as a healing force, but as a manipulative power, invading and colonising the mind, and ultimately resulting in a terrifying loss of self. The latter text, especially, is a key document of literary mesmerism. Here the magnetiser Alban, a parasitic monster who feeds on the life energy of his patient Marie, treats her with mesmeric passes for a nervous disorder which he himself had caused in the first instance through that self-same magnetic mind control. He is driven by a proto-Nietzschean will to power and justifies his desire to triumph over his female victim with the gendered anthropology of his time: 'Nature has organised the female as passive in all her tendencies. – It is this willing abandonment, this eager grasping of the other, exterior, the acceptance and veneration of the higher principle, in which the truly childlike spirit consists, and which only the female possesses. Completely to dominate and assimilate this spirit is the highest bliss.'[8] Alban's ruthless manipulations, which rob Marie of her free will and ultimately kill her, amount to an act of communicative vampirism. His portrayal unmasks the ideal of the magnetiser as a benevolent and generous purveyor of vital forces as a misogynist dream of male domination.

A number of other tales like Caroline de La Motte Fouqué's novel *Magie der Natur* (1810; *Magic of Nature*), Achim von Arnim's *Päpstin Johanna* (1810; *Pope Joan*), E. T. A. Hoffmann's 'Das öde Haus' (1817; 'The Desolate House') and also Eduard Mörike's *Maler Nolten* (1832; *Nolten the Painter*) further highlight the central importance of the Romantic gender discourse for mesmerism by experimenting with role reversals. These texts feature female magnetisers who usurp the active and authoritative magnetiser's role which in theory and practice was an all-male reserve. Without exception they are punished for their transgressive behaviour.

The second aspect exploits the potential of mesmerism for aesthetic self-reflexivity. Most literary treatments use the parallels between aesthetic and magnetic inspiration for a self-reflection of the creative process and the rapport between text and reader. In some of his music novellas like 'Ritter Gluck' (1809; 'Sir Gluck') and 'Don Juan' (1812) Hoffmann stresses the affinities between music as the 'most Romantic of all art forms'[9] and the mesmerist fluid. At their best, the most fundamental force in nature and the most artificial product of human ingenuity can work together to touch our deepest emotions, momentarily to open the soul to transcendence and foster harmony. However, his portraits of Romantic artist-magnetisers also reveal fundamental scepticism about art's capacity to fulfil such potential in the hands of more often than not self-obsessed Romantic poets who abuse their art narcissistically. A similar ambivalence is at work in Achim von Arnim's early Romantic artist novel *Hollins Liebesleben* (1802; *Hollin's Life of Love*). However, later texts like Hoffmann's last tale 'Die Genesung' (1822; 'Convalescence'), Jean Paul's *Der Komet* (1820–22; *The Comet*) and Arnim's 'Das Majorat' (1820; 'The Inheritance') are again more optimistic, if never unambiguously so, about the power of both art and mesmerism to help reintegrate the subject into a larger whole. In these texts Hardenberg's 'transcendental physician' tentatively re-emerges as artist-magnetiser.

The third important aspect of literary mesmerism takes this dimension even further, expressing the hopes of some late Romantics that the mesmeric fluid could even transgress the ultimate threshold to the afterlife and put the unconscious in contact with the spirit world. After their conversion to an orthodox Catholicism, two of the most prominent representatives of early Romanticism, Clemens Brentano and Friedrich Schlegel, fused the roles of writer and magnetiser in recording the metaphysical visions of their somnambulist media in extensive diaries. With these visions they hoped to strengthen and embellish Catholic dogma and even to find indicators of the course of salvation history. With this practice they rewrote their own position as Romantic authors from that of autonomous poets, creating a universe out of their own ingenuity, to that of humble scribe of divine inspiration. However, in Brentano's ambition to find more truth about the life of Jesus in the visions of his medium, the stigmatised Westphalian nun Anna Katharina Emmerick, the rather immodest Romantic dream of writing the absolute book re-emerges esoterically reinscribed.

The occult side of mesmerism was of particular interest to the physician and poet Justinus Kerner, who in his famous *Die Seherin von Prévorst* (1829; *The Seeress of Prévorst*) saw the mesmeric medium primarily as a vehicle for contacts with the spirits of the deceased. Kerner is the most prominent transitional figure between mesmerism and its second most important successor movement beside deep psychology, spiritualism and faith healing.

Romantic tales on the threshold of maturation and initiation

The Romantic exploration of the unconscious was, of course, by no means limited to mesmerism and the phenomena surrounding it. In their tales, authors like E. T. A Hoffmann, Ludwig Tieck, Achim von Arnim or Heinrich von Kleist investigate many facets of the psychological formation of modern subjectivity. In many ways these stories depend on a knowledge of the psyche and a vocabulary of description developed during the Enlightenment. The cultivation of emotion in the age of sentiment, the celebration of unbridled passion in the Storm and Stress, the practice of minute self-scrutiny that emerged from pietism, the anthropology of the 'philosophical doctors' or empirical psychology's insistence on precise self-observation as documented in Moritz's autobiographical *Anton Reiser* (1785–90) – all these tendencies paved the way for the later, more radical Romantic explorations of the soul. Yet despite such continuities, the difference in perspective is decisive. Unlike their enlightened predecessors, these tales do not endorse moderation, balance and the ultimate superiority of reason. They often feature the crisis of adolescence of a male Romantic anti-hero as an initiation into adulthood which in most cases goes terribly wrong and ends in madness or death. These threshold narratives reject the normative script of a young man becoming a purposeful, well-integrated member of patriarchal society. Instead they portray the transition to bourgeois identity as a dangerous and problematic process and stage a Romantic protest against the shallow optimism of the Enlightenment, the stultifying quality of everyday life and oppressive philistine smugness. They show sympathy and fascination with the abnormal and the pathological, put the terrifying powers of our unconscious impulses on display and explore the conditions under which inspiration can turn into madness and enthusiasm into disaster. Their dark visions and unsettling storylines have not lost their appeal to our fears and desires. It is no coincidence that Hoffmann was one of the most important forefathers of the modern horror story and a central influence on Edgar Allen Poe. Today it is certainly a special attraction of these scenarios of self-loss and self-search that their psychological constellations and poetic language in many ways pre-configure some of the central tenets of Freud's theories of psychosexual development. One is of course reluctant to speak of the Romantics as pre-empting a theory of the psyche invented a hundred years later. Indeed, it might well be the other way round, since Freud is known to have taken inspiration from literature of the Classical and Romantic periods. In any case, these stories present a complex 'proto-psychoanalytical structural field',[10] in which defining traumas and conflicts of the bourgeois nuclear family are given artistic expression. Their transgressive and synaesthetic symbolic imagery resembles in many respects the dream logic identified by Freud in his *Die Traumdeutung* (1900; *Interpretation of Dreams*), as does their narrative logic, with its ambivalent distinction of dream and reality or the fantastic and the everyday. Equally significant are the frequent and disturbing *Doppelgänger* and shape-shifter figures. Overall the highly innovative aesthetic of these tales manifests the constitutive ambiguity of Romantic prose which is so apt for depicting the landscape of the troubled psyche.

Anselmus, protagonist of E. T. A. Hoffmann's masterpiece 'Der goldene Topf' (1814; 'The Golden Pot'), is a prime example of the Romantic anti-hero who must negotiate his identity between that of a respected bourgeois with family and career and that of a Romantic artist, who seeks inspiration and insight, but seems borderline insane. 'Der goldene Topf' is also particularly saturated in Romantic nature philosophy. Its subtitle, 'a fairy tale from modern times', suggests that the fantastic and the miraculous are not exiled in a distant past but anchored in the present, in this case early nineteenth-century Dresden. In its opening scene the student Anselmus, who is presented as an awkward misfit, prone to melancholy and eccentric behaviour, is on his way to the beer-garden, where he intends to have a good time like everybody else, enjoy a beer and perhaps a flirtation. However, he is distracted by strange music from an elder tree, where he has an enchanting vision of three small greenish-gold serpents. The people around him regard him as mad, but he falls in love with one of them – much to the displeasure of Veronika Paulmann, who wants him to become a Hofrat (senior civil servant), so that she can marry him. The story thus unfolds as the initiation of a poet and the conflict between his artistic vocation and the demands of society. While the burghers see Anselm as psychologically unstable, Archivist Lindhorst, father of the three daughters who have manifested themselves in serpent form and himself an inhabitant of both worlds, employs Anselm as a scribe. Lindhorst is at one and the same time a respected Privy Councillor and a mythological beast – a salamander – and apparently has no problems negotiating these different identities. He sees Anselmus's psychological fragility as the promising hint of an emerging 'childlike poetic disposition'[11] or, in other words, Schubert's latent 'inner poet'. In his so-called palm room the young man's task is to copy ancient, hieroglyphic manuscripts. He cannot decipher the signs, but if he is in tune with himself and his beloved Serpentina he can grasp their meaning intuitively. The story is full of alchemistic and cabbalistic symbolism, cited with typical Romantic self-reflexivity (in alchemy palms are a symbol of ancient wisdom). Copying old manuscripts, the meaning of which has been lost in time, and which only the gifted outsider can recuperate, is presented simultaneously as Anselmus's initiation into the secret language of nature and poetry. But it can only proceed in a dream-like state. The creative process is depicted as a trance, and Romantic art is here seen as a rediscovery of a long-lost arcana. Anselmus's path also symbolises the Romantic philosophy of history, with the poet as redeemer from present alienation and messiah of the once and future paradise Atlantis. When Anselmus withstands the lures of a bourgeois existence and devotes himself totally to the poetic, he wins both Serpentina's love and the golden pot, alchemistic symbol of totality and the unity of nature. Throughout the novella the real and the fantastic blur as in a dream. Hoffmann invests all his artistic ingenuity to keep unresolved the ambiguity as to whether the fantastic elements are real or imagined, and whether Anselmus's exalted states are inspiration or madness. However the optimistic end of this modern fairy tale suggests that his happiness in the regained Atlantis is nothing less than the process of writing and reading itself.

Most of Hoffmann's psychological tales do not end so well, and the split between Romantic longing and the demands of modern society can only be reconciled in a fairy tale. In many ways his famous 'Die Bergwerke zu Falun' (1818; 'The Mines at Falun') is a counter-narrative to 'Der goldene Topf'. After having lost his beloved mother, the protagonist Elis Fröbom is embarking on a new career as a miner. There he is torn between the love for the blonde Ulla, daughter of the mine's owner, who himself wants the talented Elis as son-in-law and as his successor, and the strong attraction he feels for the mysterious mountain queen, whom he encounters deep in the mine. Elis yearns to become one with mother earth, personified by this mythical goddess, who may or may not be a product of Elis's over-stimulated imagination. While Anselmus was attracted to the secrets of poetry, Elis is drawn to the secrets of nature. On his wedding day with Ulla, Elis in a fit of madness descends deep into the mine. He wants to fetch the most beautiful jewels for Ulla as a wedding present, or so he says. Instead he seeks a sexual-mystical union with the mountain queen: it comes at a high price, as he is buried in a collapsed shaft and never returns. The longing to lose one's everyday self, to break free from the burden of subjectivity and return to nature, is a typical motif of Romanticism. Under the conditions of modernity, however, such longing can only lead to madness and destruction, and unity with nature is achievable only in death. In Romanticism the mine is a potent symbol of the unconscious, and the descent into the womb of nature is always also a dangerous journey of self-discovery, a descent into one's own concealed phantasies. Like 'Der goldene Topf', the story can be read on one level as a subtle psychological study on the pitfalls of the transition to adulthood: the young man is afraid of commitment to a real woman and does not want to enter into a fixed and limiting profession as yet. He rather idolises a fantasmatic dream woman. But there is also a more general comment on bourgeois society and its values: The modern miner is in search of profit. He descends into the mine to find material wealth. Gold is no longer a symbol of self-perfection and unity of nature, as it was in alchemy, but a means to an end, a commodity. In previous centuries, the quest was for the secrets of nature and for closeness to mother earth. Mining was a ritualised process. Its rituals expressed an awareness that it entailed a violation and exploitation of nature, akin to the rape of mother earth. Elis undertakes mining in a similar spirit of affection and even awe, and his encounters with the mountain queen have strong erotic undertones, yet it is also an initiation into a pre-modern concept of nature's wholeness, which in modern times as the return of the repressed takes the form of madness.

This mountain queen is of course a powerful mother figure, her lure symbolises the unconscious refusal to sever the oedipal bond. A very different Oedipal narrative is at the centre in one of Hoffmann's most famous psychological tales, 'Der Sandmann' (1816; 'The Sandman'). This enigmatic story has attracted countless interpretations, many of them psychoanalytical, starting with Sigmund Freud's essay on the uncanny of 1919. Like 'Die Bergwerke zu Falun' it can be read on the level of individual psychology, but also on that of cultural commentary. At the heart of the story is an early childhood trauma of the protagonist Nathanael. He is caught observing the alchemical experiments of his father and an uncanny acquaintance Coppelius, who Faust-like are trying to create the homunculus. As punishment, Coppelius threatens to remove the eyes of this unwelcome observer of an all-male surrogate of the sexual act. In a psychotic experience of fragmentation Nathanael imagines that Coppelius really does dismember and reassemble his body. Freud reads this fantasy as an illustration of castration anxiety. The simultaneously beloved and threatening father is split, into a benevolent and a malevolent father *imago*. Years later, these fears revisit the student Nathanael, who becomes convinced that an itinerant peddler of glassware called Coppola is the demonic revenant or *Doppelgänger* of Coppelius, returned to destroy his happiness with his fiancée. In a Freudian reading, the oedipal fear of the paternal rival on the threshold of adulthood prevents a mature relationship with a woman. Nathanael, however, encounters tremendous difficulties in communicating this trauma to Clara, his level-headed fiancée, whose name marks her out as a representative of enlightened sobriety. She never takes his confession seriously, rejects any supernatural explanation of his fears and opts for psychology. Yet this Enlightenment woman lacks the Romantic empathy for his unconscious anxieties and suggests simply rationalizing them. With its intricate narrative structure, in which letters from various standpoints and an authorial voice provide polyperspectivist accounts of Nathanael's mental disturbance, the tale is also a Romantic critical commentary on the difficulty of communicating madness or accessing it from the outside position of reason. Misunderstood and isolated, Nathanael slides into madness. Rejecting Clara, he falls in love with Olimpia, the mysterious and uncanny daughter of Professor Spalanzani. This enigmatic, strangely reticent and stiff young woman turns out to be an automat, constructed by his academic father-figure Spalanzani and Coppola, who repeat the childhood constellation of dual father figures. The lifeless robot proved ideal for the projection of his narcissism. Nobody understood him better, nobody appreciated his poetry more than she did. At this point the psychological tale turns into a cultural critique of both modern male hubris and romantic imagination. In an Oedipal challenge to the ultimate father figure, God, the physicist and the technician have taken over from the alchemists the patriarchal obsession with creating artificial humanity, outdoing the natural order and replacing female fertility with technology. Thus the final catastrophe of the story, Nathanael's suicide in a fit of madness, also highlights the fatal consequences of being in love with modern technology. The fantasies and projections of the young Romantic poet Nathanael are shown to be congruent with the dreams of his fathers, the alchemists and the engineers.

Overall, tales like these seem to suggest a great affinity between Romantic and Freudian concepts of the unconscious. However, one must not overlook fundamental differences. Central to the Romantic unconscious is its metaphysical dimension, its tendency towards connectivity and wholeness. In that it is much closer to C. G. Jung's idea of the collective unconscious than to Freud's theories, which firmly situate the unconscious in this world only and in the drives (*Triebschicksal*) of the individual. In a far-reaching study, Odo Marquard has described the development from Romantic concepts of (human) nature to that of Freud as one during which the essentially benevolent 'nature' of Romanticism has been reduced to a threatening, instinctual 'nature'. Romantic science fully subscribes to what Marquard aptly calls 'Romantiknatur', and authors close to it like Achim von Arnim or Jean Paul embellish it aesthetically.[12] As we have seen, others, like E. T. A. Hoffmann, treat it with a suspicion and Romantic irony, in many ways pre-empting Freudian scepticism. This is certainly one of the reasons why these authors still intrigue us today. However, this preponderance of a modern psychological perspective should not lead us to overlook other important elements of the lasting legacy of Romantic science and psychology. Some aspects of the Romantic protest against the onset of modernity 200 years ago, such as its insistence on the subjective factor in scientific investigation, its keen eye for the interrelatedness of mind and body, and its emphasis on the intimate bond of man and nature are still of relevance to us late moderns.

NOTES

1. H. Steffens, *Zur Geschichte der heutigen Physik* (Breslau: Max, 1829), p. 118.
2. H. Steffens, 'Ueber die Vegetation', in *Schriften: Alt und Neu*, vol. II (Breslau: Max, 1821), p. 102.
3. J. W. Ritter, *Fragmente aus dem Nachlasse eines jungen Physikers* (Heidelberg: Schneider, 1810), vol. I, p. 33.
4. Ibid. vol. II, p. 205.
5. Jean Paul, 'Selina', in *Sämtliche Werke*, Section 1, vol. VI, ed. Norbert Miller (Munich: Hanser 1970), p. 1182.
6. N. Saul, 'Nachwort', in N. Saul (ed.), *Die deutsche literarische Romantik und die Wissenschaften* (London: Institute of Germanic Studies; Munich: Iudicium, 1991), pp. 306–18, here p. 314.
7. Gotthilf Heinrich Schubert, *Symbolik des Traumes* (Bamberg: Kunz, 1814), p. 3.
8. E. T. A. Hoffmann, 'Der Magnetiseur', in *Fantasie- und Nachtstücke*, ed. Walter Müller-Seidel (Munich: Winkler, 1960), pp. 141–78, here p. 173.
9. E. T. A. Hoffmann, 'Kreisleriana', in *Fantasie- und Nachtstücke*, pp. 39, 41.
10. H. Böhme, 'Romantische Adoleszenzkrisen: Zur Psychodynamik der Venuskult-Novellen von Tieck, Eichendorff und E. T. A. Hoffmann', in *Literatur und Psychoanalyse. Vorträge des Kolloqiums am 6. und 7. Oktober 1980,* eds. K. Bohnen, S. A. Jørgensen, F. Schmoë (Copenhagen and Munich: Fink, 1981), pp. 133–76, here p. 136.
11. E. T. A Hoffmann, 'Der goldne Topf', in *Fantasie- und Nachtstücke* (1960), pp. 179–255, here p. 230.
12. O. Marquard, *Transzendentaler Idealismus: Romantische Naturphilosophie: Psychoanalyse* (Cologne: Jürgen Dinter, 1987), p. 198.

FURTHER READING

Auhuber, F., *In einem fernen dunklen Spiegel: E. T. A. Hoffmanns Poetisierung der Medizin* (Opladen: Westdeutscher Verlag, 1986)

Barkhoff, Jürgen, *Magnetische Fiktionen: Literarisierung des Mesmerismus in der Romantik* (Stuttgart and Weimar: Metzler, 1995)

Bell, Matthew, *The German Tradition of Psychology in Literature and Thought, 1700–1840* (Cambridge: Cambridge University Press, 2005)

Böhme, H., 'Geheime Macht im Schoß der Erde: Das Symbolfeld des Bergbaus zwischen Sozialgeschichte und Psychohistorie', in *Natur und Subjekt* (Frankfurt am Main: Suhrkamp, 1988), pp. 67–144

Cunningham, Andrew and Nicholas Jardine (eds.), *Romanticism and the Sciences* (Cambridge: Cambridge University Press, 1990)

Ellenberger, Henri F., *The Discovery of the Unconscious: The History and Evolution of Dynamic Psychiatry* (New York: Basic Books, 1970)

Engelhardt, D. von, 'Natural Science in the Age of Romanticism', in A. Faivre and J. Needleman (eds.), *Modern Esoteric Spirituality* (New York: Crossroad, 1992), pp. 101–31

Kremer, D., *Prosa der Romantik* (Stuttgart and Weimar: Metzler, 1997) (Ch. 9: 'Psychologische Konturen')

Mahlendorf, U., 'Die Psychologie der Romantik', in *Romantik-Handbuch*, ed. H. Schanze (Stuttgart: Alfred Kröner, 1994), pp. 590–604

Neubauer, J., *Bifocal Vision: Novalis's Philosophy of Nature and Disease* (Chapel Hill: University of North Carolina Press, 1971)

Reuchlein, G., *Bürgerliche Gesellschaft, Psychiatrie und Literatur: Zur Entwicklung der Wahnsinnsthematik in der deutschen Literatur des späten 18. und frühen 19. Jahrhunderts* (Munich: Fink, 1986)

Rommel, G., 'Romanticism and Natural Science', in *The Literature of German Romanticism, The Camden House History of German Literature*, ed. D. F. Mahoney, vol. VIII (Rochester: Camden House, 2004), pp. 209–27

Wiesing, U., *Kunst oder Wissenschaft? Konzeptionen der Medizin in der deutschen Romantik* (Stuttgart: frommann-holzboog, 1995)

Ziolkowski, T., *German Romanticism and Its Institutions* (Princeton, N.J.: Princeton University Press, 1990) (Ch. 2: 'The Mine', Ch. 4: 'The Madhouse')

14

RICHARD LITTLEJOHNS

German Romantic painters

A new aesthetic

The work of German Romantic artists consistently reflects, directly or indirectly, the new aesthetic propagated by Romantic writers, critics and theorists. The two most significant painters of the epoch, Caspar David Friedrich and Philipp Otto Runge, were not given to issuing manifestos, preferring to set out their artistic agenda in letters to friends and relatives. Yet their paintings manifest the same tensions between empirical reality and spiritual vision which inform not only the poetic work of Romantic authors but also the theories of art enunciated by Romantics as diverse as Wackenroder and Friedrich Schlegel. Art was no longer conceived as a medium of entertainment, edification or even aesthetic gratification; rather, its function was to body forth insights into the transcendental. It was to be evaluated, not by the criterion of (good) taste, but according to its visionary intensity.

In the *Herzensergießungen eines kunstliebenden Klosterbruders* (1797; *Heartfelt Outpourings of an Art-Loving Friar*), which Wackenroder wrote with the assistance of Tieck, art is described as 'Hieroglypenschrift' ('hieroglyphic script').[1] The term was topical, since contemporary scholars were on their way to deciphering the Egyptian hieroglyphs. It implied a medium of communication which employed recognisable characters whilst remaining only partially comprehensible and thus offered tantalising but incomplete glimpses into ancient and arcane wisdom. Friedrich Schlegel echoed Wackenroder's thought in his *Gespräch über die Poesie* (1800; *Conversation on Poetry*), asserting that all Romantic visions were in essence a 'Hieroglyphe der Einen ewigen Liebe' ('hieroglyph of indivisible eternal love') (*KFSA* II, p. 334). In other words, all forms of art, visual as well as literary, should be symbolic, adumbrating spiritual truths through the code of material forms. Infinite truths were by definition not accessible to human reason, but in the hieroglyph of art they might be fleetingly and imperfectly intuited. The artist did portray material reality, whether human or natural, but this reality should 'intimate immortality'.

Such conceptions challenged and overthrew the doctrines of neo-classicism, according to which the arts existed to offer an idealised and harmonised reproduction of the physical world and its inhabitants, as for instance in the Arcadian landscapes of Claude Lorraine and Ruisdael or the pastoral idylls of Salomon Gessner. The idealisation sought by the neo-classicists had been best exemplified, according to the influential theories of Winckelmann and Anton Raphael Mengs, in the classical works of the ancients, and it was incumbent on modern artists to imitate and combine the timeless merits of these various models. Wackenroder was contemptuous of such eclecticism, substituting for its contrivance and derivativeness a new Romantic concept of inspiration. The artist was to be fired, not by models and copied skills, but by a personal and spontaneous afflatus, metaphorically a moment of 'unmittelbaren göttlichen Beystand' ('direct divine support')[2] arriving unpredictably and uncontrollably. Genius was to take the place of taste. The implications for the painter of this new Romantic subjectivism were later spelt out by Caspar David Friedrich in his injunction to painters to 'Schließe dein leibliches Auge, damit du mit dem geistigen Auge zuerst siehst dein Bild' ('close your bodily eye so that you may see your picture first with the spiritual eye').[3] Latent spiritual meaning could only be perceived through the inner vision of the inspired artist.

Romantic painters thus did not in general favour the history painting which in the eighteenth century had been viewed as the apogee of artistic practice, whether its subject matter was modern history or, as most often, classical mythology. Philip Otto Runge, having unsuccessfully submitted a drawing of a subject from Homer in the annual painting competition organised by the circle of 'Weimar Friends of Art' surrounding Goethe, turned away in indignation from such classical subjects. 'Wir sind keine Griechen mehr,' he wrote to his brother, 'können das Ganze schon nicht mehr so fühlen, wenn wir ihre vollendeten Kunstwerke sehen, viel weniger selbst solche hervorbringen' ('we are no longer Greeks, we can no longer sense the whole thing when we see their perfected works of art, much less produce such works ourselves').[4] He went on in the same letter to declare his preference for landscape, specifically for landscape with a symbolic import. The only true works of art, he argued, were those in which the artist was moved by a sense that his subject had a transcendental significance, 'einen Zusammenhang mit dem Universum' ('a connection with the universe').

The new view of landscape painting had already been set out in Ludwig Tieck's *Franz Sternbalds Wanderungen* (1798; *The Wanderings of Franz Sternbald*), an artist novel planned with Wackenroder, much admired by Runge and enthusiastically received by the Romantic generation in Germany in general. The eponymous hero, a journeyman artist in sixteenth-century Germany, encounters a hermit painter who declares that it is the task of the artist to discern the signature of God in nature, the 'geheime Ziffer' ('secret cypher') concealed in every stone. The artist then responds to this encoded transcendental meaning and, in an act of unconscious inspiration, reflects it in his finished work: 'heimlich sind Blumen hineingewachsen, von denen der Künstler selber nicht weiß, die Gottes Finger hineinwirkte' ('flowers have grown into it, unknown to the artist himself and worked in by God's finger').[5]

Pictorially, the new aesthetic was dramatically and controversially manifested in 1808 in Caspar David Friedrich's painting *Das Kreuz im Gebirge* (*The Cross in the Mountains*). Apart from the cropping of foreground and middle ground, involving the viewer emotionally with an uncomfortable directness inconceivable in neo-classical landscape, this picture was revolutionary in its juxtaposition of two entirely disparate images. On the one hand, we see a tract of Northern European landscape, realistically depicted, albeit in stylised form: a craggy mountain peak with an outgrowth of pine trees. At the same time, the peak is surmounted, at first sight incongruously, by a motif drawn from New Testament iconography: Christ on the cross. The fusion of the two elements, conspicuously European topography and the Passion of Christ in the Holy Land, is emphasised by the ivy spiralling up the crucifix and the symmetrical resemblance between the tall cross and the pines below it. A long denunciation of this picture was immediately published by Basilius von Ramdohr, a neo-classicist theoretician whom Wackenroder and Tieck in the *Herzensergießungen* had singled out for particular disapproval. Ramdohr rejected the picture on two counts: allegory, as he calls it, should not be introduced into landscapes, since it moves the viewer 'pathologically' rather than engaging a purely aesthetic interest; and secondly, the picture exemplifies the contemporary craze for religious mysticism, in which symbols and fantasies purport to be painterly and poetic images and classical antiquity is rejected in favour of 'Gothic' aberrations. The controversy clearly marks the threshold between neo-classical and Romantic art. Ramdohr spoke for an outdated school of thought, and Romantic painters were already producing landscapes which were charged with 'pathological', in other words emotional intensity, and in which 'allegorical' significance was everywhere apparent.

Figure 1. *Das Kreuz im Gebirge* (*The Cross in the Mountains*), 1808 (oil on canvas) by
Caspar David Friedrich (1774–1840) (Galerie Neue Meister, Dresden, Germany)

Romantic landscape

As early as 1803 a set of Romantic landscapes had been created, at least in the form of drawings, which abandoned any attempt at mimetic reproduction of the natural world and aimed entirely at the expression of transcendental meaning: Runge's four *Zeiten* (*Times* – of Day and/or Seasons). Runge's main focus is on the depiction of symbolic vegetation. The times of day are represented by outsize flowers: morning, (mid)day and evening by an ascending, dominant or sinking lily respectively, night by a poppy. Seated on the flowers and their stems, in symmetrical pairs or embracing clusters and no larger than the blooms, are androgynous *putti* making music. They celebrate the wondrous and everlasting alternation of night, ambiguously portrayed as a period not only of dormancy but of menace, and pristine and regenerate day. All creation participates in an eternally unbroken and secure cycle of burgeoning (morning/spring), maturity (day/summer), decay (evening/autumn) and extinction (night/winter). This predominantly pantheistic vision of sublimely self-perpetuating nature is lent Christian significance by the framework panels of the drawings, in which icons of Jehovah, Christ and the Trinity suggest divine protection of the terrestrial cycle.[6] In later coloured versions of *Morgen* (*Morning*) Runge adhered to the same symbolic procedure: above the primeval earth the lily now merges with a giant figure of Aurora, the goddess of dawn.

The *Zeiten* are the most well-known of Runge's landscapes, but in fact they only constitute the most conspicuous application of techniques which are apparent in a number of his works. In the frame of *Die Lehrstunde der Nachtigall* (1805; *Instruction of the Nightingale*), for instance, we see again the stylised figures which reflect the influence on Runge of the two-dimensional sculptures and outline drawings of the English artist John Flaxman. *Quelle und Dichter* (also 1805; *The Source and the Poet*) offers another symbolic landscape, employing luxuriant vegetation and more *putti* figures to convey the religious belief, derived from the German mystic Jacob Böhme, that terrestrial creation strives towards divine light. The notion of light, or whiteness, as the embodiment of goodness or the divine is explicitly developed in Runge's simultaneously technical and rhapsodic treatise *Farbenkugel* (*Sphere of Colours*) of 1810 and is exemplified in paintings such as *Die Ruhe auf der Flucht* (1806; *Rest on the Flight into Egypt*), in which the infant Christ lies irradiated by a sky flooded with preternatural whiteness. Like Turner in Britain, Romantic painters in Germany discovered luminosity as a means to convey the transcendental.

In a whole series of landscapes by Caspar David Friedrich brightness, varying from pale patches in a leaden sky to yellow or red light suffusing an

Figure 2. *Morgen* (*Morning*), 1803 (ink on paper) by Philipp Otto Runge (1777–1810) (Hamburger Kunsthalle, Hamburg, Germany).

entire scene, appears in the distance or background, whilst nearer the viewer an individual traveller or a group in procession make their way towards it, often through a church archway or some other portal. The symbolism is clear: struggling in earthly adversity, mortals can attain to redemption through the means of faith. One of the only two works by Friedrich held in Britain, *Winterlandschaft* (probably 1811; *Winter Landscape*) in the National Gallery, offers a striking example of this recurrent configuration: a solitary pilgrim in a snowy wilderness has dispensed with his crutches on sighting a wayside crucifix, whilst in the distance the outline of an extravagantly Gothic church beckons to a heaven indicated by a mist illuminated with pink brightness. In paintings such as *Das grosse Gehege* (1832; *The Great Enclosure*) or the startling early work *Mönch am Meer* (1809; *Monk on the Seashore*) Friedrich uses a panoramic and luminous sky to suggest the majesty of the cosmos and the insignificance of humanity in relation to it. This last painting attracted admiration and amazement from Romantic writers, Kleist remarking that the vastness of the scene created a sensation 'als ob einem die Augenlider weggeschnitten wären' ('as if one's eyelids had been cut away'),[7] referring to Friedrich's renewed cropping of the foreground. In other maritime paintings, such as *Auf dem Segler* (1818–19; *On the Sailing Boat*), Friedrich again portrays a passage towards redemptive light.

Employing the metaphor of the journey of life, Friedrich also painted scenes of ships sailing into the distance, cruising towards the shore, or safely at anchor. A more enigmatic example of this category is *Die Lebensstufen* (1834–5; *The Stages of Life*), in which Friedrich depicts a group of five ships approaching a shoreline on which we see a corresponding group of five family members of representative different ages. This is again a clearly symbolic seascape, as the mannered gestures and postures of the family indicate, perhaps with a coded political message. A perhaps more realistic scene is the subject of *Kreidefelsen auf Rügen* (1818; *Chalk Cliffs on Rügen Island*), in which a trio of friends peers over a cliff edge at the rocks and shore below in what appears to be a holiday memory or genre picture. But here too the perspective opens up on a wide and bright expanse of water, just as in the nocturnal woodland scene of *Zwei Männer in Betrachtung des Mondes* (1819; *Two Men Observing the Moon*) the friends gaze in awe at the full moon in the distance, or in *Der Wanderer über dem Nebelmeer* (1818; *The Walker above the Sea of Mist*) the solitary spectator stands on high and stares away from us at a seemingly unending panorama of mountain peaks. Everywhere in Friedrich's work landscapes and seascapes imply a numinous dimension beyond the topographical data. His numerous disciples and imitators – Carl Gustav Carus, Ferdinand Oehme, Julius Leypold, the Norwegian Johann Christian Clausen Dahl – rehearse his Romantic images and themes but rarely achieve his evocative power. Carus's painting *Kahnfahrt auf der Elbe* (1827; *Boat Trip on the Elbe*), for example, whilst reproducing the familiar rear view of passengers gazing into a bright distance, only suggests comfortable *Biedermeier* normality, whilst the destination of this trip is nothing more mysterious than contemporary Dresden sketched in postcard style. More originality was exhibited by Carl Blechen, another follower of Friedrich and Dahl, who broke free of the clichés of Gothic ruins to produce paintings of sunlit Italian scenes but also northern landscapes with hints of industrialised reality.

Political art

Like writers such as Kleist, artists in Germany were provoked into political themes and even propaganda by the upheavals of the Napoleonic wars. Following the defeats of the Austrian Empire in 1805 and of Prussia in 1806, the ensuing French hegemony over the German states as a whole induced a wave of nationalistic sentiment. Philipp Otto Runge, who joined a patriotic society in Hamburg, sketched cover designs in 1809 for a periodical with the programmatic title *Vaterländisches Museum* (*Museum of the Fatherland*). Drawn at a point where there seemed little hope of the survival of German identity and traditions, the front cover, designated *Fall des Vaterlandes* (*Fall of the Fatherland*), was to show Germany as a male figure buried alive, naked and without a coffin, while the turf above comes under the plough. In 1815, following the wars which had led to the expulsion of the French, Georg Friedrich Kersting, another of Friedrich's Dresden associates, produced a painting entitled *Auf Vorposten* (*On Outpost Duty*), showing himself and two friends serving in a volunteer corps in the campaign against the retreating French. The subtext of the picture lies not only in the fact that the comrades in arms are wearing uniforms based on the 'old German' costume fashionable amongst young nationalists and that one of them has been decorated with the Iron Cross, but in their location in dense oak forest, a symbol of German fortitude in the face of French oppression. A similar message is conveyed by Friedrich's *Chasseur im Walde* (1812; *Chasseur in the Forest*): a solitary French cavalryman stares at an impenetrable German forest, implying the hopeless isolation of the occupying French in a resilient Germany. Under the repressive French regime political themes could only be presented through such covert allegory. A number of paintings executed by Friedrich in this period thus express patriotism obliquely by portraying monuments to German patriots from the past, whilst in one of them (*Grabmale alter Helden* (1812; *Tombs of Ancient Heroes*) a barely visible snake in the colours of the French flag slithers sacrilegiously over a German hero's grave.

In the period after the Congress of Vienna Romantic artists moved to a different political agenda, although nationalism remained the underlying focus. Reflecting the dashed hopes for German unification, the disappointment over the restoration of absolutist government, and the general pessimism of the post-Napoleonic era, Friedrich painted *Das Eismeer* (1824; *The Polar Sea*): a sailing ship with the significant name 'The Hope' lies capsized, crushed by the inexorable force of huge slabs of ice, its broken masts projecting out into a desolate Arctic wilderness. Other artists sought comfort in traditional German folk themes, in celebration of German provincial culture, or in re-creation of medieval splendour. The Viennese painter Moritz von Schwind exploited German folklore, illustrating fairy tales and romances, as in his vivid painting (1845) of the grotesque sprite Rübezahl; another typical work, *Kuno von Falkenstein* (1843–4), shows the legendary knight guiding his horse up to a medieval castle from which a fair damsel leans out, while dwarves and hobgoblins scramble up the path behind him. Similar scenes were painted by Adrian Ludwig Richter, such as *Die heilige Genoveva im Wald* (1841; *St Genevieve in the Forest*), although he tended more to favour sentimental subject matter drawn from rustic German life, often in the medium of woodcuts. The architect Karl Friedrich Schinkel painted medieval castles which are entirely imaginative pastiche, such as *Dom über einer Stadt am Wasser* (1813; *Cathedral above City Waterfront*), in which a Gothic church of massive proportions and impossibly intricate arches and spires dominates a dramatic medieval city. One of Richter's most well-known pictures, *Die Überfahrt am Schreckenstein* (1857; *Crossing the River by the Schreckenstein*), shows a party of pilgrims and tourists being rowed past a Gothic castle perched on a crag. Since Goethe's essay on Strasburg Cathedral (1773) Gothic architecture had been supposed, erroneously, to be a characteristically German phenomenon; and, in an epoch where campaigns to complete the unfinished Cologne Cathedral were linked closely to continuing aspirations for German unity, historical fantasies such as those of Schinkel and Richter had unmistakable political implications.

Rediscovered religion

Gothic church architecture, often in picturesquely ruined form, figures ubiquitously in the work of Friedrich and his followers and there too has patriotic connotations; but, as we have seen above, in these cases its significance is primarily religious. Sometimes only residual church facades are portrayed, as in Friedrich's *Abtei im Eichwald* (1809–10; *Abbey in an Oak Forest*), where a procession of monks makes its way across a snow-covered graveyard through two archways into the light of eternity, or

Oehme's *Gotische Kirchenruine im Walde* (1841; *Gothic Church Ruin in the Forest*), or Carus's *Fenster am Obyn bei Mondschein* (1828; *Window on the Obyn in the Moonlight*), where a pair of lovers gazes at the moon through an overgrown Gothic arch. Sometimes an entire church appears in ethereal two-dimensional form, as in Friedrich's *Kreuz im Gebirge* (1812, *Cross in the Mountains*) or his *Die Kathedrale* (1817; *The Cathedral*): visions of the glory of heaven. Sometimes there is a view from outside into a church, as in Oehme's *Dom im Winter* (1821; *Cathedral in Winter*), where the brilliantly illuminated altar offers the warmth of salvation, or a church interior is shown, as in Blechen's *Gotische Kirchenruine* (1826; *Gothic Church Ruin*). A ruined Gothic window frame provides a site for individual meditation in Friedrich's *Der Träumer* (1835–6; *The Dreamer*) and, with additional patriotic significance, in his *Huttens Grab* (1823; *The Grave of Ulrich von Hutten*). The ruined monastery of Eldena was painted repeatedly by both Friedrich and, less mysteriously, by Carus (1823), and in Friedrich's case it combines in one picture with a mountainous background to symbolise redemption in double form.

The religious significance for Romantic artists of mountains or mountain ranges is made spectacularly explicit in Friedrich's *Morgen im Riesengebirge* (1830–4; *Morning in the Riesengebirge*). In the foreground a tall crucifix surmounts the peak of the highest of a wide sweep of mountains, and a female figure assists her male companion in scrambling up to the foot of the cross. Christian faith is the rock on which human beings climb to marvel at the prospect of heavenly salvation, symbolised again by the brilliant light of the dawn rising over the mountains and illuminating the climbers as they emerge from the dark shadow of the earthly side of the peak. Similar iconography operates in Friedrich's *Gebirgslandschaft mit Regenbogen* (1810; *Mountain Landscape with Rainbow*), in which a solitary climber finds rest on a rock illuminated by the rainbow. Often the sheer scale and magnificence of a mountain peak or peaks are enough to suggest the sublime, as in Friedrich's *Felsenschlucht* (1823; *Rocky Chasm*), or in pictures of the Watzmann mountain as painted by Richter (1824) and Friedrich (1825), or in Oehme's painting *Das Wetterhorn* (1829). In these last three works snow-covered peaks tower over rocky foothills, densely wooded middle ground, and waterfalls plunging down to form rushing streams in the foreground, reminiscent of Eichendorff's poem 'Sehnsucht' ('Yearning') with its description of an Alpine landscape with 'schwindelnde Felsenschlüfte' ('dizzying rocky abysses') and springs which 'von den Klüften sich stürzen in die Waldesnacht' ('plunge from the chasms into the night of forests'). Both Romantic artists and writers envisaged such mountain vistas as symbols of a sublime spiritual world in contrast to imperfect social reality. Josef Anton

Koch's *Der Schmadribachfall* (1821–2; *The Schmadribach Falls*) appears almost like an illustration to Eichendorff's poem.

In the *Herzensergießungen* Wackenroder had concentrated on the religious art of the Renaissance, suggesting that it was of at least equal value to the art of antiquity which neo-classicist theorists had extolled as the ideal. Raphael's madonnas, so he proclaimed, were lifted and inspired by the religious devotion which underpinned them. Friedrich Schlegel went a step further in the art-historical essays which he published in his journal *Europa* (1803–5), at a time when he was on his way to conversion from a form of pantheism to Catholicism, maintaining that the criterion by which works of art should be judged was not their aesthetic appeal but their 'hohe, ja göttliche Bedeutung' ('high, indeed divine meaning', *KFSA* IV, p. 93). Whilst Friedrich, Runge, and their Protestant associates in North Germany used landscape as a means of indirectly symbolizing their religious convictions, another group of artists emerged in Vienna in 1809 who put Schlegel's assertion into practice, painting overtly religious and even devotional subjects and thus in part returning to history painting: the so-called Nazarenes.

Initially calling themselves the 'Lukasbrüder' ('Brethren of St Luke'), this group of artists was led by Franz Pforr and Friedrich Overbeck. Rejecting the sterile classicism of the Vienna Academy, they aspired to imitate the primitive and pious art of Raphael and his predecessors. In 1810 the brotherhood moved to Rome and took up residence in the monastery of San Isidoro, where they affected a monastic style of dress and way of life, which seems to be the origin of the designation 'Nazarenes'. Perhaps the most typical of their quasi-religious paintings is Pforr's *Sulamith und Maria* (1811), a diptych showing on the left Shulamit as the embodiment of the South, a figure redolent of Raphael madonnas and seated in front of an Italian landscape, and on the right Maria as the personification of the North, combing her hair in a Gothic chamber recalling domestic scenes by Dürer. A similar parallelism is evoked in Overbeck's *Italia und Germania* (1811–28), where two pious maids in flowing medieval costumes are set against contrasting backgrounds of Italian and German architecture respectively. Overbeck's *Der heilige Sebastian* (1813–16; *St Sebastian*) shows the martyr as a Christ-like figure in a state of holy repose against a background of Italian church buildings. From the beginning the Nazarenes also took to painting scenes from German medieval history and legend, as in Pforr's *Der Graf von Habsburg und der Priester* (1810; *The Count of Habsburg and the Priest*), a picture strikingly primitivist in its flatness and two-dimensionality. His *Einzug Rudolfs von Habsburg in Basel* (1810; *Entry of Rudolf von Habsburg into Basel*) is a crowded and colourful medieval scene which might have been painted by

Dürer or an artist of the Flemish school, with buildings and their occupants in the background shown flat and without perspective.

Not all of the original 'brothers' accompanied Pforr and Overbeck to Rome, but they were joined there by important new members of the Nazarene school, in particular Peter Cornelius and Julius Schnorr von Carolsfeld. Cornelius had already made his name as the illustrator of Goethe's *Faust* in appropriately 'old German', medievalizing style, and in Rome he took up the Nazarenes' preoccupation with religious themes, illustrating parables such as *Die klugen und die törichten Jungfrauen* (1813; *The Wise and the Foolish Virgins*) and completing a range of Old Testament history paintings in Renaissance style, for example *Joseph deutet die Träume Pharaos* (1816; *Joseph Interprets the Pharaoh's Dreams*). The paintings relating the story of Joseph were part of a cycle of frescos for the Casa Bartholdi, a collaborative project which also involved Overbeck, Wilhelm Schadow, Philipp Veit and Franz Catel. For Schnorr von Carolsfeld religious subjects were of less interest, although he did later paint *Die Hochzeit zu Kana* (1819; *The Marriage at Cana*) in the naive Renaissance manner which the Nazarenes cultivated. Schnorr's strength lay in medieval history paintings, as exemplified by his dramatic *Reiterkampf auf Lipadusa* (1816; *Cavalry Battle on Lipadusa*) with its bold symmetrical composition, and he also produced the remarkable portrait of Bianca von Quandt playing the lute (1819–20), the medieval costume, loggia setting and Italian landscape background of which make it one of the most characteristic products of the Nazarene group.

Other German artists in Rome gravitated into the circle surrounding the Nazarenes. The Riepenhausen brothers, Franz and Joseph, had already emigrated to Rome in 1805, having made a reputation with illustrations to Tieck's *Genoveva* in Flaxman's outline style, and they now became interested principally in producing art with Christian themes. Another pair of brothers, Ferdinand and Friedrich Olivier, painted portraits and medievalising urban scenes in the Nazarene style. Joseph Anton Koch, an older Swiss painter who had begun painting according to neo-classical conventions, collaborated in some of the Nazarenes' fresco projects and in the 1820s turned, as we have seen, to landscape painting in a Romantic manner akin to the work of Friedrich. In the context of the conversion to Catholicism of a number of Romantic writers, the activities of the Nazarenes and their circle induced a sharp condemnation in 1817 by Goethe (and/or by his ally Meyer) of the mysticism of what they termed the 'neu-deutsche religiös-patriotische Kunst' ('new-German religious-patriotic art') of the day; but the Nazarenes laid the foundations of major schools of art in Germany in the nineteenth century, particularly in Düsseldorf, and were important models for the Pre-Raphaelites in England.

Conclusion

In the work of Friedrich and his followers such as Kersting there are a number of paintings of interiors which seem to have only private importance, in particular scenes beside windows or simply plain square windows without human presence. But here too symbolism is at work. In Friedrich's *Frau am Fenster* (1822; *Woman at the Window*) we again encounter a figure facing away from the spectator, gazing out from a window on to a river scene and a sunlit wood on the far bank. As in the writings of Kleist and Eichendorff at this time, the window is significant as a threshold, the point at which those unsettled in a restrictive domestic circle or social environment can escape into visions of freedom. It is no accident that *Frau am Fenster*, an interior, resembles *Wanderer über dem Nebelmeer*, set in the most open of panoramas: in both cases a reflective individual communes with a bright beyond. In his two paintings entitled *Caspar David Friedrich in seinem Atelier* (1811 and 1819) Kersting showed Friedrich himself at work beside a window, the sunlight pouring through on to the easel, and by implication into the painted scene, in an otherwise austerely bare room. The symbolism of the window is at work too in paintings by Kersting such as *Die Stickerin* (1812; *The Embroideress*), but here *Biedermeier* composure and even sentimentality outweigh Romantic longing.

In Runge's portrait of Luise Perthes (1805) the little girl stands on a chair facing a window and is illuminated by rays of sunshine, an embodiment of childish innocence with divine endorsement. In his picture of the three Hülsenbeck children (1805–6) the innocence of the siblings is celebrated not only by the light of dawn but by their domination of a garden world uncorrupted by adults and urban civilisation. In this way Runge's innovative portraits too are intensified by symbolism. He does not paint wealthy patrons, but portrays family and friends in intimate and often nervous stances, as in *Wir Drei* (1810; *We Three*), showing himself with his wife and brother, pensive individuals huddling together in politically turbulent times, or in *Die Eltern des Künstlers* (1806; *The Artist's Parents*), where the elderly couple seem apprehensive and discomfitted by the happy grandchildren at their feet. In this last work the sense of vulnerability, political as well as personal, is further symbolised by threatening red clouds gathering in the sky above the sea behind the house.

Thus in numerous ways Romantic art in Germany follows the same agenda as in literature: empirical reality is acknowledged and portrayed, but it is shown to be imperfect and in need of transcending spiritual visions which can only be suggested through symbolism. One final but especially striking illustration of this phenomenon may be cited: again and again

Friedrich paints landscapes which at first sight represent topographic reality, such as *Dorflandschaft bei Morgenbeleuchtung* (1822; *Village Landscape in Morning Light*) or *Ruine im Riesengebirge* (1830–34; *Ruin in the Riesengebirge*), but in the former the tree dominating the scene is a stock feature taken from Friedrich's sketchbooks, whilst in the latter the ruin is Eldena, situated hundreds of miles away near Greifswald. In the final phases of Romanticism altogether more realistic techniques began to be employed, as in the Viennese rural scenes painted by Ferdinand Waldmüller. Romantic painting in Germany came to an end with the wryly observed social scenes painted by Carl Spitzweg, in which he affectionately but also sardonically shows the descent of grand Romantic gesture into provincial *kitsch*. In *Der arme Poet* (1837; *The Poor Poet*), perhaps his most well-known work, the Romantic poet has become a sad eccentric stuck in his garret; Friedrich's sunlit window is still there, but the poet finds no vision looking out of it, instead he cowers away from it in his bed and creates poetry in the least Romantic fashion imaginable – reckoning metre on his fingers.

NOTES

1. Wilhelm Heinrich Wackenroder, *Sämtliche Werke und Briefe*, eds. Silvio Vietta and Richard Littlejohns (Heidelberg: Carl Winter, 1991), vol. I, p. 98.
2. Ibid., p. 58.
3. *Caspar David Friedrich in Briefen und Bekenntnissen*, ed. Sigrid Hinz (Munich: Rogner & Bernhard, 1974), p. 83.
4. Philipp Otto Runge, *Hinterlassene Schriften*, ed. Johann Daniel Runge, 2 vols. facsimile edition (Göttingen: Vandenhoeck & Ruprecht, 1965 [1840–1]), vol. I, p. 6.
5. *Franz Sternbalds Wanderungen*, ed. Alfred Anger (Stuttgart: Reclam, 1966), pp. 252–3.
6. For more detailed interpretation of these drawings, see my article 'Philipp Otto Runge's *Tageszeiten* and their relationship to Romantic Nature Philosophy', *Studies in Romanticism*, 42 (2003), pp. 55–74.
7. Heinrich von Kleist, *Sämtliche Werke und Briefe*, ed. Helmut Sembdner, 4 vols. (Munich: Hanser, 1982), vols. III, p. 327.

FURTHER READING

Allert, Beate, 'Romanticism and the Visual Arts', in *The Literature of German Romanticism*, ed. Dennis F. Mahoney (Columbia, S.C.: Camden House, 2004), pp. 273–306

Andrews, Keith, *The Nazarenes: A Brotherhood of German Painters in Rome* (Oxford: Clarendon Press, 1964)

Bisanz, Rudolf M., *German Romanticism and Philipp Otto Runge* (DeKalb: Northern Illinois University Press, 1970)

Hartley, Keith, Henry Meyric Hughes, Peter-Klaus Schuster and William Vaughan (eds.), *The Romantic Spirit in German Art 1790–1990* (London: Thames and Hudson, 1994)

Honour, Hugh, *Romanticism* (Harmondsworth: Penguin, 1979)

Rewald, Sabine (ed.), *The Romantic Vision of Caspar David Friedrich* (New York: Metropolitan Museum of Art, 1990)

Schrade, Hubert, *German Romantic Painting* (New York: Harry N. Abrams, 1977)

Vaughan, William, *German Romantic Painting* (New Haven and London: Yale University Press, 1980)

Walther, Angelo, *Caspar David Friedrich* (Berlin: Henschel Verlag, 1985)

15

ANDREW BOWIE

Romanticism and music

Absolute music

During the second half of the eighteenth century in Europe a remarkable change occurred in the evaluation and understanding of music. From being widely regarded as something to be used to accompany social and religious occasions, rather than be listened to and played for its own sake, music came to be regarded by some influential writers, philosophers and composers as the source of revelations that were inaccessible to any other form of human expression. This change in the reception of music paralleled the remarkable flowering in the production of music in Germany from the later eighteenth to the end of the nineteenth century in the work of, among others, Joseph Haydn, Wolfgang Amadeus Mozart, Ludwig van Beethoven, Franz Schubert, Felix Mendelssohn, Robert Schumann, Johannes Brahms and Richard Wagner.

The status of music in this period is connected to new interpretations of language and subjectivity associated with Romanticism, and these interpretations affect many widely held theoretical assumptions. Philosophical accounts of music still, for example, tend to assume that music is a mystery which needs to be explained in a philosophical theory. However, conceptual and aesthetic developments associated with Romanticism already put this assumption into question, because it depends on the idea that the primary function of language is to represent the objective world. This idea makes the relationship between verbal language and music hard to understand, because a great deal of music obviously does not function representationally. One major aspect of the philosophical Romanticism which emerges in the wake of Kant is the idea that if the subject always plays some role in how the world is constituted, language can be understood in a much broader sense, namely as the means by which those subjects *respond* to the world and to other subjects, rather than just 'represent' it. In this Romantic view music therefore need not be regarded as something to be explained primarily in other terms, and so can itself become the source of new relationships between ourselves and the world.

Distinctions between differing ways in which the term 'Romantic' is used are particularly significant in this area (on defining 'Romanticism', see Chapter 11). 'Romantic music' is often characterised by means of a contrast with 'classical music', the latter being seen as concerned to sustain balance within musical forms in a manner which the former abandons in the name of individual subjective expressiveness. However, the contrast is not as straightforward as this distinction might make it appear. Composers who are widely seen as epitomising Romanticism in music, like Schubert and Schumann, sometimes employ quite conventional formal structures when composing in certain genres. The sonata movements of Schubert's piano sonatas, for example, frequently follow the pattern of exposition (initial statement of the thematic material) development (variation of the initial thematic material), and recapitulation (return of the initial thematic material) in a schematic manner, although what happens within the sections of the form can be highly expressive and innovative. In contrast, Beethoven, who is seen by some as belonging to the classical tradition, employs a variety of very differing schemes for his sonata movements. Moreover, the famous opening Adagio movement of his Sonata Opus 27, No. 2 (the 'Moonlight') is said by T.W. Adorno already to contain the essence of Romanticism. Apparent contradictions of this kind are also evident in the fact that some commentators see the end of Romanticism in music as occurring early in the twentieth century, in the work of the 'second Viennese School' of Arnold Schoenberg, Alban Berg and Anton Webern. Other commentators argue, though, that Schoenberg is actually 'the last Romantic', the end of Romanticism coming instead with the revolt, in the neo-classicism of Igor Stravinsky and others, against the musical 'expressionism' which emerged in the wake of Wagner. There are, then, no uncontested criteria for Romanticism in music.

Even in the early phases of Romanticism, the application of the term 'Romantic' to music is hardly straightforward. E. T. A. Hoffmann, himself a composer of some of the first music that is still generally agreed to be Romantic, takes up philosophical ideas that emerged in the 1790s when he claims in the early 1800s that Mozart, Haydn and Beethoven, who are all these days widely assumed to be classical composers, are the epitome of Romanticism. Hoffmann refers in this context to music as 'die romantischste aller Künste' ('the most Romantic of all arts'), thus implying that music and what he means by Romanticism are inseparable. The reasons why are indicated by a comment in his famous review in 1808 of Beethoven's Fifth Symphony, the hearing of which, he asserts, leads one to leave behind 'alle durch Begriffe bestimmbaren Gefühle … um sich dem Unaussprechlichen hinzugeben' ('all feelings that can be determined by concepts ... in order to devote oneself to the unsayable').[1] Hoffmann concentrates on word-less instrumental music because for him and others at this time music is no longer considered merely to be the servant of words, and music which lacks words is thought of as being capable of expressing what words cannot express. What music expresses is the essence of Romanticism, therefore, precisely because it cannot be said in words.

Hoffmann himself changes his mind about wordless music in 1814, when he applies to church vocal music deriving from Palestrina ideas very similar to those he applied to instrumental music. This change suggests, though, how the main Romantic idea here can be taken in significantly different ways. The 'unsayable' can be understood in religious and mystical terms, as a realm only accessible by means which resist rational analysis, but it can also be understood as something which has to be 'shown', because words do not capture what is essential about it. In the latter case it may, for example, just be a matter of using an appropriate gesture to express something that words, or words alone, fail to convey. Analogously, the organisation of the words in a poem, rather than their propositional content, can be regarded as showing what cannot be said. Hardenberg talks in this respect of the idea of 'Gedichte – bloß *wohlklingend* und voll schöner Worte – aber auch ohne allen Sinn und Zusammenhang ... wie lauter Bruchstücke aus den ver-schiedenartigsten Dingen. Höchstens kann wahre Poësie einen *allegorischen* Sinn im Großen haben und eine indirecte Wirckung wie Musik etc. thun' ('Poems, just *pleasant-sounding* and full of beautiful words, but also with-out any meaning or context ... like fragments of the most diverse things. True poetry can at the most have an *allegorical* meaning as a whole and an indirect effect, like music, etc.', NS III, p. 572, No. 113). Later Romantic-influenced thinkers, like Adorno and Wittgenstein, will consider music to be a 'language of gestures', and both connect it to poetry. This tension between the mystical and religious and other senses of the unsayable is echoed in the contrasting ways in which philosophy relates to music from the Romantics onwards.

Why, though, should such ideas emerge at all in this period? The answer has in part to do with certain philosophical and religious debates of the time. In those debates, the sense that the 'Absolute', the understanding of which would explain the true relationship between mind and world, might be inaccessible to philosophy, leads to the idea of the Absolute as 'unsay-able'. The idea of musical 'unsayability' therefore follows, as the quotation from Hoffmann indicates, from the sense that the highest things cannot be captured in concepts.[2] However, it would be mistaken to regard what happens in relation to music as just deriving from philosophical sources.

If music becomes an essential means of responding to the world, it may be fulfilling needs which philosophy (and religion) cannot, or can no longer, fulfil. In Germany in particular the parallel development of music from Haydn and Mozart to Wagner, and of philosophy from Kant to Nietzsche suggests that establishing how music and Romanticism relate depends on how the relationships between differing spheres of modern culture are conceived. German Romanticism is central to this issue because it is concerned both to differentiate cognitive, ethical and aesthetic dimensions of human life, and to see how they can inform and influence each other.

Language and 'longing'

One of the most hyperbolic Romantic claims about music is made by Hardenberg's friend, J. W. Ritter, in his *Fragmente aus dem Nachlasse eines jungen Physikers* (1810, *Fragments from the Unpublished Works of a Young Physicist*): 'Des Menschen Wesen und Wirken ist Ton, ist Sprache. Musik ist gleichfalls Sprache, *allgemeine*; die *erste* des Menschen. Die vorhandenen Sprachen sind Individualisierungen der Musik; nicht individualisierte Musik, sondern, die zur Musik sich verhalten, wie die einzelnen Organe zum organisch Ganzen ... Die *Musik zerfiel* in Sprachen' ('The essence and working of humankind is sound, is language. Music is language as well, *universal* language; the *first* language of humankind. Existing languages are individualisations of music; not individualised music, rather they relate to music as the individual organs relate to the organic whole ... *Music disintegrated* into languages').[3] To understand such remarks one needs to consider how the emergence of new attitudes towards music in the eighteenth century is linked to the emergence of the interest in the origin of language exemplified by Jean-Jacques Rousseau, J. G. Hamann, and J. G. Herder. This interest comes about in part because traditional assumptions about the divine origin of language prove hard to defend.[4] These three thinkers all suggest, albeit in different ways, that the first language was 'music'. Instead of language being thought of as a 'logos' established by God, which manifests an inherent rational order of things, it is now what characterises us as human beings. As such, language must be able to express all dimensions of human existence. If responses to the world in early human societies are primarily based on pleasure, pain and fear, it follows that language will be primarily affective. Language in its early forms was therefore thought of as closer to what we encounter in the expressive form of music, rather than to the classifying, referential aspects of verbal language.

These versions of the idea that music is the first language raise the issue of how we are to understand the move from the pre-semantic to the semantic, from instinctual expression to conventionalised social articulation.[5] The idea also implies that the move to conventionalised forms of language may entail a loss of expressive immediacy, because the generality inherent in using words to designate things reduces things to what they have in common. The individuality of things and the specificity of how people relate to them may consequently be neglected. Cognitive advances in modernity can therefore be interpreted as involving a loss of the direct, particular relationships to the world which are essential to aesthetic understanding. The language of music is then felt as a compensation for this loss, because it can sustain or restore affective immediacy in a world which threatens to destroy it. This feeling is the key to one aspect of music's relationship to Romanticism.

Regarding music in this manner depends on a sense of what has been lost, otherwise its appeal as a counter to that loss would be incomprehensible. This sense of loss is part of what leads music to be connected, as it is in Hoffmann, to 'longing' (*Sehnsucht*). The notion of longing is central to the philosophical work of Friedrich Schlegel, and he links his philosophical concern to music in the dictum that 'Musik ist am meisten Sehnsucht' ('Music is most of all longing'; *KFSA* X, p. 551). Longing can be interpreted in a variety of ways, but its connection to music has to do with the feeling that we are no longer 'at home' in the modern world, which itself depends on a prior sense of what it would be to be at home. Hardenberg-Novalis sums up the idea here in his suggestion that philosophy is 'eigentlich Heimweh – *Trieb überall zu Hause zu seyn*' ('really homesickness – *drive to be at home everywhere*'; *NS* III, p. 434, No. 857), and that music allows the mind to be 'auf diese kurzen Augenblicke in seiner irdischen Heymath' ('for short moments in its earthly home'; *NS* III, p. 283, No. 245). Schlegel's friends, Wilhelm Heinrich Wackenroder and Ludwig Tieck, the authors of *Phantasien über die Kunst* (1799, *Fantasias on Art*) make the analogous claim that 'Ohne Musik ist die Erde wie ein wüstes, noch nicht fertiges Haus, in dem die Einwohner mangeln' ('Without music the earth is like a desolate, as yet incomplete house that lacks its inhabitants').[6] In this Romantic view music is a vital part of what it is to dwell in the world.

How, though, does such metaphorical and speculative thinking relate to the actual music of the time? Carl Dahlhaus talks of the 'paradox that around 1800 there was neither a classical music-aesthetic to correspond to the classical music of Haydn and Mozart, nor a romantic music to correspond to the romantic music-aesthetic of Wackenroder and Tieck. Reflection and compositional practice were widely divergent'.[7] Romantic musical practice in this sense only emerges around 1810 with the music of Hoffmann, Carl Maria von Weber, Schubert and, slightly later, of Mendelssohn, Schumann and others. However, if music comes to be seen as its own kind of language in this period, the implications of this divergence become more complex. Music and philosophy can be linked in ways which do not rely on a direct correspondence between musical theory and practice. The idea of longing, for example, becomes philosophically significant soon after resolution of harmonic tension becomes the central structuring principle of music in the second half of the eighteenth century. Tonal melody relies on moving away from and returning to a tonic note, but the resolution of tension is less decisive in the polyphonic music of the Baroque, in which counterpoint can seem to symbolise a unchanging order of things, than it is in the dynamic shifts of harmony in sonata form. These shifts constitute the core of early classical music and play a vital role in the development of Romantic music. In sonata form the move away from the 'home' key creates a sense of lack, of 'longing', which can only be overcome by a return to that key. The more complex the return, the more the music becomes able to express shadings and contrasts of affective and other aspects of life in new ways. Romantic music can be characterised in this respect by its increased use of chromaticism, dissonance and modulation, as means of extending the range of musical expression.

The use of tonality in sonata form in particular involves what will be construed by Adorno and others as a kind of teleology, in which the reasons for the musical tensions become fully comprehensible in the reconciliation that occurs at the end of the piece. Adorno associates this teleology with the 'heroic' music of the middle Beethoven in particular (and with Hegel's philosophy), which he regards as 'affirmative' at a time when the injustices of the history suggest that critical music (and philosophy) would be more appropriate.[8] However, the return to the home key is anyway only a temporary symbol of reconciliation, and it is not clear how it relates to other kinds of reconciliation in the social and political sphere. The status of these differing forms of reconciliation is a major factor in understanding music and Romanticism.

F. W. J. Schelling suggests one reason why the idea of reconciliation is so significant when, from around 1810, he links music to ontological reflections about the nature of reality as it is prior to becoming accessible to rational thought: 'kann die Tonkunst allein ein Bild jener uranfänglichen Natur und ihrer Bewegung seyn, wie auch ihr ganzes Wesen im Umlauf besteht, da sie von einem Grundton ausgehend, durch noch so viele Ausschweifungen zuletzt immer in den Anfang zurückkehrt' ('only music can be an image of that primal nature and its movement, for its whole essence also consists in circulation, as it, beginning from a tonic, always finally returns to the beginning, however many variations it may go through').[9] Following Schelling, Arthur Schopenhauer, who has a decisive influence on the music of Richard Wagner from the 1850s onwards, develops the idea of the resolution of harmonic tension in music as the basis of his account of the underlying nature of reality, which he terms 'the Will'. Schopenhauer claims that the 'Wesen des Willens an sich, ein endloses Streben ist' ('the essence of the Will in itself ... is an endless striving').[10] Because music is the direct 'image' (*Abbild*) of the Will, it is 'zu allem Physischen der Welt das Metaphysische, zu aller Erscheinung das Ding an sich ... Man könnte demnach die Welt eben so wohl verkörperte Musik, als verkörperten Willen nennen' ('the metaphysical to everything physical in the world, the thing in itself to every appearance ... One could accordingly just as well call the world embodied music as embodied Will').[11] His reasons for this claim are based on examples of music's move from harmonic tension to resolution (which means that the argument does not work for non-diatonic music, that is, music which is not in any key and so cannot resolve to a home key). Although reality for Schopenhauer always involves endless dissatisfaction, each fulfilment just making space for the next lack, the aesthetic experience of music allows one temporarily to escape this cycle, even as music is also a symbol of it.

Music, nature, and the subject

Schopenhauer's restrictive philosophical conception of music's significance is, however, hard to square with the ways in which music becomes linked to more and more aspects of the world in the classical and Romantic period. The 'programme music' of Franz Liszt and others, which emerges around the late 1840s and introduces the idea of the 'symphonic poem' on themes such as places, or literary figures, like Hamlet, is just one manifestation of this tendency. Another such manifestation, in some respects less significant in Germany than in Russia or Czechoslovakia (Bohemia), is the emergence of the association of music with new ideas of national identity. This association is accompanied by attention to the idea of 'folk music', which already begins with Herder and others in the 1770s, and which is vital for the development of German *Lied*. Such phenomena suggest how the 'language of music' now responds to needs which are not fully satisfied by verbal language. Music's new connections to the world are, moreover, not divorced from the ways in which it is felt to enact the establishing of reconciliation from tension. This is apparent when Romantic composers seek new ways of expressing and responding to nature. The songs of Schubert and Schumann, the vast land-scapes of Anton Bruckner's symphonies, and many passages in Wagner's music dramas introduce a radically new musical relationship to nature.

The idea of the beauty of wild nature only becomes widespread in the second half of the eighteenth century, when substantial technological control of nature becomes a reality. Until then nature's threat to human survival meant that it generally did not become an object of pleasurable contemplation for its own sake. The emergence of philosophical aesthetics and nature's new importance for music are closely connected: both involve the idea of relationships between humankind and nature that transcend what can be understood in conceptual terms. As knowledge-based control of nature advances, so does the sense that this control may be both a blessing and a curse. In earlier forms of music natural phenomena, such as storms, were not responded to primarily in terms of the subject's affective relationship to them, being regarded predominantly as events to be imitated in sound. The ambivalent relationships to nature in Romanticism lead, in contrast, to a growing fascination with capturing the 'moods' evoked by nature. One of the most famous attempts to do so can help to establish an important distinction. Beethoven composes the 'Pastoral' Symphony as a celebration of the value of nature for his spiritual well-being. The symphony is, therefore, in one sense of the word, a 'Romantic' one. The relationship to nature evoked by the 'Pastoral' is, however, unambiguously positive: the ferocious storm of the fourth movement gives way to a pantheistic sense of harmony in the shepherd's song of the last movement. In this respect the music, like some of Beethoven's other middle period works, seems closer to a German Idealist, Spinoza-inspired attitude to humankind's relationship to nature (see Chapter 11).

The early Romantic idea of homelessness suggests, in contrast, a different attitude to nature. Here nature does not promise any kind of ultimate harmony, and, along with its potential for emotional enrichment, also involves forces which cannot be mastered. A notable musical example of this latter sense of nature is Carl Maria von Weber's opera *Der Freischütz* (1821, *The Enchanted Huntsman*), particularly the scene in the Wolf's Glen, which helps to initiate a new kind of sinister music that will be developed by Wagner and others. This music exemplifies the Romantic idea of the 'uncanny', the German word for this being, precisely, *das Unheimliche* (literally: the 'unhomely').[12] The sense of the uncanniness of certain states of external nature is also echoed in the feeling that we are not wholly at home with our internal nature, because it is in some respects an alien part of ourselves.

The idea of the 'unconscious' is a product of Romantic thought. It plays a role, for instance, in the philosophy of Schelling, who talks, in his *Naturphilosophie* and *System des transcendentalen Idealismus* (1801, *System of Transcendental Idealism*), of nature's 'unconscious productivity', which gives rise to living, organic forms from inanimate material bound by the laws of physics and chemistry. He links this unconscious productivity to 'genius', the artist's capacity to produce work which transgresses rules and yet still succeeds aesthetically.[13] In a more disturbing vein, Hoffmann suggests in many of his literary works how the powers that make possible creative artistic transgression can also drive the subject to madness: his fictional composer, Johannes Kreisler, both needs music and is at risk of losing his mind through it. The notion of the unconscious points as well to the idea that the border between the inside and the outside of the subject is not fixed: external states of nature give rise to internal states, and internal states change the apprehension of external states. Nature 'in us' and nature 'outside of us' become inextricably linked, in a manner which can be both disturbing and inspiring. The complexities of this link lead to the need for new expressive resources, which are evident, for example, in how Romantic poetry about and painting of nature both echoes and informs musical responses to the world, and vice versa. Nietzsche captures some of what happens here when he says of Wagner in 1874 that 'er allem in der Natur, was bis jetzt nicht *reden* wollte, eine Sprache gegeben hat: er glaubt nicht daran, daß es etwas Stummes geben müsse. Er taucht auch in Morgenröte, Wald, Nebel, Kluft, Bergeshöhe, Nachtschauer, Mondesglanz hinein und merkt ihnen ein heimliches Begehren ab: sie wollen auch tönen' ('he has given a language to everything in nature which did not until now wish to *speak*: he does not believe that there has to be anything that is speechless. He also plunges into dawn, wood, fog, ravine, mountain heights, nocturnal shudders, moonlight, and sees in them a secret desire: they too wish to sound').[14] Wagner's ability to do this is related to musical developments that can still usefully be termed 'Romantic'. How, then, should we talk about Romantic music?

Romantic music

These days the epithet 'Romantic' is almost a term of abuse in some music criticism. 'Romantic' performances are said to have tempi that are too slow, phrasing which ignores the supposed original manner of phrasing and the sound of the instruments in the period of the work's composition, etc. (It is, though, worth remembering here Charles Rosen's remark that 'authentic' performance practice confuses what the composer got with what s/he wanted.) Even in everyday usage, calling music 'Romantic' can mean that it is excessively sentimental. One source of such critical uses of the word is no doubt the role played by the idea of individual subjective expressiveness in the history of 'Romanticism'. However, the use of Romantic as a term of opprobrium is largely irrelevant to a real understanding of 'Romantic music'. The interesting issue is rather the development of attitudes towards musical expression in the modern period, of which the recent concern with period styles is another manifestation. Adorno sees modern music in terms of a dialectic between 'expression' and 'convention'. It is not that music prior to the later part of the eighteenth century was not expressive: what is at issue is rather the particular musical vocabulary employed in the name of expression. Adorno illustrates the dialectic of expression and convention by the example of Beethoven's use of the diminished seventh chord (the chord C, E-flat, G-flat, A, in the key of C), which involves considerable harmonic tension and makes modulation into other keys easy. In Beethoven the effect is novel and highly expressive, but the same chord will not that long afterwards become a conventional cliché in salon music. Romantic music is in part a result of what is epitomised by this example. In modernity what begins life in art of all kinds as a means of individual expression can rapidly become a convention that denotes being expressive, rather than really being expressive. This situation leads to a constant pressure to innovate if the artist is not just to repeat schematic formulae. However, much the same problem occurs, for example, in the history of jazz, and this means that the drive for novelty of expression is not sufficient to characterise music as 'Romantic'.

A related aspect of music more specifically characterisable as 'Romantic' is, as Charles Rosen (1998) has shown, the breakdown of 'closed', classical forms, a breakdown which can be connected to the Romantic sense that a complete philosophical system may be just an unattainable ideal. The combination of a given musical form with the feeling that the form may break down or mutate is characteristic of some of the most important Romantic music. Rosen offers an example of this which can serve as a metaphor for characterising a key aspect of Romanticism in music, namely Schumann's ending of the first song of his song cycle *Dichterliebe* (1840; *Poet's Love*) with an unresolved dominant seventh chord (the chord C-sharp, F, G-sharp, B).[15] In contrast to songs prior to this one, where the end is generally marked by a return to the tonic chord (the chord of the 'home' key), the ending on the dominant, which gives a sense of a missing conclusion, forces the listener to listen and think beyond the confines of the song. The effect of this device is added to by the fact that other songs in the cycle often end with a piano postlude which takes the song's significance beyond what the words of the song can express. In one startlingly original case the final postlude echoes the postlude of a song earlier in the cycle, creating the impression that the composer is trapped in the mood evoked by the first occurrence of the material, even though the songs are quite different. There is no formal musical reason for such occurrences – they are not meant to make the cycle cohere in the way a sonata coheres via its recapitulation – so they result from the primacy of expression over formal convention. Similarly, piano works like Schumann's 'Humoreske' involve sudden radical changes of mood which are not prepared by the music that precedes them. These pieces break with the kind of Classical model in which moods tend to change in accordance with a musical pattern that structures the piece. The result is a widening of expressive possibilities, sometimes accompanied by a sense of threatening disintegration. The turbulent, almost atonal, passage that occurs in the slow movement of Schubert's A major piano sonata, D 959, for example, suggests a kind of panic at where music can lead when it abandons established forms.

These changes are connected to the new role of the *Lied*, as composed and notated art song, rather than as orally transmitted folk-song, established above all by Schubert from around 1815. *Lieder* move in Romantic music from being based on the collectively generated, formally quite limited, resources of folk-song to being a highly developed, individualised genre which can involve complex changes of mood and musical material, and very varying dimensions. Schubert's late setting of Heine's 'Der Doppelgänger', is, for example, so harmonically ambiguous that critics are still unsure of how best to analyse it, and it points to musical possibilities based on the abandonment of harmonic resolution that are characteristic of musical modernism. The decisive aspect here is that particular songs may establish a unique configuration which offers new possibilities for composition beyond established melodic and other structures. The demands both of the organisation of the words of the song and of the meanings of the text bring about an expansion of musical resources that affects chamber music, the symphony, and other musical forms.

Such developments in Romantic music make possible perhaps the most controversial, and influential, Romantic move beyond classical forms, namely Richard Wagner's music dramas. These highlight many of the issues which arise with regard to the new perception of music's relationship to language in Romanticism. Wagner's much-cited assertion in 'Oper und Drama' (1851, 'Opera and Drama'), that 'der Irrthum in dem Kunstgenre der Oper bestand darin, *daß ein Mittel des Ausdruckes (die Musik) zum Zwecke, der Zweck des Ausdruckes (das Drama) aber zum Mittel gemacht war*' ('the mistake in the artistic genre of opera was *that it made a means of expression (music) into the end, but made the end of expression (drama) into the means*'),[16] does *not*, however, as has often been maintained, mean that for Wagner the *text* should be the end, and the music the means.[17] His point is rather that 'drama' should involve a complex interaction of the significances generated by text, dramatic action and music. Wagner himself changes his mind throughout his career on the relationship between words and music. He later says, for example, in 'Über die Benennung Musikdrama' (1872; 'On the Name Music-Drama'), that 'ich meine Dramen gern als *ersichtlich gewordene Thaten der Musik* bezeichnet hätte' ('I would have liked to call my dramas *acts of music which have become visible*').[18] The crucial point here is that Romantic music is seen as capable of having performative cultural effects.

Dahlhaus maintains that it was 'the effect of [Wagner's] music itself from which consequences for cultural politics emerged. One can, exaggerating only a little, actually talk of the emergence of the "*Kulturkritik*" of the end of the century from the spirit of music – Wagnerian music'.[19] Neither Wagner's libretti nor his sometimes rather turgid theoretical texts could have had this effect. The libretti are mainly based on Nordic sagas and on tales of the Middle Ages, but they are accompanied by technically advanced music which makes them into a profound reflection on the *modern* world. The economic, political, psychological and social crises of Wagner's era are explored in a manner which involves both nostalgia for the past and a radical aesthetic modernism.

This combination of reference to the past and radical contemporaneity suggests why Wagner's works are both the culmination of musical Romanticism and what leads to musical modernism. By further breaking down existing limitations in music in the wake of his Romantic predecessors Wagner opens the way to the realisation that there are no ultimate constraints on how music is organised, even as he tries to sustain order by the employment of forms based on myth. The dilemma for subsequent music lies in how to maintain forms of order which allow music to communicate with a wider public without the music then becoming merely conventional and repetitive. Romantic music represents a moment in modernity where it seemed possible for individual expressive freedom to be compatible with forms of expression which allow a collective reception. We are still living with the consequences of the breakdown of what made this moment possible, and this means that understanding what was at stake in music's relation to Romanticism is not just an issue for music.[20]

NOTES

1. See E. T. A, Hoffmann, *Schriften zur Musik: Singspiele* (Berlin, Weimar: Aufbau, 1988), p. 23. All translations are my own.
2. See C. Dahlhaus, *Die Idee der absoluten Musik* (Munich and Kassel: dtv, 1978).
3. J. W. Ritter, *Fragmente aus dem Nachlasse eines jungen Physikers* (Leipzig: Kiepenhauer, 1984), p. 272.
4. Hamann still adheres to the idea of the divine origin, but he does so in a thoroughly unorthodox manner. He describes language, in terms which prefigure Heidegger, as the revelation of being. God does not give definitive names to things, so the proliferation of different ways of articulating things made possible by his creation of language is the essence of language.
5. See D. A. Thomas, *Music and the Origins of Language: Theories from the French Enlightenment* (Cambridge: Cambridge University Press, 1995), A. Bowie, *Music, Philosophy, and Modernity* (Cambridge: Cambridge University Press, 2007) (Chapter Two).

6. W. H. Wackenroder and L. Tieck, *Phantasien über die Kunst* (Stuttgart: Reclam, 1973), p. 102.
7. C. Dahlhaus, *Klassische und romantische Musikästhetik* (Laaber: Laaber, 1988), p. 86.
8. Beethoven himself, of course, becomes less 'affirmative' in much of his later work, not least because of his disappointment at political and social developments after the Vienna Congress.
9. F. W. J. Schelling, *Die Weltalter* (Munich: Biederstein, 1946), p. 40.
10. A. Schopenhauer, *Die Welt als Wille und Vorstellung*, in *Sämtliche Werke*, ed. W. Frhr. von Löhneysen, 5 vols. (Frankfurt am Main: Suhrkamp, 1986), vol. I, p. 240.
11. Ibid., p. 366.
12. Weber's opera actually has a 'happy ending', but this is widely seen as jarring with what has been revealed in the preceding scenes. On the complexities of interpreting this work, see L. Finscher, 'Weber's *Freischütz*: Conceptions and Misconceptions', *Proceedings of the Royal Musical Association*, 110 (1983–4), pp. 79–90.
13. See Bowie, *Aesthetics and Subjectivity: From Kant to Nietzsche* (Manchester: Manchester University Press, 2003), and Bowie, *Schelling and Modern European Philosophy* (London and New York: Routledge, 1993).
14. F. Nietzsche, *Werke*, ed. K. Schlechta, 10 vols. (Berlin: Directmedia, 2000), vol. I, p. 418.
15. See also B. Perrey, *Schumann's Dichterliebe and Early Romantic Poetics: Fragmentation of Desire* (Cambridge: Cambridge University Press, 2002).
16. R. Wagner, *Gesammelte Schriften und Dichtungen*, 10 vols. (Leipzig: Siegel, 1903), vol. III, p. 231.
17. See C. Dahlhaus, *Wagners Konzeption des musikalischen Dramas* (Munich and Kassel: dtv, 1990).
18. R. Wagner, *Gesammelte Schriften und Dichtungen*, vol. IX, p. 306.
19. C. Dahlhaus, *Zwischen Romantik und Moderne: Vier Studien zur Musikgeschichte des späteren 19. Jahrhunderts* (Munich: Musikverlag Katzbichler, 1974), p. 13.
20. This essay was written with the support of a Major Research Fellowship from the Leverhulme Foundation.

FURTHER READING

Bent, Ian (ed.), *Music Theory in the Age of Romanticism* (Cambridge: Cambridge University Press, 2005)
Dahlhaus, Carl, *Richard Wagners Musikdramen* (Velber: Friedrich, 1971)
Daverio, John, *Nineteenth-Century Music and the German Romantic Ideology* (New York: Schirmer, 1993)
Donovan, Siobhan and Robin Elliott (eds.), *Music and Literature in German Romanticism* (New York: Camden House, 2004)
Rosen, Charles, *The Romantic Generation* (Cambridge, Mass.: Harvard University Press, 1998)
Whittall, Arnold, *Romantic Music: A Concise History from Schubert to Sibelius* (London: Thames and Hudson, 1990)

16

MARGARETE KOHLENBACH

Transformations of German Romanticism 1830–2000

Overview

German Romanticism emerged before the great ideologies and social movements that would shape German and European life in much of the nineteenth and twentieth centuries. In the Germany of 1800, nationalist conservatism, democratic liberalism and internationalist socialism, or a political dichotomy between right and left, did not exist. Accordingly, the intrinsic concerns of early Romanticism are at odds with many of the issues that dominate subsequent political and cultural controversies. Friedrich von Hardenberg (Novalis) uses words like 'monarchy' and 'republic' not to denote particular forms of state constitution but as metaphors that evoke the creation of a common, spiritually full life. His vision is informed by the oppositions between poetic and prosaic forms of existence, and between transcendental, spiritual insight and instrumental, worldly prudence. The French Revolution, the Ancien Régime and the realities of Prussian Absolutism all come down on the latter side. And in its reliance on philosophical reflection, the cultural revival Hardenberg envisages differs from traditionalist conceptions of natural growth. These philosophical, spiritual and apolitical features of early Romanticism provide an alternative frame of reference that allows us to question, qualify or reject the methods and goals of modern politics. In the politicised contexts of modern societies, however, these features can in effect support, or be appropriated for, political ends that are alien to early Romanticism.

The emergence of a conservative and nationalist right and a radical-democratic or socialist left during the nineteenth century was accompanied by interpretations of Romanticism that ignored, misunderstood or reinterpreted the apolitical, philosophical, non-traditionalist and aesthetically innovative concerns of early Romanticism. The resulting image of Romanticism as an anti-modern and conservative movement remained dominant until the 1960s. Ironically, later Romantic authors at both ends of the emerging political spectrum were instrumental in shaping this image, notably Adam Müller and Joseph von Eichendorff on the conservative side, and Heinrich Heine – with subsequent support from the Young Hegelians Theodor Echtermeyer and Arnold Ruge – on that of radical liberalism and emerging Marxism. In Heine's *Die romantische Schule* (1833 and 1836; *The Romantic School*), the political rejection of Romanticism as reactionary and outdated is linked to earlier, neo-classical condemnations of the movement. Directly or indirectly, Heine relies on Johann Heinrich Voß's polemical equations of Romanticism with an immoral, if not decadent, mysticism, on Goethe's charge that the essence of Romanticism is 'the sick', and on Hegel's criticism of Romantic irony as an arbitrary indulgence in irrational subjectivism.[1] On the conservative side, Eichendorff actually accepts the verdict of subjectivism for many features of Romantic literature. However, for him these features are accidental and the essence of Romanticism coincides with the truly objective nature of Catholicism.[2]

Rudolf Haym's 1870 history of (early) Romanticism was the first work systematically to question the dichotomies underlying the political interpretations of Romanticism.[3] Haym presented early Romanticism as a cultural formation that aimed to reconcile the diverging interests of philosophy, religion, literature and science, had strong roots in the eighteenth century, including the Enlightenment, and was closely related to the concerns of Goethe, Weimar Classicism and Hegel's philosophy. But if Haym was right in rejecting the dichotomies on which the political interpretations relied, he was wrong in assuming that Romanticism and its political receptions were things of the past.

Around the turn of the twentieth century, sections of the educated middle class increasingly doubted that the cultural and intellectual paradigms which had dominated the second half of the nineteenth century were capable of dealing with the social and existential effects of modernity. This scepticism about traditional religion, bourgeois morality, philosophical materialism, scientific world views and the beliefs in progress and evolution contributed to a broad, multi-faceted and frequently mystical cultural reorientation to which contemporaries referred as 'new Romanticism' or 'neo-Romanticism'. After the present overview, I shall discuss in some detail the continuities and discontinuities between Romanticism and 'neo-Romanticism', and the latter's both innovative and traditionalist features.

Here, it is important to note that politically 'neo-Romanticism' was rather amorphous, and that much of this political indeterminacy continued to characterise its repercussions well into the Weimar period. Reinterpretations of the Romantic concept of national spirit, for instance, figured prominently not only in right-wing German nationalism, but also in Gustav Landauer's socialist anarchism and the work of the Jewish philosopher Erich Unger. Yet this actual indeterminacy of 'neo-Romanticism' did not prevent politicians and theorists adapting the nineteenth-century image of a conservative or 'reactionary' Romanticism to the political realities of the interwar period. On the right, conservatives made 'Romanticism' a major source for their anti-liberal and anti-socialist politics. On the orthodox left, Georg Lukács elaborated Heine's linkage of political 'progress' with neo-Classical aesthetics to establish socialist realism as the obligatory mode of communist art. Accordingly, Lukács placed Romanticism, 'neo-Romanticism' and the modernist adoptions of Romantic techniques of defamiliarisation and fragmentation in the genealogy of fascism. My discussion below will reflect the political indeterminacy of 'neo-Romanticism' by dealing with neo-Romantic positions in different political contexts. After the analysis of the Austrian writer Hugo von Hofmannsthal's path from *fin-de-siècle* 'neo-Romanticism' to his call, in 1927, for a 'conservative revolution' I shall treat the receptions of Romanticism in the neo-Marxist tradition of the Frankfurt School (see pp. 267–71 and pp. 271–5 respectively).

National Socialism appropriated and thereby discredited many German traditions. In the case of Romanticism, the damage was particularly great because the political conservatism which had helped Hitler into power counted, for both supporters and opponents, as *the* heir of *the* Romantic tradition despite the fact that radical conservatism, neo-Romantic orientation and support for National Socialism had not been fully congruent.[4] It is therefore not surprising that in both East and West Germany sustained and publicly debated engagements with Romanticism nearly came to a halt between 1945 and, approximately, 1965. During the last decades of the twentieth century, however, the received image of German Romanticism underwent a dramatic change. Four factors mainly were responsible for this. First, the critical editions of the complete writings of Friedrich Schlegel (begun in 1958) and Hardenberg (begun in 1960) made available material which had so far been unpublished or published only in misleading editorial arrangements. These newly edited sources suggested that the early Romantic concerns with 'feeling' and intuition, far from demonstrating an irrational subjectivism, actually contained an epistemological critique of Fichte's Subjective Idealism. And they also showed that to a large extent the early Romantic insistence on irony and fragmentary forms of representation resulted from the attempt to reconcile modern, progressive notions of historical time with neo-Classical ideals of perfection. Second, from the 1960s onwards the West German reception of Jewish neo-Marxist thinkers such as Walter Benjamin and Theodor W. Adorno, whose works displayed strong affinities with Romanticism, undermined the view of Romanticism as 'reactionary' and 'proto-fascist'. Hardenberg and the early Friedrich Schlegel came to be adopted, as it were, by the New Left. Third, after 1965 sporadic relaxations in the state's enforcement of socialist realism permitted East German writers cautiously to re-engage with the Romantic tradition. Finally, the end of the Cold War and the unification of Germany in 1990 further weakened the political dichotomy between right and left, which had dominated the reception of Romanticism for so long.

Today it is widely accepted that German Romanticism was a modern movement engaged in a modern critique of modernity. Of course, the Romantic critique of central features of modern society – notably its functional differentiation and the absence of a comprehensive religious or metaphysical foundation – could be conceived only in modernity. But recent scholarship emphasises that German Romanticism actually contributed to the modernisation of European life. The Romantic insistence on the autonomy of art and on self-referential artistic techniques helped to establish the status of art as a relatively independent, self-regulating sub-system in modern society, notwithstanding the fact that the Romantics' holistic criticisms of modern differentiation also demanded the unity of art with all other dimensions of human life. Romantic experiments with 'new mythologies' and non-institutionalised religiosity reinforced the modern disintegration and privatisation of religion, which Romantic authors also deplored. And the Romantic emphasis on the subject and its experiences and feelings actually radicalised and extended Enlightenment individualism although it was accompanied by Hardenberg's and Jean Paul's criticisms of Fichte's Subjective Idealism and by communal conceptions of society. Even the aestheticisation of nature, the engagement with dreams and the imaginary, and the poetic constructions of a peaceful medieval life – traditionally regarded as evidence of a Romantic 'escapism' from modern reality – are now increasingly understood as genetically and functionally related to the very fabric of modernity.[5] I shall conclude the present essay by relating this new scholarly understanding of the movement to recent literary engagements with Romanticism.

'Neo-Romanticism'

Empirical research into the natural world that ran counter to the Romantic conception of nature in human and spiritual terms rapidly gained in influence after 1850. The cultural dominance it finally achieved rested less on the success of the natural sciences as such than on the fact that the empirical perspective on nature was widely accepted *as a matter of principle*. Accordingly, powerful schools of thought such as nineteenth-century philosophical materialism and positivism frequently aimed for comprehensively scientific world views. Thus not only nature but also the human world – history, society, culture and everyday life – came to be seen as a causally determined realm devoid of all 'spirit' and 'meaning'. Especially after the German unification of 1871, this process coincided with rapid phases of industrialisation and urbanisation that destroyed traditional ways of life, frequently leading to social destitution and brutal exploitation, but offering no existential orientation. The Naturalist writers of the 1880s, who rejected Romantic literature as a misleading, idealistic transfiguration of modern reality, relentlessly monitored modern everyday life and sometimes expressed outrage at the human and social costs of modernisation. As a mode of writing, however, Naturalism was itself strongly indebted to scientific world views and thus incapable of filling what was increasingly perceived as the 'void' of modern existence.

In the late 1880s, and partly in response to the unresolved tensions within Naturalism, critics and writers like Hermann Bahr (1863–1934) and Heinrich Mann (1871–1959) started to use 'Romanticism', 'new Romanticism' and 'neo-Romanticism' as catchwords to demand a cultural reorientation.[6] By the turn of the century, Eugen Diederichs (1867–1930) found it profitable to present his publishing house as the leading voice of a 'neo-Romanticism' that answered to 'the soul's longing for a meaning and content in life' and replaced Naturalism, materialism and the fragmentations of modern knowledge by a holistic world view.[7] Ludwig Coellen's *Neuromantik*, which classified contemporary writers like Hofmannsthal (1874–1929), Stefan George (1868–1933) and Richard Dehmel (1863–1920) as 'neo-Romantics' was published with Diederichs in 1906. However, 'neo-Romanticism' meant more than a new literary orientation or even a new world view. The term also referred to the cultural practice of numerous reform movements which emerged around 1900 and which adopted, at least in part, Romantic conceptions of nature, child or woman: the Jugendbewegung (Youth Movement) and the movement for educational reform, the so-called Lebensreform (Life Reform) and early environmentalism and feminism.

Today, 'neo-Romanticism' is still used to characterise the cultural atmosphere around 1900 with its various anti-Naturalist, neo-Idealist and holistic tendencies. However, the term can be misleading. Although Romantic texts were republished and on the whole found a positive reception, 'neo-Romanticism' was not a revival of Romanticism in the sense that its literary and cultural manifestations were always or primarily based on a direct and sustained engagement with Romantic writings. Diederichs's broad understanding of the term is symptomatic in that it includes not only Goethe but also the culture of the Renaissance among the historical allies of 'neo-Romanticism'. In other words, 'neo-Romanticism' opposed late nineteenth-century rationalism and materialism by eclectically appealing, in a vaguely 'romantic' manner, to different periods and traditions of the past, including Romanticism.

The transformations of German Romanticism throughout the nineteenth century contributed to both the traditionalist and the innovative features of 'neo-Romanticism'. Three developments were particularly important in this regard: the continuing reception of Romantic literature in Germany after 1830, the transformations of the Romantics' concerns with 'life' in the philosophies of Arthur Schopenhauer (1788–1860) and Friedrich Nietzsche (1844–1900) and, finally, the literary reception of the German Romantics in French Symbolism.

The reception of Romantic literature in Germany after 1830

Although German Romanticism as a dominant and innovative literary movement came to an end around 1830, when Heine declared it dead, elements of its literary production retained a strong presence in German culture throughout the nineteenth century. Notably Romantic poems, frequently as part of the Romantic *Lied*, continued to be widely received and performed. Eichendorff's poetry, for instance, often served that nostalgic flight from modern reality for which its critics blamed Romanticism as a whole. (Ironically, Heine's poems suffered a similar fate.) In one of its dimensions, 'neo-Romanticism' around 1900 consisted in the strengthening of these traditionalist tendencies in response to the increasing pressures of modernisation. Here, 'neo-Romantic' literature merged with *Heimatkunst* – the broad stream of regionalist literature and art in Imperial Germany – and the related aesthetic appreciation of the German countryside in conservationist associations such as the Bund Heimatschutz (founded in 1904). Hermann Hesse's first literary success, *Peter Camenzind* (1904), stands for many contemporary novels that centre on romantically inspired vagabonds and present their life on the margins of modern society in an inoffensive and inconsequential manner. This literature continues the domestication of the Romantics' sometimes bitter solidarity with outsiders in Eichendorff's treatment of the *Wanderer* motif. Camenzind eventually withdraws from the wider world and returns to his native village, where he finds a true life embedded in the beauties of the surrounding countryside. The contributions to the journal *Berliner Romantik* (1918–25) show that these traditionalist elements of 'neo-Romanticism' sometimes survived the First World War.

Transformations in the notion of life

In early Idealism and Romanticism, the notion of life had been used to criticise the *ossifications* of late eighteenth-century rationalism. 'Life' had denoted not an opposite of reason but the medium of its true realisation in human morality, freedom and happiness. This changed with Schopenhauer's metaphysical Pessimism, which, through the mediation of Nietzsche, Richard Wagner (1813–83) and Eduard von Hartmann (1842–1906), became a major reference point for 'neo-Romanticism'. According to Schopenhauer, an unconscious, irrational and impersonal 'will to life' is the substance of the world. The reality of objects, human individuality, truth and moral values are merely subjective representations and have no part in 'the will'. This drive of self-preservation runs counter to human aspirations for happiness and itself represents the guilt pertaining to all life. Redemption from the suffering caused by 'the will' can be achieved only by a Buddhist abnegation of life and, ultimately, in death. Compassion and charity are ethical because they are ascetic exercises in support of this abnegation.[8]

In *Die Geburt der Tragödie* (1872; *The Birth of Tragedy*), Nietzsche uses the polarity between the 'Apolline' and the 'Dionysian' to explain both the genesis of Greek tragedy and the dynamics of artistic production in general. This polarity still resonates with the old opposition of 'classical' limitation and 'Romantic' infinity, which Nietzsche reinterprets, however, on the basis of Schopenhauer's philosophy. While Friedrich Schlegel had located Dionysus and 'the agility of life' – which correspond to Nietzsche's 'Romantic' pole – in Greek Old Comedy,[9] the early Nietzsche finds Dionysus and 'life' in tragedy. Accordingly, Nietzsche's notion of Dionysian art coincides with a deeply tragic world view. Like Schopenhauer's 'will', the ground of being revealed by Dionysian art is essentially hostile to all human needs. The only 'justification' of existence lies in the amoral beauty and depth of its expressions and representations in art. The later Nietzsche dismissed both Schopenhauer's Pessimism and his own earlier aesthetic reinterpretation of it as a 'Romantic' flight from the present. 'Life' and its 'wills to power', as he now maintained, must be affirmed. Buddhism and any search for an aesthetic justification of existence were signs of weakness. This rejection of Pessimism in no way represented a return to early Romanticism and Idealism. Nietzsche's 'wills to power' still conformed to Schopenhauer's 'will' by their basic incommensurability with human reason, morality and civilisation. And Wagner's operas, in which the Nietzsche of 1872 had located the hope for a German revival of great, Dionysian art, now appeared to epitomise the modern artist's 'decadent' resentment against life.[10]

In 'neo-Romanticism', the different connotations which 'life' assumed between the early Schlegel and the later Nietzsche coexist side by side. 'Life' becomes a powerful, if oscillating, keyword in the literature and cultural debates of the time. Diederichs contrasts 'neo-Romanticism' with all ossified, 'dead' knowledge, encouraging his readers to lead a conscious life *and* considering such a life an unconscious work of art. Under the Romantic banner of a pure, innocent and full 'life', the Jugendbewegung and Lebensreform rebel against middle-class conventions, but the cultural critique of these conventions and the contemporary 'philosophy of life' frequently turn to Schopenhauer's Pessimistic notion of an evil will to life, especially in their apocalyptic variations on the theme of cultural decline.[11] Hofmannsthal's play *Das Bergwerk zu Falun* (1899; *The Mine at Falun*) presents the difference between historical Romanticism and Pessimistic neo-Romanticism in a nutshell. It centres on an objective, tragic conflict between the everyday world and that of the supratemporal Queen of the Earth, to whose realm the artist-hero Elis is attracted by a Dionysian desire 'without bounds'.[12] Elis knows that the two worlds are incompatible and that his union with the Queen requires the sacrifice of all happiness in the human world. In Hofmannsthal's Romantic source, E. T. A. Hoffmann's story 'Die Bergwerke zu Falun' (1818; 'The Mines of Falun'), the dualism between the two worlds marks Hoffmann's departure from the early Romantic postulate of the unity of *Poesie* and life; but in Hoffmann's pre-Schopenhauerian, semi-psychological story we find no tragic conflict or Pessimistic knowledge. Finally, let us turn to the margins of 'neo-Romanticism' and Thomas Mann (1875–1955). His early work is sometimes considered 'neo-Romantic', but its central conflict between 'art' and 'life' is alien to early Romanticism and deviates from 'neo-Romanticism' by Mann's placement of 'life' in conventional, middle-class existence. Yet in *Der Tod in Venedig* (1912; *Death in Venice*) even Mann draws heavily, if ironically, on Nietzsche's early tragic world view and his later theme of artistic 'decadence'.

French Symbolism

'Neo-Romanticism' had a strong psychological dimension. In his calls for a new Romanticism, Bahr envisioned both a 'new psychology' and new narrative techniques that permitted the representation of unconscious sensations and of thoughts uncontrolled by reason. He strongly appealed to prefigurations of the desired change in the work of French Symbolists and related writers. When Arthur Schnitzler wrote 'Leutnant Gustl' (1900; 'Lieutenant Gustl'), the first German narrative to consist entirely of its hero's stream of consciousness, he drew not only on the psychoanalytical method of 'free association' recently developed by Freud, but also on the Symbolist Édouard Dujardin's interior monologue *Les Lauriers sont coupés* (1887; *The Bays Are Sere*). French Symbolism actually led to a conjunction of literary and psychological interests that preceded both the literary reception of psychoanalysis and the development of stream-of-consciousness techniques in neo-Romantic and modern literature. The impact of French Symbolism on poetry was perhaps even stronger.

Baudelaire (1821–67) and after him Rimbaud (1854–91), Verlaine (1844–96) and Mallarmé (1842–98) were influenced by Hardenberg and E. T. A. Hoffmann, but radically modernised this Romantic legacy. It is primarily through this French transformation that historical German Romanticism retained an impact on early twentieth-century German modernism. In Symbolism, German Romanticism had travelled from Tieck's and Eichendorff's forest solitudes to the modern metropolis of Baudelaire's Paris. It had exchanged the synthesis of art and nature for the uncanny feasts of *l'art pour l'art*. Symbolist authors detached Hardenberg's view of *Poesie* as an 'absolute reality' from its ontological and epistemological contexts: 'absolute' *Poesie* no longer served as the mediator between humanity and nature, and thought and feeling, but justified the appreciation of art as the highest, self-contained reality. For Hardenberg, the self-referential play of language mirrors the dynamic relations between things and expresses the soul of the world. For the Symbolists and their aestheticist heirs, it created a world apart. But if art was now the only true 'life', nature took its revenge in the 'decadent' after-shocks of Symbolism: reduced to ugliness, decay, illness and death, it re-emerged as a spell-binding focus of the poet's 'nervous' and morbid fascination.

Stefan George was instrumental in making Baudelaire and Symbolism known in Germany. A famous poem from the collection *Algabal* (1892) marks his distance from German Romanticism: strolling through his self-made, sacred, yet lifeless garden, the lyrical 'I' longs not to find Ofterdingen's blue flower but to engender the 'black flower' of death.[13] George knew that with the barren magnificence of *Algabal*'s artificial paradises aestheticism had reached an extreme and an end. In his later work, he abandoned radical aestheticism, reducing Symbolist imagery and using a more abstract and didactic language to create a quasi-religious cult of art that promised a new life of beauty and heroic greatness outside the mediocrities of modern mass existence. He assumed the role of a charismatic leader and prophet in a both elitist and influential circle of poets and academics. The private religiosity of the circle differed from the affinity between poetry and prophecy in early Romanticism by its authoritarian structure and George's calculated use of homoerotic attraction.

In 1896 Hofmannsthal, who refused to be drawn into the circle around George, explicitly contrasted the Symbolist programme underlying his early, 'neo-Romantic', poetry with the Romantic poetry of Uhland and Eichendorff.[14] And certainly, poems like Hofmannsthal's 'Erlebnis' (1892; 'Experience') and 'Weltgeheimnis' (1894; 'World Mystery') not only display a greater technical refinement and symbolic density than most Romantic ones, but also use their new powers of expression to mourn the loss of any knowledge of, and sustainable life within, the mystery of nature which in Eichendorff enriched and renewed traditional piety. By its precise and 'nervous' modulation of minute sensations, Hofmannsthal's poetry creates configurations of existential disorientation, melancholic longing and psychophysical pain that in their near-musical intensity surpass the expressions of longing in historical Romanticism.

While Hofmannsthal started from a Symbolist, self-consciously modern and 'nervous' Romanticism, the early poems of Rainer Maria Rilke (1875–1926) are still close to Eichendorff's Romantic piety. However, the sense of a divine foundation of life, which in *Das Buch der Bilder* (1902–6; *The Book of Images*) and the semi-devotional *Das Stunden-Buch* (1905; *The Book of Hours*) underlies the representation of transience, is shattered in the experience of the modern metropolis. In Rilke's partly autobiographical *Die Aufzeichnungen des Malte Laurids Brigge* (1910; *The Notebooks of Malte Laurids Brigge*) the narrator is subjected to a chaos of fragmented impressions that can no longer be apprehended in any meaningful synthesis. The setting of this disorientation is contemporary Paris, and it is in Paris that Rilke, as the secretary of the sculptor Auguste Rodin, engaged in semi-religious exercises of depersonalisation. His search for a new poetic practice in which 'feelings' are replaced by 'experiences',[15] and in which the poet becomes the impersonal recipient of an objective revelation, coincides with his increasingly refined adoption of Symbolist techniques. This desire for impersonality and objectivity notwithstanding, Rilke's poetry retains unmistakably Romantic features. Romantic inwardness is still present in his evocation, around 1914, of an *inner* space that reaches through all beings. Yet this evocation of *Weltinnenraum* proceeds with a nearly archaic, 'mythic' objectivity from which both a language of nature and the reflections and emotions of the subject are absent: the birds fly through this space, but silently, and 'the tree grows *in* me'.[16] In Eichendorff, the poet's word is to unbind the 'song' residing in all things; in Hardenberg, the observation of the reflecting subject ought to bring the reflection within the object to life, and reveal the object's true nature as a 'Thou'. By contrast, in Rilke there is no conscious mediation between subject and object: *Weltinnenraum* discloses itself in the mode of an incomprehensible grace. Therefore his engagement with Romanticism marks less a revival of Romanticism than 'a crisis of the Romantic'.[17] Given that the Romantics never actually succeeded in establishing the intended mediation between subject and object, it may also mark a modern radicalisation of a crisis within Romanticism.

In German neo-Romantic poetry influenced by French Symbolism, then, we find different degrees of closeness to historical German Romanticism: George is perhaps most remote from, and Rilke closest to, Romanticism. Yet however problematic the Romantic legacy had become for George and Hofmannsthal, and however 'modern' their poetry was, both propagated, in different ways, a view of the poet as a spiritual leader in which the Romantic association of poetry and prophecy was linked to authoritarian forms of social practice. In 'neo-Romanticism' as a whole, this view of the poet combined with pre-modern and non-Western conceptions of charismatic authority. Many groups of the Jugendbewegung, for instance, encouraged the formation of spiritual (and erotic) bonds between a leader and followers who were supposed to experience their obedience as self-fulfilment. The continuing attraction of charismatic authority after World War One was a major cultural factor in creating or sustaining a widespread contempt for liberal politics that contributed to the failure of the Weimar Republic.

Hofmannsthal: from 'neo-Romanticism' to radical conservatism

Hofmannsthal repeatedly defined the modernity of his own time with reference to Romanticism. In 1893, at the age of nineteen, he criticised the intellectual disposition of contemporary aestheticism, which was also his own, as over-refined, 'nervously Romantic' and hostile to any true or full life.[18] This critique led him to work in more popular and representative genres, notably comedy and, in collaboration with the composer Richard Strauß, opera. Two years before his death, in the so-called *Schrifttumsrede* (1927), he conceived the cultural revival that was to regain a true and full life for German and Austrian society as a 'conservative revolution' and a reversal, but also a continuation, of Romanticism.[19] Hofmannsthal's reflections differ from both dogmatically anti-Romantic and naively 'neo-Romantic' stances and are among the most instructive conservative sources in our context. In particular, his deeply unstable engagement with Romanticism epitomises what Martin Greiffenhagen has called the dilemma of conservatism: the impossibility, in modernity, of restoring pre-modern values like tradition or traditional belief without contravening, by the very attempt at restoration, the conservative ideal of natural, unreflective growth.

I have already noted that Hofmannsthal's play *Das Bergwerk zu Falun* marks the difference between Romanticism and neo-Romantic Pessimism.

The fact that Hofmannsthal treated the play as a fragment after its completion in 1899 shows that he considered it problematic. Indeed, the play fails to unify its conflicting recourses to Hoffmann's story and to one of Hoffmann's own sources, Hardenberg's *Heinrich von Ofterdingen*. In line with the Symbolist reception of Hardenberg, which reduces the distance between Hardenberg and Hoffmann's concern with the uncanny, Hofmannsthal reinforces the destructive, 'Gothic' elements of Hoffmann's narrative, at times to the point of sharing the infatuation with bodily decomposition that thrills the 'decadent' heirs of Symbolism. Yet with its insistence on the reality of the Queen's underworld, the play also confirms Hardenberg's metaphysical orientation, which was largely ignored in French Symbolism. Although Hofmannsthal's Pessimism prevents him adopting Hardenberg's pietistic unity of the mythic-religious and the everyday in Chapter 5 of *Heinrich von Ofterdingen*, he is not prepared to abandon the existential, religious and social orientation of Hardenberg's vision. The famous Chandos letter of 1902 places these tensions in Hofmannsthal's engagement with Romanticism into the context of modern rationalisation and fragmentation.

In this fictitious letter,[20] Hofmannsthal's persona, Lord Chandos, explains to his mentor, 'Francis Bacon', why he can no longer produce any literary works. In particular, Chandos has abandoned the plan to write '*Nosce te ipsum*': an encyclopaedic, eminently Romantic work in which the representation of self-knowledge would have coincided with that of the world's spiritual and physical unity. Thus Chandos's failure to think or talk coherently in particular reflects his inability to apprehend or express any Romantic unity of self and world. Accordingly, the quasi-mathematical and musical nature of the self-referential language in which Hardenberg located the soul of the world is for Chandos an empty, aestheticist play, alien to both worldly life and innermost self. The Chandos letter presents this aestheticist death of the Romantic vision as the symptom of a larger, existential crisis. It is not just that Chandos can no longer produce Romantic literature or appreciate aestheticist excellence; the crisis of language he experiences is marked by alienation and destroys both his sense of identity and his participation in any form of cultural and social life. Self-consciousness, philosophical reflection, religious meaning, political judgement, moral values and everyday, private communication all fall prey to an atomised perception.

Chandos compares this perception to the view through a magnifying glass that shows a piece of one's skin as an open field of caves and furrows. This comparison links his alienation to the experimental attitude towards nature evident in the writings of Francis Bacon (1561–1626). By its experiment-based removal of traditional 'prejudices', Bacon's 'new science' undermined pre-modern world views in which nature figured both as the largely unexamined setting of human life and a dimension in which humans participated in cosmic, mythic or religious, orders. Bacon thus seems to stand at the beginning of that fragmentation and loss of meaning which for Hofmannsthal and 'neo-Romanticism' in general receive a contemporary urgency from late nineteenth-century positivism. The similarities between Chandos's loss of self and the positivist psychology of Ernst Mach (1838–1916), who rejected any synthesising agency underlying the punctual sensations in human perception, have frequently been noted. On their own, however, neither Baconian empiricism nor Machian positivism can account for Chandos's crisis. Rather, this crisis reflects the effects of analytical and sceptical dispositions when they gain hold over a person's habitual perception and the traditional concepts, norms and conventions underlying his and his society's sense of reality and self. Chandos shares these dispositions and a 'modern' attention to detail not only with scientists but also with any poetry that, like Hofmannsthal's own, centres on the communication of minute sensations. By subjecting all life and thought to this kind of attention, Chandos refuses to behave differently in different regards: nature, the psyche, human thought, politics, language and the traditional beliefs informing everyday life – all are treated in the same way. Without this holistic, and Romantic, refusal to do without one all-encompassing approach to the world, modern 'fragmentation' could not be experienced as a crisis.

Accordingly, the Romantic vision of cosmic unity that precedes Chandos's crisis does not vanish completely. At his moments of revelation, it recurs in a transformed way. Chandos finds 'the most sublime presence' of a 'divine feeling', which dissolves the borders between subject and object in his perceptions, memories and fantasies of despised creatures – cripples, rats, ugly dogs – and in banal objects detached from their uses in practical life. These moments of 'feverish thinking' connect him to 'the whole of existence'. Like the disclosure of *Weltinnenraum* in Rilke, this revelation of the world's unity cannot be provoked or controlled. Moreover, in its fluid and glowing immediacy it defies the fixations of conceptual language. Yet while Chandos pleads impossibility of expression, Hofmannsthal's portrayal of Chandos as a mystic without mysticism in masterly fashion outlines a modern, post-Romantic construction of 'epiphany' outside the realms of traditional religions and communities. Since similar constructions are widespread in modern literature, the Chandos letter can be read not only as documenting a writer's crisis, but also as a poetological programme characterised less by a general scepticism concerning language than by its specific poetic challenge to the rationalised languages of modernity.

While the Chandos letter links post-Romantic epiphany to an ethos of mystical silence, Hofmannsthal does not forsake literature but tries to overcome modern fragmentation in the writer's visions of wholeness. Increasingly, however, his recourse to literary notions of cultural revival becomes part of concerns which he considers social and even political. The interpretation of the First World War as a spiritual event from which would spring the regeneration of German and Austrian culture, shared by many German writers of the time, provides the most important context of this 'politicisation' of his cultural critique. After the war, his constructions of epiphanic wholeness as the source of a new national life become even more pronounced. While these constructions are in structural agreement with the early Romantic postulate that *Poesie* be 'sociable', their significance in the early twentieth century deviates from the ethos of early Romanticism. The German dissociation of liberalism and nationalism during the last decades of the nineteenth century means that Hofmannsthal's embrace of spiritual politics as part of a *national* revival entails the rejection of the liberal and emancipatory potentials in early Romanticism.

The concept of 'counter-experience' in the 1920 speeches on Beethoven makes this rejection explicit. On the one hand, Hofmannsthal binds the desired change in contemporary society to the experience of that spirituality which between 1750 and 1800 led to Enlightenment humanism, the emancipation of the individual and the esteem for, and refinement of, individual experience. On the other hand, any twentieth-century revival must oppose the central tendency of that time, and of Romanticism in particular. The Romantics rebelled against the overwhelming constraints of traditional society, but in the early twentieth century there is too much freedom and an anarchic wealth of spiritual aspirations without any normative force. The construction of cultural revival as 'counter-experience', then, appeals to an essentially anti-traditional spirituality for the sake of establishing a normative spiritual tradition.

With his 1927 call for a 'conservative revolution', Hofmannsthal responds to the dilemma of an anti-traditional establishment of tradition by combining an implicitly religious conception of tradition with a strongly authoritarian position. In the *Schrifttumsrede*, he insists on both the absence of any true tradition in German society and the need to overcome the arbitrariness of neo-Romantic spirituality by the acceptance of an unquestionable authority. Germans need to bind 'themselves to necessity, but to the highest one, which resides above all statutes and is the geometrical locus, as it were, of all thinkable statutes'. The normative force of the desired tradition must be based on the highest necessity which precedes, and is the 'absolute' source of, any binding agreements and statutes in society. But a necessity to which one first has to bind oneself is, of course, no necessity. As presented in the *Schrifttumsrede*, the modern search for a tradition and, to put it bluntly, God, differs from Romantic appeals to the Absolute by aiming not for freedom but 'for true constraint'. Moreover, hardened by the school of nineteenth-century science, positivism and metaphysical scepticism, Hofmannsthal's modern seeker of the Absolute displays the rigorous features of masculinity, and not the vague, gentle and child-like disposition of the Romantics. Yet this new masculinity is still informed by Romantic inwardness: for the conservative revolutionary, the depth of his own soul is the only *true* reality. His revolution starts from the inward and poetic unification of the divisions and fragments of modern reality, and finishes by projecting the resulting inner wholeness onto the external world. According to Hofmannsthal's own diagnosis, however, this mythic conception of revolution cannot be realised. If, as he insists, the world becomes a unity only to those who in themselves are 'whole', the world will not become a unity. The *Schrifttumsrede* makes it perfectly clear that wholeness is precisely what modern, neo-Romantic individuals lack.

The Frankfurt School

The critical theory developed between 1930 and 1970 by the members and associates of the Frankfurt Institute of Social Research comprises a great diversity of approaches to the problems of modern society and culture. Equally diverse is the reception of Romanticism within the School. Critical theory as a whole both subjects the Romantic tradition to a Marxist ideology critique and tries to salvage its 'progressive' or Utopian potentials: Romantic visions of the unity of humanity and nature conceal and support the domination over humans and nature in capitalism (and in modernity as a whole) *and* transmit images of a reconciliation between the classes and between mankind and nature that cannot be realised in – and in this sense transcend – capitalism (and modernity). The markedly different engagements with Romanticism within this critical framework to some extent reflect the ways in which particular aspects of the Romantic tradition influenced particular critical theorists before and during their alignment with the political left.

Herbert Marcuse (1898–1979) became a Marxist theorist through his enthusiastic reading of Marx's 'Ökonomisch-Philosophische Manuskripte' (1844; 'Economic and Philosophic Manuscripts') immediately after their first publication in 1932.[21] Marcuse's Marxism is itself Romantic, for the 1844 manuscripts show Marx's early thought to be strongly influenced by Romanticism: communism amounts to the reconciliation of humanity and nature, or 'humanism' and 'naturalism', and Romantic conceptions of creativity clearly inform the author's understanding of non-alienated labour as the realisation of human essence. This early-Marxist and Romantic image of a nature the 'liberation' of which coincides with the realisation of human essence guides Marcuse's reinterpretation of Freudian psychoanalysis in *Eros and Civilisation* (1955) and his critique of modern technology and advanced capitalism in *One-Dimensional Man* (1964). Both books strongly influenced student activism in the late 1960s in Germany and the United States. They use and develop, but hardly reflect upon, the humanist elements of Romanticism. In other words, Marcuse in his version of critical theory adopts a basically optimistic kind of Romanticism which tends to be exempted from critical discussion by its early-Marxist credentials.

Early Marxism was an important reference point for all major critical theorists. However, in the Frankfurt office of Max Horkheimer (1895–1973), who became director of the Institute in January 1931, hung a portrait not of Marx but of Schopenhauer.[22] The alignment of Schopenhauer's Pessimism and his emphasis on 'compassion' with social criticisms of the conditions of working-class life in Horkheimer's earliest writings precedes the positive references to Schopenhauer throughout his critical career. In Horkheimer's and Adorno's *Dialektik der Aufklärung* (1947; *Dialectic of Enlightenment*), probably the most influential publication of the Frankfurt School, compassion appears in dialectical parlance as 'a kind of sensuous awareness of the identity of general and particular' alongside 'the immediate social universal' that is solidarity.[23] The authors present Schopenhauer's mistrust of humanism and civilisation as proto-fascist, but their own critique of Enlightenment heavily draws on Schopenhauer's equation of self-preservation with guilt. The later Horkheimer interpreted critical theory as agreeing with a Romantic 'longing for the totally Other'[24] which cannot be fulfilled in this world. Student activists who felt heartened by Marcuse's optimistic Romanticism perceived Horkheimer's Romantic pessimism and religious orientation as a betrayal of critical theory. They were wrong. In his programmatic essay 'Traditionelle und kritische Theorie' ('Traditional and Critical Theory') of 1937 Horkheimer had already emphasised the strictly theoretical character of critical theory by disclaiming any interest in social improvements within contemporary society. Combined with the critical axiom that true emancipation required the overcoming of 'instrumental reason' and purposive action as such, this rejection of practical aims in fact ruled out not only the option of social reform but also any non-mystical concept of revolution.

The importance of non-instrumentality in critical theory reflects its indebtedness to early Romanticism. Friedrich Schlegel's demand that society become 'poetic' and *Poesie* 'sociable' implies the idea that the freedom from purpose and utility which Kant had restricted to the pure judgement of taste, and which for the early Romantics pertained to all *Poesie* and art, ought to inform social life as a whole. Perhaps even more than Horkheimer, Adorno (1903–69) insisted on the incompatibility of true freedom with instrumental reason and purposive action. Adorno's critical path did not lead to religion but started and ended with modern art. Deeply impressed by Arnold Schönberg's development from a 'neo-Romantic' composer to the master of dodecaphony, Adorno developed a version of critical theory that focused on the social meaning of modernist techniques in the high art of his time.

For Adorno, the social meaning of art results neither from a direct representation of society as attempted by socialist realism nor from the expression of a leftist or existentialist commitment. Rather, modern art achieves true social significance only through its autonomous construction of self-enclosed configurations that by their very existence protest against the adoption of the principle of utility in both society and art. These configurations must not harbour a comprehensive metaphysics. Rather, 'authentic' art must do justice to the fact that 'the whole' is absent in modernity's transcendental homelessness. It does so by radicalising the Romantic techniques of fragmentation and defamiliarisation. Only through this radicalisation can the modernist work of art implicitly and indirectly express the hope for a meaningful life that traditional metaphysics presented as fulfilled. Adorno did not establish this normative conception of modern art in a conventionally academic philosophy. His last work *Ästhetische Theorie* (written 1961–9; *Aesthetic Theory*) was precisely that: less a philosophical work about aesthetics than a philosophical meditation that itself was aesthetic and thus represented a twentieth-century adoption of the postulate of the unity of philosophy and *Poesie* that Friedrich Schlegel and Schelling had first formulated at the time of historical Romanticism.

In his adoption of an aesthetic manner of philosophising Adorno was strongly influenced by Walter Benjamin (1892–1940), who became an associate of the Institute in 1935. In 1923, when the two thinkers first met, Benjamin already had a history of sustained engagements with German Romanticism. From its emergence in the context of the Jugendbewegung, Benjamin's affinity with Romanticism included the rejection of neo-Romantic emotionalism and nationalism: the new youth, whose culture would coincide with true, non-institutionalised and cosmopolitan religion, was to be both Romantic and sober, or rather, the true Romanticism of youth itself was sober. Youth needed both the inspiration by an enthusiastic will to beauty, truth and deed and the freedom from the 'idealist narcotism' typical of philistine sentimentality. This early Romantic insistence on both enthusiasm and level-headedness stayed with Benjamin after his dissociation from the Jugendbewegung. It informed the emphasis on sobriety, thinking and on 'prose' as the idea of Romantic *Poesie* in his 1919 doctoral thesis on Romanticism. And it still informed his support for communism in the Surrealism essay of 1929, which bound the revolution to both the energies of intoxication and the rationality of a methodological and disciplined preparation. The so-called 'profane illumination' at the basis of revolutionary practice was to reveal the interpenetration of the everyday and the mysterious, of the known and the unknown. That is, it was to reveal what Hardenberg considered the result of 'romanticisation'.

Benjamin's doctoral thesis *Der Begriff der Kunstkritik in der deutschen Romantik (The Concept of Art Criticism in German Romanticism)* probably represents the boldest German reinterpretation of Romanticism in the early twentieth century. With considerable chutzpah, the author breaks the historical continuities between early Romanticism and its afterlife in Catholic conservatism. Moreover, he severs the 'reflection' and 'irony' within the Romantic work of art from both the (Fichtean) notion of 'I' and the Schlegelian context of Dionysian 'ecstasy' and disillusionary techniques. Romantic 'reflection' is exclusively conceived as the transforming – and ultimately destructive – activity of reflecting upon an aesthetic form; Romantic 'irony' is essentially formal; and 'immanent criticism' perfects the ironic destruction of form within the work and thereby, paradoxically, salvages the work in the idea. The formalist and destructive features of Benjamin's discussion, which ignores or minimises central early Romantic concerns like subjectivity, 'feeling', 'genius' or the hermeneutical relationship between author and reader, perhaps explain why both his thesis and a Romanticism conceived along its lines were interpreted as anticipations of structuralism and poststructuralism.[25] However, the concept of a destructive and yet redemptive criticism derived by Benjamin from his conceptual montage relies too heavily on his own messianism and linguistic mysticism to be compatible with any consistently secular theory.

In the *Ursprung des deutschen Trauerspiels* (1925; *Origin of the German Tragic Drama*), Benjamin complements the formalism of his thesis with a historical dimension. In contrast to the idea of the great, timelessly valid work of art, Baroque works are from the very beginning designed to decompose in the course of time. It is in this orientation towards historical decay that Benjamin now locates the prefiguration, *within* the works, of redemptive critique. This historical modification of the concept of an immanent, destructive and redemptive criticism marks the last stage of Benjamin's engagement with Romanticism before his alignment with left-wing politics.

Influenced by Bertolt Brecht and caught up in fascist Europe, the earlier activist of the *Jugendbewegung* tried to identify with 'the proletariat' as the agent of a new civilisation more strongly than perhaps any philosopher of the Frankfurt School. Yet Benjamin's interpretation of Brechtian theatre contains hidden contemplative and semi-religious elements that become manifest through the parallels with his work on Franz Kafka from the same period. Within the Frankfurt School, Marcuse's openness for real political movements is perhaps closest to Benjamin's position. However, Benjamin is separated from Marcuse's Romantic optimism by an intensive and utterly pessimistic reflection upon Romantic poetics and thought, which corresponds to his apocalyptical placement of hope in decay and destruction rather than life. His 'destructive' and anti-subjective reception of Romanticism precedes the shrill celebration, in the Surrealism essay, of the destruction of the individual, on whose aesthetic sensibilities Adorno rests his hopes for true emancipation. Accordingly, Benjamin searches for liberation from the 'barbarism' of bourgeois culture in popular art forms like the cinema – a search that can be compared to Hofmannsthal's move towards popular genres – which for Adorno epitomise the alienation of capitalist culture. But this search for a positive meaning in the destruction of the 'aura' surrounding the great work of art rests on Benjamin's 1925 modification of the Romantic concept of criticism and still represents, as he acknowledges, a search for Hardenberg's 'blue flower in the land of technology'.[26]

Recent Romanticisms

The present-day view of German Romanticism as a critical and modern movement in the tradition of the Enlightenment rightly emphasises the importance of early Romanticism. To a large extent, however, this view merely inverts the dominant perception of the whole movement before the 1960s. This fact may account for its limitations, at least as long as the relationships between early Romanticism and the association of later phases of the movement with Catholic and nationalist conservatism receive relatively little attention. Recent literary engagements with Romanticism support the notion that German Romanticism is a complex historical configuration with strong anti-modern and escapist as well as critical and enlightened potentials.

Between 1970 and today, the early Romantic play with the text's own textuality entered light fiction and children's literature. International bestsellers like Michael Ende's *Die unendliche Geschichte* (1979; *The Neverending Story*) and Cornelia Funke's *Tintenherz* triology (2003–7; *Inkheart* triology) skilfully use textual self-reference to engage their readers in simulated experiences of an essentially unproblematic and enjoyable unity of myth and reality. At least for adult readers, this literature compensates for the dissatisfactions of modern life no less than did Eichendorff's poetry in Imperial Germany. There is no law that links critical reflection to early Romantic techniques.

Neither is there a law that excludes critical reflection from traditionalist Romantic genres. Modern German nature poetry, which upheld the spiritual orientation of the Romantic philosophy of nature, was tolerated in Nazi Germany and survived as a largely unbroken tradition between the 1920s and 1950s. After 1945, its increased popularity reflected the widespread reluctance to engage with political issues, especially the Nazi crimes. Yet from the mid-1950s onwards East and West German poets – notably Peter Huchel (1903–81), Johannes Bobrowski (1917–65) and Günter Eich (1907–72) – fruitfully used even this traditionalist genre for social critique and historical reflection.

Works by Peter Handke (b. 1942) and Botho Strauß (b. 1944) figure among the most noteworthy recent engagements with Romanticism. Both authors combine creative recourses to Romantic techniques and motifs with critical reflections on National Socialism. Yet even in this combination, the enlightened potentials of early Romanticism can in fact be rejected.

Strauß's *Der junge Mann* (1984; *The Young Man*) presents itself as a 'RomanticReflectionNovel' and ironically introduces its own subversions of linear time as a comfort people need in the absence of a universal and timeless truth.[27] With great virtuosity, Strauß radicalises textual self-reference and generic plurality to the point of subjecting these early Romantic techniques themselves to an ironic deconstruction. This deconstruction has a thematic counterpart in the critique of Romantic features in the life of contemporary 'alternative' subcultures, which are targeted in the novel's quasi-anthropological comments on 'the Syks'. The multinational Syks live in an economically dependent 'reservation' inside modern society. They enact a Romantic world view in rites that combine the celebration of non-instrumental female knowledge with a playful, persistently provisional *bricolage* in mythic story-telling and social experimentation. Strauß's fictitious anthropologist repeats Hofmannsthal's critique of 'neo-Romanticism' by objecting to the arbitrariness of the Syks' Romantic mythologising. Like Hofmannsthal, he insists that humans must submit to a 'higher necessity'.[28] In *Der junge Mann*, radical conservatism is only one of several options in the face of the instability that early Romantic religiosity shares with its postmodern re-enactments. After the collapse of the GDR, Strauß embraced this option wholeheartedly. He interpreted the dissolution of the Soviet empire as an event that by its incommensurability with all previous experience had the power to re-establish the pre-modern division between the sacred and the profane. Accordingly, he rejected French Symbolism, deconstruction and, implicitly, early Romantic irony in favour of an aesthetic fundamentalism that agreed with the Catholic Eucharist in suggesting the 'real' presence of the divine. Strauß comdemned Enlightenment and liberal politics as such, and declared Romanticism deeply Catholic. The route that led Friedrich Schlegel from early Romanticism to Catholic Restoration, then, can still be travelled today.[29]

Handke's *Der Bildverlust, oder Durch die Sierra de Gredos* (2002; *Crossing the Sierra de Gredos*) shows that a passionate and differentiated engagement with the Romantic tradition does not have to take that route. This ambitious, modern *Don Quixote* shares a number of devices and concerns with *Der junge Mann*, for example the fictionalisation of anthropology, the exploration of non-linear conceptions of time or the critique of media culture. More importantly, *Der Bildverlust* is the rich, aesthetically fascinating and morally mature outcome of Handke's earlier engagements with Romanticism. Its markedly experimental search for a full life in modernity, both adventurous and contemplative, rules out any religious or 'aesthetic' fundamentalism. Handke leaves the dichotomy of pure art and social commitment behind to reflect, in the open form of his narrative, on the interrelations between religious fervour and terrorism, and confronts the present Western arrogance towards Islamic societies by respectful references to Arab culture. His Romanticism is set against the undeclared wars of our time and the military and economic power of the West, yet affirms its own powerlessness in the knowledge of the disasters that political romanticisms can entail. *Der Bildverlust* deserves the closest attention of anyone interested in the modernity of Romanticism.

NOTES

1. Heinrich Heine, *Die romantische Schule*, in *Schriften zur Literatur und Politik I*, ed. U. Schweikert (Darmstadt: Wissenschaftliche Buchgesellschaft, 1992), pp. 259–394, esp. pp. 276–80, 283–304, 310–11, 365–6; Johann Heinrich Voß, 'Für die Romantiker', *Morgenblatt für die gebildeten Stände*, 12 (14 January 1808), pp. 45–7; 'Beitrag zum Wunderhorn', *Morgenblatt*, 283 (25 November 1808), pp. 1129–30 and 284 (26 November 1808), pp. 1133–4; J. P. Eckermann, *Gespräche mit Goethe*, ed. C. Michel (Frankfurt am Main: DKV, 1999), p. 324; G. W. F. Hegel, *Vorlesungen über die Ästhetik I*, eds. E. Moldenhauer, K. M. Michel (Frankfurt am Main: Suhrkamp, 1970), pp. 92–9, 136; Theodor Echtermeyer and Arnold Ruge, 'Der Protestantismus und die Romantik', *Hallische Jahrbücher*, 245–310 (1839) and 53–64 (1840), *passim*.
2. Theodor Eichendorff, 'Zur Geschichte der neuern romantischen Poesie in Deutschland' (1846), in *Geschichte der Poesie*, ed. H. Schultz (Frankfurt am Main: DKV, 1990), pp. 13–60, esp. pp. 37–42; Adam Müller, *Vorlesungen über die deutsche Wissenschaft und Literatur* (1806), in *Kritische, ästhetische und philosophische Schriften*, eds. Walter Schröder and Werner Siebert (Neuwied: Luchterhand, 1967), vol. I, esp. pp. 27–9, 55–8, 99–102, 111–12.

3. Rudolf Haym, *Die romantische Schule* (Berlin: Weidmannsche Buchhandlung, 1906), esp. pp. 3–16, 862–4.

4. The radical conservative philosopher of law Carl Schmitt, who came to support Nazism, rejected political Romanticism. Hans Zehrer, the radical conservative chief-editor of the journal *Die Tat*, published by the 'neo-Romantic' Eugen Diederichs Verlag, opposed Nazism.

5. C. Klinger, *Flucht, Trost, Revolte: Die Moderne und ihre ästhetischen Gegenwelten* (Munich: Hanser, 1995), pp. 9–67. Outside Romanticism scholarship, there is a corresponding disinclination to oppose 'modernity' or conceptions of modern rationality to post-Romantic, twentieth-century holism and cultural critique. See, for instance, A. Harrington, *Reenchanted Science: Holism in German Culture from Wilhelm II to Hitler* (Princeton, N.J.: Princeton University Press, 1996), and T. Rohkrämer, *Eine andere Moderne?: Zivilisationskritik, Natur und Technik in Deutschland 1880–1933* (Paderborn: Schöningh, 1999).

6. Hermann Bahr, *Zur Überwindung des Naturalismus*, ed. G. Wunberg (Stuttgart: Kohlhammer, 1968), pp. 10–13, 87, 99–102; Heinrich Mann, 'Neue Romantik', *Die Gegenwart*, 42:29 (1892), pp. 40–2.

7. Eugen Diederichs, 'Zur Jahrhundertwende' (1900), repr. in J. H. Ulbricht and M. G. Werner (eds.), *Romantik, Revolution und Reform: Der Eugen Diederichs Verlag im Epochenkontext 1900–1949* (Göttingen: Wallstein, 1999), p. 82.

8. Arthur Schopenhauer, *Die Welt als Wille und Vorstellung* (1819–59), 2 vols., in *Sämtliche Werke*, ed. P. Deussen (Munich: R. Piper, 1911), esp. vol. II, pp. 398–410 and 690–726.

9. Schlegel, 'Vom ästhetischen Werte der griechischen Komödie' (1794), in *KFSA* I, pp. 19–33.

10. Friedrich Nietzsche, *Die Geburt der Tragödie* and 'Versuch einer Selbstkritik' (1886), in *Sämtliche Werke*, vol. I, eds. G. Colli and M. Montinari (Munich: dtv, 1980), pp. 9–156; *Der Fall Wagner*, in *Sämtliche Werke*, vol. VI, pp. 9–53.

11. H. Schnädelbach, *Philosophy in Germany 1831–1933* (Cambridge: Cambridge University Press, 1984), pp. 139–60; F. Stern, *The Politics of Cultural Despair* (Berkeley: University of California Press, 1974).

12. Hugo von Hofmannsthal, 'Das Bergwerk zu Falun', in *Sämtliche Werke*, vol. VI, ed. H.-G. Dewitz (Frankfurt am Main: Fischer, 1995), p. 75.

13. Stefan George, 'Mein garten bedarf nicht luft und nicht wärme', in *Gedichte*, ed. E. Osterkamp (Frankfurt am Main: Insel, 2005), p. 45.

14. 'Poesie und Leben', in Hugo von Hofmannsthal, *Prosa*, 4 vols., ed. H. Steiner (Frankfurt am Main: Fischer, 1950–5), vol. I, p. 265.

15. Rainer-Maria Rilke, *Die Aufzeichnungen des Malte Laurids Brigge*, in *Werke*, vol. III, ed. A. Stahl (Frankfurt am Main: Insel, 1996), pp. 466–7.

16. Rilke, 'Es winkt zu Fühlung', in *Werke*, vol. II, eds. M. Engel and U. Fülleborn (Frankfurt am Main: Insel, 1996), p. 113.

17. L. Ryan, 'Die Krise des Romantischen bei Rainer Maria Rilke', in W. Paulsen (ed.), *Das Nachleben der Romantik in der modernen deutschen Literatur* (Heidelberg: Stiehm, 1969), pp. 130–51.

18. Hugo von Hofmannsthal, 'Gabriele D'Annunzio' (1893), in *Prosa*, vol. I, pp. 149, 155.

19. Hugo von Hofmannsthal, 'Das Schrifttum als geistiger Raum der Nation', in *Prosa*, vol. IV, pp. 390–413.

20. Hugo von Hofmannsthal, 'Ein Brief', in *Sämtliche Werke*, vol. XXXI, ed. E. Ritter (Frankfurt am Main: Fischer, 1991), pp. 45–55.

21. R. Wiggershaus, *Die Frankfurter Schule* (Munich: dtv, 1989), pp. 120–2.

22. Ibid., p. 66.

23. Max Horkheimer and Theodor W. Adorno, *Dialektik der Aufklärung* (Frankfurt am Main: Fischer, 1977), pp. 91, 23.

24. Max Horkheimer, 'Die Sehnsucht nach dem ganz Anderen' (1970), in *Gesammelte Schriften*, eds. A. Schmidt and G. Schmid Noerr (Frankfurt am Main: Fischer, 1985–96), vol. VII, pp. 384–404. For a Romantic use of the phrase 'ein ganz Anderer' ('a totally Other') as a reference to God, see H. F. Jacobi (ed.), *Jacobi an Fichte* (Hamburg: Friedrich Perthes, 1799), p. 30.

25. W. Menninghaus, *Unendliche Verdopplung: Die frühromantische Grundlegung der Kunsttheorie im Begriff absoluter Selbstreflexion* (Frankfurt am Main: Suhrkamp, 1987), pp. 115–31; P. Lacoue-Labarthe, J.-L. Nancy, *The Literary Absolute: The Theory of Literature in German Romanticism* (Albany, N.Y.: SUNY Press, 1988 [1978]), p. 124.

26. Walter Benjamin, 'Das Kunstwerk im Zeitalter seiner technischen Reproduzierbarkeit', in *Gesammelte Schriften*, vol. I.2, p. 495.

27. B. Strauß, *Der junge Mann* (Munich: Hanser, 1984), pp. 14–15.

28. Ibid., pp. 120–1.

29. B. Strauß, *Der Aufstand gegen die sekundäre Welt* (Munich: Hanser, 2004), pp. 39–40, 41–50, 57–78 and 112.

FURTHER READING

Armstrong, C., *Romantic Organicism: From Idealist Origins to Ambivalent Afterlife* (Basingstoke: Palgrave Macmillan, 2003)

Barker, A., K. McPherson and H. Gaskill (eds.), *Neue Ansichten: The Reception of Romanticism in the Literature of the GDR* (Amsterdam: Rodolphi, 1990)

Behler, E. and J. Hörisch (eds.), *Die Aktualität der Frühromantik* (Paderborn: Schöningh, 1987)

Bowie, A., *From Romanticism to Critical Theory: The Philosophy of German Literary Theory* (London: Routledge, 1997)

Hanssen, B. and A. Benjamin (eds.), *Walter Benjamin and Romanticism* (New York: Continuum, 2002)

Huch, R. O., *Blüthezeit der Romantik* (Leipzig: H. Haessel, 1899)
Ausbreitung und Verfall der Romantik (Leipzig: H. Haessel, 1902)

Kerbs, D. and J. Reulecke (eds.), *Handbuch der deutschen Reformbewegungen 1880–1933* (Wuppertal: Peter Hammer, 1988)

Kohlenbach, M., *Walter Benjamin: Self-Reference and Religiosity* (Basingstoke: Palgrave Macmillan, 2002)

Peter, K., 'History and Moral Imperatives: The Contradictions of Political Romanticism', in Dennis F. Mahoney (ed.), *The Literature of German Romanticism* (Rochester, N.Y.: Camden House, 2004), pp. 191–208

Pipkin, J. (ed.), *English and German Romanticism: Cross-Currents and Controversies* (Heidelberg: Carl Winter, 1985)

Saul, N., 'The Reception of German Romanticism in the Twentieth Century', in *The Literature of German Romanticism*, ed. Dennis F. Mahoney (Rochester, N.Y.: Camden House, 2004), pp. 327–59

'Hofmannsthal and Novalis', in *Fin de Siècle Vienna*, eds. G. J. Carr and E. Sagarra (Dublin: Trinity College Dublin, 1985), pp. 26–62

Seyhan, A., *Representation and Its Discontents: The Critical Legacy of German Romanticism* (Berkeley, Los Angeles and Oxford: University of California Press, 1992)

Sommerhage, C., *Romantische Aporien: Zur Kontinuität des Romantischen bei Novalis, Eichendorff, Hofmannsthal und Handke* (Paderborn and Munich: Ferdinard Schöningh, 1993)

Vordtriede, W., *Novalis und die französischen Symbolisten* (Stuttgart: Kohlhammer, 1963)

KEY AUTHORS AND THEIR WORKS

ARNIM, LUDWIG ACHIM VON (1781–1831). Minor nobility, studied at Göttingen, friend and collaborator of Clemens Brentano, husband of Bettine B.-von Arnim. Author of major novels *Gräfin Dolores* (1810; *Countess Dolores*), *Die Kronenwächter* (1817; *Guardians of the Crown*), co-author of folk-lyric collection *Des Knaben Wunderhorn* (1806–8; *The Boy's Magic Horn*), founder (1811) of anti-Semitic, nationalistic Christlich-teutsche Tischgesellschaft (Christian-German Dining Society), friend of Romanies.

BOISSERÉE, JOHANN SULPIZ VON (1783–1854). Wealthy Cologne family, son-in-law of Brentanos, with brother Melchior (1786–1851) art historian and connoisseur. Friendship with F. Schlegel and Goethe, collector and restorer of medieval and renaissance fine art, collections today in Cologne Wallraf-Richartz Museum and Munich Alte Pinakothek.

BRENTANO, CLEMENS MARIA (1778–1842). Patrician Italian-German son of Frankfurt am Main, brother of Bettine Brentano, studies at Halle, Jena, Göttingen, friend of early Romantics and close friend of Arnim. First marriage to Sophie Mereau. Author of major novel *Godwi* (1802), peerless lyrics (*Lore Lay*), co-author of folk-lyric collection *Des Knaben Wunderhorn* (1806–8; *The Boy's Magic Horn*), of fine novellas and *Märchen*, of the comedy *Ponce de Leon* (1803) and the Romantic drama *Die Gründung Prags* (1813; *The Founding of Prague*).

BRENTANO-VON ARNIM, BETTINE (1785–1859). Mercurial sister of Clemens, wife of Arnim, youthful intimate of aged Goethe, bosom friend of Günderrode. Published writings, subtle, semi-fictive 'letter-novels', only after Arnim's decease: the literary monuments *Goethe's Briefwechsel mit einem Kinde* (1835; *Goethe's Correspondence with a Child*), *Die Günderrode* (1840; *Günderrode*), *Clemens Brentano's Frühlingskranz* (1844; *A Vernal Wreath for Clemens Brentano*) and the social critique *Dies Buch gehört dem König* (1843; *This Book Belongs to the King*).

CHAMISSO, ADELBERT VON (1781–1838). Son of French aristocratic *émigrés*, Berlin. Bi-cultural friend of Fouqué, Varnhagen. Natural-scientific studies. Circumnavigator of globe with Romanzov expedition 1815–1818, author of *Doppelgänger* novella *Peter Schlemihl* (1814), *Reise um die Welt* (1819; *A Voyage Around the World*), ballads.

CREUZER, FRIEDRICH (1771–1858). Professor of classical philology at Marburg and Heidelberg. Married lover of Günderrode, withheld publication of her last volume *Melete*. Acquaintance of Brentanos, Arnim, Görres. Author of important comparative study *Symbolik und Mythologie der alten Völker, besonders der Griechen* (1812; *Symbolism and Mythology of the Ancient Peoples, especially the Greeks*).

EICHENDORFF, JOSEPH VON (1788–1857). Silesian minor nobility, later Prussian civil servant. Studies in Halle and Heidelberg, friendship with Arnim, Brentano, Görres. Patriotic service with Lützow Rangers in Wars of Liberation. Author of whimsical yet existential novella *Aus dem Leben eines Taugenichts* (1826; *From the Life of a Good-for-Nothing*), novels *Ahnung und Gegenwart* (1815; *Presentiment and Presence*) and *Dichter und ihre Gesellen* (1834; *Poets and their Pupils*), best known for deep, seemingly artless lyrics such as *Wünschelrute* (1815; 'Magic Wand').

ESCHENMAYER, CARL AUGUST VON (1768–1852). Swabian, medical studies in Göttingen and Tübingen, Professor at Tübingen. Influence of Schelling. Author of *Versuch die scheinbare Magie des thierischen Magnetismus aus physiologischen und psychischen Gesetzen zu erklären* (1816; *Essay in Explanation of the Apparent Magic of Animal Magnetism by Physiological and Psychological Causes*)

FICHTE, JOHANN GOTTLIEB (1762–1814). Key philosopher of Romanticism. Professor at Jena, inaugural Professor at Berlin (1810). Author of pioneering texts on subjectivism *Grundlage der gesammten Wissenschaftslehre* (1795; *Foundation of the Complete Theory of Knowledge*) and resurgent nationalist patriotism *Reden an die deutsche Nation* (1809; *Addresses to the German Nation*).

FORSTER, GEORG (1754–94). Danzig natural philosopher, ethnologist, travel writer, journalist, revolutionary. Accompanied Cook on second voyage around the world in 1772, Fellow of the Royal Society. Professorship in Kassel, then Mainz. Support for Revolution. Died of pneumonia in Paris of Terror. Author of *Reise um die Welt* (1778–80; *A Voyage round the World*, originally written in English) and *Ansichten vom Niederrhein* (1791–4; *Views of the Lower Rhineland*).

FOUQUÉ, CAROLINE DE LA MOTTE (1774–1831). Berliner. Wife of Carl. Numerous novellas and works of women's education. Author of *Briefe über Zweck und Richtung weiblicher Bildung* (1811; *Letters on the Aim and Direction of Women's Education*) and the novel *Resignation* (1831).

FOUQUÉ, FRIEDRICH HEINRICH CARL DE LA MOTTE (1777–1843). Prussian aristocrat and soldier, friend of Kleist. Author of tragic novella *Undine* (1811), historical tragedies and historical novels.

FRIEDRICH, CASPAR DAVID (1774–1840). Soapmaker's son from Greifswald. Studies in art at Greifswald, Copenhagen. Friend of Runge, Georg Friedrich Kersting, G. H. Schubert. Perhaps leading landscape painter of Romanticism, also figures and portraits. *Der Mönch am Meer* (1808–9; *Monk by the Sea*) inspired C. Brentano and Kleist; also *Kreidefelsen auf Rügen* (1818; *Chalk Cliffs at Rügen*).

GOETHE, JOHANN WOLFGANG VON (1749–1832). Patrician son of Frankfurt am Main, later courtier and minister of statelet Sachsen-Weimar. Central writer of epoch often defined against him. Humanist, friend and literary ally of Schiller. Author of numerous classics, including novels *Werther* (1775), *Wilhelm Meister* (1795–6, 1820–9) and *Die Wahlverwandtschaften* (1810; *Elective Affinities*), lyrics from *Erlkönig* (1770; *Elf-King*) to *West-östlicher Divan* (1819; *West-eastern Divan*) and *Vermächtnis* (1832; *Testament*), dramas (*Faust*, 1808–32), and natural science (anti-Newtonian *Farbenlehre* (1810; *Theory of Colour*).

GÖRRES, JOSEPH VON (1776–1848). Firebrand republican from the Palatinate, later mystical Catholic publicist and academic. Friend of Brentano and Arnim. Author of amusing and learned satires, ferocious political pamphlets, pioneering expositions of chapbooks and German myths. Died as Professor in Munich. 'Sympoetic' co-author with C. Brentano (Brentano-Görres) of *BOGS, der Uhrmacher* (1807; *Watchmaker BOGS*).

GRIMM, JACOB (1785–1863). Academic, philologist, brother of Wilhelm. Librarian at Kassel 1808, Professor at Göttingen 1830, 1837. one of the 'Göttingen Seven' who resigned office in protest at unconstitutional action of King. Friend of Savigny, Brentano. Co-author of dictionary, myth and fairy-tale collections with Wilhelm, also of important texts on the history and theory of language, law and sagas.

GRIMM, WILHELM (1786–1859). Brother of Jacob. Member of 'Göttingen Seven'. Co-author of dictionary, fairy-tale and myth collections. Individual work on ancient Germanic philology and runes.

GÜNDERRODE, KAROLINE VON (1780–1806). Patrician daughter of Frankfurt am Main. Close friend of Brentanos. Most gifted woman writer and thinker of the age. Tragic love-affairs with Savigny and Creuzer. Author as 'Tian' of fine lyrics, including suicide song 'Die malabarischen Witwen' (1805; 'The Widows of Malabar'), philo-sophical monodramas and novellas and the interesting religious tragedy *Mahomet, der Prophet von Mekka* (1805; *Mohammed, Prophet of Mecca*).

HAMANN, JOHANN GEORG (1730–88). Königsberg customs man, biblical fundamen-talist and philosopher of language. 'Magus of the North'. Friend of Herder. Dense, esoteric-allusive style, designed to lead the reader through a labyrinth to the truth. Author of *Sokratische Denkwürdigkeiten* (1759; *Socratic Sententia*), *Kreuzzüge des Philologen* (1762; *Philological Crusades*).

HARDENBERG, GEORG PHILIPP FRIEDRICH VON (Novalis; 1772–1801). Minor Saxon aristocrat, law studies in Wittenberg, natural sciences at Freiberg Mining Academy, later mining engineer. With friend F. Schlegel one of leading early Romantic writers and thinkers. Author of anti-Goethean novel *Heinrich von Ofterdingen* (1800–2), profound existential narrative lyric *Hymnen an die Nacht* (1799; *Hymns to Night*), pithy *Fragment* collections, rich unpublished writings.

HEGEL, GEORG WILHELM FRIEDRICH (1777–1831). Swabian student at Tübingen Hochstift with friends Hölderlin and Schelling. Professor at Heidelberg and Berlin.

The philosopher of absolute subjectivity, yet fierce critic of Romantic idealism. Possible co-author of the *Ältestes Systemprogramm* (1796; *Oldest System Programme*), made his name with *Phänomenologie des Geistes* (1807; *Phenonomenology of Spirit*); mature philosophy in aesthetics, right, logic, history published as lecture transcripts after death.

HEINE, HEINRICH (1797–1856). German-Jewish son of Düsseldorf, studies in Bonn, Göttingen, pro forma baptism 1825. Late Romantic. Political exile in Paris 1831. Writer of lyrics, lyrical cycles and anthologies, *Buch der Lieder* (1827; *Book of Songs*), *Romanzero* (1851), travelogues (*Reisebilder* (1826–31; *Pictures from My Travels*)), satirical epics *Deutschland. Ein Wintermärchen* (1844; *Germany. A Winter's Tale*), a fragmentary novel *Der Rabbi von Bacherach* (1840; *The Rabbi of Bacherach*), intellectual and literary history *Die romantische Schule* (1833; *The Romantic School*), *Geschichte der Religion und Philosophie in Deutschland* (1856; *History of Religion and Philosophy in Germany*).

HERDER, JOHAN GOTTFRIED (1744–1803). Son of an East Prussian schoolteacher. Literary theoretician, philosopher, critic, historian, translator, poet, theologian, pastor, later General-Superintendent (religious head) at Weimar. *The* pre-Romantic theoretician of cultural anthropology. Author of *Shakespeare* (1770), *Über den Ursprung der Sprache* (1772; *On the Origin of Language*), *Ideen zur Philosophie der Geschichte der Menschheit* (1784–91; *Ideas on the Philosophy of History of Humanity*).

HOFFMANN, ERNST THEODOR AMADEUS [WILHELM] (1776–1822). Son of middle-class Königsberg (Kaliningrad), friend of Werner. Lawyer, *Kapellmeister* at Bamberg, finally criminal judge at Berlin. Opponent of Biedermeier political repression. Aesthetic multi-talent as graphic artist, conductor and composer, and writer. Opera *Undine* (1822; after Fouqué), author of numerous fantastic novellas and two great nineteenth-century novels, *Die Elixire des Teufels* (1814–15; *The Devil's Elixirs*) and *Lebens-Ansichten des Katers Murr* (1820–22; *The Life and Opinions of Tomcat Murr*).

HÖLDERLIN, FRIEDRICH (1770–1843). Student and friend at Tübingen Hochstift of Hegel and Schelling. Philosopher, literary theoretician, poet. Author of lyric novel *Hyperion* (1797–9), tragic drama *Empedokles* (1797–1800), superlative philosophical lyrics. Cruel onset of mental illness 1805.

HUFELAND, CHRISTOPH WILHELM (1762–1836). Berlin physician and natural philosopher. First Director of Charité hospital. Critic of Mesmer. First proponent of vitalistic macrobiotic remedies. Author of *Die Kunst, das Leben zu verlängern* (1796; *The Art of Prolonging Life*), leading medical doctor of age.

HUMBOLDT, ALEXANDER VON (1769–1859). Brother of Wilhelm, Prussian aristocrat and scholar, polymathic natural philosopher and socialist. Pioneering explorations of S. America with Bonpland 1799–1804, Russia 1829. Author of fundamental works *Voyage aux régions équinoxiales du Nouveau Continent* (1805–34; *Journey to the Equatorial Regions of the New Continent*, 30 vols.), *Ansichten der Natur* (1808;

Perspectives on Nature), *Kosmos – Entwurf einer physischen Weltbeschreibung* (1845–62; *Cosmos – Project for a Physical Description of the Universe*). Friend of Thomas Jefferson.

HUMBOLDT, WILHELM VON (1767–1835). Brother of Alexander. Prussian aristocrat, multi-faceted scholar, later diplomat, politician and minister. Author of important work on gender anthropology, aesthetics, language. *Über die Verschiedenheit des menschlichen Sprachbaus und seinen Einfluß auf die geistige Entwicklung des Menschengeschlechts* (1836; *On the Difference in Structure of Human Language and Its Influence on the Intellectual Development of the Human Species*).

JACOBI, FRIEDRICH HEINRICH (1743–1829). Middle-class son of Düsseldorf. So-called philosopher of faith. Fierce critic of Kantian epistemology on this basis. Author of *David Hume über den Glauben, oder Idealismus und Realismus* (1787; *David Hume on Faith, or Idealism and Realism*).

KANT, IMMANUEL (1724–1804). Professor of philosophy at Königsberg (Kaliningrad). Chief proponent and critic of the Enlightenment. Author of fundamental critiques of pure reason, practical reason and judgement 1781–90, later on religion and reason, anthropology and political theory. His theory of subject offered a basis of Romantic thought.

KLEIST, HEINRICH VON (1777–1811). Minor Prussian aristocrat and soldier, turned writer and thinker. Friend of Adam Müller. Greatest outsider of age, author, possibly motivated by Kant-critique, of complex and subversive novellas, lyrics, dramas and theoretical discourses, including *Die Verlobung in St Domingo* (1811; *The Betrothal at St Domingo*), *Der zerbrochene Krug* (1811; *The Broken Jug*), *Über das Marionettentheater* (1810; *On the Puppet Theatre*). Editor of *Phöbus* (1807), *Berliner Abendblätter* (1810–11; *Berlin Evening Gazette*).

KLINGEMANN, AUGUST (1777–1831). Dramatist from Braunschweig, popular dramas but author also of extraordinary black Romantic novel *Nachtwachen* (1805; *Night Watches*).

KLUGE, CARL ALEXANDER FERDINAND (1782–1844). Berlin physician, later Director of Charité hospital. Author of influential study on animal magnetism *Versuch einer Darstellung des animalischen Magnetismus als Heilmittel* (1811; *Essay at an Account of Animal Magnetism as a Remedy*).

KÖRNER, CARL THEODOR (1791–1813). Dresden, son of close friend of Schiller. Study of natural science at Freiberg Mining Academy, then history and philosophy at Leipzig and Berlin. Later Vienna, acquaintance of F. Schlegel and Eichendorff. Joined Lützow Rangers in Wars of Coalition, fell. Author of fervent, quasi-religious patriotic songs (*Leyer und Schwert* (1813; *Lyre and Sword*)) and Schillerian sacrifice drama *Zriny* (1813).

LENAU, NIKOLAUS (1802–50). Born near Timisoara, youth in Hungary. Law, philosophy studies in Vienna, Altenburg, Heidelberg. Friend of Uhland, Kerner in Stuttgart.

Late Romantic author of *Faust* (1836), ballad *Die drei Zigeuner* (1844; *The Three Gypsies*).

LESSING, GOTTHOLD EPHRAIM (1729–1781). Pastor's son from Lausitz. Leading late Enlightenment figure. All-round verve as critic of aesthetic, historical, philosophical and theological orthodoxy. Author of model realist drama (1755; *Miß Sara Sampson*), of decisive critique of historical biblical hermeneutics *Die Erziehung des Menschengeschlechts* (1781; *The Education of the Human Race*), of model drama on religious tolerance *Nathan der Weise* (1781; *Nathan the Wise*).

MENDELSSOHN BARTHOLDY, FELIX (1809–1847). Studies with Carl Friedrich Zelter. Music Director in Düsseldorf, Leipzig, *Kapellmeister* in Berlin. Extensive travel to Britain, also Paris. Acquaintance of Klingemann, Immermann, Goethe; influence of Shakespeare. Promoted Bach to nineteenth century. Works: *Lieder ohne Worte* (1829; *Songs without Words*); *Die Hebriden* (1832, *The Hebrides*); *Paulus* (1832; *Paul*); *Sommernachtstraum* (1843; *Midsummer Night's Dream*).

MEREAU-BRENTANO, SOPHIE (1770–1806). First independent woman writer in Germany. Committed republican, social centre in Jena. Lyrics published by Schiller, later own journal *Kalathiskos*, translator of Boccaccio. Author of feminist novels *Das Blüthenalter der Empfindung* (1794; *The Flowering of Sentiment*) and *Amanda und Eduard* (1802). Second marriage to Clemens Brentano, gender-experimental co-authorship of texts.

MORITZ, KARL PHILIPP (1756–93). Upbringing in poverty, education through Pietism to Berlin Enlightenment. Friend of leading Enlightenment figures, Goethe. Influential aesthetic writings *Über die bildende Nachahmung des Schönen* (1788; *On the Formative Imitation of the Beautiful*). Above all, influence on Romantics through empirical psychology, co-editor of journal *Zeitschrift für Erfahrungsseelenkunde* (1783–92; *Journal of Empirical Psychology*), semi-autobiographical psychological novel *Anton Reiser* (1785–90).

MÜLLER, ADAM VON (1779–1829). Berliner, studied political sciences at Göttingen, civil servant, politician, philosopher, aesthetician, political scientist, diplomat. Conversion to Roman Catholicism, migration to Vienna. Close friend of Kleist. Author of influential work of philosophy *Die Lehre vom Gegensatz* (1804; *Theory of Antithesis*), of *Elemente der Staatskunst* (1809; *Elements of Governance*), *Zwölf Reden über die Beredsamkeit und deren Verfall in Deutschland* (1816; *Twelve Addresses on the Art of Eloquence and Its Decline in Germany*).

NOVALIS: see HARDENBERG, GEORG PHILIPP FRIEDRICH VON.

PAUL, JEAN: see RICHTER, JOHANN PAUL FRIEDRICH.

REIL, JOHANN CHRISTIAN (1759–1813). Pastor's son, Ostfriesland, medical studies in Göttingen, Halle. Influenced by Hufeland and Schelling, vitalism. Author of *Rhapsodieen über die Anwendung der psychischen Kurmethode auf Geisteszerrüttungen* (1803; *Rhapsodies on the Application of the Psychological*

Method for Healing Mental Disturbances), influential on Hoffmann and other Romantics.

REINHOLD, CARL LEONHARD (1757–1823). Viennese, joined Jesuits early, influence of Herder, conversion to Protestantism, then leading representative of Austrian Enlightenment. Married Wieland's daughter, move to Weimar, philosophy Chair at Jena, then Kiel. At Jena influence of Jacobi, Fichte. Author of *Versuch einer neuen Theorie des menschlichen Vorstellungsvermögens* (1789; *Essay at a New Theory of the Human Faculty of Representation*), pioneering critique of ground of Kant's account of subjectivity.

RICHTER, JOHANN PAUL FRIEDRICH (Jean Paul, 1763–1825). Pastor's son, studies in Leipzig, teaching, then popular and influential writer in Weimar and (mainly) Bayreuth. Acquaintance of leading figures of age (Romantics, Goethe, Schiller), but always independent. Gifted theologian, *Das Kampaner Thal* (1797; *The Vale of Campano*) and aesthetician, *Vorschule der Ästhetik* (1804; *Aesthetic Primer*), series of critical novels on tendencies of age including *Der Titan* (1802; *Titan*).

RITTER, JOHANN WILHELM (1776–1810). Silesian, apprentice apothecary, then studies at Jena. Influence of Schelling, influence on Hardenberg and other early Romantics. Speculative and experimental natural philosophy on inner, universal forces of nature, galvanism, electricity, magnetism, divination. Author of *Fragmente aus dem Nachlasse eines jungen Physikers* (1810; *Fragments from the Unpublished Works of a Young Physicist*).

RUNGE, PHILIPP OTTO (1777–1810). Pomeranian. Influenced by Jacob Böhme, Tieck, Hardenberg. Author of influential low German fairy tales and anti-Newtonian colour theory theory with parallels to that of Goethe, the *Farbenkugel* (1810; *Colour Sphere*), close friend of Brentano, correspondent of Goethe. Chief works of art with characteristically esoteric symbolism: *Die Zeiten* (1802–03; *The Times of Day*, cycle of drawings, later partially executed in oils), portraits and self-portraits, biblical scenes.

SAVIGNY, FRIEDRICH CARL VON (1779–1861). Patrician son of Frankfurt am Main, lover of Günderrode, husband of Gunda Brentano, intimate friend of Grimm brothers, Brentano, Görres. Leading philosophical jurist of age, historistic-Romantic approach, Professor in Marburg, later Berlin. Author of *Vom Beruf unserer Zeit für Gesetzgebung und Rechtswissenschaft* (1814; *On the Vocation of our Age for Legislation and Jurisprudence*).

SCHELLING, FRIEDRICH WILHELM JOSEPH (1776–1854). Pastor's son from Swabia, theological and philosophical studies at Tübingen Hochstift, Professor of philosophy at Jena, then Würzburg, Erlangen, Munich, Berlin. Married Caroline Schlegel, close links with Schlegel brothers, Hardenberg, Goethe, Fichte. Chief meta-critic of Fichte, supplanted Fichte's one-sided subjectivism with philosophy of nature. Author of *Vom Ich als Princip der Philosophie* (1795; *On the Ego as Principle of Philosophy*), *Ideen zu einer Philosophie der Natur* (1797; *Ideas on a Philosophy of Nature*), *Von der Weltseele* (1797; *On the World Soul*), *System des transcendentalen Idealismus* (1800;

System of Transcendental Idealism), *Philosophie der Kunst* (1802–3; *Philosophy of Art*), later anti-Hegelian writings on mythology and religion.

SCHILLER, FRIEDRICH CARL (1759–1805). Swabian middle-class, medical training, then rebellious poet. Later friend and ally of Goethe, great theoretician of classical literature *Über die ästhetische Erziehung des Menschen* (1795–6; *On the Aesthetic Education of Humanity*), *Über naive und sentimentalische Dichtung* (1796; *On Naive and Reflective Poetry*) and author of peerless historical tragedies *Don Carlos* (1796), *Wallenstein* (1799–1800), *Maria Stuart* (1801).

SCHLEGEL, AUGUST WILHELM (1767–1845). Son of Hanover pastor, brother and collaborator of Friedrich. Friend and adviser (on prosody) of Goethe. Populariser of Romantic literary theory in successful lectures and writings. With Tieck author of canonical Shakespeare translation. Later friend and house guest of Mme de Staël. Major translator of Spanish theatre into German. Later Professor at Bonn, mediator of Indian culture.

SCHLEGEL, CARL FRIEDRICH (1772–1829). Son of Hanover pastor, brother and collaborator of August Wilhelm. Studies at Göttingen, Leipzig. Intimate, 'symphilosophical' friend of Hardenberg, wed Dorothea Mendelssohn. Enemy of Schiller. *The* theoretician of early Romanticism. Early work on classical and modern literature, theory of Romanticism, co-editor and author of journal *Athenaeum* (1797–1800) and others, author of *Fragment* collections, erotic novel *Lucinde* (1799), later philosophy of history, conversion to Roman Catholicism, Sanscrit studies, diplomatic and political activities.

SCHLEGEL-SCHELLING, CAROLINE BÖHMER (1763–1809). Daughter of Göttingen theologian Johann David Michaelis. Republican sympathies at Mainz 1792, friendship with Georg Forster. Married A.W. Schlegel 1796, social and intellectual centre of brilliant early Romantic circle at Jena, brilliant correspondence and critical activity. Married Schelling 1803.

SCHLEGEL, DOROTHEA MENDELSSOHN-VEIT (1764–1839). Daughter of Berlin Jewish Enlightenment philosopher Moses Mendelssohn. Lived with F. Schlegel from 1799, *vie de bohème* at Jena in early Romantic circle, baptism and marriage 1804, Roman Catholicism 1808. Author of novel *Florentin* (1800), feminist riposte to husband's *Lucinde*.

SCHLEIERMACHER, FRIEDRICH DANIEL ERNST (1768–1834). Silesian, Pietistic upbringing, theology at Halle. Reformed Chaplain at Berlin Charité hospital, later one of leading evangelical theologians of the age. Intimate friend of F. Schlegel at Berlin, contributor to early Romantic *Fragmente*. Crystallised early Romantic religiosity in *Über die Religion* (1799; *On Religion*). Important later homiletic and dogmatic writings.

SCHUBERT, FRANZ (1797–1828). Schoolteacher's son, Vienna. Studies with Salieri. Friend of Grillparzer, Bauernfeld, Moritz von Schwind. Opera *Rosamunde* (1823), string quartet *Der Tod und das Mädchen* (1825–6; *Death and the Maiden*), *Die schöne Müllerin* (1823; *The Miller's Beautiful Wife*), *Winterreise* (1827; *A Winter's Journey*), eight symphonies, numerous *Lieder*.

SCHUBERT, GOTTHILF HEINRICH (1780–1860). Saxon pastor's son and *Naturphilosoph*. Study of theology at Leipzig, then medicine at Jena. Influence of Ritter and Schelling, private tutor, then Professor at Erlangen, Munich. Seminal public lectures at Dresden *Ansichten von der Nachtseite der Naturwissenschaft* (1808; *Views of the Dark Side of the Natural Science*), seminal *Symbolik des Traumes* (1814; *Symbolism of Dream*). Influence on all later Romantics, especially Hoffmann.

SCHUMANN, ROBERT (1810–1856). Son of Zwickau publisher. Law studies at Leipzig. *Kreisleriana* (after Hoffmann, 1838). Music Director of Düsseldorf. Numerous individual *Lieder* and cycles, including *Dichterliebe* (1840; *Poet's Love*, after Heine), piano pieces including *Carnaval* (1835), opera *Genoveva* (1850), four symphonies.

SOLGER, KARL WILHELM FERDINAND (1780–1819). Aesthetician and philosopher. Studies at Halle, Jena. Influence of Schelling. Later Professor at Berlin. Author of *Erwin: Vier Gespräche über das Schöne und die Kunst* (1817; *Erwin. Four Dialogues on Beauty and Art*). Ironic aesthetics said to be influential on Hegel.

STEFFENS, HENRIK (1773–1845). Philosopher, natural scientist, poet. Studies of natural philosophy at Kiel, Jena (Schelling's influence) and Freiberg. Chairs in Copenhagen, Breslau (Wroclaw) and Berlin. Author of *Grundzüge der philosophischen Naturwissenschaft* (1806; *Outlines of Natural Philosophy*), *Anthropologie* (1824) and valuable memoirs *Was ich erlebte* (1840–5; *What I Experienced*).

TIECK, LUDWIG (1773–1853). Berlin ropemaker's son. Theology studies, then hack Gothic writer, then first Romantic generation, leading poet and critic. Intimate friend of Wackenroder, also of Hardenberg. Pioneering study of marvellous in Shakespeare, first artist novel in *Franz Sternbalds Wanderungen* (1798; *The Wanderings of Franz Sternbald*). Fine psychological novellas, first genuine Romantic drama *Der gestiefelte Kater* (1797; *Puss-in-Boots*), interesting generic experiments (1800; *Genoveva*). Later realism and historical novels. With A. W. Schlegel canonical translation of Shakespeare.

VARNHAGEN VON ENSE, FRIEDRICH LUDWIG (1785–1858). Son of Düsseldorf doctor. Man of letters, diarist, diplomat, husband of Rahel V. Author of important memoires (*Denkwürdigkeiten*, 1837f.)

VARNHAGEN VON ENSE, RAHEL LEVIN (1771–1833). Daughter of Berlin Jewish merchant, wife of K. A. Varnhagen, literary salon, connections with all major figures of the epoch. Extensive correspondence in semi-literary form on the problem of women's and Jewish self-definition.

WACKENRODER, WILHELM HEINRICH VON (1773–1798). Son of Berlin advocate. Early friendship with Tieck, co-founder of Berlin Romanticism. Co-author of *Herzensergießungen* (1795; *Heartfelt Outpourings*) and *Phantasien über die Kunst* (1796; *Fantasias on Art*).

WEBER, CARL MARIA VON (1786–1826). Born in Eutin, Schleswig-Holstein. Opera Director in Prague, Dresden. Best known for operas *Der Freischütz* (1821; *The Enchanted Huntsman*), *Euryanthe* (1823).

WERNER, FRIEDRICH LUDWIG ZACHARIAS (1768–1823). Patrician family in Königsberg (Kaliningrad), later Warsaw and Berlin. Early friendship with Hoffmann. Freemason. Leading dramatist of Romantic movement. Friendship, then enmity, of Goethe. Conversion to Roman Catholicism 1810, ordination Rome 1814, Viennese Redemptorists, star preacher of Congress of Vienna 1815. Author of weighty, mystical historical dramas *Die Söhne des Thals* (1803–4; *The Sons of the Vale*), *Das Kreuz an der Ostsee* (1806; *The Cross on the Baltic*), of powerful fate drama *Der 24. Februar* (1809; *The 24th February*), and many virtuoso sonnets.

WOLZOGEN, CAROLINE VON (1763–1847). Minor Thuringian aristocrat. Schiller's sister-in-law, member of Classical Weimar circle. Author of sentimental novel *Agnes von Lilien* (1796; in Schiller's *Horen*), *Schiller's Leben* (1830; *Life of Schiller*), also of several good novellas, including *Die Zigeuner* (1802; *The Gypsies*).

FURTHER READING

Editions

Arnim, Bettine von, *Sämtliche Werke und Briefe*, eds. Konrad Feilchenfeldt *et al.* (Stuttgart, Berlin, Cologne, Mainz: Kohlhammer, 1990–)

Werke und Briefe, eds. Walter Schmitz and Sibylle von Steinsdorff, 4 vols. (Frankfurt am Main: Deutscher Klassiker Verlag, 1986–2004)

Arnim, Ludwig Achim von, *Werke und Briefwechsel: Historisch-kritische Ausgabe*, eds. Roswitha Burwick *et al.* (Tübingen: Niemeyer, 1999–)

Werke, eds. Roswitha Burwick *et al.*, 6 vols. (Frankfurt am Main: Deutscher Klassiker Verlag, 1989–94)

Brentano, Clemens *Werke*, eds. Wolfgang Frühwald, Bernhard Gajek and Friedhelm Kemp, 4 vols. (Munich: Hanser, 1963–8)

Sämtliche Werke und Briefe, eds. Jürgen Behrens, Wolfgang Frühwald, Detlev Lüders, 36 vols. (Stuttgart, Berlin, Cologne, Mainz: Kohlhammer, 1975–)

Chamisso, Adelbert von, *Sämtliche Werke*, eds. Jost Perfahl and Volker Hoffmann, 2 vols. (Munich: Winkler, 1975)

Eichendorff, Joseph von, *Werke*, eds. Wolfgang Frühwald, Brigitte Schillbach and Hartwig Schultz, 6 vols. (Frankfurt am Main: Deutscher Klassiker Verlag, 1985–93)

Fichte, Johann Gottlieb, *Werke*, eds. G. Jacobs and Peter Lothar Oesterreich, 2 vols. (Frankfurt am Main: Deutscher Klassiker Verlag, 1997)

Fouqué, Friedrich de la Motte, *Ausgewählte Werke: Ausgabe letzter Hand*, 12 vols. (Halle: Schwetschke, 1841–2)

Fouqué, Caroline de la Motte, *Ausgewählte Werke*, ed. Petra Kabus, 4 vols. (Hildesheim: Georg Olms, 2003–6)

Goethe, Johann Wolfgang von, *Sämtliche Werke, Briefe, Tagebücher und Gespräche*, eds. Henrik Birus *et al.*, 40 vols. (Frankfurt am Main: Deutscher Klassiker Verlag, 1985–)

Görres, Joseph, *Gesammelte Schriften*, ed. Wilhelm Schellberg (Cologne: Gilde-Verlag, 1926–)

Ausgewählte Werke, ed. Wolfgang Frühwald, 2 vols. (Freiburg im Breisgau, Basel and Vienna: Herder, 1978)

Grimm, Jacob and Wilhelm Grimm, *Gesamtausgabe der Werke von Jacob und Wilhelm Grimm*, ed. L. E. Schmitt (Hildesheim: Olms, 1963–)

Günderrode, Karoline von, *Der Schatten eines Traumes: Gedichte, Prosa Briefe, Zeugnisse von Zeitgenossen*, ed. with an essay by Christa Wolf (Darmstadt and Neuwied: Luchterhand, 1979)

Sämtliche Werke und Ausgewählte Studien, ed. Walter Morgenthaler, 3 vols. (Frankfurt am Main: Roter Stern/Stroemfeld, 1990–91)

Hegel, G.W.F., *Werke*, ed. Eva Moldenhauer and Karl Markus Michel, 20 vols. (Frankfurt am Main: Suhrkamp, 1970)

Heine, Heinrich, *Historisch-kritische Gesamtausgabe*, ed. Manfred Windfuhr, 16 vols. (Hamburg: Hoffmann & Campe, 1973–97)

Hoffmann, E.T.A., *Sämtliche Werke*, eds. Hartmut Steinecke *et al.*, 6 vols. (Frankfurt am Main: Deutscher Klassiker Verlag, 1985–2004)

Hölderlin, Friedrich, *Werke, Briefe, Dokumente*, ed. Pierre Botaux (Munich: Winkler, 1963)

Sämtliche Werke, ed. Friedrich Beissner, 8 vols. (Stuttgart: Kohlhammer, 1943–85)

Sämtliche Werke, ed. D. E. Sattler (Frankfurt: Stroemfeld/Roter Stern, 1975–)

Sämtliche Werke und Briefe, ed. Jochen Schmidt, 3 vols. (Frankfurt am Main: Deutscher Klassiker Verlag, 1992–2004)

Sämtliche Werke und Briefe, ed. Michael Knaupp, 3 vols. (Munich and Vienna: Hanser, 1992–3)

Humboldt, Wilhelm von, *Werke*, eds. Andreas Fischer and Klaus Giel, 5 vols. (Stuttgart: Cotta, 1960–81)

Jacobi, Friedrich Heinrich, *Jacobi an Fichte* (Hamburg: Friedrich Perthes, 1799)

Die Hauptschriften zum Pantheismusstreit zwischen Jacobi und Mendelssohn, ed. Heinrich Scholz (Berlin: Reuther & Reichard, 1916)

Jean Paul [Johann Paul Friedrich Richter], *Sämtliche Werke: Historisch-Kritische Ausgabe*, eds. Eduard Berend *et al.* (Weimar: Böhlau, 1927–, Berlin: Akademie-Verlag, 1952–)

Werke, ed. Norbert Miller, 6 vols. (Munich: Hanser, 1959–63)

Kant, Immanuel, *Werkausgabe*, ed. Wilhelm Weischedel, 10 vols. (Frankfurt: Suhrkamp, 1968)

Kleist, Heinrich von, *Sämtliche Werke und Briefe in vier Bänden*, eds. Ilse-Marie Barth, Klaus Müller-Salget, Stefan Ormans and Hinrich C. Seeba (Frankfurt am Main, Deutscher Klassiker Verlag, 1987–97)

Klingemann, August, *Nachtwachen von Bonaventura*, ed. with an afterword by Jost Schillemeit (Frankfurt am Main: Insel, 1974)

Lenau, Nikolaus, *Werke und Briefe*, eds. Helmut Brandt *et al.*, 7 vols. (Vienna: Deuticke, Stuttgart: Klett-Cotta 1989–2004)

Mereau-Brentano, Sophie, *Werke und autobiographische Schriften*, ed. Katharina von Hammerstein, 3 vols. (Munich: dtv, 1997)

Müller, Adam, *Kritische, ästhetische und Philosophische Schriften*, eds. Walter Schröder and Werner Siebert, 2 vols. (Neuwied and Berlin: Luchterhand, 1967)

Schelling, Friedrich Wilhelm Joseph, *Sämmtliche Werke*, ed. K.F.A. Schelling, (Stuttgart: Cotta, 1856–61)

Werke, ed. Manfred Schröter, 12 vols. (Munich: Beck, 1946–59)

Schiller, Friedrich, *Werke*, eds. Julius Petersen, Lieselotte Blumenthal, Benno von Wiese, Norbert Oellers and Siegfried Seidel (Weimar: Böhlau, 1943–)

Schlegel, August Wilhelm, *Kritische Schriften und Briefe*, ed. Edgar Lohner (Stuttgart: Metzler, 1966)

Schlegel, Dorothea, *Florentin: Ein Roman herausgegeben von Friedrich Schlegel*, ed. Wolfgang Nehring (Stuttgart: Reclam, 1993)

Schleiermacher, Friedrich Daniel Ernst, *Kritische Gesamtausgabe*, eds. Hans-Joachim Birkner *et al.* (Berlin and New York: de Gruyter, 1984–)
Tieck, Ludwig, *Schriften*, eds. Manfred Frank *et al.*, 12 vols. (Frankfurt am Main: Deutscher Klassiker Verlag, 1985–)
Varnhagen, Rahel Levin, *Gesammelte Werke*, eds. Konrad Feilchenfeldt, Uwe Schweikert, Rahel E. Steiner, 10 vols. (Munich: Matthes & Seitz, 1983)
Briefwechsel mit Pauline Wiesel, ed. Barbara Hahn (Munich: Beck, 1997)
Wackenroder, Wilhelm Heinrich, *Sämtliche Werke und Briefe*. Historisch-kritische Ausgabe, eds. Silvio Vietta and Richard Littlejohns, 2 vols. (Heidelberg: Carl Winter, 1991)
Werner, Zacharias, *Ausgewählte Werke*, 15 vols. (Grimma: Verlags-Comptoir, n.d. [=1840–41])

Works in English

Arnim, Achim von, *Gentry by Entailment*, trans. Alan Brown (London: Atlas, 1990)
Novellas of 1812, trans. Bruce Duncan (Lewiston, N.Y.: Edwin Mellen Press, 1997)
Chamisso, Adelbert von, *A Voyage Around the World*, trans. and ed. Henry Kratz (Honolulu: University of Hawaii Press, 1986)
Eichendorff, Joseph von, *Life of a Good-For-Nothing*, trans. J. G. Nichols (London: Hesperus, 2002)
Fichte, Johann Gottlieb, *Addresses to the German Nation*, trans. George Armstrong Kelly (New York: Harper and Row, 1968)
Goethe, Johann Wolfgang von, *Collected Works*, eds. Victor Lange, Eric A. Blackall, Cyrus Hamlin, 12 vols. (Princeton, N.J.: Princeton University Press, 1994–5)
Hardenberg, Friedrich von, *Novalis: Philosophical Writings*, trans. Margaret Mahony Stoljar (Albany: State University of New York Press, 1997)
Henry von Ofterdingen: A Novel, trans. Palmer Hilty (Prospect Heights, Ill.: Waveland Press, 1990)
Pollen and Fragments. Selected Poetry and Prose of Novalis, trans. A. Versluis (Grand Rapids, Miss.: Phanes, 1999)
Heine, Heinrich, *Deutschland: A Winter's Tale*, trans. T. J. Reed (London: Angel, 1986)
Hoffmann, E.T.A., *The Golden Pot and Other Tales*, trans. and ed. Ritchie Robertson (Oxford: Oxford University Press, 1992)
Selected Writings of E. T. A. Hoffmann, ed. and trans. Leonard J. Kent and Elizabeth C. Knight, 2 vols. (Chicago: University of Chicago Press, 1969)
Hölderlin, Friedrich, *Selected Poems*, trans. David Constantine (Newcastle upon Tyne: Bloodaxe, 1990)
Jean Paul, *A Reader*, ed., with essay and commentary Timothy J. Casey, trans. Erika Casey (Baltimore and London: Johns Hopkins University Press, 1992)
Kleist, Heinrich von, *The Marquise of O. and Other Stories*, trans. and with an introduction by David Luke and Nigel Reeves (Harmondsworth: Penguin, 1978)
Selected Writings, trans. David Constantine (London: Dent, 1997)
Klingemann, August, *The Night Watches of Bonaventura*, ed. and trans. Gerald Gillespie (Edinburgh: Edinburgh University Press, 1972)

Müller, Adam, *Twelve Lectures on Rhetoric*, trans., with a critical essay by Dennis R. Bormann and Elisabeth Leinfellner (Ann Arbor: University of Nebraska Press/ University Microfilms International, 1978)

Romantic Fairy Tales, trans. and ed. by Carol Tully (London: Penguin Books, 2000)

Savigny, Friedrich Carl von, *Of the Vocation of our Age for Legislation and Jurisprudence*, trans. A. Hayward (Kitchener: Batoche, 1999)

Schiller, Friedrich, *On the Aesthetic Education of Man*, eds. and trans. with an introduction, commentary and glossary of terms by Elizabeth M. Wilkinson and L. A. Willoughby (Oxford: Clarendon Press, 1967)

On the Naive and Sentimental in Literature, trans. Helen Watanabe (Manchester: Carcanet, 1981)

Schlegel, Dorothea, *Florentin: A Novel*, trans., annotated, and introduced by Edwina Lawler and Ruth Richardson (Lewiston, N.Y.: Edwin Mellen Press, 1988)

Schlegel, Friedrich, *Lucinde and the Fragments*, trans. Peter Firchow (Minneapolis: University of Minnesota Press, 1971)

Dialogue on Poetry and Literary Aphorisms, trans. and eds. Ernst Behler and Roman Struc (University Park and London: Pennsylvania State University Press, 1968)

Six German Romantic Tales. Heinrich von Kleist, Ludwig Tieck, E. T. A. Hoffmann, trans. with an introduction by Ronald Taylor (London: Angel, 1985)

Tieck, Ludwig, *The Land of Upside Down*, trans. by Oscar Mandel in collaboration with Maria Kelsen Feder (Rutherford: Fairleigh Dickinson University; London: Associated University Presses, c.1978)

Wackenroder, Wilhelm Heinrich and Ludwig Tieck, *Outpourings of an Art-Loving Friar*, trans. and with an introduction by Edward Mornin (New York: Ungar, c.1975)

Wheeler, Kathleen M. (ed.), *German Aesthetics and Literary Criticism: Romantic Ironists and Goethe* (Cambridge: Cambridge University Press, 1984)

Secondary Literature

General

Andrews, Keith, *The Nazarenes: A Brotherhood of German Painters in Rome* (Oxford: Clarendon Press, 1964)

Behler, Ernst, *Frühromantik* (Berlin and New York: de Gruyter, 1992)

Beiser, Frederick C., *The Romantic Imperative: The Concept of Early German Romanticism* (Cambridge, Mass.: Harvard University Press, 2003)

Berlin, Isaiah, *The Roots of Romanticism* (London: Chatto and Windus, 1999)

Brinkmann, R. (ed.), *Romantik in Deutschland: Ein interdisziplinäres Symposion* (Stuttgart: Metzler, 1978)

Brown, Marshall, *The Shape of German Romanticism* (Ithaca, N.Y.: Cornell University Press, 1979)

Dürbeck, Gabriele, '"Sibylle", "Pythia" oder "Dame Lucifer": Zur Idealisierung und Marginalisierung von Autorinnen der Romantik in der Literaturgeschichtsschreibung des 19. Jahrhunderts', *Zeitschrift für Germanistik*, 2 (2000), pp. 258–80

Eichner, Hans (ed.), *'Romantic' and its Cognates: The European History of a Word* (Manchester: Manchester University Press, 1972)

Frank, Manfred, *Einführung in die frühromantische Ästhetik* (Frankfurt am Main: Suhrkamp, 1989)

Hartley, Keith, Henry Meyric Hughes, Peter-Klaus Schuster and William Vaughan (eds.), *The Romantic Spirit in German Art 1790–1990* (London: Thames and Hudson, 1994)

Hoffmeister, Gerhard, *Deutsche und europäische Romantik* (Stuttgart: Metzler, 1978)

Honour, Hugh, *Romanticism* (Harmondsworth: Penguin, 1979)

Huch, Ricarda, *Blüthezeit der Romantik* (Leipzig: H. Haessel, 1899)
Ausbreitung und Verfall der Romantik (Leipzig: H. Haessel, 1902)

Hughes, Glyn Tegai, *Romantic German Literature* (London: Arnold, 1979)

Kluckhohn, Paul, *Das Ideengut der deutschen Romantik* (Tübingen: Niemeyer, 1961)

Kremer, Detlev, *Romantik* (Stuttgart: Metzler, 2007)

McGann, Jerome J., *The Romantic Ideology: A Critical Investigation* (Chicago: University of Chicago Press, 1983)

Mahoney, Dennis F. (ed.), *The Literature of German Romanticism* (Rochester, N.Y.: Camden House, 2004)

Menhennet, Alan, *The Romantic Movement* (London: Croom Helm, 1981)

Pikulik, Lothar, *Frühromantik: Epoche – Werk – Wirkung* (Munich: Beck, 1992)

Pipkin, J. (ed.), *English and German Romanticism: Cross-Currents and Controversies* (Heidelberg: Carl Winter, 1985)

Prawer, S. S., *The Romantic Period in Germany* (London: Weidenfeld and Nicolson, 1970)

Reed, T. J., *The Classical Centre: Goethe and Weimar 1775–1832* (London: Croom Helm, 1980)

Safranski, Rüdiger, *Romantik: Eine deutsche Affäre* (Munich: Hanser, 2007)

Schrade, Hubert, *German Romantic Painting* (New York: Harry N. Abrams, 1977)

Seyhan, Azade, *Representation and Its Discontents: The Critical Legacy of German Romanticism* (Berkeley and Oxford: University of California Press, 1992)

Stopp, E. C., *German Romantics in Context: Selected Essays 1971–86*, collected by P. Hutchinson, R. Paulin, and J. Purver (London: Bristol Classical Texts, 1992)

Vaughan, William, *German Romantic Painting* (New Haven and London: Yale University Press, 1980)

Vietta, Silvio (ed.), *Die literarische Frühromantik* (Göttingen: Vandenhoeck & Ruprecht, 1983)

Authors

Adorno, Theodor W., 'Zum Gedächtnis Eichendorffs', in *Noten zur Literatur* (Frankfurt am Main: Suhrkamp, 1981), pp. 69–94
'Die Wunde Heine', in *Noten zur Literatur* (Frankfurt am Main: Suhrkamp, 1981), pp. 95–100

Constantine, David, *Hölderlin* (Oxford: Clarendon Press, 1988)

Bäumer, Konstanze and Hartwig Schultz, *Bettina von Arnim* (Stuttgart and Weimar: Metzler, 1995)

Bisanz, Rudolf M., *German Romanticism and Philipp Otto Runge* (DeKalb: Northern Illinois University Press, 1970)

Bowie, Andrew, *Schelling and Modern European Philosophy* (London, New York: Routledge 1993)

Enzensberger, Hans Magnus, *Brentanos Poetik* (Munich: Hanser, 1961)

Feldges, B. and U. Stadler, *E. T. A. Hoffmann. Epoche – Werk – Wirkung* (Munich: Beck, 1986)

Fetzer, John, *Romantic Orpheus: Profiles of Clemens Brentano* (Berkeley: University of California Press, 1974)

Hamburger, Michael, 'Novalis', in *Reason and Energy: Studies in German Literature* (London: Weidenfeld and Nicolson, 1970), pp. 66–100

Hechtfischer, Ute *et al.* (eds.), *Metzler Autorinnen Lexikon* (Stuttgart and Weimar: Metzler, 1998)

Hille, Markus, *Karoline von Günderrode* (Reinbek: Rowohlt, 1999)

Kastinger-Riley, H. M., *Clemens Brentano* (Stuttgart: Metzler, 1985)

Kemper, Dirk, *Sprache der Dichtung: Wilhelm Heinrich Wackenroder im Kontext der Spätaufklärung* (Stuztgart and Weimar: Metzler, 1993)

Kremer, Detlef, *E. T. A Hofmann zur Einführung* (Hamburg: Junius, 1998)

Loster-Schneider, Gudrun and Gaby Pailer (eds.), *Lexikon deutschsprachiger Epik und Dramatik von Autorinnen (1730–1900)* (Tübingen and Basel: Francke, 2006)

Mahoney, Dennis F., *Friedrich von Hardenberg (Novalis)* (Stuttgart: Metzler, 2001)

Müller, Götz, *Jean Paul im Kontext: Gesammelte Aufsätze*, ed. by Wolfgang Riedel (Würzburg: Königshausen & Neumann, 1996)

Neubauer, John, *Novalis* (Boston: Twayne, 1980)

Paulin, Roger, *Ludwig Tieck: A Literary Biography* (Oxford: Oxford University Press, 1985)

Phelan, Anthony, *Reading Heinrich Heine* (Cambridge: Cambridge University Press, 2007)

Rewald, Sabine (ed.), *The Romantic Vision of Caspar David Friedrich* (New York: Metropolitan Museum of Art, 1990)

Ries, F. X., *Zeitkritik bei Joseph von Eichendorff*, ed. Bernd Engler, Volker Kapp, Helmuth Kiesel and Günter Niggl (Berlin: Duncker & Humblot, 1997)

Saul, Nicholas, 'The Body, Death, Mutilation and Decay in Zacharias Werner', in *German Life and Letters*, n. s. 52 (1999), pp. 255–70

Schultz, Hartwig; *'Unsre Lieb aber ist ausserkohren': Die Geschichte der Geschwister Clemens und Bettine Brentano* (Frankfurt am Main: Insel, 2004)

Schwarzer Schmetterling: Zwanzig Kapitel aus dem Leben des romantischen Dichters Clemens Brentano (Berlin: Berlin Verlag, 2000)

Schulz, Gerhard, *Kleist: Eine Biographie* (Munich: Beck, 2007)

Stephens, Anthony, *Heinrich von Kleist: The Dramas and the Stories* (Oxford: Berg, 1994)

Uerlings, Herbert, *Novalis* (Stuttgart: Reclam, 1998)

Walther, Angelo, *Caspar David Friedrich* (Berlin: Henschel Verlag, 1985)

Wingertszahn, Christof, *Ambiguität und Ambivalenz im erzählerischen Werk Achim von Arnims: Mit einem Anhang unbekannter Texte aus Arnims Nachlaß* (Frankfurt am Main: R. G. Fischer, 1990)

Genres

Behler, Ernst, *Die Zeitschriften der Brüder Schlegel: Ein Beitrag zur Geschichte der deutschen Romantik* (Darmstadt: Wissenschaftliche Buchgesellschaft, 1983)

Blackall, Eric A., *The Novels of the German Romantics* (Ithaca, N.Y., and London: Cornell University Press, 1983)

Bohrer, Karl-Heinz, *Der romantische Brief: Die Entstehung ästhetischer Subjektivität* (Munich: Suhrkamp, 1987)

Cox, J. N., *In the Shadows of Romance: Romantic Drama in Germany, England, and France* (Athens: Ohio University Press, 1987)

Engel, Manfred, *Roman der Goethezeit* (Stuttgart: Metzler, 1993)

Fetzer, John, 'Die romantische Lyrik', in *Romantik-Handbuch*, ed. Helmut Schanze, 2nd edn (Stuttgart: Kröner, 2003), pp. 312–36

Frühwald, Wolfgang, *Gedichte der Romantik* (Stuttgart: Reclam, 1984

Gallas, Helga, and Magdalena Heuser (eds.), *Untersuchungen zum Roman von Frauen um 1800* (Tübingen: Niemeyer, 1990)

Gillespie, Gerald, (ed.), *Romantic Drama* (Amsterdam and Philadelphia: Benjamin, 1994)

Gorman, David, 'A bibliography of German Romantic Literary Criticism and Theory in English', *Style* (Winter 1994) (FindArticles.com, accessed 12 August 2007. http://www.engl.niu.edu/style/)

Hardy, Swana L., *Goethe, Calderón und die romantische Theorie des Dramas* (Heidelberg: Winter, 1965)

Jacobs, Jürgen, *Wilhelm Meister und seine Brüder: Untersuchungen zum deutschen Bildungsroman* (Munich: Wilhelm Fink Verlag, 1978)

Japp, Uwe, Stefan Scherer and Claudia Stockinger (eds.), *Das romantische Drama: Produktive Synthese zwischen Tradition und Innovation* (Tübingen: Niemeyer, 2000)

Kaminski, Nicola, *Kreuzgänge: Romanexperimente der deutschen Romantik* (Paderborn: Ferdinand Schöningh, 2001)

Kluge, Gerhard, 'Das romantische Drama', in *Handbuch des deutschen Dramas*, ed. Walter Hinck (Düsseldorf: Bagel, 1980), pp. 186–99

Kord, Susanne, *Ein Blick hinter die Kulissen: Deutschsprachige Dramatikerinnen im 18. und 19. Jahrhundert* (Stuttgart: Metzler, 1992)

Kremer, Detlev, *Prosa der Romantik* (Stuttgart and Weimar: Metzler, 1997)

Mahoney, Dennis F., *Der Roman der Goethezeit* (Stuttgart: Metzler, 1988)

Malinowski, Bernadette, 'German Romantic Poetry in Theory and Practice', in *The Literature of German Romanticism*, ed. Dennis F. Mahoney (Rochester, N.Y.: Camden House, 2004), pp. 147–69

Minden, Michael, *The German Bildungsroman: Incest and Inheritance* (Cambridge: Cambridge University Press, 1997)

Ostermann, Eberhard, *Das Fragment: Geschichte einer ästhetischen Idee* (Munich: Fink, 1991)

Paulin, Roger, *The Brief Compass: The Nineteenth-Century German Novelle* (Oxford: Clarendon Press, 1985)

Rodger, Gillian, 'The Lyric', in *The Romantic Period in Germany*, ed. S. S. Prawer (London: Weidenfeld and Nicolson, 1970), pp. 147–72

Rölleke, Heinz, 'Nachwort', in *Des Knaben Wunderhorn: Alte deutsche Lieder, gesammelt von Achim von Arnim und Clemens Brentano*, ed. Heinz Rölleke, Kritische Ausgabe, 3 vols. (Stuttgart: Reclam, 1987), vol. III, pp. 557–81

Schultz, Hartwig, 'Eichendorffs Lyrik', in Joseph von Eichendorff, *Werke*, eds. Wolfgang Frühwald, Brigitte Schillbach and Hartwig Schultz, 6 vols. (Frankfurt am Main: Deutscher Klassiker Verlag, 1985–93), vol. I, pp. 715–800

Schulz, Gerhard, 'Das romantische Drama: Befragung eines Begriffes', in *Das romantische Drama: Synthese zwischen Tradition und Innovation*, eds. Uwe, Japp, Stefan, Scherer, Claudia, Stockinger (Tübingen: Niemeyer, 2000), pp. 1–19

Ulshöfer, Robert, *Die Theorie des Dramas in der deutschen Romantik* (Berlin: Junker & Dünnhaupt, 1935)

Themes

Allert, Beate, 'Romanticism and the Visual Arts', in *The Literature of German Romanticism*, ed. Dennis F. Mahoney (Rochester, N.Y.: Camden House, 2004), pp. 273–306

Alvarez, A., *The Savage God: A Study of Suicide* (Harmondsworth: Penguin, 1971)

Améry, Jean, *Hand an sich legen: Diskurs über den Freitod* (Stuttgart: Klett-Cotta, 1976)

Anderson, Benedict, *Imagined Communities: Reflections on the Origin and Spread of Nationalism*, 2nd edn (London: Verso, 1991)

Anz, Thomas, 'Der schöne und der häßliche Tod: Klassische und moderne Normen literarischer Diskurse über den Tod', in *Klassik und Moderne: Die Weimarer Klassik als historisches Ereignis und Herausforderung im kulturgeschichtlichen Prozeß: Walter Müller-Seidel Zum 65. Geburtstag*, eds. Karl Richter and Jörg Schönert (Stuttgart: Metzler, 1983), pp. 409–32

Armstrong, C., *Romantic Organicism: From Idealist Origins to Ambivalent Afterlife* (Basingstoke: Palgrave Macmillan, 2003)

Auhuber, F., *In einem fernen dunklen Spiegel: E. T. A. Hoffmanns Poetisierung der Medizin* (Opladen: Westdeutscher Verlag, 1986)

Aurnhammer, Achim, *Androgynie: Studien zu einem Motiv in der europäischen Literatur* (Cologne and Vienna: Böhlau, 1986)

Balke, Friedrich, *Der Staat nach seinem Ende: Die Versuchung Carl Schmitts* (Munich: Fink, 1996)

Bänsch, D. (ed.), *Zur Modernität der Romantik* (Stuttgart: Metzler, 1977)

Barker, A., K. McPherson and H. Gaskill (eds.), *Neue Ansichten: The Reception of Romanticism in the Literature of the GDR* (Amsterdam: Rodolphi, 1990)

Barkhoff, Jürgen, *Magnetische Fiktionen: Literarisierung des Mesmerismus in der Romantik* (Stuttgart and Weimar: Metzler, 1995)

Baxa, J., *Einführung in die romantische Staatswissenschaft*, 2nd edn (Jena: Gustav Fischer, 1931)

Becker-Cantarino, Barbara, *Schriftstellerinnen der Romantik: Epoche – Werk – Wirkung* (Munich: Beck, 2000)

Behler, Ernst, 'Die Wirkung Goethes und Schillers auf Die Brüder Schlegel', in *Unser Commercium: Goethes und Schillers Literaturpolitik*, eds. Wilfried Barner, Eberhard Lämmert, and Norbert Oellers (Stuttgart: Cotta, 1984), pp. 559–83

German Romantic Literary Theory (Cambridge: Cambridge University Press, 1993)

Behler, Ernst and Jochen Hörisch (eds.), *Die Aktualität der Frühromantik* (Paderborn, Munich, Vienna: Schöningh, 1987)

Bent, Ian (ed.), *Music Theory in the Age of Romanticism* (Cambridge: Cambridge University Press, 2005)

Beiser, Frederick C., *Enlightenment, Revolution, and Romanticism: The Genesis of Modern German Political Thought, 1790–1800* (Cambridge, Mass., London: Harvard University Press, 1992)

(ed.), *The Early Political Writings of the German Romantics* (Cambridge: Cambridge University Press, 1996)

Bell, Matthew, *The German Tradition of Psychology in Literature and Thought, 1700–1840* (Cambridge: Cambridge University Press, 2005)

Benjamin, Walter, *Der Begriff der Kunstkritik in der deutschen* Romantik, ed. Hermann Schweppenhäuser (Frankfurt am Main: Suhrkamp, 1973; first edn, 1920)

Berman, Antoine, *The Experience of the Foreign: Culture and Translation in Romantic Germany*, trans. S. Heyvaert (Albany: State University of New York Press, 1992)

Berman, R. A., *Enlightenment or Empire: Colonial Discourse in German Culture* (Lincoln and London: Nebraska University Press, 1998)

Bock, Gisela, *Frauen in der europäischen Geschichte: Vom Mittelalter bis zur Gegenwart* (Munich: Beck, 2000)

Böhme, H., 'Geheime Macht im Schoß der Erde: Das Symbolfeld des Bergbaus zwischen Sozialgeschichte und Psychohistorie', in *Natur und Subjekt* (Frankfurt am Main: Suhrkamp, 1988), pp.67–144

Bohrer, Karl Heinz, *Mythos und Moderne: Begriff und Bild einer Rekonstruktion* (Frankfurt am Main: Suhrkamp, 1983)

Borchmeyer, Dieter, 'What Is Classicism?', in *The Literature of Weimar Classicism*, ed. Simon Richter (Rochester, N.Y.: Camden House, 2005), pp.44–61

Bormann, A. von (ed.), *Volk–Nation–Europa: Zur Romantisierung und Entromantisierung politischer Begriffe* (Würzburg: Königshausen & Neumann, 1998

Bovenschen, Silvia, *Die imaginierte Weiblichkeit: Exemplarische Untersuchungen zu kulturgeschichtlichen literarischen Präsentationsformen des Weiblichen* (Frankfurt am Main: Suhrkamp, 1979)

Bowie, Andrew, *From Romanticism to Critical Theory: The Philosophy of German Literary Theory* (London and New York: Routledge, 1997)

Introduction to German Philosophy from Kant to Habermas (Cambridge: Polity, 2003)

Aesthetics and Subjectivity: From Kant to Nietzsche (Manchester: Manchester University Press, 2003)

Music, Philosophy, and Modernity (Cambridge: Cambridge University Press, 2007)

Boyle, Nicholas, *Goethe: The Poet and the Age*, 2 vols. (Oxford: Clarendon Press, 1991, 2000)

Brandom, Robert, *Making It Explicit* (Cambridge, Mass., and London: Harvard University Press, 1994)

Tales of the Mighty Dead (Cambridge, Mass., and London: Harvard University Press, 2002)

Brecht, C., *Die gefährliche Rede: Sprachreflexion und Erzählstruktur in der Prosa Ludwig Tiecks* (Tübingen: Niemeyer, 1993)

Breger, Claudia, *Ortlosigkeit des Fremden: 'Zigeunerinnen' und 'Zigeuner' in der deutschsprachigen Literatur um 1800* (Cologne, Weimar, Vienna: Böhlau, 1998)

Brinker-Gabler, Gisela (ed.), *Deutsche Literatur von Frauen* (Munich: Beck, 1988)

Brinkmann, Richard (ed.), *Deutsche Literatur und Französische Revolution: Sieben Studien* (Göttingen: Vandenhoeck & Ruprecht, 1974)

Brown, H. M., E. T. A. *Hoffman and the Serapiontic Principle: Critique and Creativity* (Rochester, N.Y.: Camden House, 2006)

Brown, Marshall, *The Shape of German Romanticism* (Ithaca, N.Y.: Cornell University Press, 1979)

Calhoon, Kenneth S., *Fatherland: Novalis, Freud, and the Discipline of Romance* (Detroit, Mich.: Wayne State University Press, 1992)

Cavell, Stanley, *Must We Mean What We Say?* (Cambridge: Cambridge University Press, 1976)

Cunningham, Andrew and Nicholas Jardine (eds.), *Romanticism and the Sciences* (Cambridge: Cambridge University Press, 1990)

Dahlhaus, Carl, *Richard Wagners Musikdramen* (Velber: Friedrich, 1971)

Daverio, John, *Nineteenth-Century Music and the German Romantic Ideology* (New York: Schirmer, 1993)

Dawson, Ruth P., 'Im Reifrock den Parnaß besteigen: Die Rezeption von Dichterinnen im 18. Jahrhundert', in *Frauensprache – Frauenliteratur? Für und wider einer Psychoanalyse literarischer Werke*, ed. Inge Stephan and Carl Pietzcker (Tübingen; Niemeyer, 1986), pp. 24–9 (=*Akten des VII. Internationalen Germanisten-Kongresses Göttingen 1985*, ed. Albrecht Schöne, 11 vols. (Tübingen: Niemeyer, 1986), vol. VI)

De Man, Paul, *The Rhetoric of Romanticism* (New York: Columbia University Press, 1984)

Donovan, Siobhan and Robin Elliott (eds.), *Music and Literature in German Romanticism* (New York: Camden House, 2004)

Dougherty, F. W. P., *Gesammelte Aufsätze zu Themen der klassischen Periode der Naturgeschichte / Collected Essays on Themes from the Classical Period of Natural History* (Göttingen: Norbert Klatt, 1996)

Eigen, S. and M. Larrimore (eds.), *The German Invention of Race* (Albany: State University of New York Press, 2006)

Eldridge, Richard, *Living a Human Life: Wittgenstein, Intentionality, and Romanticism* (Chicago: University of Chicago Press, 1997)

Ellenberger, Henri F., *The Discovery of the Unconscious: The History and Evolution of Dynamic Psychiatry* (New York: Basic Books, 1970)

Engelhardt, D. von, 'Natural Science in the Age of Romanticism', in A. Faivre and J. Needleman (eds.), *Modern Esoteric Spirituality* (New York: Crossroad, 1992), pp. 101–31

Engell, James, *The Creative Imagination: Enlightenment to Romanticism* (Cambridge, Mass.: Harvard University Press, 1981)

Epstein, Klaus, *Die Ursprünge des Konservativismus in Deutschland: Der Ausgangspunkt: Die Herausforderung durch die Französische Revolution 1770–1806* (Frankfurt and Berlin: Propyläen, 1973)

Feilchenfeldt, Konrad *et al.* (eds.), *Zwischen Aufklärung und Romantik: Neue Perspektiven der Forschung: Festschrift für Roger Paulin* (Würzburg: Königshausen & Neumann, 2006)

Fischer, B., *Das Eigene und das Eigentliche: Klopstock, Herder, Fichte, Kleist: Episoden aus der Konstruktionsgeschichte nationaler Intentionalitäten* (Berlin: Erich Schmidt, 1995)

Frank, Manfred, *Der kommende Gott: Vorlesung über die neue Mythologie I* (Frankfurt am Main: Suhrkamp, 1982)

Freud, Sigmund, *Jenseits des Lustprinzips*, in *Studienausgabe*, eds. Alexander Mitscherlich *et al.*, 14 vols. (Frankfurt am Main: Suhrkamp, 1982), vol. III, pp. 217–72

Das Unbehagen in der Kultur, in *Studienausgabe*, eds. Alexander Mitscherlich *et al.*, 14 vols. (Frankfurt am Main: Suhrkamp, 1982), vol. IX, pp. 191–270

Frevert, Ute, *'Mann und Weib, und Weib und Mann': Geschlechterdifferenzen in der Moderne* (Munich: Beck, 1995)

Gaus, Detlef, *Geselligkeit und Gesellige: Bildung, Bürgertum und bildungsbürgerliche Kultur um 1800* (Stuttgart: Metzler, 1998)

Gerhard, Ute (ed.), *Frauen in der Geschichte des Rechts* (Munich: Beck, 1997)

Guilloton, Doris Starr, 'Schiller and Friedrich Schlegel: Their Controversial Relationship', in *Friedrich von Schiller and the Drama of Human Existence*, eds. Alexej Ugrinsky and Wolfgang Wittkowski (New York: Greenwood, 1988), pp. 149–54

Hahn, Barbara, *Unter falschem Namen: Von der schwierigen Autorschaft der Frauen* (Frankfurt am Main: Suhrkamp, 1991)

'Der Mythos vom Salon: Rahels "Dachstube" als historische Fiktion', in *Salons der Romantik: Beiträge eines Wiepersdorfer Kolloquiums zu Theorie und Geschichte des Salons*, ed. Hartwig Schultz (Berlin, New York: de Gruyter 1997), pp. 213–34

Hanssen, B. and A. Benjamin (eds.), *Walter Benjamin and Romanticism* (New York: Continuum, 2002)

Heipcke, Corinna, *Autorhetorik: Zur Konstruktion weiblicher Autorschaft im ausgehenden 18. Jahrhundert* (Frankfurt am Main: Peter Lang, 2002)

Henrich, Dieter, *Fichtes ursprüngliche Einsicht* (Frankfurt am Main: Suhrkamp, 1967)

Herrmann, H.P., H.-M. Blitz and S. Moßmann, *Machtphantasie Deutschland. Nationalismus, Männlichkeit und Fremdenhaß im Vaterlandsdiskurs deutscher Schriftsteller des 18. Jahrhunderts* (Frankfurt am Main: Suhrkamp, 1996)

Hobsbawm, Eric J., *Nations and Nationalism since 1780: Programme, Myth, Reality* (Cambridge: Cambridge University Press, 1992)

Horstkotte, Silke, *Androgyne Autorschaft: Poesie und Geschlecht im Prosawerk Clemens Brentanos* (Tübingen: Niemeyer, 2004)

Izenberg, Gerald N., *Impossible Individuality: Romanticism, Revolution, and the Origins of Modern Selfhood* (Princeton, N.J.: Princeton University Press, 1992)

Kaiser, Gerhard, *Pietismus und Patriotismus im literarischen Deutschland: Ein Beitrag zum Problem der Säkularisation*, 2nd edn (Frankfurt am Main: Athenäum, 1973)

Kerbs, D. and J. Reulecke (eds.), *Handbuch der deutschen Reformbewegungen 1880–1933* (Wuppertal: Peter Hammer, 1988)

Kittler, Wolf, *Die Geburt des Partisanen aus dem Geist der Poesie: Heinrich von Kleist und die Strategie der Befreiungskriege* (Freiburg: Rombach Verlag, 1987)

Köhler, Astrid, *Salonkultur im klassischen Weimar: Geselligkeit als Lebensform und literarisches Konzept* (Stuttgart: Metzler, 1996)

Körner, Josef, *Romantiker und Klassiker: Die Brüder Schlegel in ihren Beziehungen zu Schiller und Goethe* (Berlin: Askanischer Verlag, 1924)

Kohlenbach, M., *Walter Benjamin: Self-Reference and Religiosity* (Basingstoke: Palgrave Macmillan, 2002)

Kohn, Hans, *Prelude to Nation-States: The French and German Experience, 1789–1815* (Princeton, N.J.: Van Nostrand, 1967)

Kontje, Todd, *Women, the Novel, and the German Nation 1771–1871* (Cambridge: Cambridge University Press, 1998)

Kunisch, Hermann, 'Friedrich Schlegel und Goethe', in *Kleine Schriften* (Berlin: Duncker & Humblot, 1968), pp. 189–204

Kuzniar, Alice, A., *Delayed Endings: Nonclosure in Novalis and Hölderlin* (Athens: University of Georgia Press, 1987)

Lepenies, Wolf, *Das Ende der Naturgeschichte: Wandel kultureller Selbstverständlichkeiten in den Wissenschaften des 18. und 19. Jahrhunderts* (Munich and Vienna: Hanser, 1976)

Librett, J. S., *The Rhetoric of Cultural Dialogue: Jews and Germans from Moses Mendelssohn to Richard Wagner and Beyond* (Palo Alto, Calif.: Stanford University Press, 2000)

Mahlendorf, U., 'Die Psychologie der Romantik', in *Romantik-Handbuch*, ed. H. Schanze (Stuttgart: Alfred Kröner, 1994), pp. 590–604

Matala de Mazza, Ethel, *Der verfaßte Körper: Zum Projekt einer organischen Gemeinschaft in der Politischen Romantik* (Freiburg: Rombach Verlag, 1999)

Matt, Peter von, *Die Augen der Automaten: E.T.A. Hoffmanns Imaginationslehre als Prinzip seiner Kunst* (Tübingen: Niemeyer, 1971)

Minois, Georges, *History of Suicide: Voluntary Death in Western Culture*, trans. Lydia G. Cochrane (Baltimore and London: Johns Hopkins University Press, 1999; Ist edn, Paris: Fayard, 1995)

Molnár, Geza von, *Romantic Vision, Ethical Context: Novalis and Artistic Autonomy* (Minneapolis: University of Minnesota Press, 1987)

Müller, Götz, *Gegenwelten: Die Utopie in der deutschen Literatur* (Stuttgart: Metzler, 1989)

Neubauer, J., *Bifocal Vision: Novalis's Philosophy of Nature and Disease* (Chapel Hill: University of North Carolina Press, 1971)

Neumann, Gerhard and Günter Oesterle (eds.), *Bild und Schrift in der Romantik* (Würzburg: Königshausen & Neumann, 1999)

O'Brien, William Arctander, *Novalis: Signs of Revolution* (Durham, N.C., and London: Duke University Press, 1995)

Peter, K., 'History and Moral Imperatives: The Contradictions of Political Romanticism', in *The Literature of German Romanticism*, ed. Dennis F. Mahoney (Rochester, N.Y.: Camden House, 2004), pp. 191–208

Pfefferkorn, Kristin, *Novalis: A Romantic's Theory of Language and Poetry* (New Haven, Conn.: Yale University Press, 1988)

Plessner, Helmuth, *Die verspätete Nation: Über die politische Verführbarkeit bürgerlichen Geistes*, 5th edn (Frankfurt am Main: Suhrkamp, 1994)

Redfield, Marc, *The Politics of Aesthetics: Nationalism, Gender, Romanticism* (Palo Alto: Stanford University Press, 2003)

Reuchlein, G., *Bürgerliche Gesellschaft, Psychiatrie und Literatur: Zur Entwicklung der Wahnsinnsthematik in der deutschen Literatur des späten 18. und frühen 19. Jahrhunderts* (Munich: Fink, 1986)

Rommel, G., 'Romanticism and Natural Science', in *The Literature of German Romanticism*, ed. Dennis F. Mahoney (Rochester, N.Y.: Camden House, 2004), pp. 209–27

Rosen, Charles, *The Romantic Generation* (Cambridge, Mass.: Harvard University Press, 1998)

Runge, Anita, *Literarische Praxis von Frauen um 1800: Briefroman, Autobiographie, Märchen* (Hildesheim: Olms, 1997)

Saul, Nicholas, 'Hofmannsthal and Novalis', in *Fin de Siècle Vienna*, eds. G. J. Carr and E. Sagarra (Dublin: Trinity College Dublin, 1985), pp. 26–62

(ed.), *Die deutsche literarische Romantik und die Wissenschaften* (London: Institute of Germanic Studies; Munich: Iudicium, 1991)

'Prediger aus der neuen romantischen Clique': Zur Interaktion von Romantik und Homiletik um 1800 (Würzburg: Königshausen & Neumann 1999)

'The Pursuit of the Subject: Literature as Critic and Perfecter of Philosophy 1790–1830', in *German Philosophy and Literature 1700–1990* (Cambridge: Cambridge University Press, 2002), pp. 57–101

'The Reception of German Romanticism in the Twentieth Century', in *The Literature of German Romanticism*, ed. Dennis F. Mahoney (Rochester, N.Y.: Camden House, 2004), pp. 327–59

'Morbid? Suicide, Freedom, Human Dignity and the German Romantic Yearning for Death', in *Historical Reflections / Réflexions historiques* (2006), pp. 579–99

Sommerhage, Claus, *Romantische Aporien: Zur Kontiuität des Romantischen bei Novalis, Eichendorff, Hofmannsthal und Handke* (Paderborn and Munich: Ferdinand Schöningh, 1993)

Strohschneider-Kohrs, I., *Die romantische Ironie in Theorie und Gestaltung* (Tübingen: Niemeyer, 1977; first edn, 1960)

Taylor, Charles, *Human Agency and Language* (Cambridge: Cambridge University Press, 1985)

Vietta, Silvio, 'Frühromantik und Aufklärung', in *Die literarische Frühromantik* (Göttingen: Vandenhoeck & Ruprecht, 1983), pp. 7–84

Vietta, Silvio and Dirk Kemper (eds.), *Ästhetische Moderne in Europa: Grundzüge und Problemzusammenhänge seit der Romantik* (Munich: Fink, 1998)

Vogl, Joseph (ed.), *Gemeinschaften: Positionen zu einer Philosophie des Politischen* (Frankfurt am Main: Suhrkamp, 1994)

Vordtriede, W., *Novalis und die französische Symbolisten* (Stuttgart: Kohlhammer, 1963)

Whittall, Arnold, *Romantic Music: A Concise History from Schubert to Sibelius* (London: Thames and Hudson, 1990)

Wiesing, U., *Kunst oder Wissenschaft? Konzeptionen der Medizin in der deutschen Romantik* (Stuttgart: frommann-holzboog, 1995)

Wöbkemeier, Rita, *Erzählte Krankheit: Medizinische und literarische Phantasien um 1800* (Stuttgart: Metzler, 1990)

Zammito, J.H., *Kant, Herder, and the Birth of Anthropology* (Chicago and London: University of Chicago Press, 2002)

Ziolkowski, Theodor, *German Romanticism and Its Institutions* (Princeton, N.J.: Princeton University Press, 1990)

INDEX

Cambridge Companions To...

AUTHORS

Edward Albee edited by Stephen J. Bottoms

Margaret Atwood edited by Coral Ann Howells

W. H. Auden edited by Stan Smith

Jane Austen edited by Edward Copeland and Juliet McMaster

Beckett edited by John Pilling

Aphra Behn edited by Derek Hughes and Janet Todd

Walter Benjamin edited by David S. Ferris

William Blake edited by Morris Eaves

Brecht edited by Peter Thomson and Glendyr Sacks (second edition)

The Brontës edited by Heather Glen

Frances Burney edited by Peter Sabor

Byron edited by Drummond Bone

Albert Camus edited by Edward J. Hughes

Willa Cather edited by Marilee Lindemann

Cervantes edited by Anthony J. Cascardi

Chaucer, second edition edited by Piero Boitani and Jill Mann

Chekhov edited by Vera Gottlieb and Paul Allain

Kate Chopin edited by Janet Beer

Coleridge edited by Lucy Newlyn

Wilkie Collins edited by Jenny Bourne Taylor

Joseph Conrad edited by J. H. Stape

Dante edited by Rachel Jacoff (second edition)

Daniel Defoe edited by John Richetti

Don DeLillo edited by John N. Duvall

Charles Dickens edited by John O. Jordan

Emily Dickinson edited by Wendy Martin

John Donne edited by Achsah Guibbory

Dostoevskii edited by W. J. Leatherbarrow

Theodore Dreiser edited by Leonard Cassuto and Claire Virginia Eby

John Dryden edited by Steven N. Zwicker

W. E. B. Du Bois edited by Shamoon Zamir

George Eliot edited by George Levine

T. S. Eliot edited by A. David Moody

Ralph Ellison edited by Ross Posnock

Ralph Waldo Emerson edited by Joel Porte and Saundra Morris

William Faulkner edited by Philip M. Weinstein

Henry Fielding edited by Claude Rawson

F. Scott Fitzgerald edited by Ruth Prigozy

Flaubert edited by Timothy Unwin

E. M. Forster edited by David Bradshaw

Benjamin Franklin edited by Carla Mulford

Brian Friel edited by Anthony Roche

Robert Frost edited by Robert Faggen

Elizabeth Gaskell edited by Jill L. Matus

Goethe edited by Lesley Sharpe

Thomas Hardy edited by Dale Kramer

David Hare edited by Richard Boon

Nathaniel Hawthorne edited by Richard Millington

Seamus Heaney edited by Bernard O'Donoghue

Ernest Hemingway edited by Scott Donaldson

Homer edited by Robert Fowler

Ibsen edited by James McFarlane

Henry James edited by Jonathan Freedman

Samuel Johnson edited by Greg Clingham

Ben Jonson edited by Richard Harp and Stanley Stewart

James Joyce edited by Derek Attridge (second edition)

Kafka edited by Julian Preece

Keats edited by Susan J. Wolfson

Lacan edited by Jean-Michel Rabaté

D. H. Lawrence edited by Anne Fernihough

Primo Levi edited by Robert Gordon

Lucretius edited by Stuart Gillespie and Philip Hardie

David Mamet edited by Christopher Bigsby

Thomas Mann edited by Ritchie Robertson

Christopher Marlowe edited by Patrick Cheney

Herman Melville edited by Robert S. Levine

Arthur Miller edited by Christopher Bigsby

Milton edited by Dennis Danielson (second edition)

Molière edited by David Bradby and Andrew Calder

TOPICS

www.ingramcontent.com/pod-product-compliance
Ingram Content Group UK Ltd.
Pitfield, Milton Keynes, MK11 3LW, UK
UKHW042154280225
455719UK00001B/339